American Homes

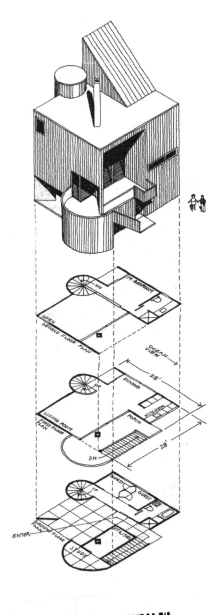

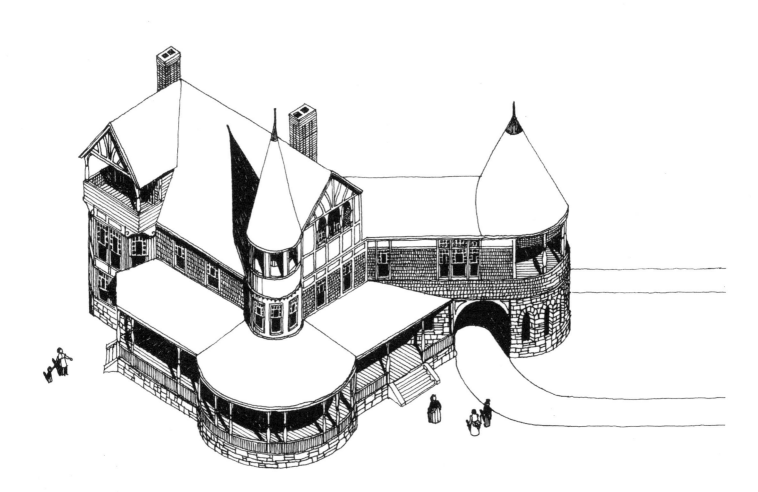

American Homes

The Landmark Illustrated Encyclopedia of Domestic Architecture

LESTER WALKER
Preface by Charles Moore

BLACK DOG
& LEVENTHAL
PUBLISHERS
NEW YORK

Published by
Black Dog & Leventhal Publishers, Inc.
151 West 19th Street
New York, NY 10011

Distributed by
Workman Publishing Company
225 Varick Street
New York, NY 10014

First Black Dog & Leventhal Publishers hardcover edition 2002; first paperback edition 2014.
Originally published under the title *American Shelter: An Illustrated Encyclopedia of the American Home*

Manufactured in The United States of America

Cover and interior design by Sheila Hart Design

ISBN-13: 978-1-57912-992-7

h g f e d c b a

Library of Congress Cataloging-in-Publication Data available on file.

To my Mother and Father

TABLE OF CONTENTS

PREFACE. 11

INTRODUCTION 13

THE AMERICAN INDIANS 19

THE SETTLERS 37

GLOSSARY. 328

BIBLIOGRAPHY. 332

INDEX TO ARCHITECTS 336

THE INDIANS

Page	Style & Date
20	Earth Lodge 300
22	Pueblo 700
24	Pole and Thatch 800
26	Tipi 1200
28	Longhouse 1400
30	Wigwam 1600
32	Hogan 1750
34	Plank House 1800

THE SETTLERS

Page	Style & Date
38	Spanish Cottage 1580
40	English Cottage 1623
44	Medieval 1635
48	Log Cabin 1638
54	Stone Ender 1640
56	Dutch Colonial 1650

Page	Style & Date
60	Cross House 1650
62	Jacobean 1655
64	Garrison House 1660
66	Saltbox 1670
70	German Colonial 1675
74	Southern Colonial 1680
76	New England Farmhouse 1690
80	Plantation Colonial 1700
86	Cape Cod 1710
90	French Colonial 1720
92	Georgian 1720
96	Federal 1765
98	Jeffersonian Classicism 1770
102	Adam 1800
104	Regency 1815
106	Greek Revival 1820

Page	Style & Date		Page	Style & Date
110	Spanish Colonial 1825		146	Second Empire 1870
112	Shaker 1830		148	High Victorian Gothic 1875
114	Egyptian Revival 1835		150	Queen Anne 1880
116	Monterey 1835		154	Eastlake 1880
118	Shacks and Shanties 1840		156	Richardsonian Romanesque 1885
120	Early Gothic Revival 1840		158	Norman 1885
124	Cottage 1845		160	Shingle 1885
126	Carpenter Gothic 1850		166	Baled Hay and Sod 1890
130	Steamboat Gothic 1855		168	Chateauesque 1890
132	Italian Villa 1855		170	Georgian Revival 1895
134	Swiss Cottage 1855		172	Mission 1895
136	Italianate 1855		174	Tudor 1900
138	Octagon 1860		176	Classic Revival 1905
140	False Front 1860		178	Craftsmen 1905
142	Renaissance Revival 1860		180	Wrightian 1905
144	Stick 1865		184	Bungalow 1910

Page	Style & Date		Page	Style & Date
190	Bay Region 1910, 1930, 1960		246	High Tech 1955
194	Prairie 1915		248	Roof Architecture 1955
196	Pueblo Revival 1920		250	A-Frame 1955
198	Colonial Revival 1925		252	Contractor Modern 1955
200	Fantasy 1925		256	Neocolonial 1955
208	Spanish Colonial Revival 1925		262	Split Level 1960
210	Period 1930		266	Converted Train Car 1960
214	International 1930		268	Pole House 1960
218	Art Moderne 1935		270	Brutalism 1960
220	Northwestern 1945		272	Free Form 1965
222	Rammed Earth 1945		274	Geodesic Dome 1970
224	Quonset Hut 1945		280	Modular 1970
226	Mobile Home 1950		282	Silo and Yurt 1970
232	California Ranch 1950		284	Floating House 1970
236	Miesian 1950		288	New Shingle 1970
240	Prefabricated 1950		296	International Revival 1970

Page	Style & Date
300	Inflatable 1975
302	Passive Solar 1975
304	Active Solar 1975
306	Earth Sheltered 1975
308	Post Modern 1978
312	Deconstruction 1988
316	Neomodern 1990
320	Everyday and the Ordinary 1992
326	Space 2000

Preface

This engaging book of drawings and descriptions of pleasant American houses is far more epochal than perhaps it seems: Not many years ago, the compilers of a book of houses would have been exercising their opportunity to preach to us, to "educate" us, to explain why some decisions were correct and others were not, based on some criteria probably assumed rather than made explicit, like "honesty of structure." Now, such is the state of our new-non architectural freedom that Les Walker draws fondly, even lovingly, an extraordinary disparate group of houses, plain and fancy, large and small, straightforward and exotic, without even suggesting favoritism. He seems to enjoy them all, exhibiting a broadness of mind, catholicity of taste, a generously eclectic spirit which makes this compendium come alive.

Not many years ago there would have been special praise for houses which explicitly exhibited their structural systems. Now, in an era when architects are frequently called on to restructure old buildings, to meet new requirements without changing the looks of a beloved old place, there is as much virtue in structural deception as in structural explicitness. That makes it easier for us to enjoy all kinds of romantic enthusiasms without having to regard them as regrettable lapses from classic purity.

The other part of our liberation is a renewed joy in surfaces and pattern and ornament, the pleasure in all kinds of enrichment, from the patterns at the corners of a log cabin to the recollection by way of systems of ornament of civilizations distant in time and space. This volume is full of both those kinds of joy, and is a genuine feast for the eyes and mind.

Charles Moore
Los Angeles, California

Introduction

The idea for this book began with my publisher's request for a handbook of American housing styles that would be of interest to architects, historians, anthropologists, builders, real estate agents, and anyone else interested in how the shape and character of dwellings came about. What seemed to him to be a relatively straightforward proposition was, I knew, a most difficult and time-consuming project. My investigations of the Dutch Colonial stone houses scattered about my neighborhood in Ulster County, New York, had given me vivid experience as to the research required to fully reveal the reasons why a group of people from another culture would build a house of the shape and style with the materials and floor plan that the Dutch built along the west shore of the Hudson River. I must have read fifteen books, ranging from a documented history of Kingston, New York, to architecture in the Netherlands before 1700, in studying this one single housing style. Did I have the ability to condense all this information, some of it quite technical, into one or two pages that could be easily understood, or the energy to devote to a book of this length and complexity?

I decided to prove to both of us whether or not the project was possible by spending two or three weeks in the library to establish an approximate idea as to how many significant styles I would need to include, and, of course, how much research would be necessary for each. It proved impossible to compile quickly an accurate list of how much research time I would need. At that time, I felt I would find perhaps seventy-five significant styles and it would take two weeks to research, write, and complete the art work for each style. As a test I researched and mocked up a four-page section on the Cape Cod house. Learning new detailed information about this beautiful New England dwelling held its own fascination but when I

actually began to draw what I had learned, and saw the structure come to life, I had a sense of such joy, that I immediately decided to do the book, no matter how much time it would take. My publisher agreed and felt that my interest in structure, plan development, and shape, if stressed and clearly illustrated, would lead to a book which filled a need in that history and architecture, in the most human sense, would interrelate.

The next step was to compile a file folder filled with pertinent information including pictures, plans, essays, and a brief select bibliography of as many house styles as I could find. This was done with the able assistance of a good friend and colleague, Richard Bouchard, who enriched the compilation with his "Sgt. Pepper section"—a title we used for such nontraditional, often whimsical styles like Converted Train Cars, Domes, Floating Houses, and Quonset Huts. I found that journals such as *American Builder* and *Popular Science* gave valuable information regarding structure (the bones of the building), and architecture magazines like *Architectural Record* gave contextual information regarding stylistic influences and decoration (the skin of the building), and history texts gave factual and cultural information regarding shape, material, and plan development.

As the reader will see, the work is organized chronologically, beginning with the American Indians and early settlers, and perhaps you will experience, as I did, the flow of American housebuilding history as it happened. In the end, five years after I began, I felt as much a reporter as an architectural historian. I saw my role as commonsensically interpreting and condensing knowledge for a wide variety of readers. At first I was overwhelmed, but as time passed and more and more finished work accumulated, I began to relax and really enjoy an almost dreamlike participation in American housebuilding.

Each house discussed in the book grew from an idea. The idea at first was one of simple shelter and expedient use of available tools and materials. Many anthropologists believe that American Indians, living as long ago as 10,000 B.C., didn't begin to leave their natural shelters to build their own dwellings until A.D. 300. At that time they began to leave their caves and cliffs and settle into areas with plentiful food supplies. There they built permanent small villages of single-family dwellings made primarily from earth and logs. Over the years the American Indians learned to use the natural materials available to them to create structures that related to climate, their construction abilities, and their cultures. The Plains tribes developed lightweight, portable, conical structures (tipis) because these American Indians were always on the move. The tribes located in New York State evolved a dwelling made primarily of saplings and bark that could be built over one hundred feet long and that could have held as many as fifty members of an extended family (longhouse). Tribes living in the South used reeds and grass to keep cool, and the

American Indians of the great Southwest used earth to make adobe bricks for strong, cool dwellings.

There are eight primary American Indian shelter styles, each with a special, individual, primitive idea derived from the straightforward, expedient use of indigenous materials used to construct a shape reflective of the tribe's culture and lifestyle.

The first European settlers brought housebuilding ideas from their native countries and adapted them to the new locale. Settlements were established in four regions, each with a distinctly different culture. The first was in New England, settled by the English, who developed their housebuilding skills in wood. The second was in the Chesapeake Bay area, settled by a generally wealthier, more dependent group of English who used brick to build houses in the Medieval Style popular then in England. The third region was developed by the Germans and Scotch/Irish in the Delaware River valley, where they built primarily in stone, influenced somewhat by the architecture of their homeland. The fourth region, the Hudson River valley, was settled by the Dutch, who used a variety of materials to build their dwellings.

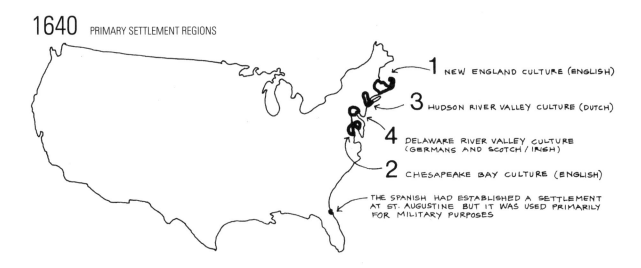

1640 PRIMARY SETTLEMENT REGIONS

1 NEW ENGLAND CULTURE (ENGLISH)

3 HUDSON RIVER VALLEY CULTURE (DUTCH)

4 DELAWARE RIVER VALLEY CULTURE (GERMANS AND SCOTCH / IRISH)

2 CHESAPEAKE BAY CULTURE (ENGLISH)

THE SPANISH HAD ESTABLISHED A SETTLEMENT AT ST. AUGUSTINE BUT IT WAS USED PRIMARILY FOR MILITARY PURPOSES

By 1700 three of these four culture regions were growing along migratory trails influenced by geography and climate. The New England culture pushed westward across New York State and north into Maine; the Delaware Valley culture followed a frontier to the west across Pennsylvania, southwest along the Appalachian Mountains, and south into North and South Carolina; and the Chesapeake Bay culture moved westward and southward. Only the Dutch culture in the Hudson River valley remained static and had little influence outside its region.

New settlements blossomed all along the migratory trails with dwellings built according to climate, skills, available materials, and, most importantly, housebuilding knowledge gained from the original culture region.

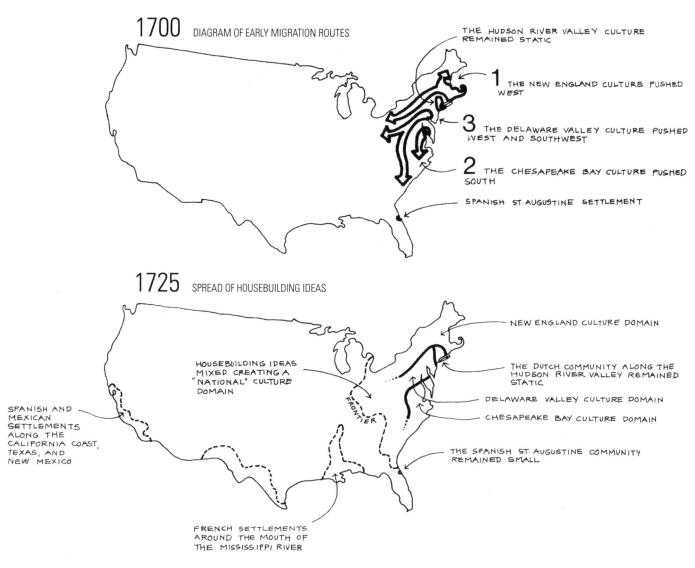

1700 DIAGRAM OF EARLY MIGRATION ROUTES

THE HUDSON RIVER VALLEY CULTURE REMAINED STATIC

1 THE NEW ENGLAND CULTURE PUSHED WEST

3 THE DELAWARE VALLEY CULTURE PUSHED WEST AND SOUTHWEST

2 THE CHESAPEAKE BAY CULTURE PUSHED SOUTH

SPANISH ST·AUGUSTINE SETTLEMENT

1725 SPREAD OF HOUSEBUILDING IDEAS

HOUSEBUILDING IDEAS MIXED CREATING A "NATIONAL" CULTURE DOMAIN

SPANISH AND MEXICAN SETTLEMENTS ALONG THE CALIFORNIA COAST, TEXAS, AND NEW MEXICO

FRONTIER

NEW ENGLAND CULTURE DOMAIN

THE DUTCH COMMUNITY ALONG THE HUDSON RIVER VALLEY REMAINED STATIC

DELAWARE VALLEY CULTURE DOMAIN

CHESAPEAKE BAY CULTURE DOMAIN

THE SPANISH ST·AUGUSTINE COMMUNITY REMAINED SMALL

FRENCH SETTLEMENTS AROUND THE MOUTH OF THE MISSISSIPPI RIVER

In the early eighteenth century, as homesteaders spread westward into the heart of America, their ideas mixed to create hybrid house designs influenced primarily by the three original culture regions. The new area was a true melting pot of housebuilding ideas, the beginning of what might be termed a national culture.

At the same time, the French were settling in the southern portion of their vast empire flanking the Mississippi River. In this hot, damp climate they invented new forms and building techniques that later influenced housebuilding in the Deep South. Spanish-speaking people were also settling in California, Texas, and New Mexico, in small religious communities designed to convert the American Indian to Catholicism. Their colonial architecture ideas were to influence greatly the California and Florida regions during the nineteenth and twentieth centuries.

Most housing styles that developed after the American Revolution were the result of national or international trends rather than regional concepts. Ideas were conveyed throughout the country in housebuilding journals and books. Travelers such as Thomas Jefferson brought back new European ideas, and architecture became an elite profession. In the late nineteenth and twentieth centuries, new technologies were developed inspiring a wide variety of new housebuilding ideas. The Quonset hut and the geodesic dome, developed during World War II; the free form house, possible because of the development of lightweight concrete; and the solar house, using new mechanical devices and techniques, were house ideas born from technological advancement. It is interesting to me that the last style in this book, except for the theoretical look into space, is an eclectic one that borrows from all other preceding styles and ideas. What a wonderful way to end—with a style that seeks to be a summary.

There are many books on the history of American architecture. Most of them classify different building types or styles under a chronological listing of periods beginning with a medieval period and ending with a modern period. Some use geographical location or primary building materials such as stone, brick, or wood as a way to categorize the various styles. Others use the wars or turns of centuries as beginning or ending points such as "pre- or post-Civil War" or "pre- or post-eighteenth century" to group building types. I preferred not to do this for several reasons. First, I wanted to make the book as easy to understand as possible. I felt that the best way to accomplish this was simply to list the styles in the order in which they occurred beginning with the

Indians and ending with Space. This would create a book that could function as a traveler's guide to house-watching, a collection of one hundred short stories, and a reference indexed according to time. Second, it was often impossible to place a style into a broad category. For example the Nebraska sod house was built during the Victorian period but it was not Victorian in style. Finally, I wanted to treat each style equally. The Shacks and Shanties Style was as interesting to me as the Greek Revival Style. In the end, I began to view the history of the American house as a chronological series of one hundred parts, each with its own special set of reasons and influences.

I hope this book will provide an in-depth volume of information as to why, how, and when a particular house style was built; a reference for students, builders, architects, and house lovers; a field guide for those interested in recognizing and classifying house styles; and an enjoyable text for students of American architecture and architectural history.

Lester Walker
Woodstock, New York

I would especially like to thank Richard Bouchard for his valuable assistance in helping with the research; Sylvia Wright, the City College of New York School of Architecture librarian, and her staff for cooperation above and beyond the call of duty; Charles Moore for his inspiration; Peter Mayer, Mark Gornpertz, and Tracy Carns at The Overlook Press for their continuous monitoring of the work; and Jess Walker for his invaluable assistance with the most contemporary parts of the book.

The American
Indians

Earth Lodge

Prairies and Northwest
A.D. 300–Present

Archeologists think that the first crude attempts at housebuilding in America occurred about A.D. 300 in New Mexico and Arizona. These dwellings were partially excavated pits that were roofed over with branches and mud. They became known as earth lodges or pit houses. They were found primarily in the prairie and had the appearance of a huge grass-covered mound in summer and a rounded snow drift in winter. But the plume of smoke emitted from the top of each mound gave them away.

The earth lodge evolved into a cone-shaped wooded frame covered with willow brush ten to twenty inches thick and thatched grass or pine needles supporting a six-inch deep layer of sod. These houses were about forty feet in diameter with the floor sunk by digging from one to eight feet below the ground. They had earth covered tunnel-like passageways with buffalo skin doors. They gained heat from the earth below and from a central fire. An extended family, sometimes as many as forty people, often inhabited a single dwelling.

There were several types of earth lodges, but they all had a similar tentlike structural system. Lighting was surprisingly good with just an opening in the roof (smoke hole) and doorway. The Kalapuya tribe in the Northwest plateau region also used the smoke hole as an entrance by climbing over the lodge and using a notched log to serve as a ladder.

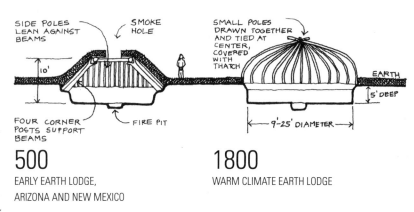

500
EARLY EARTH LODGE,
ARIZONA AND NEW MEXICO

1800
WARM CLIMATE EARTH LODGE

The Mandan of the upper Missouri River built circular, timber framed earth lodges that could accommodate five or six families, embracing thirty to forty people. The lodge was subdivided into "houses" for each family with partitions of willow mat or dehaired skin.

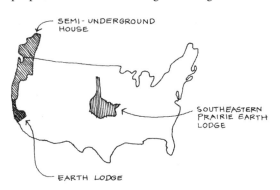

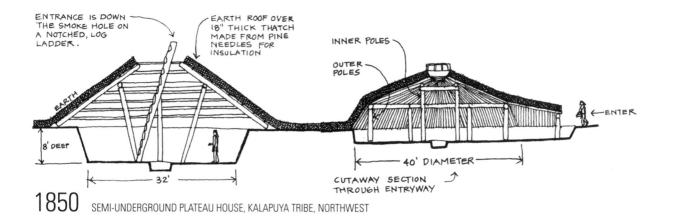

ENTRANCE IS DOWN THE SMOKE HOLE ON A NOTCHED, LOG LADDER.

EARTH ROOF OVER 18" THICK THATCH MADE FROM PINE NEEDLES FOR INSULATION

INNER POLES

OUTER POLES

EARTH

8' DEEP

32'

←ENTER

40' DIAMETER

CUTAWAY SECTION THROUGH ENTRYWAY

1850
SEMI-UNDERGROUND PLATEAU HOUSE, KALAPUYA TRIBE, NORTHWEST

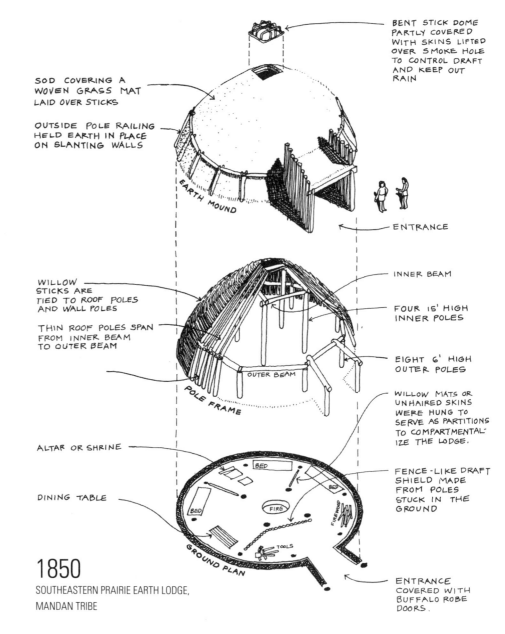

BENT STICK DOME PARTLY COVERED WITH SKINS LIFTED OVER SMOKE HOLE TO CONTROL DRAFT AND KEEP OUT RAIN

SOD COVERING A WOVEN GRASS MAT LAID OVER STICKS

OUTSIDE POLE RAILING HELD EARTH IN PLACE ON SLANTING WALLS

EARTH MOUND

ENTRANCE

WILLOW STICKS ARE TIED TO ROOF POLES AND WALL POLES

THIN ROOF POLES SPAN FROM INNER BEAM TO OUTER BEAM

OUTER BEAM

POLE FRAME

INNER BEAM

FOUR 15' HIGH INNER POLES

EIGHT 6' HIGH OUTER POLES

WILLOW MATS OR UNHAIRED SKINS WERE HUNG TO SERVE AS PARTITIONS TO COMPARTMENTAL-IZE THE LODGE.

ALTAR OR SHRINE

DINING TABLE

BED

BED

FIRE

BED

FIREWOOD

TOOLS

GROUND PLAN

FENCE-LIKE DRAFT SHIELD MADE FROM POLES STUCK IN THE GROUND

ENTRANCE COVERED WITH BUFFALO ROBE DOORS.

1850
SOUTHEASTERN PRAIRIE EARTH LODGE, MANDAN TRIBE

Pueblo

Southwest
A.D. 700–Present

The Pueblo Indians consisted of many tribes formed during prehistoric times. They lived in quiet, small, prosperous villages until they were invaded by nomadic tribes from the north. For protection, they rebuilt their villages high up on canyon walls, from where they could hurl rocks down on their enemies. They also fortified themselves by pulling their entry ladders up into these cliff dwellings.

Later, as the Pueblo grew stronger, they migrated from the areas where their culture originated. They continued to build their villages in high places, often arranging them so that the houses themselves formed a defensive wall; making it possible for them to fight from their roofs just as they had done earlier from canyon walls. They built huge "apartment buildings" (known as pueblos), sometimes in half circles with one apartment stacked on another, in broad steps. The outside of the pueblo had a clifflike appearance.

The modern pueblo is a reflection of the prehistoric Pueblo Indian culture. The apartments are still grouped together to make fortresslike protection and many apartments still have their entry ladders suspended from the roof, although there are no enemies. Building methods, even the water collection system, remain virtually unchanged. The pueblo at Taos, New Mexico, grew by accretion, adding apartments when necessary, over hundreds of years.

AREA OF RECTANGULAR FLAT ROOFED PUEBLO

1850
PART OF THE PUEBLO COMMUNITY AT TAOS, NEW MEXICO

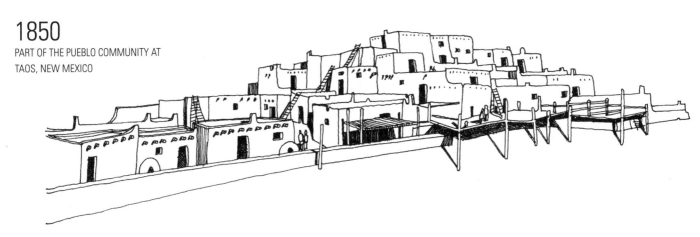

The pueblo apartment, like most simple dwellings, was primarily a place for food preparation and sleeping. During the day it was a kitchen and at night a family bedroom. The rectangular flat-roof pueblo shown below illustrates how pueblo dwellers lived in 1800, with little difference from their prehistoric ancestors.

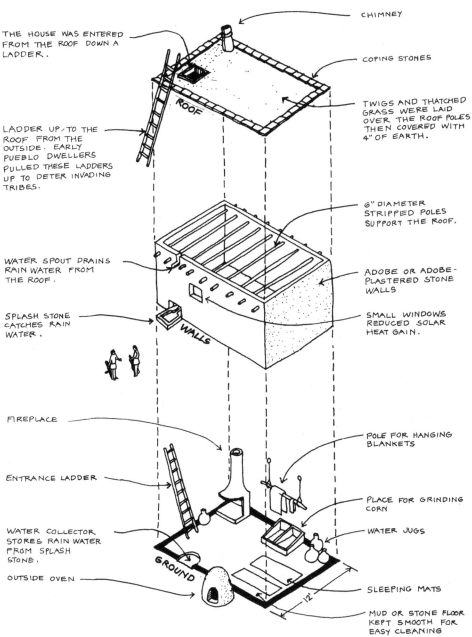

THE HOUSE WAS ENTERED FROM THE ROOF DOWN A LADDER.

CHIMNEY

COPING STONES

TWIGS AND THATCHED GRASS WERE LAID OVER THE ROOF POLES THEN COVERED WITH 4" OF EARTH.

LADDER UP TO THE ROOF FROM THE OUTSIDE. EARLY PUEBLO DWELLERS PULLED THESE LADDERS UP TO DETER INVADING TRIBES.

6" DIAMETER STRIPPED POLES SUPPORT THE ROOF.

WATER SPOUT DRAINS RAIN WATER FROM THE ROOF.

ADOBE OR ADOBE-PLASTERED STONE WALLS

SPLASH STONE CATCHES RAIN WATER.

SMALL WINDOWS REDUCED SOLAR HEAT GAIN.

FIREPLACE

POLE FOR HANGING BLANKETS

ENTRANCE LADDER

PLACE FOR GRINDING CORN

WATER JUGS

WATER COLLECTOR STORES RAIN WATER FROM SPLASH STONE.

OUTSIDE OVEN

SLEEPING MATS

MUD OR STONE FLOOR KEPT SMOOTH FOR EASY CLEANING

ROOF

WALLS

GROUND

12'

1800 RECTANGULAR FLAT-ROOFED PUEBLO, PUEBLO INDIANS

Pole and Thatch

South
A.D. 800–Present

The American Indians living in the southern prairies used their shelter as home base, developing housing technologies to suit the warm climate. Perhaps the most interesting of these is the Gothic domed thatched house of the Wichita tribe shown on the opposite page. These houses were usually occupied by several families and were larger than the tipis, averaging about twenty-five feet in diameter.

Perimeter poles were bent over an interior pole frame into a strong, pointed dome shape (thus the term "Gothic") and covered with woven heavy grass thatching. This thatching allowed the summer breeze to flow through the house and cool it, while still sheilding from heavy rains. A central fire was all the heating necessary. Smoke filtered through the roof.

The most popular dwelling in the western region of the Southwest was the rectangular domed roof house. Lines of poles with gaps between them were used for walls to allow more air to flow through the house—necessary in this hot climate. The pyramidal or hip roof rectangular house evolved in the southern section of the Southwest because the steep angle shedded the heavy rain common to that area. The rectangular gabled roof house became popular in the nineteenth century in the Southeast where it could get quite cold. This house also had a thatched roof, but its walls were made from an adobe mixture plastered against woven poles, known as mud wattle. These walls kept the house cool in summer and retained sufficient heat from a fire in winter.

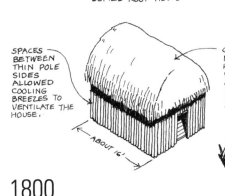

RECTANGULAR GABLED ROOF HOUSE

GOTHIC DOME THATCHED HOUSE

PYRAMIDAL OR HIPPED ROOF RECTANGULAR HOUSE

RECTANGULAR DOMED ROOF HOUSE

SPACES BETWEEN THIN POLE SIDES ALLOWED COOLING BREEZES TO VENTILATE THE HOUSE.

ABOUT 16'

1800
RECTANGULAR DOMED ROOF HOUSE, OPATA TRIBE

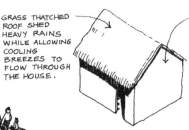

GRASS THATCHED ROOF SHED HEAVY RAINS WHILE ALLOWING COOLING BREEZES TO FLOW THROUGH THE HOUSE.

1840
RECTANGULAR GABLED ROOF HOUSE, MIDDLE MISSISSIPPI TRIBE

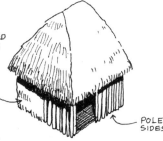

OFTEN ADOBE WAS PLASTERED AGAINST POLE SIDES TO MAKE A MORE PERMANENT DWELLING.

OFTEN THE POLE SIDES WERE WOVEN WITH GRASS TO CREATE MORE SHADE.

POLE SIDES

1850
PYRAMIDAL (HIPPED) ROOFED RECTANGULAR HOUSE, GUAYMI TRIBE

The technology of the pointed Gothic domed thatched house was quite simple. The dome was constructed with long slender poles stuck into the ground in a thirty-foot diameter circle and bent over a frame, then collected at the top in a ring made from a pliable sapling. This structure was wrapped with stick battens to create a base for the grass thatching exterior used to shed rain and keep the inside cool. The house was inhabited by one extended family and could be built in two days.

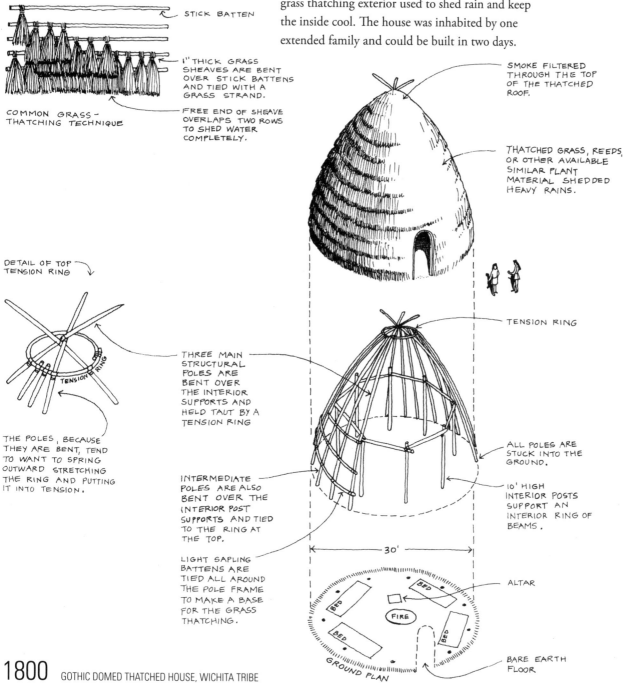

STICK BATTEN

1" THICK GRASS SHEAVES ARE BENT OVER STICK BATTENS AND TIED WITH A GRASS STRAND.

FREE END OF SHEAVE OVERLAPS TWO ROWS TO SHED WATER COMPLETELY.

COMMON GRASS-THATCHING TECHNIQUE

DETAIL OF TOP TENSION RING

TENSION RING

THE POLES, BECAUSE THEY ARE BENT, TEND TO WANT TO SPRING OUTWARD STRETCHING THE RING AND PUTTING IT INTO TENSION.

THREE MAIN STRUCTURAL POLES ARE BENT OVER THE INTERIOR SUPPORTS AND HELD TAUT BY A TENSION RING

INTERMEDIATE POLES ARE ALSO BENT OVER THE INTERIOR POST SUPPORTS AND TIED TO THE RING AT THE TOP.

LIGHT SAPLING BATTENS ARE TIED ALL AROUND THE POLE FRAME TO MAKE A BASE FOR THE GRASS THATCHING.

SMOKE FILTERED THROUGH THE TOP OF THE THATCHED ROOF.

THATCHED GRASS, REEDS, OR OTHER AVAILABLE SIMILAR PLANT MATERIAL SHEDDED HEAVY RAINS.

TENSION RING

ALL POLES ARE STUCK INTO THE GROUND.

10' HIGH INTERIOR POSTS SUPPORT AN INTERIOR RING OF BEAMS.

30'

ALTAR

BED
BED
BED
BED
FIRE

BARE EARTH FLOOR

GROUND PLAN

1800 GOTHIC DOMED THATCHED HOUSE, WICHITA TRIBE

Tipi

Great Plains A.D. 1200– Present

No dwelling stirs the imagination like the tipi of the Indians of the American Great Plains. It is one of the most economical, functional, mobile dwellings ever built. Every tribe built some kind of dwelling that was used at least part of the year. The form of these dwellings depended on the climate, the available building materials, and the character of the tribe.

The conical shape of the tipi was a logical form for the nomadic buffalo-hunting Plains Indians. It was portable, it shed water and snow and permitted smoke to escape from a central fire. The poles, cut from saplings, were light and quick to lean into a conical skeleton. Buffalo hides were plentiful and easily sewn into a relatively light, one-piece skin to fit over the skeleton.

Building the tipi was generally the woman's job. She had to shave the bark from the poles, tan, cut, and sew the hides into a tailored cover, and erect and dismantle the structure. Dogs and later horses dragged the dismantled tipi from one hunting ground to another.

Many tribes painted the outside of their tipis to announce the owner's religion and rituals. Originally the designs came from dreams and aesthetic qualities were secondary. Men were usually responsible for the painting and some became specialists. Two examples of painted coverings are shown below.

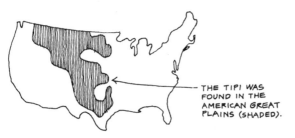

THE TIPI WAS FOUND IN THE AMERICAN GREAT PLAINS (SHADED).

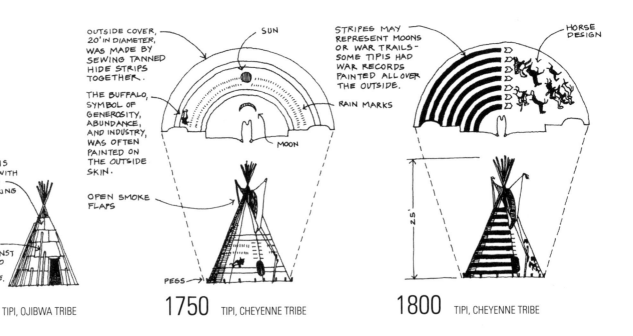

THE FIRST TIPIS WERE MADE WITH OVERLAPPING HIDES COVERING THIN POLES TIED IN A CONICAL SHAPE.

POLES WERE LEANED AGAINST THE HIDES TO HELP HOLD THEM IN PLACE.

1550 TIPI, OJIBWA TRIBE

OUTSIDE COVER, 20' IN DIAMETER, WAS MADE BY SEWING TANNED HIDE STRIPS TOGETHER.

THE BUFFALO, SYMBOL OF GENEROSITY, ABUNDANCE, AND INDUSTRY, WAS OFTEN PAINTED ON THE OUTSIDE SKIN.

OPEN SMOKE FLAPS

SUN

MOON

PEGS

1750 TIPI, CHEYENNE TRIBE

STRIPES MAY REPRESENT MOONS OR WAR TRAILS – SOME TIPIS HAD WAR RECORDS PAINTED ALL OVER THE OUTSIDE.

RAIN MARKS

HORSE DESIGN

25'

1800 TIPI, CHEYENNE TRIBE

Over the years the technology of the tipi became more and more refined. Pegs replaced heavy logs in holding the cover to the ground. An anchor rope was developed to tie down the tipi in time of high wind. A sewn one-piece, form-fitting cover or skin, replaced crude overlapping hides. The tipi has proved to be portable yet strong, lightweight, yet able to retain heat, and amazingly elegant as a living space.

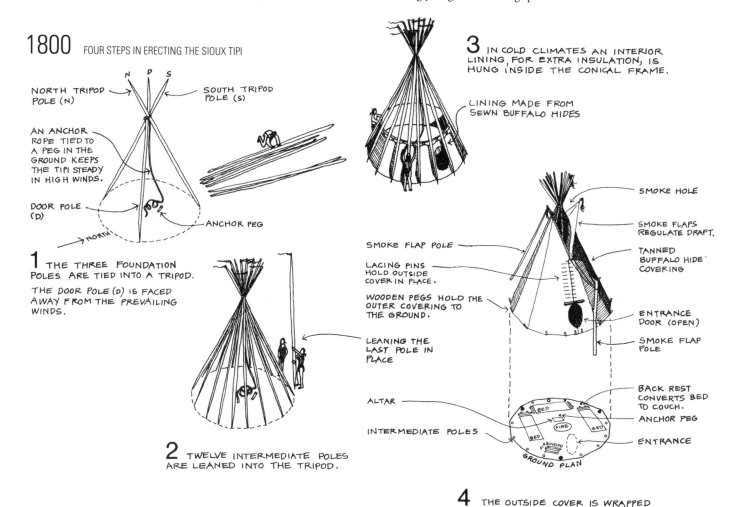

1800 FOUR STEPS IN ERECTING THE SIOUX TIPI

NORTH TRIPOD POLE (N)

SOUTH TRIPOD POLE (S)

AN ANCHOR ROPE TIED TO A PEG IN THE GROUND KEEPS THE TIPI STEADY IN HIGH WINDS.

DOOR POLE (D)

ANCHOR PEG

NORTH

1 THE THREE FOUNDATION POLES ARE TIED INTO A TRIPOD.

THE DOOR POLE (D) IS FACED AWAY FROM THE PREVAILING WINDS.

LEANING THE LAST POLE IN PLACE

2 TWELVE INTERMEDIATE POLES ARE LEANED INTO THE TRIPOD.

3 IN COLD CLIMATES AN INTERIOR LINING, FOR EXTRA INSULATION, IS HUNG INSIDE THE CONICAL FRAME.

LINING MADE FROM SEWN BUFFALO HIDES

SMOKE HOLE

SMOKE FLAPS REGULATE DRAFT.

TANNED BUFFALO HIDE COVERING

SMOKE FLAP POLE

LACING PINS HOLD OUTSIDE COVER IN PLACE.

WOODEN PEGS HOLD THE OUTER COVERING TO THE GROUND.

ENTRANCE DOOR (OPEN)

SMOKE FLAP POLE

ALTAR

INTERMEDIATE POLES

BED

FIRE

BED

BED

FIREWOOD

GROUND PLAN

BACK REST CONVERTS BED TO COUCH.

ANCHOR PEG

ENTRANCE

4 THE OUTSIDE COVER IS WRAPPED AROUND THE FRAME.

FLAPS AND DOOR CLOSED FOR RAIN RUN OFF

OPEN DOOR

NORMAL

RAINSTORM

OPEN SMOKE FLAPS

OUTER COVERING IS FOLDED UP TO CREATE NATURAL AIR VENTILATION.

OPEN DOOR

SWELTERING

SMOKE FLAPS WERE POINTED AWAY FROM THE WIND TO CREATE A DRAFT FOR SMOKE

10' HIGH PERIMETER SAPLING/BRUSH FENCE ACTED AS INSULATION.

CLOSED DOOR

BELOW ZERO

FOUR TIPI CONFIGURATIONS FOR VARIOUS WEATHER CONDITIONS

Longhouse

Northeast
1400

LOCATION OF
THE BARREL-
ROOFED LONGHOUSE

The famous longhouse of the New York Iroquois sheltered a group of small, related families. The extended family moved through the building along a central hallway. Off this hallway were partitioned rooms, or booths, where each family lived, each with a separate fireplace. This linear plan allowed a certain privacy, since the beds were located to the back of each booth, with a great deal of communal activity taking place in the central hallway. The plan also allowed for expansion, to the front or to the rear, as the family expanded. Some longhouses were over one hundred feet long.

The fires kept the longhouses warm and elm bark cladding kept it waterproof. Adequate light entered from smoke holes and doorways. Inside, the narrow hallway was flanked by a series of platforms to facilitate sitting and sleeping as seen in the section below.

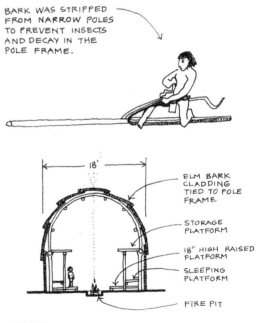

BARK WAS STRIPPED
FROM NARROW POLES
TO PREVENT INSECTS
AND DECAY IN THE
POLE FRAME.

18'

ELM BARK
CLADDING
TIED TO POLE
FRAME

STORAGE
PLATFORM

18" HIGH RAISED
PLATFORM

SLEEPING
PLATFORM

FIRE PIT

1500 CUTAWAY SECTION THROUGH IROQUOIS LONGHOUSE, NEW YORK

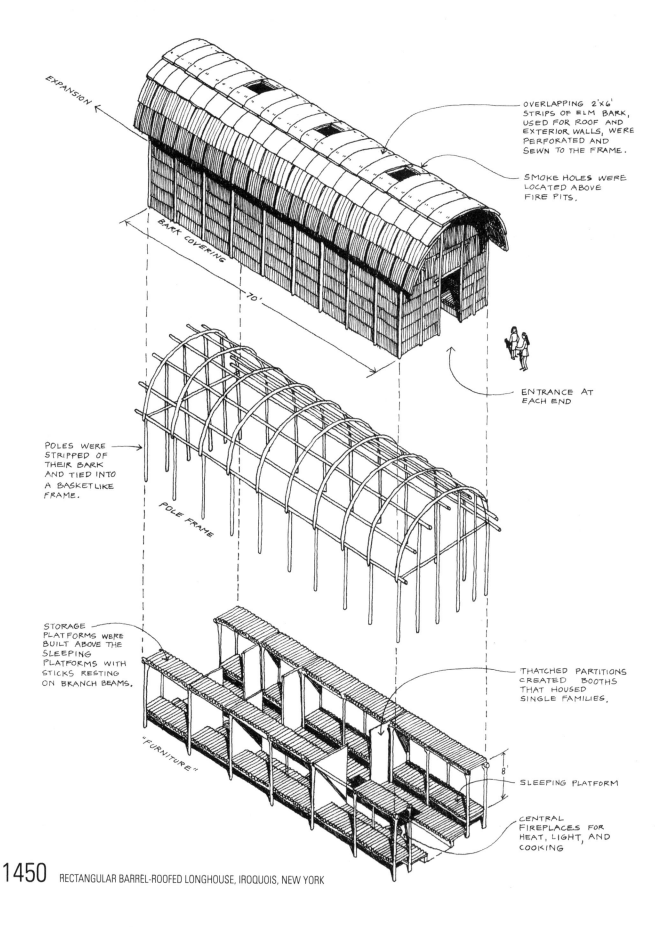

EXPANSION

OVERLAPPING 2'x6' STRIPS OF ELM BARK, USED FOR ROOF AND EXTERIOR WALLS, WERE PERFORATED AND SEWN TO THE FRAME.

SMOKE HOLES WERE LOCATED ABOVE FIRE PITS.

BARK COVERING

70'

ENTRANCE AT EACH END

POLES WERE STRIPPED OF THEIR BARK AND TIED INTO A BASKETLIKE FRAME.

POLE FRAME

STORAGE PLATFORMS WERE BUILT ABOVE THE SLEEPING PLATFORMS WITH STICKS RESTING ON BRANCH BEAMS.

THATCHED PARTITIONS CREATED BOOTHS THAT HOUSED SINGLE FAMILIES.

"FURNITURE"

8'

SLEEPING PLATFORM

CENTRAL FIREPLACES FOR HEAT, LIGHT, AND COOKING

1450 RECTANGULAR BARREL-ROOFED LONGHOUSE, IROQUOIS, NEW YORK

Wigwam

Northeast
1600

The wigwam (generally called a wickiup in the Southeast) was a bark covered shelter common in the Northeast, built in many different shapes and sizes. Single families lived in small domes or bark covered tipis and extended families lived in elliptically shaped houses, sometimes as large as twenty-five by fifteen feet. Some tribes, notably the Kiwigapawa, migrated from the Lake Michigan area in a southwestern direction to get away from white culture. In the early seventeenth century and for the next three hundred years, they gradually migrated until they reached Coahuila, Mexico, just south of the U.S. border. After all their travels, their housing form, the wigwam, remained virtually unchanged.

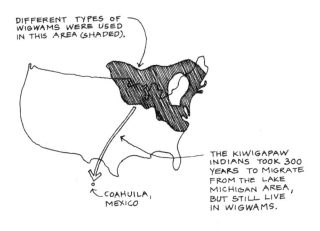

DIFFERENT TYPES OF WIGWAMS WERE USED IN THIS AREA (SHADED).

THE KIWIGAPAW INDIANS TOOK 300 YEARS TO MIGRATE FROM THE LAKE MICHIGAN AREA, BUT STILL LIVE IN WIGWAMS.

COAHUILA, MEXICO

THE EARLIEST WIGWAMS WERE MADE WITH BARK STRIPS HUNG INSIDE A BENT POLE FRAME.

1600 BIRCH BARK ROUND WIGWAM, SHAWNEE

OVERLAPPING BARK OVER A CONICAL STICK FRAME

POLES KEPT BARK FROM BLOWING OFF IN HEAVY WINDS.

1650 TIPI-SHAPED WIGWAM, MICMAC

BARK WAS SEWN TO A BENT POLE FRAME.

1650 DOMED BARK WIGWAM, CHIPPEWA

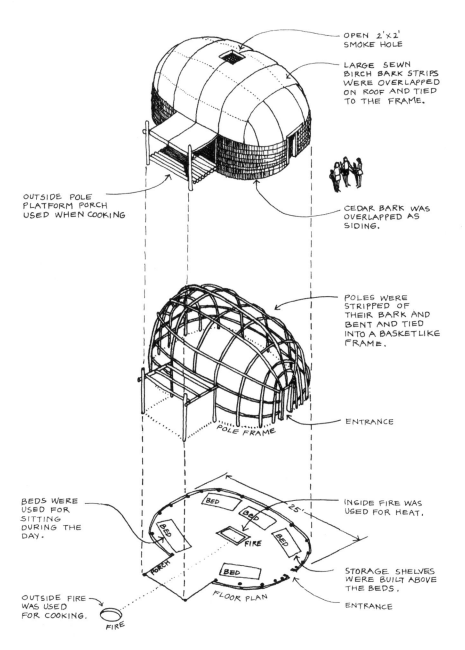

OPEN 2'X2' SMOKE HOLE

LARGE SEWN BIRCH BARK STRIPS WERE OVERLAPPED ON ROOF AND TIED TO THE FRAME.

OUTSIDE POLE PLATFORM PORCH USED WHEN COOKING

CEDAR BARK WAS OVERLAPPED AS SIDING.

POLES WERE STRIPPED OF THEIR BARK AND BENT AND TIED INTO A BASKETLIKE FRAME.

POLE FRAME

ENTRANCE

BEDS WERE USED FOR SITTING DURING THE DAY.

INSIDE FIRE WAS USED FOR HEAT.

BED
BED
BED
FIRE
BED
25'

PORCH

BED

FLOOR PLAN

OUTSIDE FIRE WAS USED FOR COOKING.

FIRE

STORAGE SHELVES WERE BUILT ABOVE THE BEDS.

ENTRANCE

1700 ELLIPTICAL WIGWAM, ALGONKIAN

Once the materials were gathered, the wigwam could be erected in a day. Unlike the tipi, it could not be taken apart and moved; the wigwam was a permanent dwelling. Most wigwams were structured around smooth sycamore saplings stuck in the ground and bent and tied into a basketlike frame. The frame was covered with birch bark on the top and cedar shingles on the sides, two materials relatively impervious to the weather.

Hogan

Southwest
1750

The Hogan is the traditional Navaho dwelling. It was, and still is, a permanent, single family house, built to retain the heat from a central fire in winter, and to keep it cool in summer. The twenty-five- to thirty-foot diameter of the dwelling provided ample room for many people to sleep or sit around the fire.

The Hogan began as a framework of five heavy poles set up in a cone shape, like the tipi, but with a small vestibule entrance like the earth lodge (p. 20). It had a smoke hole and was insulated with a heavy layer of sod. It was known as the forked stick Hogan because of the shape of the poles that held up the structure. Later, as more room was needed, it expanded into a dome shape made from earth-covered logs. These logs were stacked in circles with ever-decreasing diameters. They were called "whirling logs" because the structure resembled a wooden whirlpool when one looked up from the inside. Eventually, stone-walled hogans and the present day log-cabin walled hogan evolved because of the obvious influence of white pioneers.

LOCATION OF NAVAHO HOGAN

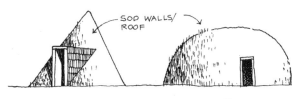

SOD WALLS/ ROOF

1500
FORKED STICK HOGAN

1550
EARTH HOGAN

STONE WALLS

LOG WITH MUD INFILL WALLS

20'

SOD ROOF

LOG WALLS

1750
STONE HOGAN

1800
SIX- OR EIGHT-SIDED LOG HOGAN

CUTAWAY SECTION

As shown below, by 1850 the Navaho had adopted, in part, the log technology of white pioneers to build the hogan's walls. But furniture arrangement, roof construction, lighting, interior functioning, and the overall shape of the building remained the same. In short, the Hogan remained an honest reflection of the domestic Navaho culture. It is interesting to compare this structure with the log octagon illustrated on page 53.

1850 EIGHT-SIDED LOG HOGAN, NAVAHO

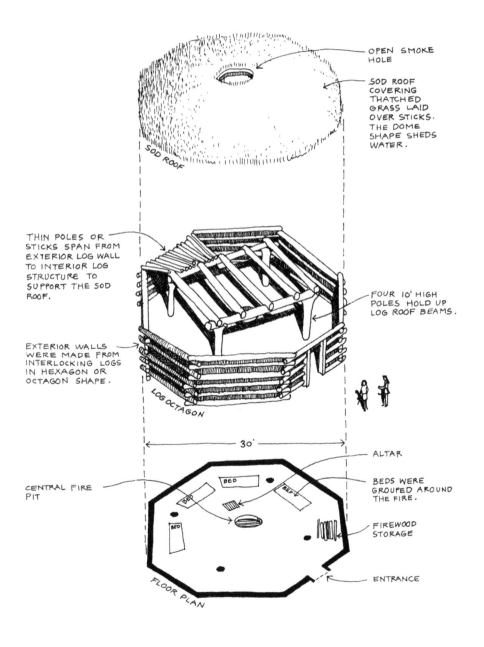

OPEN SMOKE HOLE

SOD ROOF COVERING THATCHED GRASS LAID OVER STICKS. THE DOME SHAPE SHEDS WATER.

THIN POLES OR STICKS SPAN FROM EXTERIOR LOG WALL TO INTERIOR LOG STRUCTURE TO SUPPORT THE SOD ROOF.

FOUR 10' HIGH POLES HOLD UP LOG ROOF BEAMS.

EXTERIOR WALLS WERE MADE FROM INTERLOCKING LOGS IN HEXAGON OR OCTAGON SHAPE.

LOG OCTAGON

30'

CENTRAL FIRE PIT

ALTAR

BEDS WERE GROUPED AROUND THE FIRE.

FIREWOOD STORAGE

ENTRANCE

FLOOR PLAN

BED

Plank House

Northwest
1800

The large plank houses (average size was thirty by forty feet wide by twenty feet high) of the Pacific Northwest were supported by a log framework to which wide cedar, pine, or spruce planks were attached to complete the building. They housed several families living more or less communally. Each single family had its own private space but cooked over the communal fire. The house was entered through a hole in a large carved pole, known as a totem pole, erected in honor of a fallen leader.

Coincidentally, in the early part of the nineteenth century, cladding a building with wide softwood planks over a heavy wood frame was a method employed on the Atlantic Coast by English settlers building the famous Cape Cod house (p. 86) and on the northwest Pacific Coast by the Haida Indians and other related tribes. The use of similar building methods by vastly differing cultures is found throughout history when climate considerations are alike.

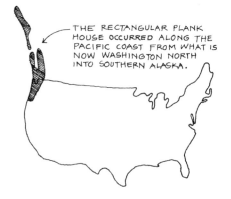

THE RECTANGULAR PLANK HOUSE OCCURRED ALONG THE PACIFIC COAST FROM WHAT IS NOW WASHINGTON NORTH INTO SOUTHERN ALASKA.

1870   OCEAN VIEW OF MINGIT VILLAGE, SITKA, ALASKA

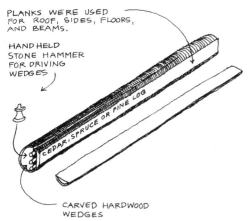

PLANKS WERE USED FOR ROOF, SIDES, FLOORS, AND BEAMS.

HAND HELD STONE HAMMER FOR DRIVING WEDGES

CEDAR, SPRUCE OR PINE LOG

CARVED HARDWOOD WEDGES

NORTHWEST INDIAN METHOD FOR MAKING WOOD PLANKS

Unlike Cape Cod pioneers who used highly evolved tools to cut planks, the Northwest American Indian used rather crude methods, but the results were the same. They selected the trees they intended to use and each tree was killed by hacking the bark away from around the trunk near the roots. After a year, the dead, dry tree was cut down and split with wooden wedges into planks.

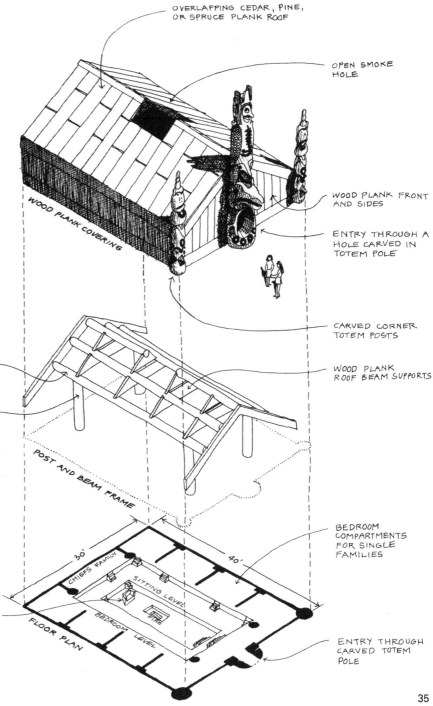

1840
RECTANGULAR PLANK HOUSE, HAIDA

OVERLAPPING CEDAR, PINE, OR SPRUCE PLANK ROOF

OPEN SMOKE HOLE

WOOD PLANK FRONT AND SIDES

ENTRY THROUGH A HOLE CARVED IN TOTEM POLE

WOOD PLANK COVERING

CARVED CORNER TOTEM POSTS

WOOD PLANK ROOF BEAM SUPPORTS

STRIPPED LOG ROOF BEAMS

THE FOUR MAIN COLUMNS WERE SOMETIMES CARVED.

POST AND BEAM FRAME

BEDROOM COMPARTMENTS FOR SINGLE FAMILIES

30'

40'

CHIEFS FAMILY

SITTING LEVEL

FIRE

BEDROOM LEVEL

CHIEF'S BENCH

FLOOR PLAN

ENTRY THROUGH CARVED TOTEM POLE

The Settlers

Spanish Cottage

Florida
1580

In 1513 Ponce de Leon landed near St. Augustine and claimed an area he called Florida for Spain. His colony lasted only a few months because of illness, lack of food, and hostile Indians, but by 1565 over two thousand Spaniards had arrived to begin the earliest permanent European settlement in America. St. Augustine began as a defense outpost to protect Spanish sailing ships. It was burned by Sir Francis Drake in 1586, but after he left, the surviving Spanish settlers rebuilt it.

Lack of prosperity, Indian raids, English harassment, and the founding of a colony at Charleston, South Carolina, by the English in 1670 inhibited the growth of the St. Augustine settlement. (By 1740 the colony had been burned four times.)

During twenty years of English occupation from 1763 to 1783, the Spanish settlers were thrown out and their houses were destroyed or remodeled. Spanish architectural influences were largely absent in Florida until their revival as an eclectic period fashion in the early twentieth century.

The first houses inhabited by the earliest settlers were one-room huts constructed of palmetto fronds and copied from the Seminole Indians. Since this house could be built in a few days, it was used throughout the history of the St. Augustine settlement as a temporary shelter, quickly built after each disaster, and inhabited until a more permanent home could be built.

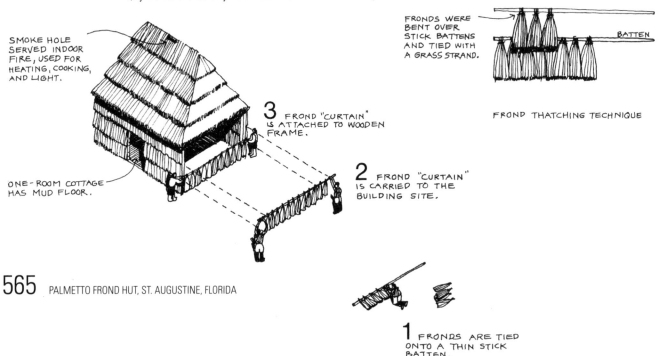

SMOKE HOLE SERVED INDOOR FIRE, USED FOR HEATING, COOKING, AND LIGHT.

ONE-ROOM COTTAGE HAS MUD FLOOR.

3 FROND "CURTAIN" IS ATTACHED TO WOODEN FRAME.

2 FROND "CURTAIN" IS CARRIED TO THE BUILDING SITE.

FRONDS WERE BENT OVER STICK BATTENS AND TIED WITH A GRASS STRAND.

BATTEN

FROND THATCHING TECHNIQUE

1565 PALMETTO FROND HUT, ST. AUGUSTINE, FLORIDA

1 FRONDS ARE TIED ONTO A THIN STICK BATTEN.

By 1586, pit sawn boards (p. 41) had been introduced and the predominant St. Augustine dwelling had become a small one-room cottage known as a board house. It was basically the same as the palmetto frond hut but used wide softwood boards for siding instead of frond curtains.

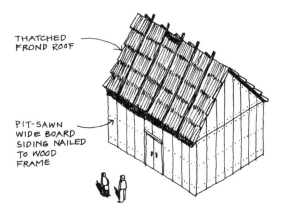

THATCHED FROND ROOF

PIT-SAWN WIDE BOARD SIDING NAILED TO WOOD FRAME

1586 BOARD HOUSE, ST. AUGUSTINE, FLORIDA

During the mid-eighteenth century, the more prosperous members of the community built so-called common houses of whitewashed lime mortar with an oyster shell aggregate. These houses shared with the palmetto hut and the board house the same overall shape. Their name derives from the use of a single room for all the functions of the house.

By the end of the eighteenth century, a house style had evolved that was dictated by the warm, humid Florida climate but still in the Spanish tradition. Built in two stories, to rise above the dampness of the earth, with rooms set aside for different functions, and cooling porches, or loggias, these houses were luxurious by the standards of the time.

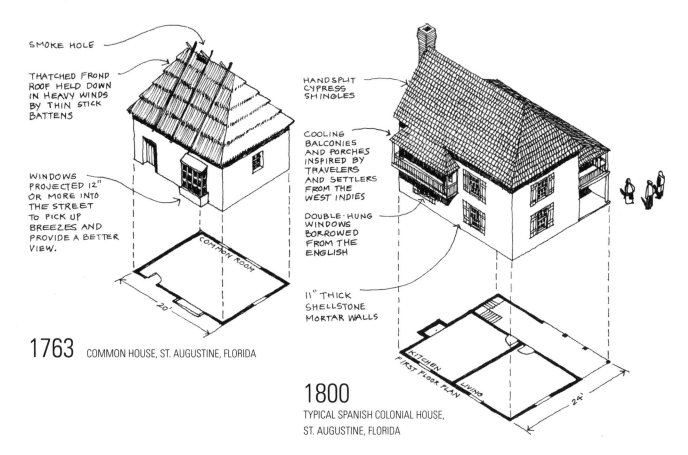

SMOKE HOLE

THATCHED FROND ROOF HELD DOWN IN HEAVY WINDS BY THIN STICK BATTENS

WINDOWS PROJECTED 12" OR MORE INTO THE STREET TO PICK UP BREEZES AND PROVIDE A BETTER VIEW.

COMMON ROOM

20'

1763 COMMON HOUSE, ST. AUGUSTINE, FLORIDA

HANDSPLIT CYPRESS SHINGLES

COOLING BALCONIES AND PORCHES INSPIRED BY TRAVELERS AND SETTLERS FROM THE WEST INDIES

DOUBLE-HUNG WINDOWS BORROWED FROM THE ENGLISH

11" THICK SHELLSTONE MORTAR WALLS

KITCHEN
LIVING
FIRST FLOOR PLAN

24'

1800
TYPICAL SPANISH COLONIAL HOUSE,
ST. AUGUSTINE, FLORIDA

English Cottage

New England
1623

America's first permanent settlers arrived in Plymouth, Massachusetts, on December 20, 1620. With the worst of winter yet to come, some sort of shelter was needed immediately. With little building experience, the Pilgrims managed to erect a few crude shelters using methods they had learned in their native England. In 1623 the Plymouth colony consisted of about twenty dwellings housing approximately sixty people.

These first houses were copies of medieval Elizabethan English cottages: a thick post and beam frame, notched and pegged for stability; thin wall studs and roof rafters notched into the frame; woven twigs (wattle) attached to the studs then covered with mud (daub) as insulation; a steep thatched grass roof to shed rain or snow; handsplit oak clapboards nailed to the walls for weatherproofing; and a huge eight foot wide stone fireplace with a wattle and daub chimney. Unlike English houses, windows were few and very small, to reduce heat loss. Glass was nonexistent, but some natural light

was necessary, so translucent oiled paper was used as a replacement in winter. The fireplace, used for cooking, heat, and light, was located inside the house, but had no damper, allowing most of the fire's heat to escape. The flammability of the thatched roof caused many early houses to burn.

These houses consisted of one room called a hall or great room on the ground floor with a storage loft above. Close to the fireplace, in a corner, a bench was placed for old people. A bed, used for sitting during the day, was located at the other end of the room. Trundle beds were brought out at night for children. Tables and chairs were small, crude, and built so they could be stored away when more space was needed.

The original Plymouth homes were built within a wooden palisade to protect the colonist from wild animals and unfriendly American Indians. New arrivals from England usually lived in wigwams or dugout caves until they could build themselves a more substantial house.

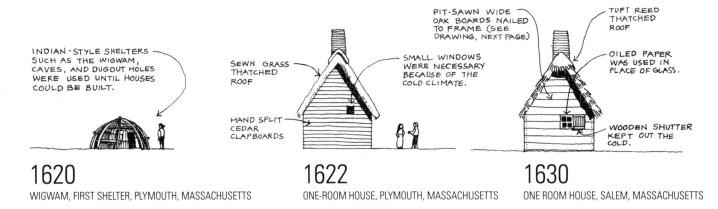

INDIAN-STYLE SHELTERS SUCH AS THE WIGWAM, CAVES, AND DUGOUT HOLES WERE USED UNTIL HOUSES COULD BE BUILT.

SEWN GRASS THATCHED ROOF

HAND SPLIT CEDAR CLAPBOARDS

PIT-SAWN WIDE OAK BOARDS NAILED TO FRAME (SEE DRAWING, NEXT PAGE)

SMALL WINDOWS WERE NECESSARY BECAUSE OF THE COLD CLIMATE.

TUFT REED THATCHED ROOF

OILED PAPER WAS USED IN PLACE OF GLASS.

WOODEN SHUTTER KEPT OUT THE COLD.

1620
WIGWAM, FIRST SHELTER, PLYMOUTH, MASSACHUSETTS

1622
ONE-ROOM HOUSE, PLYMOUTH, MASSACHUSETTS

1630
ONE ROOM HOUSE, SALEM, MASSACHUSETTS

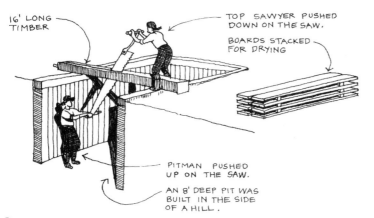

16' LONG TIMBER

TOP SAWYER PUSHED DOWN ON THE SAW.

BOARDS STACKED FOR DRYING

PITMAN PUSHED UP ON THE SAW.

AN 8' DEEP PIT WAS BUILT IN THE SIDE OF A HILL.

1630 PIT SAWING WIDE TIMBER BOARDS

The first cottages were quite crude. The floor was dirt, the stick-based chimney was a fire hazard (some of the houses had no chimney at all, just an opening in the thatched roof), and windows were closed only by shutter. Nevertheless, the timber-framing technique was to remain the most popular wood building system in America until the invention of the balloon frame in the mid-nineteenth century.

The drawings to the left and below show how the English sawed their timber into boards and thick beams and how the English cottage was constructed. Other English wood-framing techniques are shown on page 43.

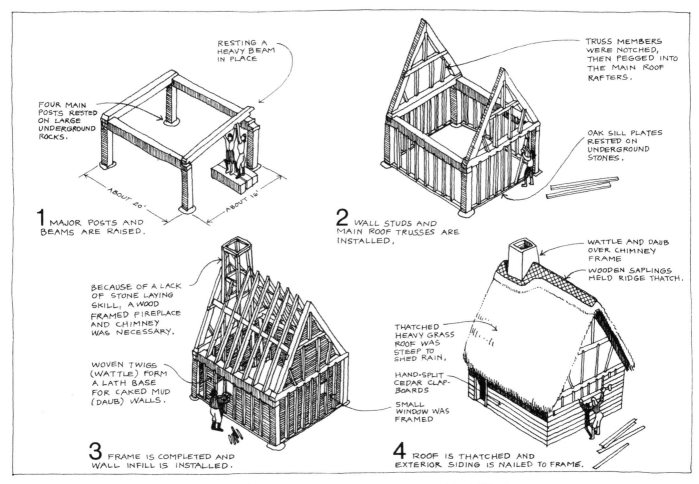

RESTING A HEAVY BEAM IN PLACE

FOUR MAIN POSTS RESTED ON LARGE UNDERGROUND ROCKS.

ABOUT 20'

ABOUT 16'

1 MAJOR POSTS AND BEAMS ARE RAISED.

TRUSS MEMBERS WERE NOTCHED, THEN PEGGED INTO THE MAIN ROOF RAFTERS.

OAK SILL PLATES RESTED ON UNDERGROUND STONES.

2 WALL STUDS AND MAIN ROOF TRUSSES ARE INSTALLED.

BECAUSE OF A LACK OF STONE LAYING SKILL, A WOOD FRAMED FIREPLACE AND CHIMNEY WAS NECESSARY.

WOVEN TWIGS (WATTLE) FORM A LATH BASE FOR CAKED MUD (DAUB) WALLS.

3 FRAME IS COMPLETED AND WALL INFILL IS INSTALLED.

WATTLE AND DAUB OVER CHIMNEY FRAME

WOODEN SAPLINGS HELD RIDGE THATCH.

THATCHED HEAVY GRASS ROOF WAS STEEP TO SHED RAIN.

HAND-SPLIT CEDAR CLAP-BOARDS

SMALL WINDOW WAS FRAMED

4 ROOF IS THATCHED AND EXTERIOR SIDING IS NAILED TO FRAME.

FOUR STEPS TO BUILDING AN EARLY SETTLER'S ENGLISH COTTAGE, PLYMOUTH, MASSACHUSETTS

Virginia was colonized in 1585 by England believing gold would be found and to expand the empire for an eventual confrontation with Spain, which claimed ownership of the entire Western Hemisphere. The first settlement at Jamestown failed largely because the settlers lacked farming and housebuilding skills. But, later colonists either acquired or arrived with necessary skills. By 1625 a protective triangular timber palisade had been erected around a community of fifteen dwellings, a church, a guardhouse, and a storehouse. It housed about one hundred people. Each family was given twenty acres outside the palisade to farm.

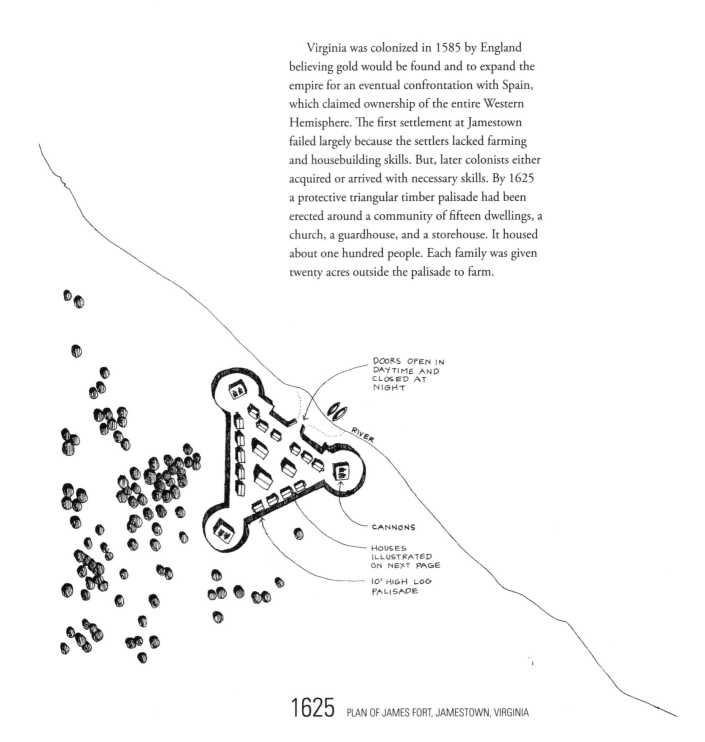

DOORS OPEN IN DAYTIME AND CLOSED AT NIGHT

RIVER

CANNONS

HOUSES ILLUSTRATED ON NEXT PAGE

10' HIGH LOG PALISADE

1625 PLAN OF JAMES FORT, JAMESTOWN, VIRGINIA

The dwelling units of the Virginia colonists were quite similar to those of the Plymouth Colony. The plan, average size, and construction methods were practically the same. However, the Virginians constructed their frame with thin, equal-sized beams, posts, and studs while the Pilgrims used thick, unmanageable corner posts and beams with light infill wall studs. Also, the Virginia house frame was left exposed with wattle and daub infill insulation finishing the walls. This style of building was known as half-timbering because of the amount of timber left showing on the outside walls.

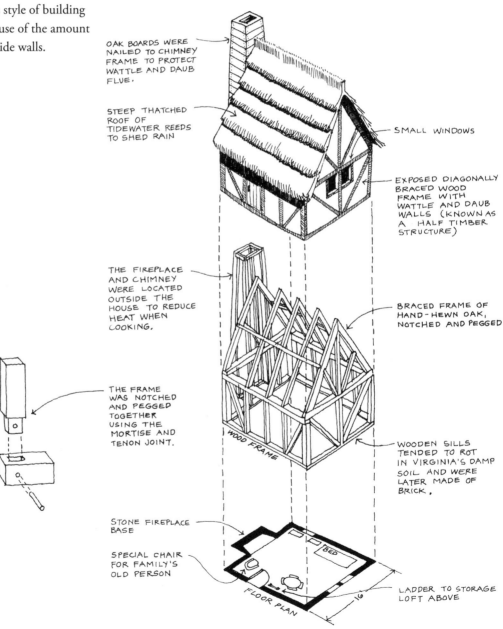

1625 ENGLISH COTTAGE, JAMESTOWN, VIRGINIA

OAK BOARDS WERE NAILED TO CHIMNEY FRAME TO PROTECT WATTLE AND DAUB FLUE.

STEEP THATCHED ROOF OF TIDEWATER REEDS TO SHED RAIN

SMALL WINDOWS

EXPOSED DIAGONALLY BRACED WOOD FRAME WITH WATTLE AND DAUB WALLS (KNOWN AS A HALF TIMBER STRUCTURE)

THE FIREPLACE AND CHIMNEY WERE LOCATED OUTSIDE THE HOUSE TO REDUCE HEAT WHEN COOKING.

BRACED FRAME OF HAND-HEWN OAK, NOTCHED AND PEGGED

THE FRAME WAS NOTCHED AND PEGGED TOGETHER USING THE MORTISE AND TENON JOINT.

WOOD FRAME

WOODEN SILLS TENDED TO ROT IN VIRGINIA'S DAMP SOIL AND WERE LATER MADE OF BRICK.

STONE FIREPLACE BASE

SPECIAL CHAIR FOR FAMILY'S OLD PERSON

BED

FLOOR PLAN

16

LADDER TO STORAGE LOFT ABOVE

Medieval

Mid-Atlantic Coast
1635

The original settlers of the Chesapeake region lived first in frail cottages similar to those described in the preceding chapter; but by 1635, they were building substantial homes of timber frame and brick walls. Most of the colonies in Maryland and Virginia were settled by farmers, tradesmen, and fishermen of modest means who were unfamiliar with the great Renaissance Revival buildings (such as those designed by Inigo Jones) then in style in England. Their architecture therefore remained medieval in style, based on the conventional English Gothic or Tudor of the sixteenth and seventeenth centuries: steep gabled roofs, tall brick chimneys, segmented brick arches over windows and doors, exposed post and beam room construction, batten doors, and leaded glass casement windows (when glass was available). Bricks were plentiful because of the excellent tidewater clay and the presence of craftsmen from England who knew how to fire bricks.

The Medieval Style one-room cottage, sometimes called a tidewater or hall, measured about sixteen by twenty feet. Except for the use of dormers to add attic light, these houses were simply substantial copies of the English cottage used by the first settlers. When the owner became rich or needed more room for a growing family, he would add a room, changing the building from a hall to a hall and parlor house (shown below). The hall and parlor house was the most popular style of shelter in Maryland and Virginia in the seventeenth century.

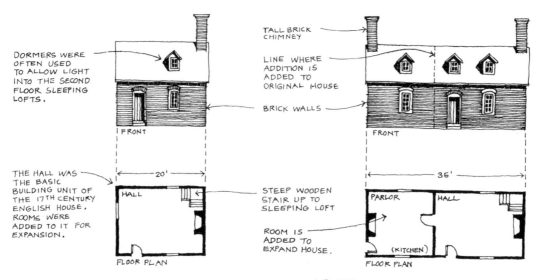

1635 ONE-ROOM HALL COTTAGE, MARYLAND

1645 HALL AND PARLOR HOUSE, MARYLAND

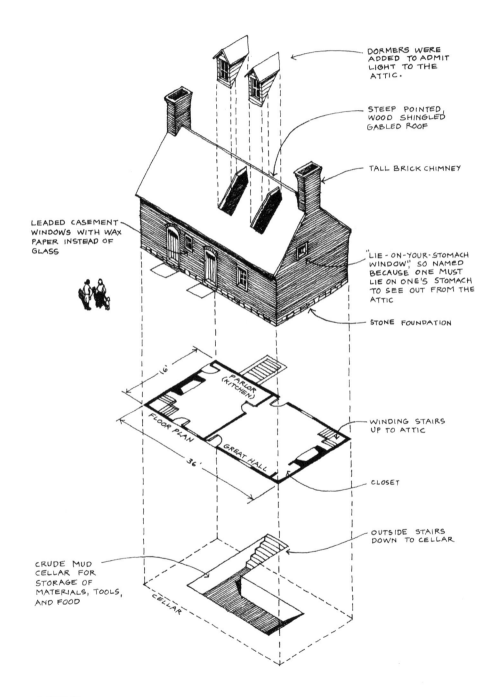

DORMERS WERE ADDED TO ADMIT LIGHT TO THE ATTIC.

STEEP POINTED, WOOD SHINGLED GABLED ROOF

TALL BRICK CHIMNEY

LEADED CASEMENT WINDOWS WITH WAX PAPER INSTEAD OF GLASS

"LIE-ON-YOUR-STOMACH WINDOW," SO NAMED BECAUSE ONE MUST LIE ON ONE'S STOMACH TO SEE OUT FROM THE ATTIC

STONE FOUNDATION

PARLOR (KITCHEN)

FLOOR PLAN

GREAT HALL

9'

36'

WINDING STAIRS UP TO ATTIC

CLOSET

OUTSIDE STAIRS DOWN TO CELLAR

CRUDE MUD CELLAR FOR STORAGE OF MATERIALS, TOOLS, AND FOOD

CELLAR

1650 TYPICAL HALL AND PARLOR HOUSE, MARYLAND AND VIRGINIA

As the Chesapeake culture grew more prosperous, the architecture reflected increasing family size, and loftier ideas about "style." By 1670, the kitchen had been moved outside into a separate building, a return to the medieval custom of carrying prepared food across a courtyard from the kitchen to the dining room, reducing heat during warm weather. With growing families, additional bedrooms were a necessity. So, an "outshot" lean-to shed was often added to the original hall and parlor house. This gave the house the shape of a medieval saltbox but was referred to as a "catslide" in the South because even a cat would lose its grip on the steep surface.

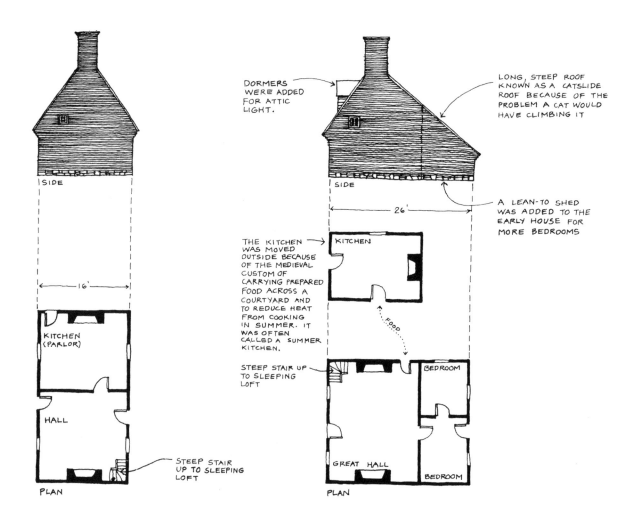

DORMERS WERE ADDED FOR ATTIC LIGHT.

LONG, STEEP ROOF KNOWN AS A CATSLIDE ROOF BECAUSE OF THE PROBLEM A CAT WOULD HAVE CLIMBING IT

SIDE

SIDE

26'

16'

A LEAN-TO SHED WAS ADDED TO THE EARLY HOUSE FOR MORE BEDROOMS

KITCHEN (PARLOR)

THE KITCHEN WAS MOVED OUTSIDE BECAUSE OF THE MEDIEVAL CUSTOM OF CARRYING PREPARED FOOD ACROSS A COURTYARD AND TO REDUCE HEAT FROM COOKING IN SUMMER. IT WAS OFTEN CALLED A SUMMER KITCHEN.

KITCHEN

FOOD

HALL

STEEP STAIR UP TO SLEEPING LOFT

BEDROOM

STEEP STAIR UP TO SLEEPING LOFT

GREAT HALL

BEDROOM

PLAN

PLAN

1645
HALL AND PARLOR HOUSE, MARYLAND AND VIRGINIA

1670
CATSLIDE ROOF HOUSE, MARYLAND AND VIRGINIA

By 1700 the Medieval Style house had grown considerably. First floor bedrooms had become apartments for older relatives of the owner. Fireplaces, popular in all first floor rooms, were used primarily for winter heat and light, but also for some cooking. Each bedroom had its own outside entrance. By 1735 the medieval house was beginning to grow upward instead of outward. A central passageway preserved each room's privacy. One can see the Georgian Style, explained on page 92, beginning here. Brick patterns, common in England in the early sixteenth century, became quite popular.

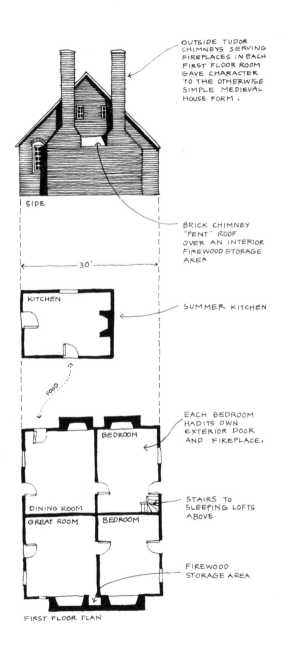

OUTSIDE TUDOR CHIMNEYS SERVING FIREPLACES IN EACH FIRST FLOOR ROOM GAVE CHARACTER TO THE OTHERWISE SIMPLE MEDIEVAL HOUSE FORM.

SIDE

BRICK CHIMNEY "PENT" ROOF OVER AN INTERIOR FIREWOOD STORAGE AREA

30'

KITCHEN

SUMMER KITCHEN

FOOD

BEDROOM

EACH BEDROOM HAD ITS OWN EXTERIOR DOOR AND FIREPLACE.

DINING ROOM

GREAT ROOM

BEDROOM

STAIRS TO SLEEPING LOFTS ABOVE

FIREWOOD STORAGE AREA

FIRST FLOOR PLAN

1700
FOUR-FIREPLACE HOUSE, MARYLAND AND VIRGINIA

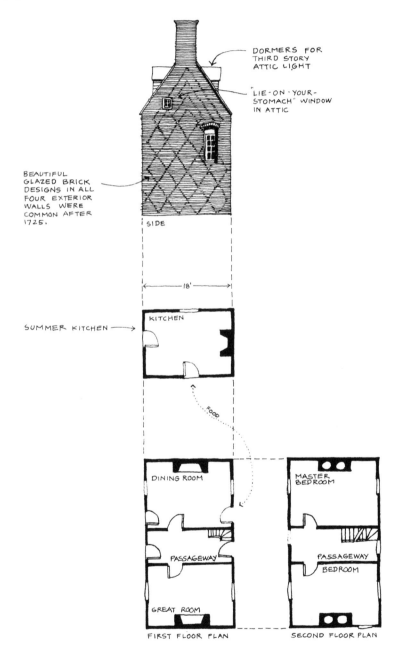

DORMERS FOR THIRD STORY ATTIC LIGHT

"LIE-ON-YOUR-STOMACH" WINDOW IN ATTIC

BEAUTIFUL GLAZED BRICK DESIGNS IN ALL FOUR EXTERIOR WALLS WERE COMMON AFTER 1725.

SIDE

18'

SUMMER KITCHEN

KITCHEN

FOOD

DINING ROOM

MASTER BEDROOM

PASSAGEWAY

PASSAGEWAY

BEDROOM

GREAT ROOM

FIRST FLOOR PLAN

SECOND FLOOR PLAN

1735
TWO-STORY HOUSE, MARYLAND AND VIRGINIA

Log Cabin

Delaware Valley
1638

The log cabin was introduced in America by the Swedes who settled along the Delaware River in 1638. New Sweden, a fur trading colony that covered parts of Pennsylvania, New Jersey, and Delaware, did not endure but its housing form, the log cabin, has survived and is still built today. It was not until the beginning of the eighteenth century that non-Swedes built log cabins; the Scotch-Irish and the German settlers in Pennsylvania were the first, sometime after 1710. The English and the Swedes had lived next to each other for over sixty years without learning each other's housing construction methods. By the Revolution, the log cabin had become the standard frontier dwelling, inhabited by all nationalities, as well as by the American Indian.

There were three basic early log cabin forms: the one-room cabin, the saddlebag, and the dogtrot. The one-room cabin had its development in Scandinavia and north Germany and was the original house built by the Swedes along the Delaware. The saddlebag seems to have taken its name from its structure, which consisted of two rooms "hung over" a single fireplace. Many saddlebags evolved from the addition of rooms to one-room cabins. The outside recesses created by the fireplace were used to stable a few head of livestock in the winter. The dogtrot was also known as "two pens and a passage" because of the breezeway separating the rooms. The pioneers also called this breezeway a possumtrot or a dogrun. The rooms were separated this way to afford privacy.

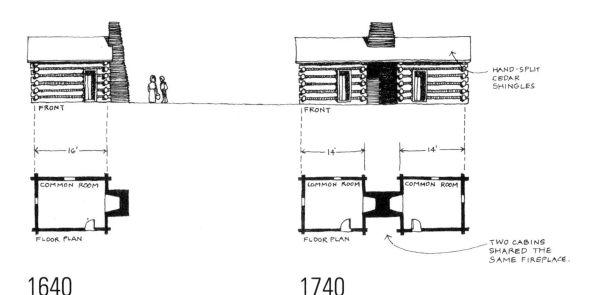

FRONT

16'

COMMON ROOM

FLOOR PLAN

1640
ONE-ROOM LOG CABIN, DELAWARE RIVER VALLEY

HAND-SPLIT CEDAR SHINGLES

FRONT

14'   14'

COMMON ROOM   COMMON ROOM

FLOOR PLAN

TWO CABINS SHARED THE SAME FIREPLACE.

1740
LOG SADDLEBAG CABIN, OHIO RIVER VALLEY

The log cabin had many features desirable to the early settlers and, later, the pioneers. It was quickly built from indigenous materials—trees and rocks cleared from land to be used for farming. With the natural insulation of thick wooden walls, a well-built log cabin was cool in the summer and warm in the winter. The log cabin was easy to build because it did not require an extra framework to hold up the walls. The fireplace was made of large stones and the chimney of sticks lined with mud. The floor was tamped earth and the roof split cedar shingles. Early log cabins were sometimes erected close to each other inside a log palisade to make a protected community.

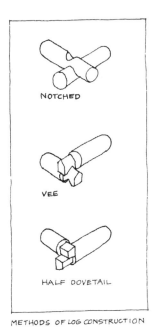

NOTCHED

VEE

HALF DOVETAIL

METHODS OF LOG CONSTRUCTION

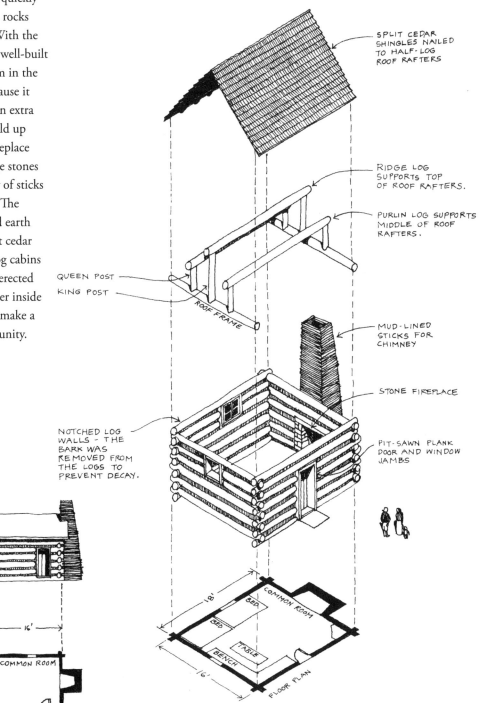

1650
SWEDISH ONE-ROOM LOG CABIN, DELAWARE RIVER VALLEY

SPLIT CEDAR SHINGLES NAILED TO HALF-LOG ROOF RAFTERS

RIDGE LOG SUPPORTS TOP OF ROOF RAFTERS.

PURLIN LOG SUPPORTS MIDDLE OF ROOF RAFTERS.

QUEEN POST

KING POST

ROOF FRAME

MUD-LINED STICKS FOR CHIMNEY

STONE FIREPLACE

NOTCHED LOG WALLS - THE BARK WAS REMOVED FROM THE LOGS TO PREVENT DECAY.

PIT-SAWN PLANK DOOR AND WINDOW JAMBS

18'

BED

BED

TABLE

COMMON ROOM

BENCH

16'

FLOOR PLAN

FIREPLACES WERE MADE WITH MUD-LINED STICKS.

FRONT

16'   10'   16'

AN OPEN BREEZEWAY, OR DOGTROT, SEPARATED THE TWO CABINS.

COMMON ROOM

COMMON ROOM

FLOOR PLAN

1840
LOG DOGTROT CABIN, SOUTHERN APPALACHIANS

There is an infinite number of log cabin variations, but the principal material, the log, remains the same. These two pages contain a few of the more interesting examples of the Log Cabin Style.

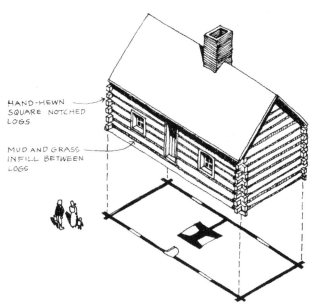

HAND-HEWN SQUARE NOTCHED LOGS

MUD AND GRASS INFILL BETWEEN LOGS

1680 TWO-ROOM SADDLEBAG LOG CABIN, NEW HAMPSHIRE

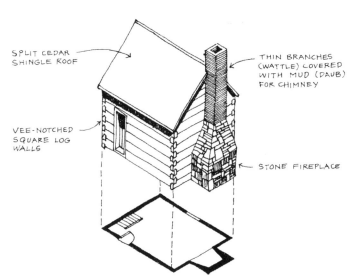

SPLIT CEDAR SHINGLE ROOF

THIN BRANCHES (WATTLE) COVERED WITH MUD (DAUB) FOR CHIMNEY

VEE-NOTCHED SQUARE LOG WALLS

STONE FIREPLACE

1780 ONE-ROOM PIONEER'S LOG CABIN, KENTUCKY

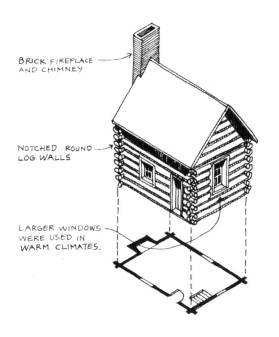

BRICK FIREPLACE AND CHIMNEY

NOTCHED ROUND LOG WALLS

LARGER WINDOWS WERE USED IN WARM CLIMATES.

1830 ONE-ROOM SLAVES LOG CABIN, VIRGINIA

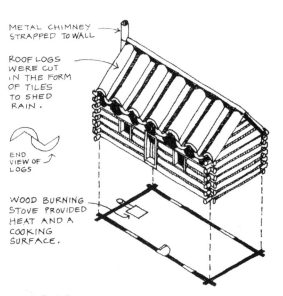

METAL CHIMNEY STRAPPED TO WALL

ROOF LOGS WERE CUT IN THE FORM OF TILES TO SHED RAIN.

END VIEW OF LOGS

WOOD BURNING STOVE PROVIDED HEAT AND A COOKING SURFACE.

1840 ONE-ROOM LUMBERJACKS' "MOSSBACK" LOG CABIN, MICHIGAN

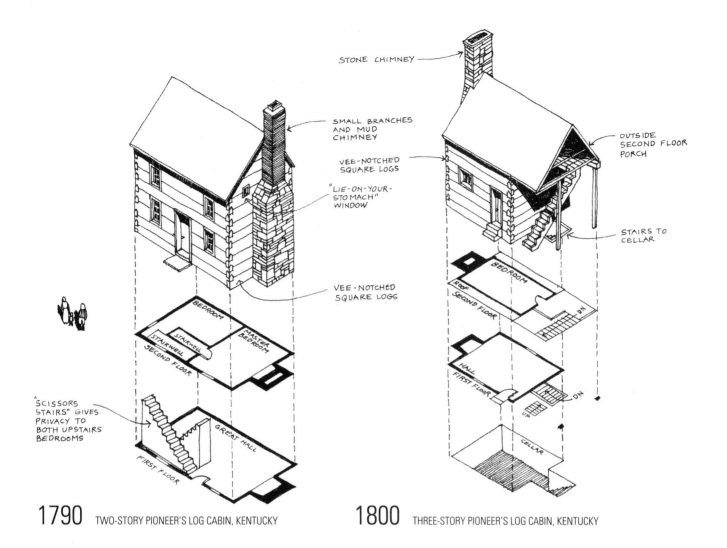

STONE CHIMNEY

SMALL BRANCHES AND MUD CHIMNEY

VEE-NOTCHED SQUARE LOGS

"LIE-ON-YOUR-STOMACH" WINDOW

OUTSIDE SECOND FLOOR PORCH

VEE-NOTCHED SQUARE LOGS

STAIRS TO CELLAR

BEDROOM

MASTER BEDROOM

STAIRWELL

SECOND FLOOR

"SCISSORS STAIRS" GIVES PRIVACY TO BOTH UPSTAIRS BEDROOMS

GREAT HALL

FIRST FLOOR

BEDROOM

ROOF

SECOND FLOOR

DN

HALL

FIRST FLOOR

UP

DN

CELLAR

1790 TWO-STORY PIONEER'S LOG CABIN, KENTUCKY

1800 THREE-STORY PIONEER'S LOG CABIN, KENTUCKY

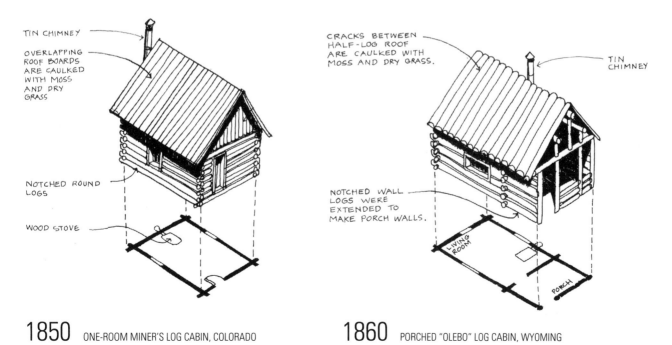

TIN CHIMNEY

OVERLAPPING ROOF BOARDS ARE CAULKED WITH MOSS AND DRY GRASS

NOTCHED ROUND LOGS

WOOD STOVE

CRACKS BETWEEN HALF-LOG ROOF ARE CAULKED WITH MOSS AND DRY GRASS.

TIN CHIMNEY

NOTCHED WALL LOGS WERE EXTENDED TO MAKE PORCH WALLS.

LIVING ROOM

PORCH

1850 ONE-ROOM MINER'S LOG CABIN, COLORADO

1860 PORCHED "OLEBO" LOG CABIN, WYOMING

The log cabin is still a popular dwelling style, especially for vacation homes in wilderness areas. Many companies in the prefabricated home industry have developed build-it-yourself kits, similar to the Lincoln Log toy, that can be built with little skill. Many of these are half-log cabins, which are designed to give the log cabin look to a standard wood framed, insulated house. (See drawing below.)

In their May/June 1977 issue, the *Mother Earth News* published an article on stackwood wall construction by Jack Henstridge. They say this method is just as easy as stacking wood, very inexpensive, and soundproof because of its thickness. It is disadvantaged by the quality of the mortar which has no insulation value.

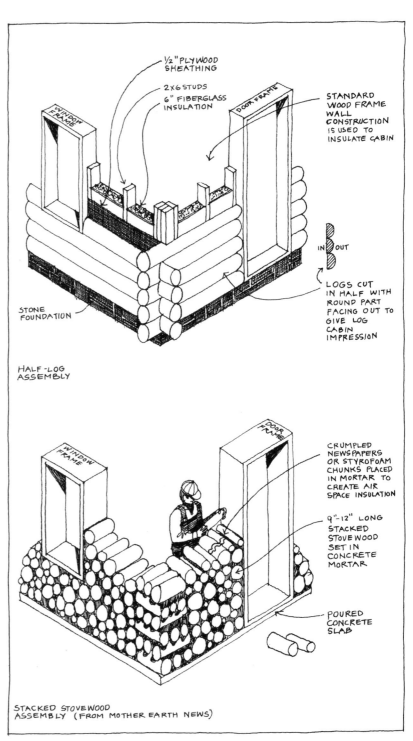

HALF-LOG ASSEMBLY

STACKED STOVEWOOD ASSEMBLY (FROM MOTHER EARTH NEWS)

1975   MODERN ADAPTIONS TO LOG CABIN CONSTRUCTION

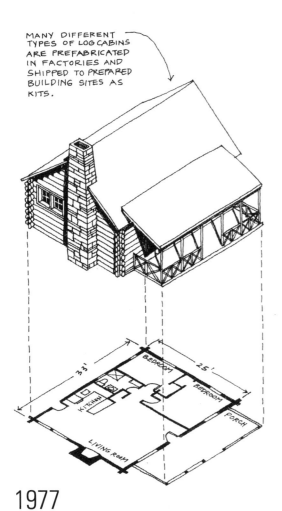

MANY DIFFERENT TYPES OF LOG CABINS ARE PREFABRICATED IN FACTORIES AND SHIPPED TO PREPARED BUILDING SITES AS KITS.

1977
WILDERNESS LOG HOMES INC. PREFABRICATED "PATHFINDER"

Homesteaders still find the log cabin one of the most economical and easy-to-build housing forms. The idea of carving out a home from the indigenous materials of a small piece of wilderness has not lost its charm since the days of the pioneers. Log cabin technology has lent itself to many innovative shapes.

One of the most popular is the octagon (used by the Navaho Indians in building the Hogan as shown on page 32) because a fairly large open space can be constructed by using relatively small, manageable logs. The 650 square foot log cabin shown below was built by an energetic couple for under $700.00 in 1977.

1977

OWNER-DESIGNED AND OWNER-BUILT LOG CABIN,
DON AND JENNY GESINGER, OWNERS, BUILDERS,
WILLIAMS LAKE, B.C., CANADA

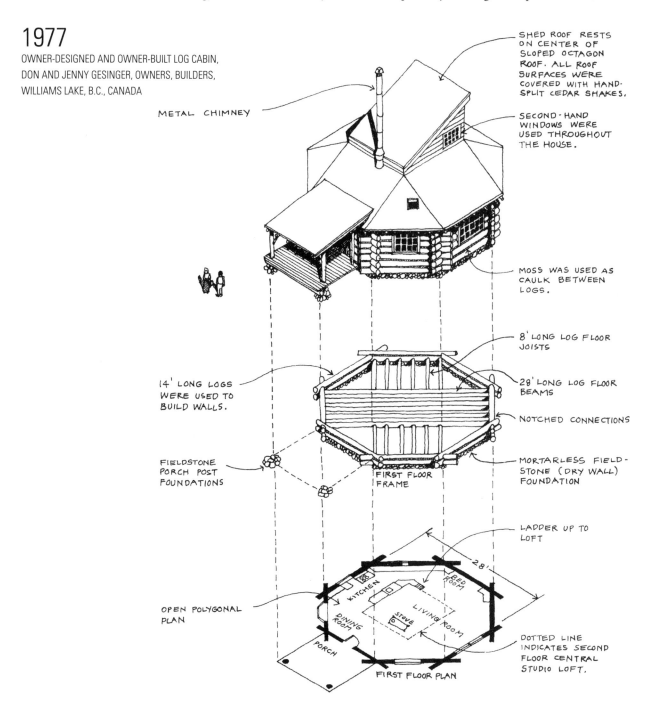

METAL CHIMNEY

SHED ROOF RESTS ON CENTER OF SLOPED OCTAGON ROOF. ALL ROOF SURFACES WERE COVERED WITH HAND-SPLIT CEDAR SHAKES.

SECOND-HAND WINDOWS WERE USED THROUGHOUT THE HOUSE.

MOSS WAS USED AS CAULK BETWEEN LOGS.

8' LONG LOG FLOOR JOISTS

28' LONG LOG FLOOR BEAMS

NOTCHED CONNECTIONS

14' LONG LOGS WERE USED TO BUILD WALLS.

FIELDSTONE PORCH POST FOUNDATIONS

FIRST FLOOR FRAME

MORTARLESS FIELD-STONE (DRY WALL) FOUNDATION

LADDER UP TO LOFT

28'

KITCHEN

BED ROOM

LIVING ROOM

STOVE

DINING ROOM

OPEN POLYGONAL PLAN

PORCH

FIRST FLOOR PLAN

DOTTED LINE INDICATES SECOND FLOOR CENTRAL STUDIO LOFT.

Stone Ender

Rhode Island
1640

By 1640 the New England settlers were building a more substantial version of the English Cottage Style known as the Rhode Island "stone ender." This house took its name from the fireplace that was built to such a size that it constituted most of, and sometimes all of, an end wall. Evidently the Puritans were convincing the settlers to rely more on fire than spirits for winter heat.

Near the end of the seventeenth century, the first change to occur in the form of the English cottage was the addition of a lean-to shed at the rear of the dwelling, providing space for a large kitchen. The result was a shape that resembled the English medieval saltbox. Thus the name "saltbox," further discussed on page 67.

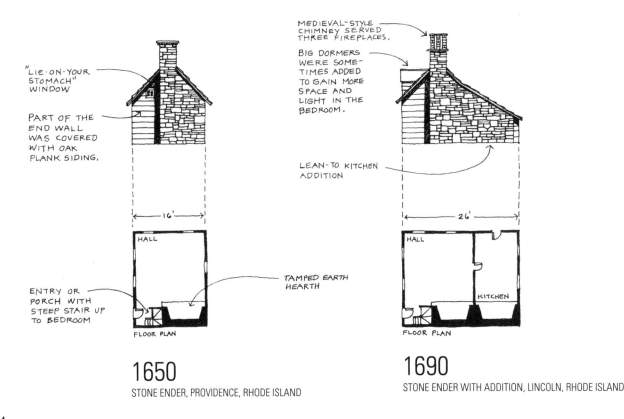

"LIE-ON-YOUR STOMACH" WINDOW

PART OF THE END WALL WAS COVERED WITH OAK PLANK SIDING.

16'

HALL

ENTRY OR PORCH WITH STEEP STAIR UP TO BEDROOM

TAMPED EARTH HEARTH

FLOOR PLAN

1650
STONE ENDER, PROVIDENCE, RHODE ISLAND

MEDIEVAL-STYLE CHIMNEY SERVED THREE FIREPLACES.

BIG DORMERS WERE SOME-TIMES ADDED TO GAIN MORE SPACE AND LIGHT IN THE BEDROOM.

LEAN-TO KITCHEN ADDITION

26'

HALL

KITCHEN

FLOOR PLAN

1690
STONE ENDER WITH ADDITION, LINCOLN, RHODE ISLAND

The pride housebuilders were beginning to take in the craftsmanship of their dwellings was manifested in the stone ender. The design of the house frame had become simpler with larger structural members spaced farther apart. Wattle and daub between the outside posts and girts were still the principal insulating materials. Windows, imported English diamond glass panes set in lead frames, swung open to the outside with wrought iron hinges. The doors, made from vertical boards nailed in a diamond-shaped design to top and bottom battens, had handcarved wooden latches. The huge end wall fireplace and chimney was built of stone above a tamped earth hearth. The fireplace contained large ovens and stock holes. The oak floorboards were pegged to floor joists spanning a dug cellar. The stair went up to the bedroom beside the chimney from the front entry or porch. With low ceilings, seven feet high, the stone ender was indeed a wellbuilt house; it kept warm in the winter and rarely burned down as did many of the earlier English cottages.

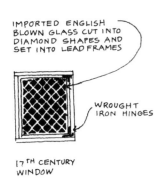

IMPORTED ENGLISH BLOWN GLASS CUT INTO DIAMOND SHAPES AND SET INTO LEAD FRAMES

WROUGHT IRON HINGES

17TH CENTURY WINDOW

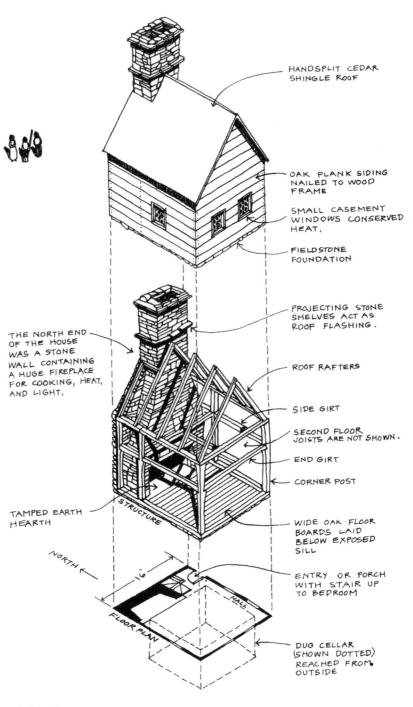

HANDSPLIT CEDAR SHINGLE ROOF

OAK PLANK SIDING NAILED TO WOOD FRAME

SMALL CASEMENT WINDOWS CONSERVED HEAT.

FIELDSTONE FOUNDATION

PROJECTING STONE SHELVES ACT AS ROOF FLASHING.

THE NORTH END OF THE HOUSE WAS A STONE WALL CONTAINING A HUGE FIREPLACE FOR COOKING, HEAT, AND LIGHT.

ROOF RAFTERS

SIDE GIRT

SECOND FLOOR JOISTS ARE NOT SHOWN.

END GIRT

CORNER POST

TAMPED EARTH HEARTH

STRUCTURE

WIDE OAK FLOOR BOARDS LAID BELOW EXPOSED SILL

ENTRY OR PORCH WITH STAIR UP TO BEDROOM

NORTH

FLOOR PLAN

HALL

DUG CELLAR (SHOWN DOTTED) REACHED FROM OUTSIDE

1650 TYPICAL STONE ENDER, RHODE ISLAND

Dutch Colonial

Hudson River Valley
1650

When the Dutch arrived in America in the 1620s, they settled along the entire length of the Hudson River, with the heaviest population living in New Amsterdam, later to become New York City. The earliest Dutch houses were dugouts, holes, or caves dug into the ground, lined with bark, and covered with reed or sod roofs. They also built temporary houses, similar to the wigwam, with a bark-covered sapling framework. The first permanent homes were small, stone, one story, one-room cottages with thatched or splitwood shingle roofs. More substantial houses, made with brick walls and tile roofs, were being built by the mid-seventeenth century in New Amsterdam and northeastern New York. These houses borrowed much of their detailing, such as the stepped gable, from Holland. But gradually there arose a variety of American Dutch Colonial styles having no European roots. In rural areas all along the Hudson, the Dutch built their houses of locally available materials in a manner totally different from the brick dwellings of the urban centers. These houses were straightforward answers to the problems of shelter and protection.

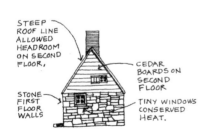

STEEP ROOF LINE ALLOWED HEADROOM ON SECOND FLOOR.

CEDAR BOARDS ON SECOND FLOOR

STONE FIRST FLOOR WALLS

TINY WINDOWS CONSERVED HEAT.

1630
ONE-ROOM COTTAGE, NEW AMSTERDAM

A BRICK FRONT FACED THE STREET HIDING A WOODEN BUILDING.

1650
EARLY ROW HOUSE, NEW AMSTERDAM

CERAMIC TILED ROOF PREVENTED CHIMNEY-SPARKED FIRES.

ARCHED WINDOWS

DOTTED LINE INDICATES ROOF LINE BEHIND STEPPED GABLE

SHUTTERS FOR INSULATION

1670
TWO STEPPED GABLE HOUSES, NEW AMSTERDAM

The development of the Dutch farmhouse began with a rural adaptation of the townhouse. The stepped gabled roof was straightened and the entrance was moved from the gable end to the side, similar to the English Medieval Style. By 1700 the flaring eave, traced to the "flying gutter" found on cottages in Flanders, began to appear on houses built at first by the Flemish and then by their Dutch and French Huguenot neighbors. The roof was extended to overhang the front and rear of the house, protecting entrances and mud mortar used in stone walls and foundations from rain. When this overhang was added to the gambrel roof (adopted from the English around 1720) providing for a front and rear veranda (adopted from the French or West Indians), the distinctive, beautiful, and popular Dutch Colonial Style was born.

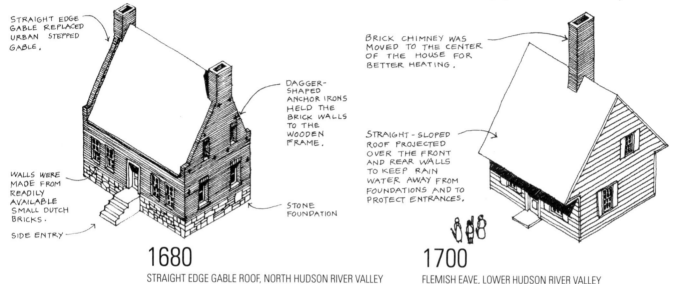

STRAIGHT EDGE GABLE REPLACED URBAN STEPPED GABLE.

DAGGER-SHAPED ANCHOR IRONS HELD THE BRICK WALLS TO THE WOODEN FRAME.

WALLS WERE MADE FROM READILY AVAILABLE SMALL DUTCH BRICKS.

SIDE ENTRY

STONE FOUNDATION

1680
STRAIGHT EDGE GABLE ROOF, NORTH HUDSON RIVER VALLEY

BRICK CHIMNEY WAS MOVED TO THE CENTER OF THE HOUSE FOR BETTER HEATING.

STRAIGHT-SLOPED ROOF PROJECTED OVER THE FRONT AND REAR WALLS TO KEEP RAIN WATER AWAY FROM FOUNDATIONS AND TO PROTECT ENTRANCES.

1700
FLEMISH EAVE, LOWER HUDSON RIVER VALLEY

After 1720 most Dutch houses had the flaring gable roof, the earlier ones without supporting posts and the late ones with them. "Doghouse dormers" (so named because of their doghouse-like shape) were sometimes added after 1740 to gain second floor bedroom space and light.

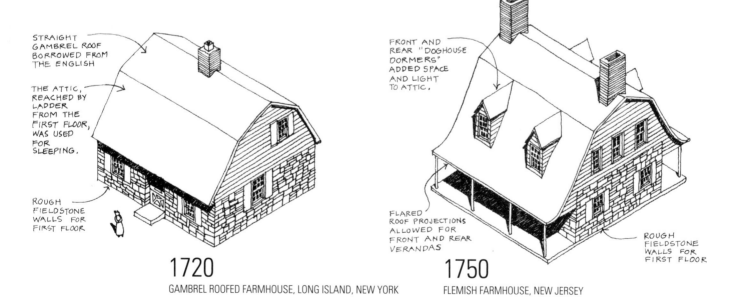

STRAIGHT GAMBREL ROOF BORROWED FROM THE ENGLISH

THE ATTIC, REACHED BY LADDER FROM THE FIRST FLOOR, WAS USED FOR SLEEPING.

ROUGH FIELDSTONE WALLS FOR FIRST FLOOR

1720
GAMBREL ROOFED FARMHOUSE, LONG ISLAND, NEW YORK

FRONT AND REAR "DOGHOUSE DORMERS" ADDED SPACE AND LIGHT TO ATTIC.

FLARED ROOF PROJECTIONS ALLOWED FOR FRONT AND REAR VERANDAS

ROUGH FIELDSTONE WALLS FOR FIRST FLOOR

1750
FLEMISH FARMHOUSE, NEW JERSEY

1690

TYPICAL DUTCH COLONIAL HOUSE,
MID-HUDSON RIVER VALLEY

One of the most innovative and unusual of the early American vernacular styles was the stone farmhouse of Ulster County (mid-Hudson River valley), built by the Dutch. The expedient and thoughtful use of a wide variety of building materials and methods that had little to do

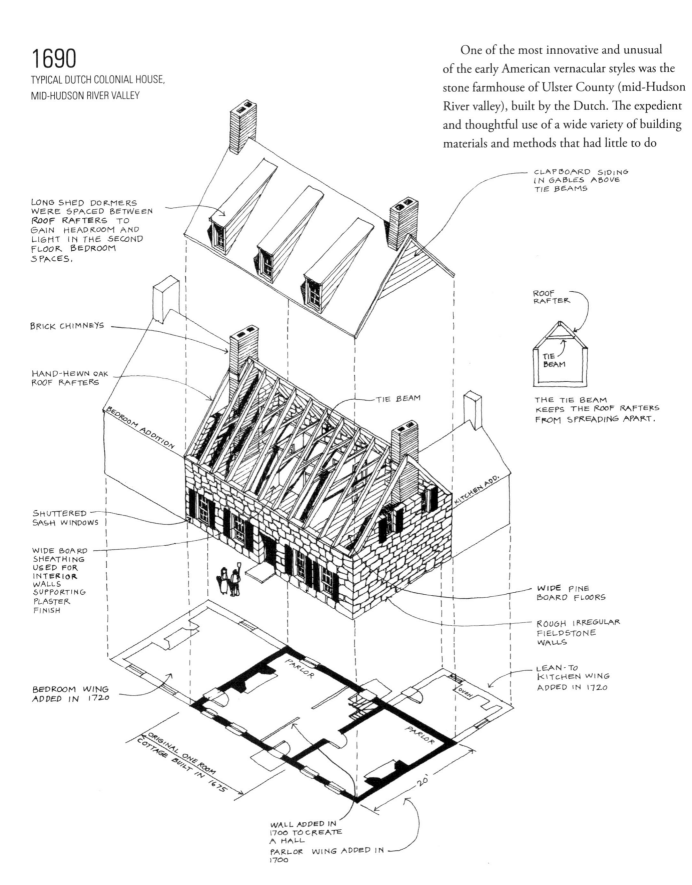

CLAPBOARD SIDING IN GABLES ABOVE TIE BEAMS

LONG SHED DORMERS WERE SPACED BETWEEN ROOF RAFTERS TO GAIN HEADROOM AND LIGHT IN THE SECOND FLOOR BEDROOM SPACES.

ROOF RAFTER

TIE BEAM

THE TIE BEAM KEEPS THE ROOF RAFTERS FROM SPREADING APART.

BRICK CHIMNEYS

HAND-HEWN OAK ROOF RAFTERS

BEDROOM ADDITION

TIE BEAM

KITCHEN ADD.

SHUTTERED SASH WINDOWS

WIDE BOARD SHEATHING USED FOR INTERIOR WALLS SUPPORTING PLASTER FINISH

WIDE PINE BOARD FLOORS

ROUGH IRREGULAR FIELDSTONE WALLS

LEAN-TO KITCHEN WING ADDED IN 1720

BEDROOM WING ADDED IN 1720

PARLOR

OVEN

PARLOR

ORIGINAL ONE ROOM COTTAGE BUILT IN 1675

20'

WALL ADDED IN 1700 TO CREATE A HALL

PARLOR WING ADDED IN 1700

with housebuilding ideas in a native country (Holland) separated these houses from others being constructed in Colonial America. Stone walls provided protection from hostile American Indians and fire. Brick was used for neat, fireproof chimneys. Cedar shingles made a roof that was easy to build, waterproof, and safe from fire compared to the thatch huts built by the first Dutch settlers.

In the early seventeenth century, the most popular Dutch Colonial dwelling in the central New Jersey area, to the south and west of the mouth of the Hudson River, was the stone gambrel-roofed center hall planned house. It is often considered to have one of the most beautiful roofs, a graceful bell-shape that combines the flaring Flemish eave, used to shed rain water, with the English gambrel, which gave more headroom to the attic floor. This house was the predecessor of the very popular twentieth-century Dutch Colonial Revival house shown on page 199.

1710
TYPICAL DUTCH COLONIAL HOUSE,
CENTRAL NEW JERSEY

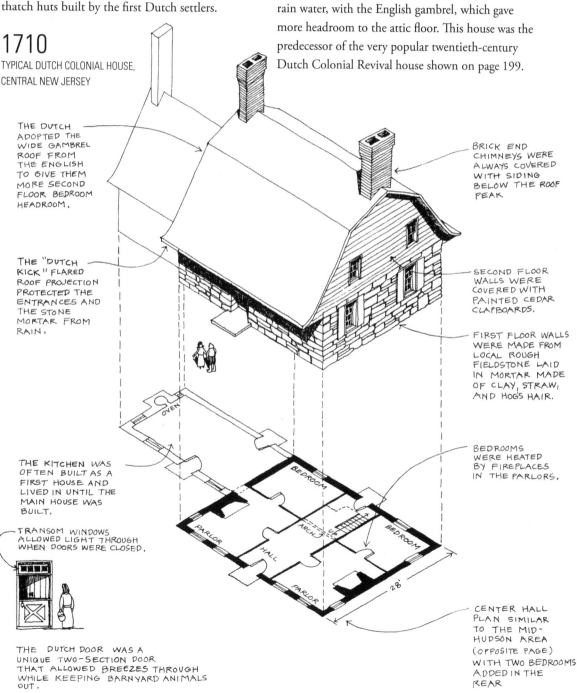

THE DUTCH ADOPTED THE WIDE GAMBREL ROOF FROM THE ENGLISH TO GIVE THEM MORE SECOND FLOOR BEDROOM HEADROOM.

THE "DUTCH KICK" FLARED ROOF PROJECTION PROTECTED THE ENTRANCES AND THE STONE MORTAR FROM RAIN.

THE KITCHEN WAS OFTEN BUILT AS A FIRST HOUSE AND LIVED IN UNTIL THE MAIN HOUSE WAS BUILT.

TRANSOM WINDOWS ALLOWED LIGHT THROUGH WHEN DOORS WERE CLOSED.

THE DUTCH DOOR WAS A UNIQUE TWO-SECTION DOOR THAT ALLOWED BREEZES THROUGH WHILE KEEPING BARNYARD ANIMALS OUT.

BRICK END CHIMNEYS WERE ALWAYS COVERED WITH SIDING BELOW THE ROOF PEAK

SECOND FLOOR WALLS WERE COVERED WITH PAINTED CEDAR CLAPBOARDS.

FIRST FLOOR WALLS WERE MADE FROM LOCAL ROUGH FIELDSTONE LAID IN MORTAR MADE OF CLAY, STRAW, AND HOGS HAIR.

BEDROOMS WERE HEATED BY FIREPLACES IN THE PARLORS.

CENTER HALL PLAN SIMILAR TO THE MID-HUDSON AREA (OPPOSITE PAGE) WITH TWO BEDROOMS ADDED IN THE REAR

OVEN

BEDROOM

PARLOR

HALL

ARCH

UP

BEDROOM

PARLOR

28'

Cross House

Mid-Atlantic Coast
1650

The cross house, the first version of the southern manor house, derived from the cruciform-shaped English parish church, but it also evolved naturally from the early settlers' Medieval Style hall and parlor house as shown below. Around 1645, a central passageway was added to the hall and parlor house to allow for privacy in each of the first floor rooms. Porches were later added to the passageway, changing the plan from a simple rectangle to a cross shape, to create a scale of grandness. The stair had its own porch or room called a "stair well." And the entry porch became a room used to enter and leave the house.

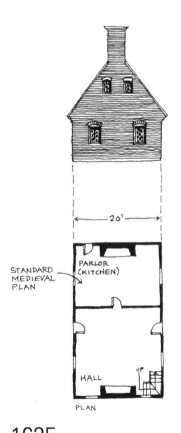

1635
HALL AND PARLOR HOUSE, MARYLAND AND VIRGINIA

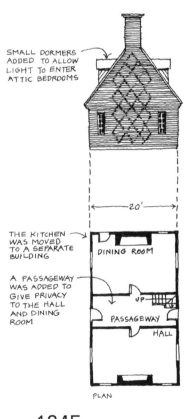

1645
CENTER HALL PLAN, MARYLAND AND VIRGINIA

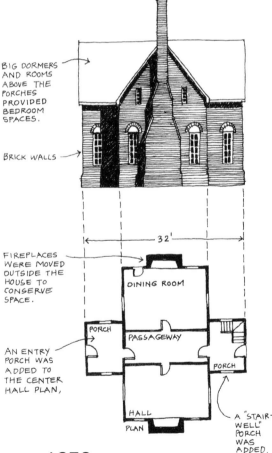

1650
CROSS HOUSE, MARYLAND AND VIRGINIA

60

Most owners of cross houses were wealthy enough to build a separate kitchen with upstairs slave quarters about ten feet from the main house. This building was connected to the hall or dining room with a passageway called a curtain, or if it had no walls, a colonnade.

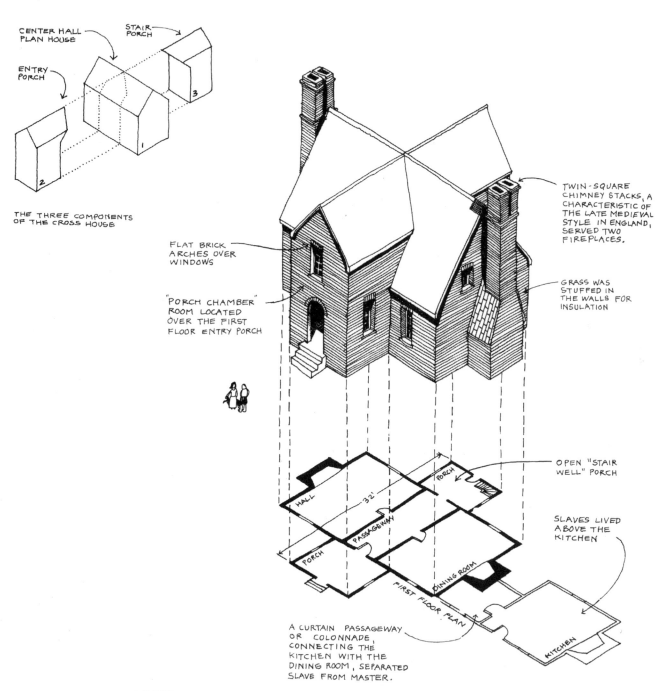

CENTER HALL PLAN HOUSE

STAIR PORCH

ENTRY PORCH

THE THREE COMPONENTS OF THE CROSS HOUSE

FLAT BRICK ARCHES OVER WINDOWS

"PORCH CHAMBER" ROOM LOCATED OVER THE FIRST FLOOR ENTRY PORCH

TWIN-SQUARE CHIMNEY STACKS, A CHARACTERISTIC OF THE LATE MEDIEVAL STYLE IN ENGLAND, SERVED TWO FIREPLACES.

GRASS WAS STUFFED IN THE WALLS FOR INSULATION

OPEN "STAIR WELL" PORCH

SLAVES LIVED ABOVE THE KITCHEN

HALL

32'

PORCH

PASSAGEWAY

PORCH

DINING ROOM

FIRST FLOOR PLAN

KITCHEN

A CURTAIN PASSAGEWAY OR COLONNADE, CONNECTING THE KITCHEN WITH THE DINING ROOM, SEPARATED SLAVE FROM MASTER.

1650 TYPICAL CROSS HOUSE, VIRGINIA

Jacobean

Mid-Atlantic Coast
1655

Much of the Early Renaissance styles of seventeenth-century England, including Jacobean, were based on the architecture of the Netherlands and Germany. In America, the Jacobean was a relatively minor style that was grafted on to the Medieval Style. Only the wealthy were interested in the decorative curvilinear gable walls, door heads, and stair balusters inherent in the style. Jacobean houses were built in the mid-Atlantic states of Maryland, Virginia, North Carolina, and South Carolina.

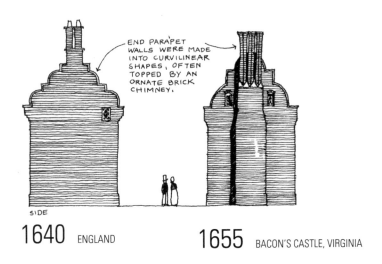

END PARAPET WALLS WERE MADE INTO CURVILINEAR SHAPES, OFTEN TOPPED BY AN ORNATE BRICK CHIMNEY.

SIDE

1640 ENGLAND

1655 BACON'S CASTLE, VIRGINIA

LOW CHIMNEY AT THE TOP OF A "CROW STEP" GABLE ROOF

1685 SOUTH CAROLINA

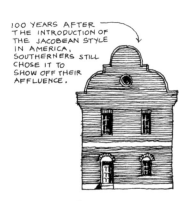

100 YEARS AFTER THE INTRODUCTION OF THE JACOBEAN STYLE IN AMERICA, SOUTHERNERS STILL CHOSE IT TO SHOW OFF THEIR AFFLUENCE.

1750 SOUTH CAROLINA

The finest example of the Jacobean Style in America is Bacon's Castle located in Surrey County, Virginia. This house was built in 1655 by Arthur Allen, who had arrived from England six years earlier. It was given its name when Nathaniel Bacon, leader of the 1676 Bacon's Rebellion against Sir William Berkeley, Virginia's corrupt governor, used the house to garrison his troops. Bacon's Castle is cruciform in plan like the cross house, borrowing many details from the Medieval Style, but primarily it reflects an attempt by the builder to make his affluence conspicuous by constructing a house in the style that was becoming so popular in England. The fantastic curved end gable walls, known as "Flemish-by-way-of-England" gables are the most obvious features but door trimmings and the stair are also Jacobean in style.

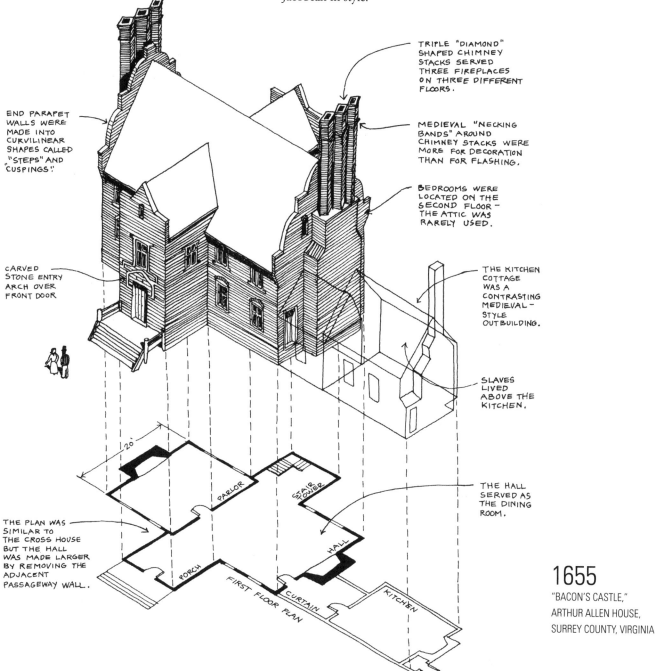

TRIPLE "DIAMOND" SHAPED CHIMNEY STACKS SERVED THREE FIREPLACES ON THREE DIFFERENT FLOORS.

MEDIEVAL "NECKING BANDS" AROUND CHIMNEY STACKS WERE MORE FOR DECORATION THAN FOR FLASHING.

BEDROOMS WERE LOCATED ON THE SECOND FLOOR – THE ATTIC WAS RARELY USED.

END PARAPET WALLS WERE MADE INTO CURVILINEAR SHAPES CALLED "STEPS" AND "CUSPINGS."

THE KITCHEN COTTAGE WAS A CONTRASTING MEDIEVAL-STYLE OUTBUILDING.

CARVED STONE ENTRY ARCH OVER FRONT DOOR

SLAVES LIVED ABOVE THE KITCHEN.

THE HALL SERVED AS THE DINING ROOM.

THE PLAN WAS SIMILAR TO THE CROSS HOUSE BUT THE HALL WAS MADE LARGER BY REMOVING THE ADJACENT PASSAGEWAY WALL.

20'

PARLOR

STAIR TOWER

HALL

PORCH

FIRST FLOOR PLAN

CURTAIN

KITCHEN

1655
"BACON'S CASTLE,"
ARTHUR ALLEN HOUSE,
SURREY COUNTY, VIRGINIA

Garrison House

New England
1660

The garrison house, an upward two-story expansion of the two-room cottage, became popular by 1670. It was quite similar to the Pennsylvania "I" (p. 72) that was developing independently at about the same time. But the garrison house had a distinctive New England character with its central chimney, second floor overhang, and the four carved pendants under the overhang. The garrison house maintained its popularity for about fifty years in Connecticut, Rhode Island, and Massachusetts.

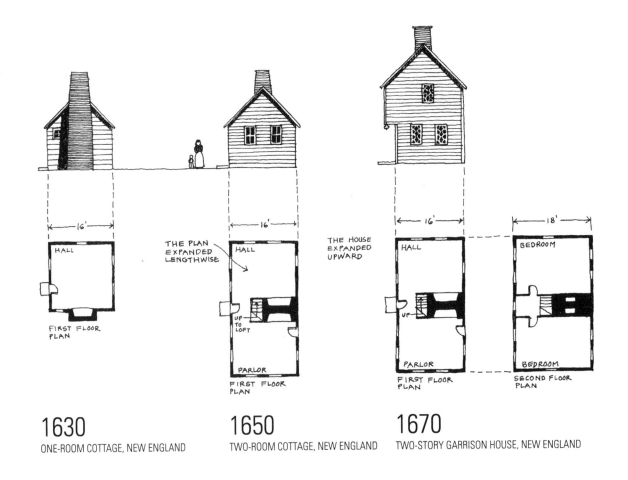

1630
ONE-ROOM COTTAGE, NEW ENGLAND

1650
TWO-ROOM COTTAGE, NEW ENGLAND

1670
TWO-STORY GARRISON HOUSE, NEW ENGLAND

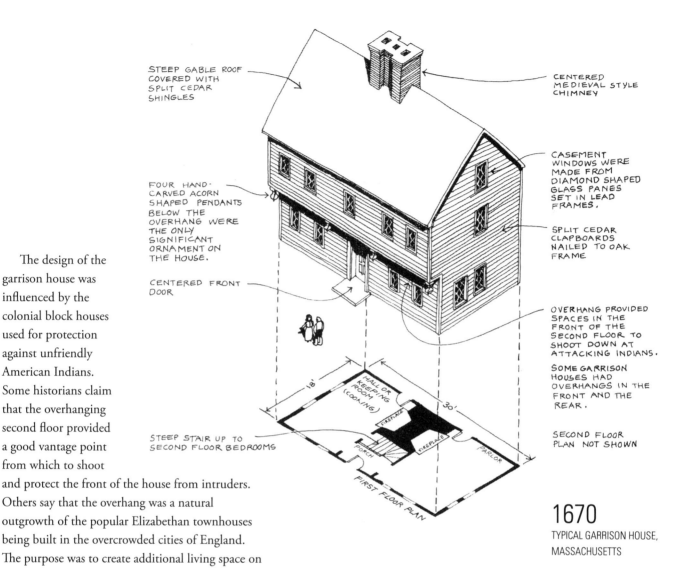

STEEP GABLE ROOF COVERED WITH SPLIT CEDAR SHINGLES

CENTERED MEDIEVAL STYLE CHIMNEY

CASEMENT WINDOWS WERE MADE FROM DIAMOND SHAPED GLASS PANES SET IN LEAD FRAMES.

FOUR HAND-CARVED ACORN SHAPED PENDANTS BELOW THE OVERHANG WERE THE ONLY SIGNIFICANT ORNAMENT ON THE HOUSE.

SPLIT CEDAR CLAPBOARDS NAILED TO OAK FRAME

CENTERED FRONT DOOR

OVERHANG PROVIDED SPACES IN THE FRONT OF THE SECOND FLOOR TO SHOOT DOWN AT ATTACKING INDIANS.

SOME GARRISON HOUSES HAD OVERHANGS IN THE FRONT AND THE REAR.

STEEP STAIR UP TO SECOND FLOOR BEDROOMS

SECOND FLOOR PLAN NOT SHOWN

HALL OR KEEPING ROOM (COOKING)

FIREPLACE

PORCH

PARLOR

FIRST FLOOR PLAN

18'

30'

The design of the garrison house was influenced by the colonial block houses used for protection against unfriendly American Indians. Some historians claim that the overhanging second floor provided a good vantage point from which to shoot and protect the front of the house from intruders. Others say that the overhang was a natural outgrowth of the popular Elizabethan townhouses being built in the overcrowded cities of England. The purpose was to create additional living space on the upper floors.

1670
TYPICAL GARRISON HOUSE, MASSACHUSETTS

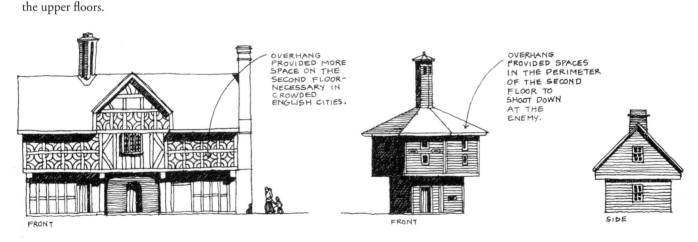

OVERHANG PROVIDED MORE SPACE ON THE SECOND FLOOR - NECESSARY IN CROWDED ENGLISH CITIES.

OVERHANG PROVIDED SPACES IN THE PERIMETER OF THE SECOND FLOOR TO SHOOT DOWN AT THE ENEMY.

FRONT

FRONT

SIDE

1570
GABLED TOWNHOUSE, LONDON, ENGLAND

1650
BLOCK HOUSE, FORT EDGECOMB, MAINE

1680
1½ STORY GARRISON HOUSE, DOVER, NEW HAMPSHIRE

Saltbox

New England 1670

Adding a single-story lean-to shed to the back of a one-and-one-half or two-story, one-room deep house was the most practical method of gaining more space. The resulting shape of this new house was that of a medieval saltbox, hence it's name. In most saltboxes the lean-to addition was divided into three rooms: a central kitchen with its new fireplace and oven; a borning room, reserved for childbirth and the ill; and a pantry. Sometimes a rear stair, located near the pantry, led up to a low-ceilinged storage space. The construction of the new fireplace and oven, always adjacent to the existing chimney, meant the addition of a new flue, resulting in a "T" shaped chimney.

By 1680, the Saltbox Style had become so popular that houses were being built with the lean-to as part of the original construction, with the roof line unbroken from the ridge to the rear wall. The saltbox grew from the early stone ender to a comfortable three-bedroom house over a period of about thirty years as families grew in size and became wealthier.

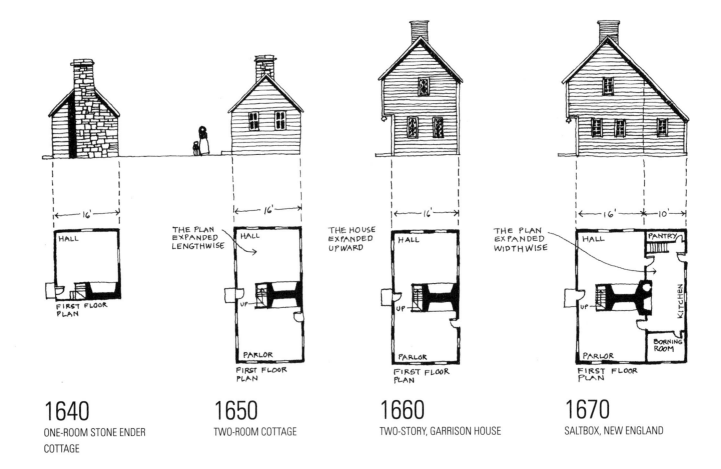

1640
ONE-ROOM STONE ENDER COTTAGE

1650
TWO-ROOM COTTAGE

1660
TWO-STORY, GARRISON HOUSE

1670
SALTBOX, NEW ENGLAND

The saltbox began as a simple rearward expansion of the plan but by 1720, lean-to additions were built to accommodate everything from animals to children.

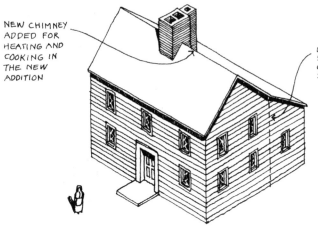

NEW CHIMNEY ADDED FOR HEATING AND COOKING IN THE NEW ADDITION

LINE OF LEAN-TO SHED ADDED TO ORIGINAL TWO-STORY HOUSE

LEAN-TO SHEDS WERE OFTEN ADDED UNTIL THE ROOF ALMOST TOUCHED THE GROUND.

1650   TYPICAL SALTBOX, CONNECTICUT

1670
DOUBLE SHED SALTBOX, CONNECTICUT

LEAN-TO SHEDS WERE ADDED TO GAIN MORE SLEEPING SPACE AS THE FAMILY GREW

CLUSTER OF LEAN-TO'S ADDED OVER THE YEARS FOR MORE SPACE

GABLED ROOF "OUT-SHOT" ATTACHED TO THE MAIN BODY OF THE HOUSE CREATED AN "L" SHAPED PLAN

1700   NANTUCKET WHALE HOUSE, NANTUCKET ISLAND, MASSACHUSETTS

1720   "OUTSHOT" HOUSE, HINGHAM, MASSACHUSETTS

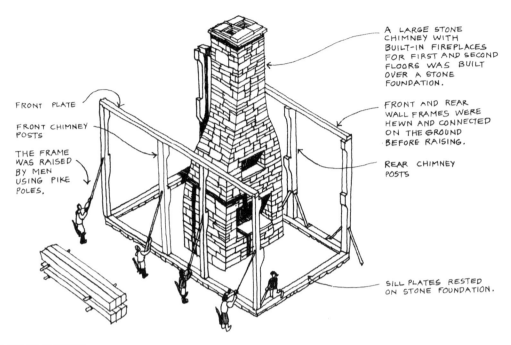

A LARGE STONE CHIMNEY WITH BUILT-IN FIREPLACES FOR FIRST AND SECOND FLOORS WAS BUILT OVER A STONE FOUNDATION.

FRONT AND REAR WALL FRAMES WERE HEWN AND CONNECTED ON THE GROUND BEFORE RAISING.

REAR CHIMNEY POSTS

FRONT PLATE

FRONT CHIMNEY POSTS

THE FRAME WAS RAISED BY MEN USING PIKE POLES.

SILL PLATES RESTED ON STONE FOUNDATION.

1
WALL FRAMES ARE RAISED
AROUND THE STONE CHIMNEY

Although many styles became popular over time, the basic construction methods of the wood-frame house remained the same for over two hundred years. This frame was hewn from on-site oak trees and was erected by most of the townspeople at a hell-raising event known as a house raising. Shown on these two pages is a four-step sequence illustrating the construction of a two-story house that was later converted into a saltbox.

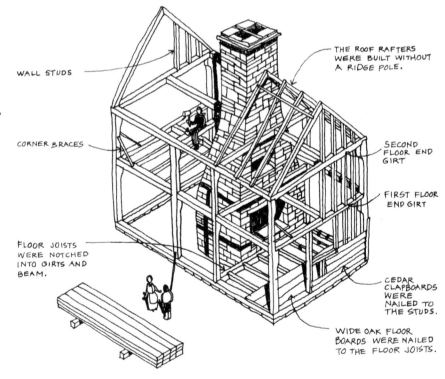

WALL STUDS

CORNER BRACES

FLOOR JOISTS WERE NOTCHED INTO GIRTS AND BEAM.

THE ROOF RAFTERS WERE BUILT WITHOUT A RIDGE POLE.

SECOND FLOOR END GIRT

FIRST FLOOR END GIRT

CEDAR CLAPBOARDS WERE NAILED TO THE STUDS.

WIDE OAK FLOOR BOARDS WERE NAILED TO THE FLOOR JOISTS.

2
THE HOUSE FRAME IS FINISHED

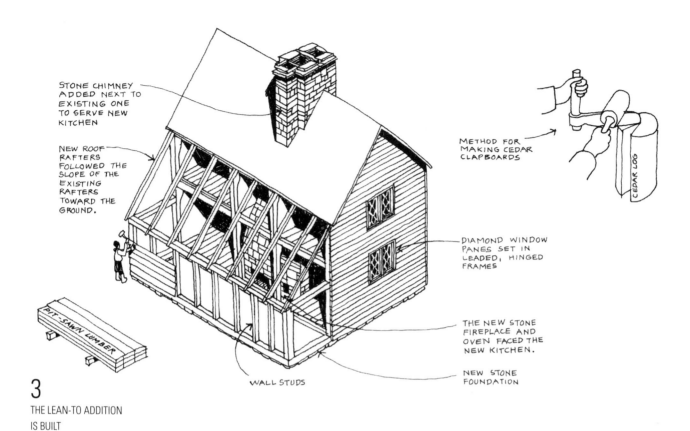

STONE CHIMNEY
ADDED NEXT TO
EXISTING ONE
TO SERVE NEW
KITCHEN

NEW ROOF
RAFTERS
FOLLOWED THE
SLOPE OF THE
EXISTING
RAFTERS
TOWARD THE
GROUND.

METHOD FOR
MAKING CEDAR
CLAPBOARDS

CEDAR LOG

DIAMOND WINDOW
PANES SET IN
LEADED, HINGED
FRAMES

THE NEW STONE
FIREPLACE AND
OVEN FACED THE
NEW KITCHEN.

PIT-SAWN LUMBER

NEW STONE
FOUNDATION

WALL STUDS

3

THE LEAN-TO ADDITION
IS BUILT

4

THE SALTBOX IS FINISHED

SPLIT CEDAR
SHINGLES
MATCHED WITH
EXISTING ONES.

SPLIT CEDAR
CLAPBOARDS
MATCHED WITH
EXISTING ONES.

REAR
ENTRY

German Colonial

Delaware River Valley
1675

During the late part of the seventeenth century, the Delaware River valley was being settled by a blend of immigrants from Sweden, Finland, Switzerland, Scotland, Ireland, England, and in the greatest number, from Germany. The popular European building technique at that time was known as half-timbered—a method whereby masonry was used as a fill material for walls inside a braced timber frame (half timber, half masonry). One might expect to find many examples of half-timbering in America, but these settlers usually copied the unique, much more expedient, log building style of the Swedes (p. 58).

A rather humorous American adaptation of the half-timbered style was the construction of a first floor in masonry and the second floor as shown below.

As families became more settled and grew larger, more substantial dwellings became necessary. Housebuilders shifted directly from logs to the readily available fieldstone as the primary building material. Their houses began as one-room stone cottages and quickly expanded to two-story farmhouses with four to eight rooms. These stone buildings were considered more attractive, more comfortable, and more durable by their owners.

1700
EARLY STONE HOUSE, PENNSYLVANIA

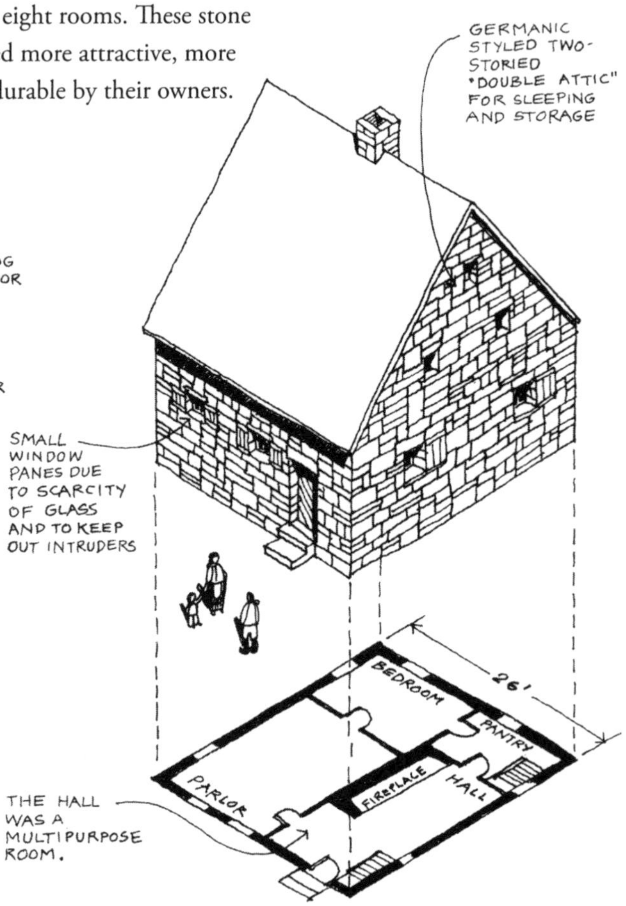

GERMANIC STYLED TWO-STORIED "DOUBLE ATTIC" FOR SLEEPING AND STORAGE

1675
HALF-TIMBER HOUSE, PENNSYLVANIA

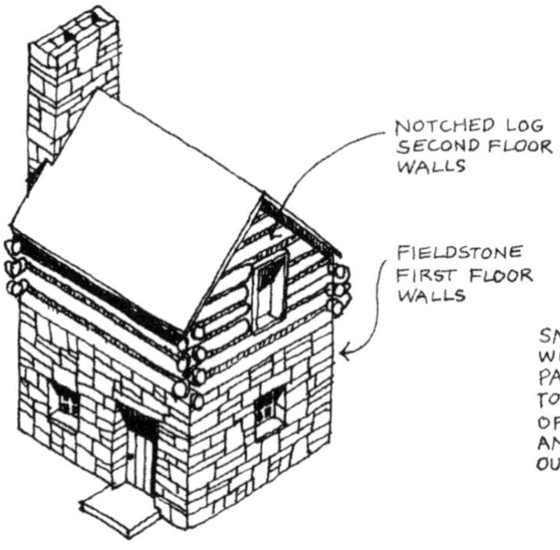

NOTCHED LOG SECOND FLOOR WALLS

FIELDSTONE FIRST FLOOR WALLS

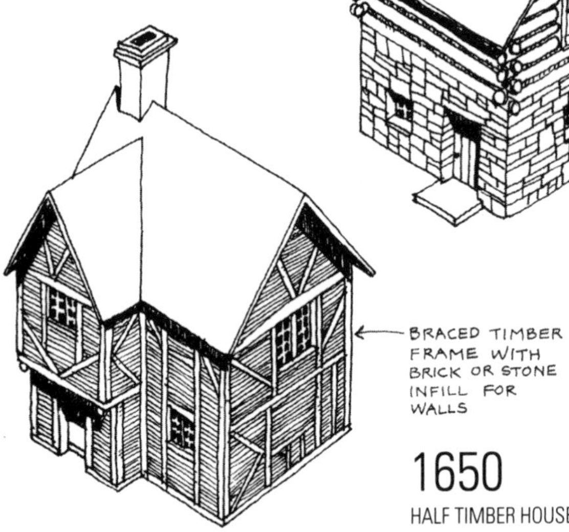

SMALL WINDOW PANES DUE TO SCARCITY OF GLASS AND TO KEEP OUT INTRUDERS

BRACED TIMBER FRAME WITH BRICK OR STONE INFILL FOR WALLS

1650
HALF TIMBER HOUSE, GERMANY

THE HALL WAS A MULTIPURPOSE ROOM.

BEDROOM

PANTRY

26'

PARLOR

FIREPLACE

HALL

Two common types of houses in early eighteenth-century eastern Pennsylvania were the bank house, a farmhouse with part of the first floor built into a hillside (bank) to keep it warm in the winter and cool in the summer, and the two-story country townhouse, a dwelling that was popular in urban centers and the Pennsylvania countryside.

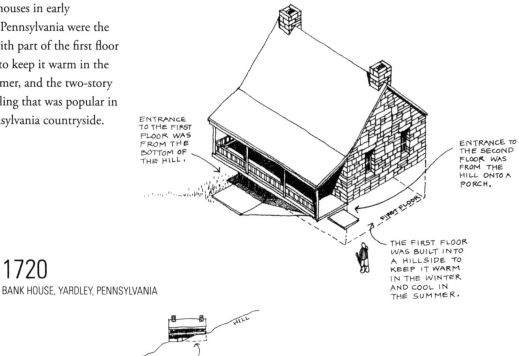

ENTRANCE TO THE FIRST FLOOR WAS FROM THE BOTTOM OF THE HILL.

ENTRANCE TO THE SECOND FLOOR WAS FROM THE HILL ONTO A PORCH.

FIRST FLOOR

THE FIRST FLOOR WAS BUILT INTO A HILLSIDE TO KEEP IT WARM IN THE WINTER AND COOL IN THE SUMMER.

1720
BANK HOUSE, YARDLEY, PENNSYLVANIA

SIDE VIEW

HILL

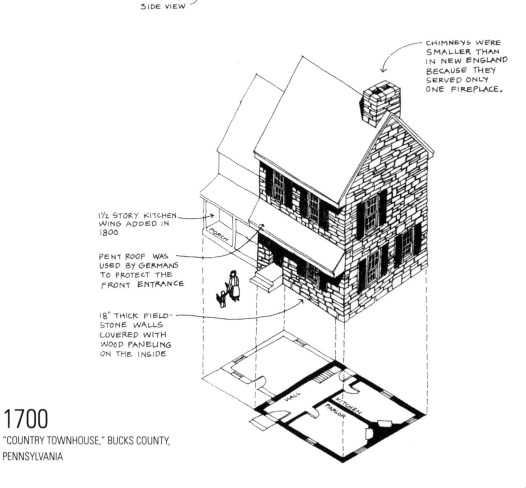

CHIMNEYS WERE SMALLER THAN IN NEW ENGLAND BECAUSE THEY SERVED ONLY ONE FIREPLACE.

1½ STORY KITCHEN WING ADDED IN 1800

PENT ROOF WAS USED BY GERMANS TO PROTECT THE FRONT ENTRANCE

18" THICK FIELDSTONE WALLS COVERED WITH WOOD PANELING ON THE INSIDE

PORCH

HALL

KITCHEN

PARLOR

1700
"COUNTRY TOWNHOUSE," BUCKS COUNTY, PENNSYLVANIA

The first settlers in Pennsylvania lived in simple one-story, one-room cottages that were soon enlarged, with the addition of another full floor, making a two-story dwelling known as a one-over-one. This house proved to be too small for growing families and a one-story kitchen was soon added.

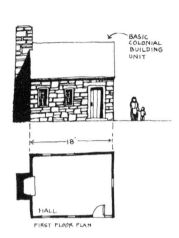

1675
ONE-ROOM COTTAGE, PENNSYLVANIA

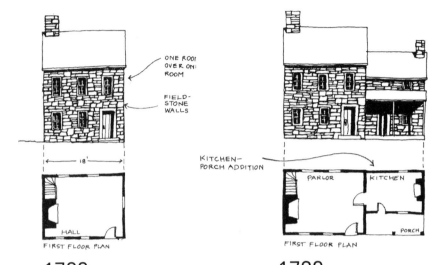

1700
ONE-OVER-ONE COUNTRY TOWNHOUSE, PENNSYLVANIA

1730
ONE-OVER-ONE WITH ADDITION, PENNSYLVANIA

Around 1730, the two-story dwelling (one-over-one) grew wider with new rooms built to one side and another set of windows to the front elevation. This type of expansion, the most common, made the house very livable, and it soon became quite popular throughout areas populated by the German and Scotch-Irish. In fact, the house became known as the "I" (pronounced "eye") house because of its great popularity in Iowa, Illinois, and Indiana in the late eighteenth century.

The earliest "I" houses presented an unbalanced appearance with one set of windows on one side of the door and two sets on the other. Around 1750 the imbalance was corrected with a symmetrical façade and the addition of a center hall. The Virginia "I", developed in that state by emigrants from Pennsylvania, is a good example of second and third generation colonial architecture. It was similar to the basic "I" house but replaced masonry with a frame construction, had three windows along the front façade rather than five, and chimneys outside the house.

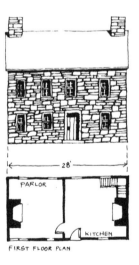

1730
PRE-CLASSICAL PENNSYLVANIA I

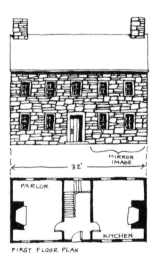

1750
CLASSICAL PENNSYLVANIA I

Houses two rooms deep were as popular as the one-room deep houses shown on the previous page. The oldest of this type, the row or townhouse, is similar to the one-over-one except it has expanded upward with two rooms on a second floor. This house could be found in every major colonial city but only in Pennsylvania was it used in villages and the countryside.

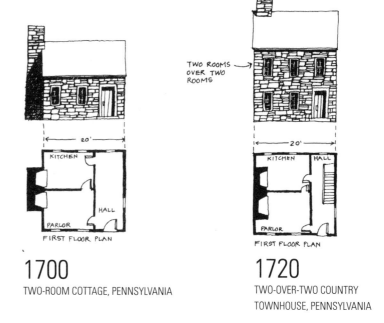

1700
TWO-ROOM COTTAGE, PENNSYLVANIA

1720
TWO-OVER-TWO COUNTRY TOWNHOUSE, PENNSYLVANIA

The country townhouse was frequently enlarged by adding a mirror image of the original portion on the side opposite the chimney. This gave the house four rooms on each floor and it came to be known as the Pennsylvania four-over-four. Like the "I" houses, the early four-over-fours had unbalanced facades that were balanced around 1760 with additional windows and a center hall. The four-over-four, a massive, boxy house similar to the New England large (p. 76) never became as popular as the Pennsylvania or Virginia "I" houses. The larger four-overfours were relatively expensive to build and the more compact "I" houses easily fit the needs of growing pioneer farm areas.

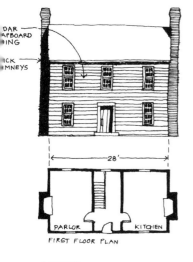

1770
VIRGINIA I, VIRGINIA AND MARYLAND

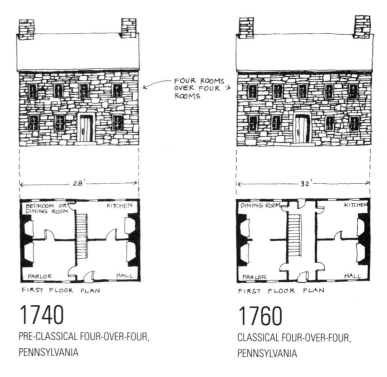

1740
PRE-CLASSICAL FOUR-OVER-FOUR, PENNSYLVANIA

1760
CLASSICAL FOUR-OVER-FOUR, PENNSYLVANIA

Southern Colonial

Southeast 1680

As the original Southern colony was settled by the wealthy, many houses were designed as mansions with kitchen and servants' living quarters located in an attached wing. The hall and parlor plan, popularized by the English (see Medieval Style, p. 44), was used with wings added to increase the house's size. The most popular method for adding these wings were the "T" shaped plan (shown below) and the "L" shaped plan, but other shapes such as the "H" and "U" were used as well. The house was always built facing the prevailing summer breeze to obtain good air circulation during hot summer days. The kitchen chimney was placed on a far exterior wall to reduce heat during cooking.

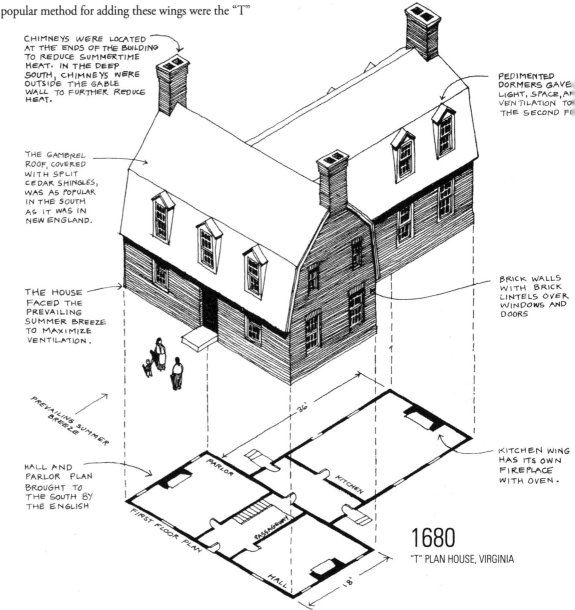

CHIMNEYS WERE LOCATED AT THE ENDS OF THE BUILDING TO REDUCE SUMMERTIME HEAT. IN THE DEEP SOUTH, CHIMNEYS WERE OUTSIDE THE GABLE WALL TO FURTHER REDUCE HEAT.

PEDIMENTED DORMERS GAVE LIGHT, SPACE, AN VENTILATION TO THE SECOND F(

THE GAMBREL ROOF, COVERED WITH SPLIT CEDAR SHINGLES, WAS AS POPULAR IN THE SOUTH AS IT WAS IN NEW ENGLAND.

THE HOUSE FACED THE PREVAILING SUMMER BREEZE TO MAXIMIZE VENTILATION.

BRICK WALLS WITH BRICK LINTELS OVER WINDOWS AND DOORS

PREVAILING SUMMER BREEZE

HALL AND PARLOR PLAN BROUGHT TO THE SOUTH BY THE ENGLISH

KITCHEN WING HAS ITS OWN FIREPLACE WITH OVEN.

PARLOR

KITCHEN

FIRST FLOOR PLAN

PASSAGEWAY

36'

8'

HALL

1680
"T" PLAN HOUSE, VIRGINIA

Many of the same features are found in these Southern houses and those being built simultaneously in New England. The design of the house was still primarily influenced by recent settlers whose ideas were formed in England. The gambrel roof, for example, imported to both areas from England, became extremely popular.

At the beginning of the eighteenth century, many areas of the South were being settled by various groups of "secondhand" colonists. Germans, Barbadians, French Protestants, Swiss, the Scotch-Irish, and the English emigrated from the North and settled in different parts of the South, below the southern border of Virginia. Many immigrants entered the country through Philadelphia and filtered south over new trails.

These people brought various housebuilding ideas and methods with them. For example, the English introduced the medieval hall and parlor house (shown below) which quickly replaced the cramped one-room cabin. The hall and parlor house then inspired many variations (depending on the culture of the builders, the available materials, and the climate) including the picturesque North Carolina coastal cottage (shown below). The Germans and the Scotch-Irish emigrating from eastern Pennsylvania, introduced the continental plan house (named for its German origin) similar to the Pennsylvania "I" house discussed in the previous chapter. The shed porch, imported from the West Indies, soon became a standard addition to all houses constructed in the South.

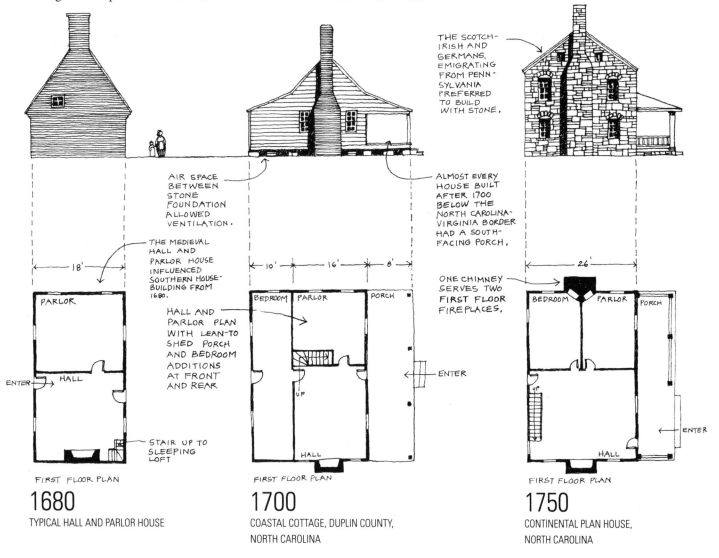

AIR SPACE BETWEEN STONE FOUNDATION ALLOWED VENTILATION.

THE MEDIEVAL HALL AND PARLOR HOUSE INFLUENCED SOUTHERN HOUSE-BUILDING FROM 1680.

HALL AND PARLOR PLAN WITH LEAN-TO SHED PORCH AND BEDROOM ADDITIONS AT FRONT AND REAR

STAIR UP TO SLEEPING LOFT

THE SCOTCH-IRISH AND GERMANS, EMIGRATING FROM PENN-SYLVANIA PREFERRED TO BUILD WITH STONE.

ALMOST EVERY HOUSE BUILT AFTER 1700 BELOW THE NORTH CAROLINA-VIRGINIA BORDER HAD A SOUTH-FACING PORCH.

ONE CHIMNEY SERVES TWO FIRST FLOOR FIREPLACES.

PARLOR
ENTER — HALL

BEDROOM PARLOR PORCH
UP
ENTER
HALL

BEDROOM PARLOR PORCH
UP
ENTER
HALL

18'

10' 16' 8'

26'

FIRST FLOOR PLAN

1680
TYPICAL HALL AND PARLOR HOUSE

FIRST FLOOR PLAN

1700
COASTAL COTTAGE, DUPLIN COUNTY, NORTH CAROLINA

FIRST FLOOR PLAN

1750
CONTINENTAL PLAN HOUSE, NORTH CAROLINA

New England Farmhouse

New England 1690

From 1690 on, the most popular New England farmhouse dwelling was the one-and-one-half, two, and two-and-one-half storied house. Times were more prosperous and the people more settled. Families were larger and could afford bigger and better houses. Ceilings grew higher, windows larger, and facades a bit more decorated with the influx of craftsmen from England where Renaissance styles were gaining popularity.

These houses marked the transition from early colonial dwellings to the Georgian Style, as shown on page 92. Their most distinctive feature was the huge central chimney that incorporated a fireplace in each room. Most houses had a whole or partial cellar, and simple ridged roofs with no dormers. The gambrel roof was common.

All these houses, including many built up to 1850, were of braced oak frame construction as shown on page 68. These frames were supported on between eight and twelve posts so that the exterior walls or interior partitions did not have to carry any weight. Exterior walls were cedar clapboards nailed into heavy oak horizontal sheathing boards that were nailed to wall studs. The inside walls were covered with lath and plaster and were otherwise uninsulated.

The second floor of the one-and-one-half story New England colonial house was partially built into the roof. All second-floor windows were in the gables with the exception of eyebrow windows located just under the roof eave in the front and rear walls. They were introduced in the early 1800s.

The two-story house was simply a vertical expansion of the one-and-one-half-story house. The floor plans remained the same but there was more headroom on the second floor.

The two-and-a-half-story house, known as the New England large, was an upward and rearward expansion of the two-story house.

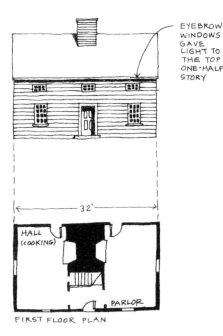

EYEBROW WINDOWS GAVE LIGHT TO THE TOP ONE-HALF STORY

32'

HALL (COOKING)

PARLOR

FIRST FLOOR PLAN

1690
ONE-AND-ONE-HALF-STORY FARMHOUSE

Two of the most popular houses in American history are the one-and-one-half-story and the two-and-one-half-story New England farmhouses shown below. Because of their simplicity, they were constructed throughout the Northeast for over 150 years. During the mid-eighteenth century, the two-and-one-half-story, the New England large, began to show some decoration, especially around the doorway. There an elaborately paneled door was framed with pilasters and capped with a deeply carved Baroque pediment. This gave the house a new "important" look, signifying the end of the New England vernacular and the beginning of the imported English Georgian Style (p. 92).

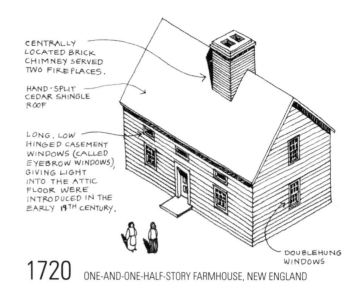

CENTRALLY LOCATED BRICK CHIMNEY SERVED TWO FIREPLACES.

HAND-SPLIT CEDAR SHINGLE ROOF

LONG, LOW HINGED CASEMENT WINDOWS (CALLED EYEBROW WINDOWS), GIVING LIGHT INTO THE ATTIC FLOOR WERE INTRODUCED IN THE EARLY 19TH CENTURY.

DOUBLEHUNG WINDOWS

1720 ONE-AND-ONE-HALF-STORY FARMHOUSE, NEW ENGLAND

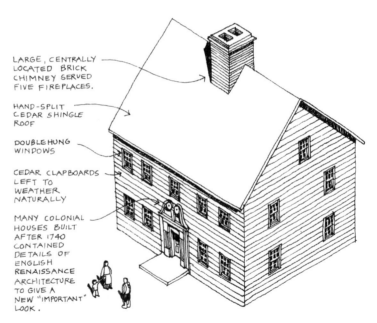

LARGE, CENTRALLY LOCATED BRICK CHIMNEY SERVED FIVE FIREPLACES.

HAND-SPLIT CEDAR SHINGLE ROOF

DOUBLEHUNG WINDOWS

CEDAR CLAPBOARDS LEFT TO WEATHER NATURALLY

MANY COLONIAL HOUSES BUILT AFTER 1740 CONTAINED DETAILS OF ENGLISH RENAISSANCE ARCHITECTURE TO GIVE A NEW "IMPORTANT" LOOK.

1740 NEW ENGLAND LARGE

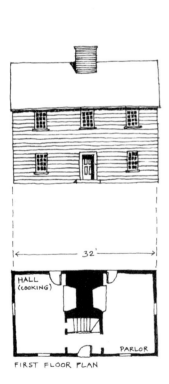

32'

HALL (COOKING)

PARLOR

FIRST FLOOR PLAN

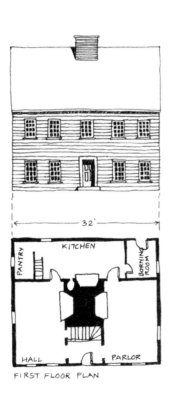

32'

PANTRY KITCHEN BORNING ROOM

HALL PARLOR

FIRST FLOOR PLAN

1720
TWO-STORY FARMHOUSE

1730
TWO-AND-ONE-HALF-STORY FARMHOUSE, THE NEW ENGLAND LARGE

The lean-to addition to the Saltbox Style, shown on page 69 became an integral part of the construction of that house around 1680. The space gained by the lean-to had become a necessity and, in fact, by 1730 many families were finding the saltbox too small for their needs. The two-and-one-half-story New England large was the last stage of the growth of the traditional early American New England Colonial farmhouse. As shown in the illustration below, the second floor above the saltbox lean-to was expanded into a full two-room-deep plan, matching the depth of the first floor. The formerly useless attic space of the lean-to was made into three new bedrooms with full headroom. The most striking feature of this change was the disappearance of the long lean-to roof of the saltbox. The New England house had developed into a rectangular box with a central chimney and a simple symmetrical roof—as utilitarian as could be.

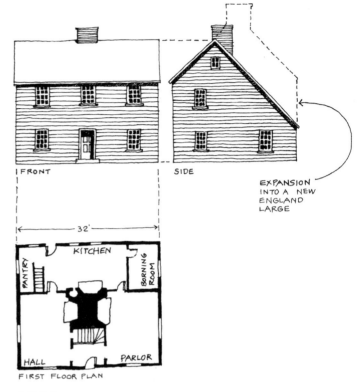

1680 SALTBOX, NEW ENGLAND

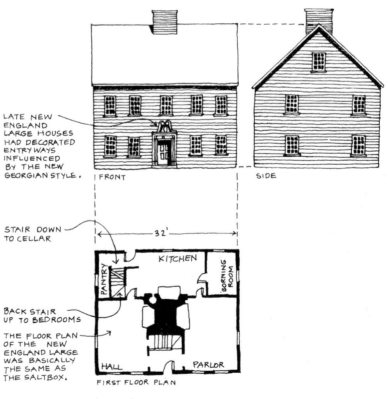

1740 NEW ENGLAND LARGE

The New England large adapted well to being built partially in the form of a one-half, three-quarter, or full house. Small families, having a limited budget but planning to expand in the future, built the one-half or three-quarter houses, then added to the house at their convenience. Today, a family in need of more space would be more inclined to either move into a larger house or build a new one.

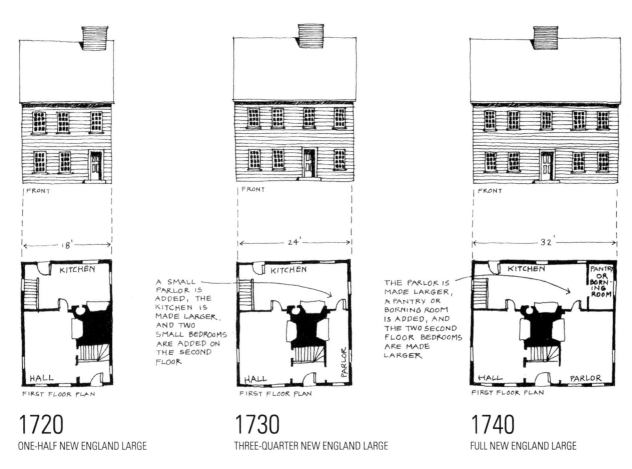

A SMALL PARLOR IS ADDED, THE KITCHEN IS MADE LARGER, AND TWO SMALL BEDROOMS ARE ADDED ON THE SECOND FLOOR

THE PARLOR IS MADE LARGER, A PANTRY OR BORNING ROOM IS ADDED, AND THE TWO SECOND FLOOR BEDROOMS ARE MADE LARGER

1720
ONE-HALF NEW ENGLAND LARGE

1730
THREE-QUARTER NEW ENGLAND LARGE

1740
FULL NEW ENGLAND LARGE

Additions were made to many of these one-and-one-half, two, and even the two-and-one-half-story farmhouses long after the original structures were built. The need for more light and space within the attic sometimes necessitated dormers. For the same reasons, many originally gable-roofed houses had their roofs changed into a gambrel shape. In rare instances a one-and-one-half-story gambrel-roofed house would be converted into a full two-story gable-roofed house.

Plantation Colonial

South
1700

After the turn of the century, plantations blossomed all along the navigable waterways of the South. At first tobacco and then rice brought prosperity to Virginia and the Carolinas where early plantation houses reflected the European origins of English, Scotch-Irish, and Huguenot (French Protestant) settlers.

The plantation house was different from the typical southern colonial house because its orientation toward the river (the much used and sometimes only highway between plantations) was just as important as toward the opposite or plantation side. The house had no conventional front or back.

The plantation house was placed on a hilltop site when possible, so that it could command a view, and it always faced the prevailing summer breeze. Large porch roofs evolved to pick up these breezes and to shade the walls of the house, so welcome in the hot southern climate. The plan of the house usually emphasized cross-ventilation, sometimes at the expense of privacy.

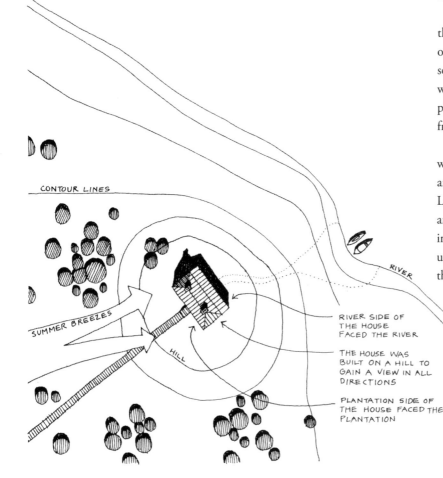

CONTOUR LINES

SUMMER BREEZES

HILL

RIVER

RIVER SIDE OF THE HOUSE FACED THE RIVER

THE HOUSE WAS BUILT ON A HILL TO GAIN A VIEW IN ALL DIRECTIONS

PLANTATION SIDE OF THE HOUSE FACED THE PLANTATION

1700
SITE PLAN OF TYPICAL PLANTATION HOUSE

The plantation house was first developed in South Carolina by the Huguenots near the end of the seventeenth century. It was unusual in that it had main entrances on the river side as well as on the plantation side. The house had no traditional front or back. The design of the house stressed cross-ventilation by placing the rooms next to each other in single file, while providing shade for the two long walls with a piazza or roofed porch, a method of cooling borrowed from the settlers from the West Indies.

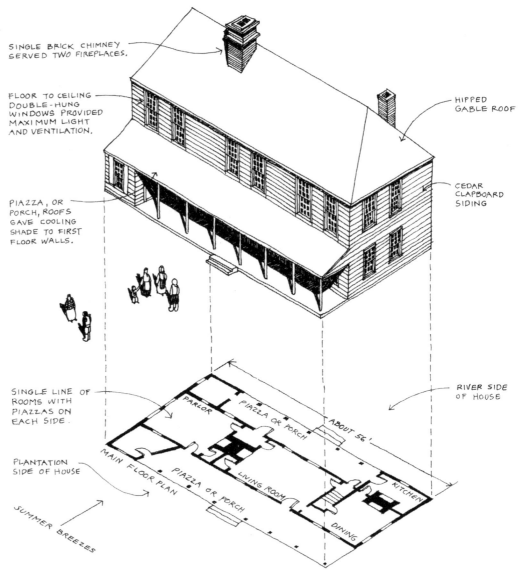

1690 HUGUENOT PLANTATION HOUSE, SOUTH CAROLINA

SINGLE BRICK CHIMNEY SERVED TWO FIREPLACES.

FLOOR TO CEILING DOUBLE-HUNG WINDOWS PROVIDED MAXIMUM LIGHT AND VENTILATION.

HIPPED GABLE ROOF

CEDAR CLAPBOARD SIDING

PIAZZA, OR PORCH, ROOFS GAVE COOLING SHADE TO FIRST FLOOR WALLS.

SINGLE LINE OF ROOMS WITH PIAZZAS ON EACH SIDE.

RIVER SIDE OF HOUSE

PARLOR

PIAZZA OR PORCH

ABOUT 56'

PLANTATION SIDE OF HOUSE

MAIN FLOOR PLAN

PIAZZA OR PORCH

LIVING ROOM

KITCHEN

SUMMER BREEZES

DINING

Possibly the most beautiful American plantation house is the home of George Washington, Mount Vernon. Although it was built in stages over a fifty-year period and it borrows from the Georgian Style, shown on page 92, and the Adam Style, shown on page 102, it remains one of the best examples of the Plantation Colonial Style.

Mount Vernon was built on a gentle hilltop on the banks of the Potamac River in Virginia, by George Washington's father, in the Medieval Style, shown on page 44. It became known as Little Hunting Creek Plantation. In 1743, Washington's half-brother, Lawrence, took deed to the house and renamed it Mount Vernon after Admiral Vernon under whom he had served in the Army. When Lawrence died in 1752, George bought the property and seven years later raised the structure to a two-and-one-half story house for his new bride, Martha Custis. In 1774 he began extensive additions and changes that took more than eleven years to complete. Mount Vernon stands today as it was when Washington finished his work.

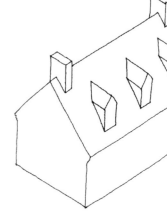

The house has two distinctly different facades: the one that faces the river has a large two-story column-supported colonnade that relates to the vast scale of the river landscape. The facade that faces the plantation emphasizes windows, doors, dormers, arcades, and dependent buildings that relate to the small scale of the human being. The building was a very successful reaction to its site and culture.

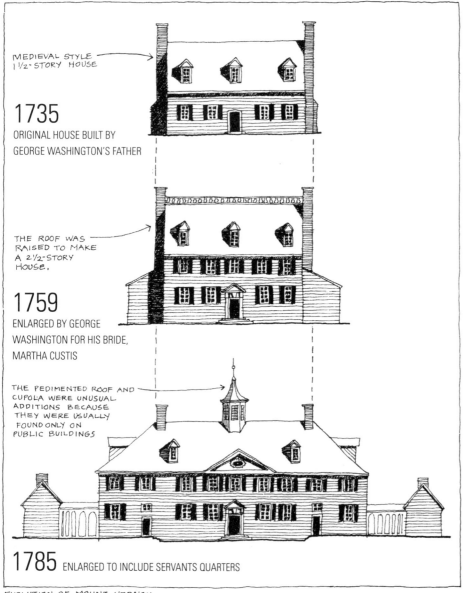

MEDIEVAL STYLE 1 1/2-STORY HOUSE

1735
ORIGINAL HOUSE BUILT BY GEORGE WASHINGTON'S FATHER

THE ROOF WAS RAISED TO MAKE A 2 1/2-STORY HOUSE.

1759
ENLARGED BY GEORGE WASHINGTON FOR HIS BRIDE, MARTHA CUSTIS

THE PEDIMENTED ROOF AND CUPOLA WERE UNUSUAL ADDITIONS BECAUSE THEY WERE USUALLY FOUND ONLY ON PUBLIC BUILDINGS

1785 ENLARGED TO INCLUDE SERVANTS QUARTERS

EVOLUTION OF MOUNT VERNON

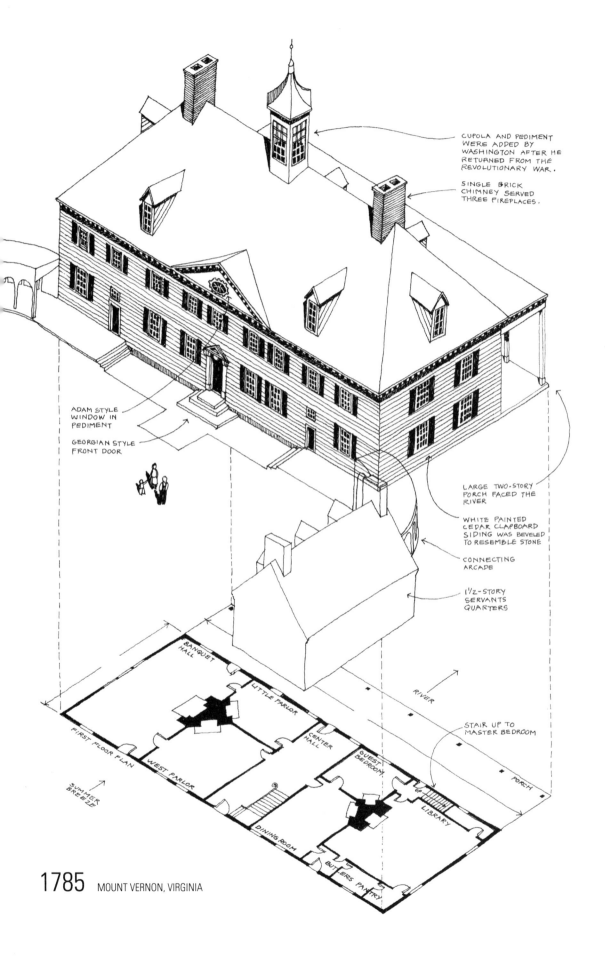

CUPOLA AND PEDIMENT
WERE ADDED BY
WASHINGTON AFTER HE
RETURNED FROM THE
REVOLUTIONARY WAR.

SINGLE BRICK
CHIMNEY SERVED
THREE FIREPLACES.

ADAM STYLE
WINDOW IN
PEDIMENT

GEORGIAN STYLE
FRONT DOOR

LARGE TWO-STORY
PORCH FACED THE
RIVER

WHITE PAINTED
CEDAR CLAPBOARD
SIDING WAS BEVELED
TO RESEMBLE STONE

CONNECTING
ARCADE

1½-STORY
SERVANTS
QUARTERS

BANQUET
HALL

LITTLE PARLOR

CENTER
HALL

RIVER

FIRST FLOOR PLAN

WEST PARLOR

GUEST
BEDROOM

STAIR UP TO
MASTER BEDROOM

PORCH

SUMMER
BREEZE

DINING ROOM

BUTLERS PANTRY

LIBRARY

1785 MOUNT VERNON, VIRGINIA

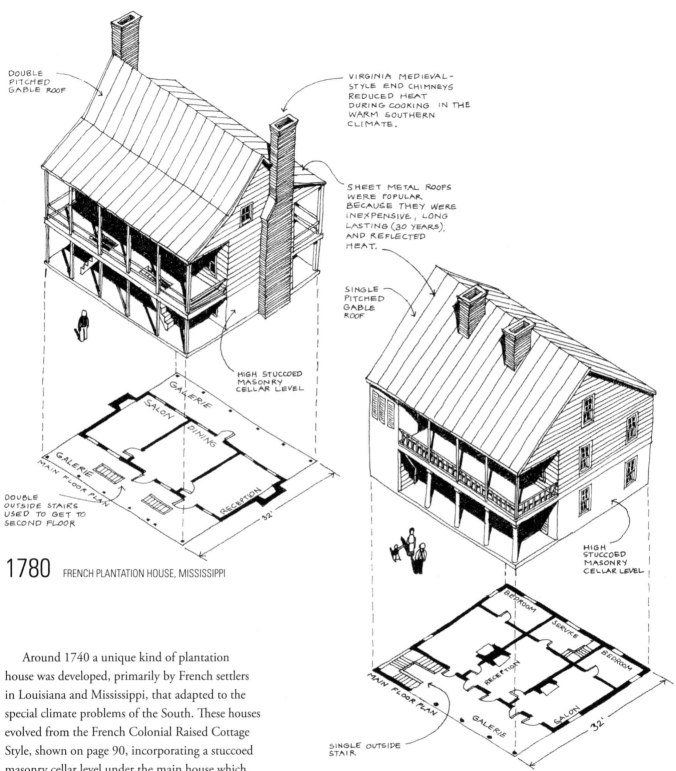

DOUBLE PITCHED GABLE ROOF

VIRGINIA MEDIEVAL-STYLE END CHIMNEYS REDUCED HEAT DURING COOKING IN THE WARM SOUTHERN CLIMATE.

SHEET METAL ROOFS WERE POPULAR BECAUSE THEY WERE INEXPENSIVE, LONG LASTING (30 YEARS), AND REFLECTED HEAT.

SINGLE PITCHED GABLE ROOF

HIGH STUCCOED MASONRY CELLAR LEVEL

GALERIE
SALON
DINING
GALERIE
MAIN FLOOR PLAN
RECEPTION
32'

DOUBLE OUTSIDE STAIRS USED TO GET TO SECOND FLOOR

1780 FRENCH PLANTATION HOUSE, MISSISSIPPI

HIGH STUCCOED MASONRY CELLAR LEVEL

BEDROOM
SERVICE
BEDROOM
RECEPTION
MAIN FLOOR PLAN
GALERIE
SALON
32'

SINGLE OUTSIDE STAIR

1720 FRENCH PLANTATION HOUSE, LOUISIANA

Around 1740 a unique kind of plantation house was developed, primarily by French settlers in Louisiana and Mississippi, that adapted to the special climate problems of the South. These houses evolved from the French Colonial Raised Cottage Style, shown on page 90, incorporating a stuccoed masonry cellar level under the main house which was usually surrounded in some form by a porchlike galerie, an idea that was brought to the South by travelers from the tropical West Indies.

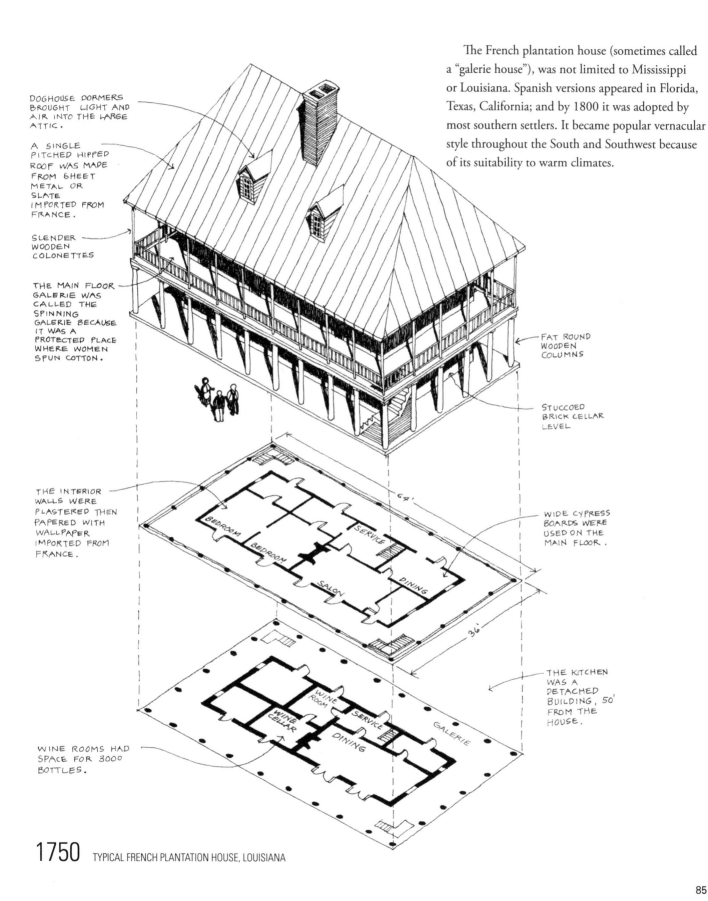

The French plantation house (sometimes called a "galerie house"), was not limited to Mississippi or Louisiana. Spanish versions appeared in Florida, Texas, California; and by 1800 it was adopted by most southern settlers. It became popular vernacular style throughout the South and Southwest because of its suitability to warm climates.

DOGHOUSE DORMERS BROUGHT LIGHT AND AIR INTO THE LARGE ATTIC.

A SINGLE PITCHED HIPPED ROOF WAS MADE FROM SHEET METAL OR SLATE IMPORTED FROM FRANCE.

SLENDER WOODEN COLONETTES

THE MAIN FLOOR GALERIE WAS CALLED THE SPINNING GALERIE BECAUSE IT WAS A PROTECTED PLACE WHERE WOMEN SPUN COTTON.

FAT ROUND WOODEN COLUMNS

STUCCOED BRICK CELLAR LEVEL

THE INTERIOR WALLS WERE PLASTERED THEN PAPERED WITH WALLPAPER IMPORTED FROM FRANCE.

WIDE CYPRESS BOARDS WERE USED ON THE MAIN FLOOR.

BEDROOM
BEDROOM
SERVICE
SALON
DINING

64'
36'

WINE ROOM
WINE CELLAR
SERVICE
DINING
GALERIE

THE KITCHEN WAS A DETACHED BUILDING, 50' FROM THE HOUSE.

WINE ROOMS HAD SPACE FOR 3000 BOTTLES.

1750 TYPICAL FRENCH PLANTATION HOUSE, LOUISIANA

Cape Cod

Massachusetts
1710

The Cape Cod cottage is a successful indigenous solution to life in a harsh natural environment based on early American building methods. It is one of the most rational, functional designs for a house in the history of architecture.

Early Cape Cods were built by ship's carpenters as though they were "land boats" made to ride shifting sands and withstand lashing wind and rain storms; they were low and broad, averaging twenty-five by forty feet, with only a seven foot ceiling height. They were built on large hewn oak sills, which steadied the house on its shifting uneven sand site. The Cape Cod had no projections or exterior extraneous decoration, so they could resist ocean gale forces.

Inside, the rooms were clustered around a huge chimney that contained as many as four fireplaces, used for heating, cooking, and light. The attic level was partitioned into numerous tiny bedrooms, each with a single window in the gable wall. A borning room was located on the first floor near the kitchen for the care of new-born children.

Many Cape Cods were ingeniously constructed so they could be partially built, then expanded when the family grew larger. The half Cape Cod was the "honeymoon cottage." The three-quarter Cape Cod was the answer when children arrived, and the full Cape Cod was used for the large family.

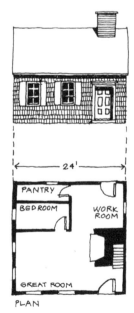

1700
HALF CAP COD (HONEYMOON COTTAGE)

1710
THREE-QUARTER CAPE COD

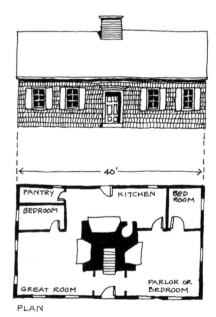

1720
FULL CAPE COD

The Cape Cod used plank construction amazingly similar to the Northwestern Indian plank houses described on page 34. Eighteen-inch wide planks, nailed to purlins on the roof and to sills and girts on the walls, not only stabilized the post-and-beam frame, but provided sheathing for shingles on the outside and plaster on the inside. They were built so sturdily that in many cases they were hauled by teams of horses across the sand or floated along the water to more suitable or desirable sites.

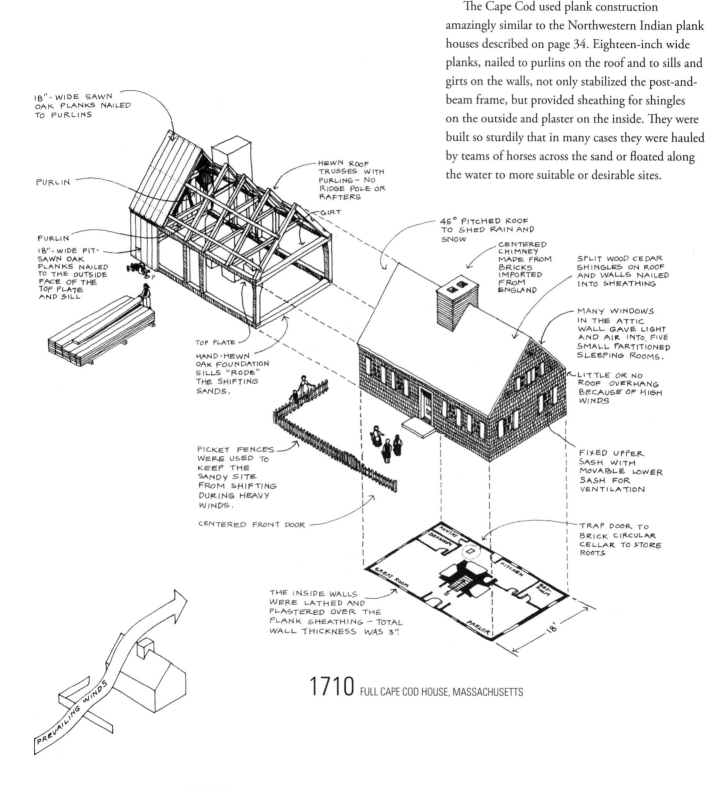

18"- WIDE SAWN OAK PLANKS NAILED TO PURLINS

PURLIN

HEWN ROOF TRUSSES WITH PURLING - NO RIDGE POLE OR RAFTERS

GIRT

PURLIN

18"- WIDE PIT-SAWN OAK PLANKS NAILED TO THE OUTSIDE FACE OF THE TOP PLATE AND SILL

TOP PLATE

HAND-HEWN OAK FOUNDATION SILLS "RODE" THE SHIFTING SANDS.

45° PITCHED ROOF TO SHED RAIN AND SNOW

CENTERED CHIMNEY MADE FROM BRICKS IMPORTED FROM ENGLAND

SPLIT WOOD CEDAR SHINGLES ON ROOF AND WALLS NAILED INTO SHEATHING

MANY WINDOWS IN THE ATTIC WALL GAVE LIGHT AND AIR INTO FIVE SMALL PARTITIONED SLEEPING ROOMS.

LITTLE OR NO ROOF OVERHANG BECAUSE OF HIGH WINDS

PICKET FENCES WERE USED TO KEEP THE SANDY SITE FROM SHIFTING DURING HEAVY WINDS.

CENTERED FRONT DOOR

FIXED UPPER SASH WITH MOVABLE LOWER SASH FOR VENTILATION

TRAP DOOR TO BRICK CIRCULAR CELLAR TO STORE ROOTS

PANTRY
BEDROOM
KITCHEN
GREAT ROOM
BEDROOM
PARLOR

18'

THE INSIDE WALLS WERE LATHED AND PLASTERED OVER THE PLANK SHEATHING - TOTAL WALL THICKNESS WAS 3".

1710 FULL CAPE COD HOUSE, MASSACHUSETTS

PREVAILING WINDS

THE CAPE COD HOUSE WAS CONSTRUCTED AND PLACED ON THE SITE SO THAT PREVAILING WINDS WOULD NOT HARM IT.

Until 1850, the basic design of the Cape Cod remained the same except for a few minor variations such as the Greek Revival's influence on the design of the front door. The Cape Cod is essentially a fisherman's cottage and during its years as a popular building type, the Cape was a successful fishing center.

Here are some of the most popular styles of the Cape Cod before 1850:

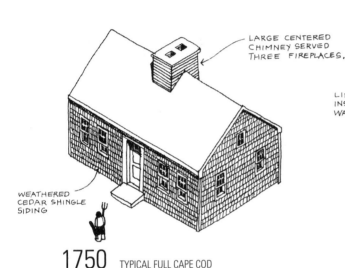

1750 TYPICAL FULL CAPE COD

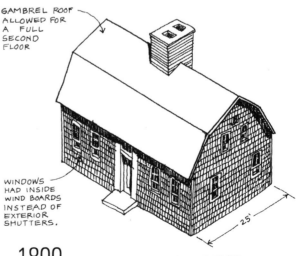

1770 DOUBLE CAPE COD BUILT BY TWO FAMILIES INTERESTED IN REDUCING HEAT LOSS

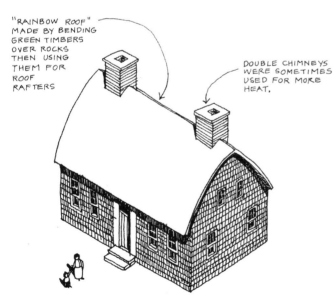

1790 BOWED ROOF CAPE COD; POPULAR AMONG SHIPWRIGHTS NEEDING MORE SECOND FLOOR SPACE

1800 CAPE ANN, A GAMBREL ROOFED CAPE COD, POPULAR IN THE CAPE ANN, MASSACHUSETTS, AREA

The era of the original Cape Cod cottage came to an end in the mid-nineteenth century when the invention of the wood-burning stove made the huge central chimney, with all its fireplaces, superfluous. But after 1930, modern versions of the Cape Cod began appearing in home magazines and soon the house became the most familiar building style of the twentieth century. As described on page 240, the style was particularly popular with the prefabricated home industry because of its simple shape and romantic past.

Below are some examples of how the Cape Cod adapted to a new culture and new building technologies:

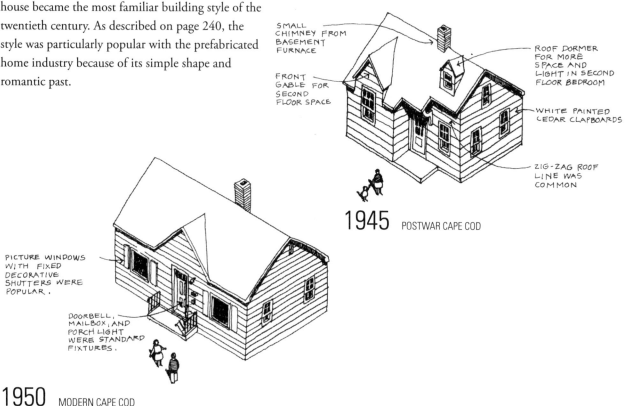

SMALL CHIMNEY FROM BASEMENT FURNACE

FRONT GABLE FOR SECOND FLOOR SPACE

ROOF DORMER FOR MORE SPACE AND LIGHT IN SECOND FLOOR BEDROOM

WHITE PAINTED CEDAR CLAPBOARDS

ZIG-ZAG ROOF LINE WAS COMMON

1945 POSTWAR CAPE COD

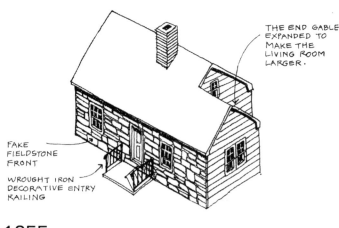

PICTURE WINDOWS WITH FIXED DECORATIVE SHUTTERS WERE POPULAR.

DOORBELL, MAILBOX, AND PORCH LIGHT WERE STANDARD FIXTURES.

1950 MODERN CAPE COD

THE END GABLE EXPANDED TO MAKE THE LIVING ROOM LARGER.

FAKE FIELDSTONE FRONT

WROUGHT IRON DECORATIVE ENTRY RAILING

1955 CONTRACTOR'S DEVELOPMENT CAPE COD

CENTRAL CHIMNEY FROM SMALL FIREPLACE

DORMERS GAVE LIGHT AND SPACE TO SECOND FLOOR BEDROOMS.

FIXED SHUTTERS

FIREPROOF ASBESTOS SHINGLE SIDING

20'

1960 BASIC "NEW" CAPE COD

French Colonial

Mississippi River Valley
1720

The French colonial empire stretched out from the Mississippi River valley, including land extending from the Allegheny Mountains to the Rockies, and from the Gulf of Mexico into northern Canada. But in this vast region there were very few towns or permanent settlers because the French built mainly forts and were itinerant fur traders with the Indians.

The few houses that were constructed during the early eighteenth century, primarily in southern towns, were a unique kind of half-timber construction called *poteaux-en-terre* (posts in earth). These houses were like the simplest Swedish colonial log cabin but built with vertical logs set into the earth. The hipped roofed main cabin was, however, surrounded by a uniquely southern galerie with a sloped roof. Its purpose was to shade the walls of the house and make optimum use of cooling breezes in the hot summer climate. The resulting double-pitched hipped roof became the most recognizable feature of the French colonial house.

Around 1725, many houses in particularly wet areas were built on brick walls six to eight feet above the ground as protection against floods. Later, even when floods were not a factor, this Raised Cottage Style persisted as a popular type of construction. The basement remained cool in the hot climate and was used as cooking, office, and service space.

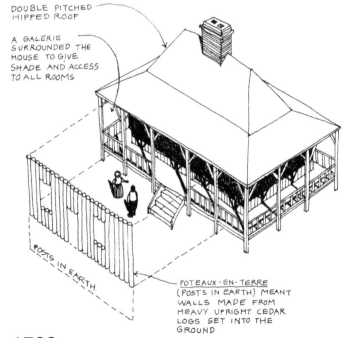

DOUBLE PITCHED HIPPED ROOF

A GALERIE SURROUNDED THE HOUSE TO GIVE SHADE AND ACCESS TO ALL ROOMS

POSTS IN EARTH

POTEAUX-EN-TERRE (POSTS IN EARTH) MEANT WALLS MADE FROM HEAVY UPRIGHT CEDAR LOGS SET INTO THE GROUND

1720   FRENCH PIONEER HOUSE, POTEAUX-EN-TERRE STYLE

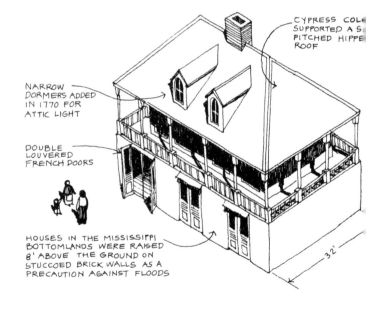

CYPRESS COL SUPPORTED A S PITCHED HIPPE ROOF

NARROW DORMERS ADDED IN 1770 FOR ATTIC LIGHT

DOUBLE LOUVERED FRENCH DOORS

HOUSES IN THE MISSISSIPPI BOTTOMLANDS WERE RAISED 8' ABOVE THE GROUND ON STUCCOED BRICK WALLS AS A PRECAUTION AGAINST FLOODS

32'

1725   FRENCH RAISED COTTAGE STYLE HOUSE

In the eighteenth century, French refugees from Acadia (now Nova Scotia), Canada, were some of the earliest settlers in Louisiana. At first they lived in small, wooden houses known as Cajun cottages ("Cajun" is a corruption of "Acadian"). Later they introduced the galleried plantation houses shown on page 84.

By 1770, the basic French Colonial house had evolved into a straightforward building without galleries. The hipped roof remained a key feature along with many louvered French doors. Stuccoed half-timbered wall construction known as *briquette-entre-poteaux* (small bricks between posts) replaced the *poteaux-en-terre*, which was more prone to rot. Louvered shutters shaded French casement windows from the hot sun in second floor dormers.

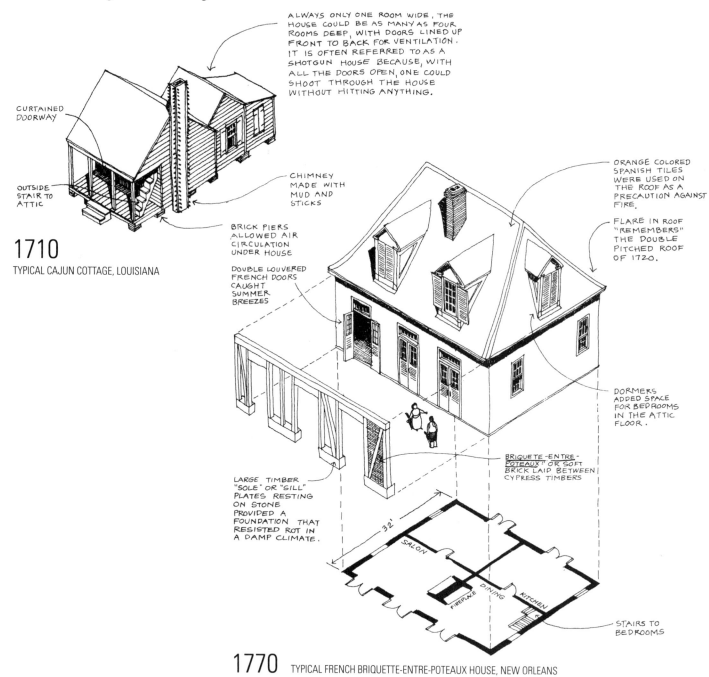

CURTAINED DOORWAY

OUTSIDE STAIR TO ATTIC

ALWAYS ONLY ONE ROOM WIDE, THE HOUSE COULD BE AS MANY AS FOUR ROOMS DEEP, WITH DOORS LINED UP FRONT TO BACK FOR VENTILATION. IT IS OFTEN REFERRED TO AS A SHOTGUN HOUSE BECAUSE, WITH ALL THE DOORS OPEN, ONE COULD SHOOT THROUGH THE HOUSE WITHOUT HITTING ANYTHING.

CHIMNEY MADE WITH MUD AND STICKS

BRICK PIERS ALLOWED AIR CIRCULATION UNDER HOUSE

1710
TYPICAL CAJUN COTTAGE, LOUISIANA

DOUBLE LOUVERED FRENCH DOORS CAUGHT SUMMER BREEZES

ORANGE COLORED SPANISH TILES WERE USED ON THE ROOF AS A PRECAUTION AGAINST FIRE.

FLARE IN ROOF "REMEMBERS" THE DOUBLE PITCHED ROOF OF 1720.

DORMERS ADDED SPACE FOR BEDROOMS IN THE ATTIC FLOOR.

BRIQUETE-ENTRE-POTEAUX" OR SOFT BRICK LAID BETWEEN CYPRESS TIMBERS

LARGE TIMBER "SOLE" OR "SILL" PLATES RESTING ON STONE PROVIDED A FOUNDATION THAT RESISTED ROT IN A DAMP CLIMATE.

32'

SALON

FIREPLACE DINING KITCHEN

STAIRS TO BEDROOMS

1770
TYPICAL FRENCH BRIQUETTE-ENTRE-POTEAUX HOUSE, NEW ORLEANS

Georgian

All Colonies
1720

Twelve major English colonies were established along the Atlantic coast by the end of the seventeenth century. Each had a unique history and separate character and were closer, in many respects, to England than to each other. The style in London set the standards for dress, art, literature, and architecture. And London, along with the rest of the western world, was greatly influenced by concepts of the Italian Renaissance.

In 1666, medieval London was virtually destroyed by fire and the city became open to large-scale architectural modernization. The Italian Renaissance influence evolved into the style known as Georgian, named after Kings George I, II, III, and IV, who ruled England from 1714 to 1830.

At the start of the eighteenth century, New England merchants, Pennsylvania businessmen, and southern planters made up America's most affluent society. This group spent money as quickly as it was made; mansions were erected in the fashionable English Georgian Style that were conspicuous symbols of the owner's wealth.

Comfort, convenience, and privacy prevailed in the American Georgian house. Separate rooms were designed for such activities as cooking, dining, entertaining, and sleeping. Houses became larger, and to keep the rooms warm, large chimneys—which inspired the symmetry and provided the framework within which the early Georgian house was built—were built at both ends of the house. A well balanced, symmetrical exterior and an ornately decorated entrance were the principal features of the house that the wealthy built to impress their friends.

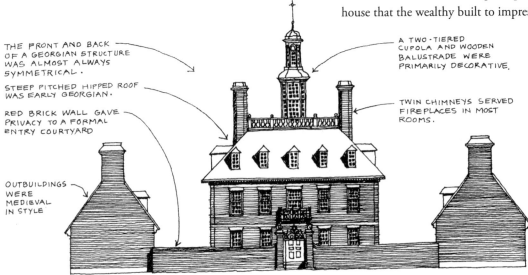

THE FRONT AND BACK OF A GEORGIAN STRUCTURE WAS ALMOST ALWAYS SYMMETRICAL.

STEEP PITCHED HIPPED ROOF WAS EARLY GEORGIAN.

RED BRICK WALL GAVE PRIVACY TO A FORMAL ENTRY COURTYARD

OUTBUILDINGS WERE MEDIEVAL IN STYLE

A TWO-TIERED CUPOLA AND WOODEN BALUSTRADE WERE PRIMARILY DECORATIVE.

TWIN CHIMNEYS SERVED FIREPLACES IN MOST ROOMS.

1720 GOVERNOR'S PALACE, WILLIAMSBURG, VIRGINIA

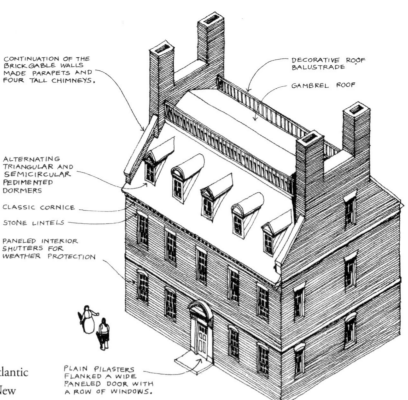

CONTINUATION OF THE BRICK GABLE WALLS MADE PARAPETS AND FOUR TALL CHIMNEYS.

DECORATIVE ROOF BALUSTRADE

GAMBREL ROOF

ALTERNATING TRIANGULAR AND SEMICIRCULAR PEDIMENTED DORMERS

CLASSIC CORNICE

STONE LINTELS

PANELED INTERIOR SHUTTERS FOR WEATHER PROTECTION

PLAIN PILASTERS FLANKED A WIDE PANELED DOOR WITH A ROW OF WINDOWS.

1725 EARLY GEORGIAN HOUSE, VIRGINIA

The Georgian Style first began in the mid-Atlantic and southern colonies, and started very late in New England because of the difficulty of translating into wood a style that owed its success to the use of stone or brick. But by 1750 it began to receive serious attention, primarily in seaport towns. Unlike the earlier "folk" designs built by unschooled colonists, the Georgian Style was transmitted by carpenters guides, architectural pattern books, and the immigration of building tradesmen, professionals, and a few trained architects from England.

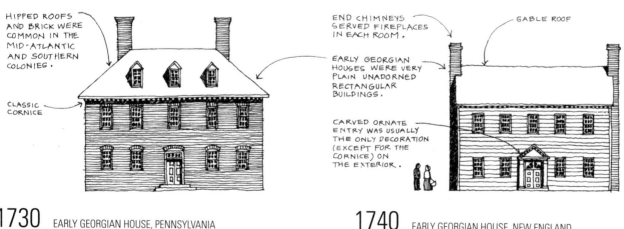

HIPPED ROOFS AND BRICK WERE COMMON IN THE MID-ATLANTIC AND SOUTHERN COLONIES.

CLASSIC CORNICE

END CHIMNEYS SERVED FIREPLACES IN EACH ROOM.

GABLE ROOF

EARLY GEORGIAN HOUSES WERE VERY PLAIN UNADORNED RECTANGULAR BUILDINGS.

CARVED ORNATE ENTRY WAS USUALLY THE ONLY DECORATION (EXCEPT FOR THE CORNICE) ON THE EXTERIOR.

1730 EARLY GEORGIAN HOUSE, PENNSYLVANIA

1740 EARLY GEORGIAN HOUSE, NEW ENGLAND

By the middle of the eighteenth century, England's enthusiasm for the Italian-based Renaissance and classical forms had become almost fanatic. Manuals and journals showing works by the great Italian architect, Andrea Palladio, and his English disciple, Inigo Jones, proliferated. The American colonies were experiencing a building boom and these Renaissance books were greatly influential.

As the Georgian Style progressed, it became more ornate and more imposing. The house grew taller and chimneys were higher and wider. Doorways were flanked by pilasters (attached columns) with either an elaborate cornice or a pediment above. The first floor hall was lit with a semicircular fanlight just above the front door. The second floor hall often had the triple sashed Palladian window, named after the Italian architect Andrea Palladio (1508–1580). The more ostentatious residences had pedimented gable roofs (shown on the opposite page) and quoins (alternating large and small square stones at the buildings' outside corners) to create an illusion of weight and solidity.

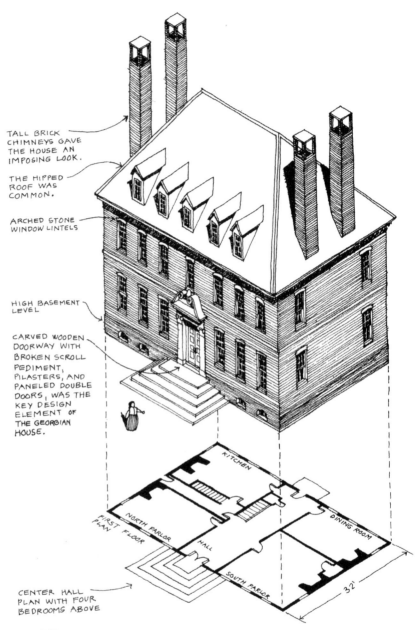

TALL BRICK CHIMNEYS GAVE THE HOUSE AN IMPOSING LOOK.

THE HIPPED ROOF WAS COMMON.

ARCHED STONE WINDOW LINTELS

HIGH BASEMENT LEVEL

CARVED WOODEN DOORWAY WITH BROKEN SCROLL PEDIMENT, PILASTERS, AND PANELED DOUBLE DOORS, WAS THE KEY DESIGN ELEMENT OF THE GEORGIAN HOUSE.

KITCHEN

NORTH PARLOR

FIRST FLOOR PLAN

HALL

DINING ROOM

SOUTH PARLOR

32'

CENTER HALL PLAN WITH FOUR BEDROOMS ABOVE

1745 TYPICAL GEORGIAN MANSION, VIRGINIA

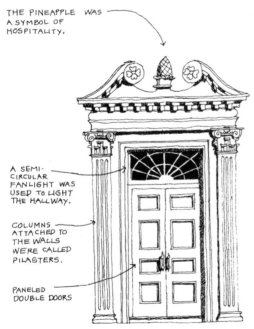

THE PINEAPPLE WAS A SYMBOL OF HOSPITALITY.

A SEMI-CIRCULAR FANLIGHT WAS USED TO LIGHT THE HALLWAY.

COLUMNS ATTACHED TO THE WALLS WERE CALLED PILASTERS.

PANELED DOUBLE DOORS

1745 GEORGIAN DOORWAY

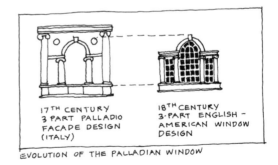

17TH CENTURY 3 PART PALLADIO FACADE DESIGN (ITALY)

18TH CENTURY 3-PART ENGLISH – AMERICAN WINDOW DESIGN

EVOLUTION OF THE PALLADIAN WINDOW

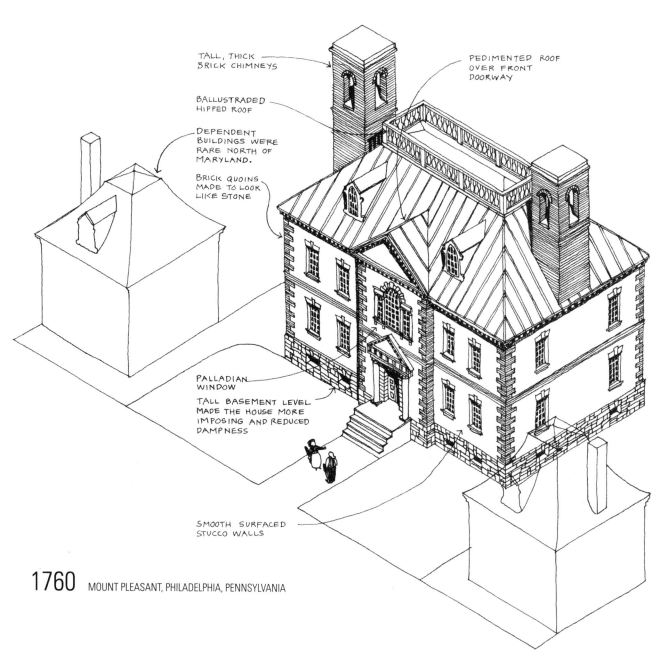

TALL, THICK BRICK CHIMNEYS

BALLUSTRADED HIPPED ROOF

DEPENDENT BUILDINGS WERE RARE NORTH OF MARYLAND.

BRICK QUOINS MADE TO LOOK LIKE STONE

PEDIMENTED ROOF OVER FRONT DOORWAY

PALLADIAN WINDOW

TALL BASEMENT LEVEL MADE THE HOUSE MORE IMPOSING AND REDUCED DAMPNESS

SMOOTH SURFACED STUCCO WALLS

1760 MOUNT PLEASANT, PHILADELPHIA, PENNSYLVANIA

Regional differences in the Georgian Style were far fewer than those in earlier architectural styles. What little variations there were came from climate and conditions of living. In New England, where masonry construction was expensive, houses were built with unpainted wood and featured the ornate doorway, tall thin end chimneys and the classical roof cornice. The middle colonies preferred stucco over stone or brick and featured Palladian detailing around the doorway and second-floor hall window, fat tall chimneys, high basement levels and sometimes paneled shutters. In the South, red brick was the primary building material on houses with hipped roofs, tall chimneys, and ornate white paneled wood detailing around the front door. In the Deep South, Georgian houses were made with tinted stucco and featured graceful iron railings and gates.

The house shown below has practically every popular device of the post-1750 Late Georgian Style: ornate doorway, second-floor Palladian window, pedimented, balustraded hipped roof, tall chimneys, quoins, and a high basement.

Federal

All Colonies 1765

Before the American Revolution in 1773, a new style of building began to evolve that rejected much of the English-inspired Georgian decoration. This style was appropriately called Federal, after the new republic.

After the war, America was a brand new country. It wanted to be as independent in literature, art, and architecture as it was politically. But, however fresh America's self-governing experiment might be, it could not quickly remove the authority of European forms. For those who could not travel abroad to absorb these forms, imports from England of every description were again available in American markets.

The influence of English Georgian architecture was difficult to resist. Houses were being designed by architects, professionally trained in Great Britain and France, who built in the Georgian Style for the wealthy in their homeland as well as in America. But slowly a new Federal Style began to take hold that stressed dignity and restraint, was much less ornamental, but retained the symmetry of the Late Georgian Style.

Architectural journals, giving complete instructions for designing and building Federal Style houses, were produced and distributed throughout the country. The first of these was *The Country Builders Assistant: Containing a Collection of New Designs of Carpentry and Architecture* by Asher Benjamin. It was published in 1796 in Greenfield, Massachusetts.

New standards of convenience, comfort, and privacy were introduced. Federal houses had butler's pantries, dressing rooms, closets of all sorts, and even indoor privies. Architects manipulated the plan to create room layouts to serve these more specific functions, but always maintained the monumental, classically symmetrical exterior.

The Federal period lasted from 1760 through 1830 and included the heavy and massive Jeffersonian Classical Style, and the light and delicate Adam and Regency Styles, discussed in the next three chapters.

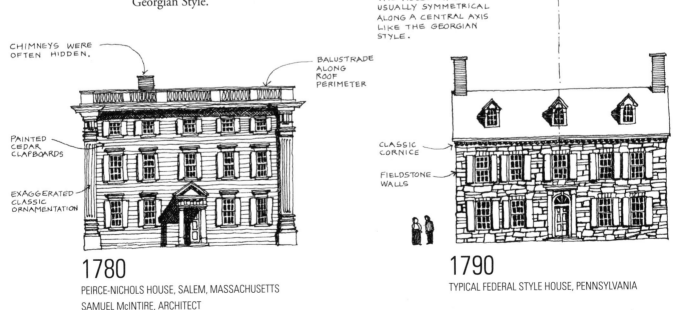

CHIMNEYS WERE OFTEN HIDDEN.

BALUSTRADE ALONG ROOF PERIMETER

PAINTED CEDAR CLAPBOARDS

EXAGGERATED CLASSIC ORNAMENTATION

THE HOUSE WAS USUALLY SYMMETRICAL ALONG A CENTRAL AXIS LIKE THE GEORGIAN STYLE.

CLASSIC CORNICE

FIELDSTONE WALLS

1780
PEIRCE-NICHOLS HOUSE, SALEM, MASSACHUSETTS
SAMUEL McINTIRE, ARCHITECT

1790
TYPICAL FEDERAL STYLE HOUSE, PENNSYLVANIA

By the early nineteenth century, Federal Style architects had stripped away most Georgian fancywork leaving a plain brick (sometimes white painted clapboards) box, upon and within which a small amount of delicate white painted wooden detailing was constructed. The place of entry (the front door and the center hall) was always given special attention: light entered into the hall through a delicately carved elliptical fanlight over the door and sidelights flanking the door. Slender columns held a semicircular, classically designed entablature over the entry. Interior stairs were sometimes curved and always delicately detailed.

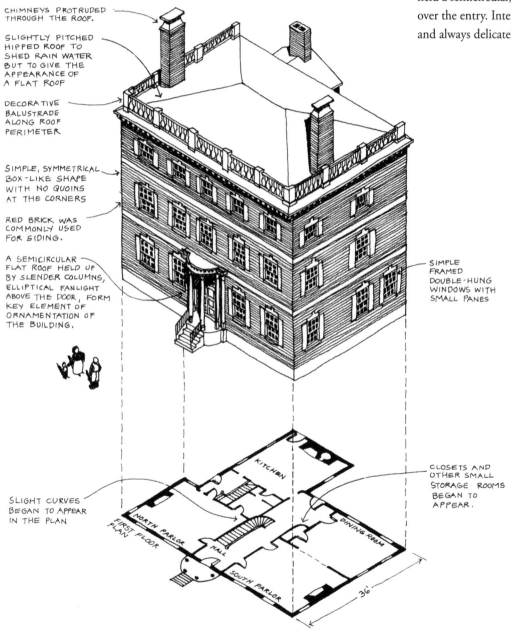

CHIMNEYS PROTRUDED THROUGH THE ROOF.

SLIGHTLY PITCHED HIPPED ROOF TO SHED RAIN WATER BUT TO GIVE THE APPEARANCE OF A FLAT ROOF

DECORATIVE BALUSTRADE ALONG ROOF PERIMETER

SIMPLE, SYMMETRICAL BOX-LIKE SHAPE WITH NO QUOINS AT THE CORNERS

RED BRICK WAS COMMONLY USED FOR SIDING.

A SEMICIRCULAR FLAT ROOF HELD UP BY SLENDER COLUMNS, ELLIPTICAL FANLIGHT ABOVE THE DOOR, FORM KEY ELEMENT OF ORNAMENTATION OF THE BUILDING.

SIMPLE FRAMED DOUBLE-HUNG WINDOWS WITH SMALL PANES

CLOSETS AND OTHER SMALL STORAGE ROOMS BEGAN TO APPEAR.

SLIGHT CURVES BEGAN TO APPEAR IN THE PLAN

KITCHEN

FIRST FLOOR PLAN

NORTH PARLOR

HALL

DINING ROOM

SOUTH PARLOR

36'

1804

PINGREE HOUSE, SALEM, MASSACHUSETTS
SAMUEL McINTIRE, ARCHITECT

Jeffersonian Classicism

Virginia 1770

Thomas Jefferson was one of America's most original and most prolific architects. He practiced architecture in both its theoretical and practical aspects, his work beginning before the Revolution and continuing until his death in 1826. He had strong reservations about Georgian architecture because it was so identifiably "English" and because it seemed crude to him by classical standards. His appreciation of Roman architecture during his European travels (as American minister to France, 1785–1789) had convinced him that the Roman orders were the fundamental discipline of architectural design and he based all of his buildings on these classic principles. In fact, sometimes this style is referred to as the

MAISON CARRÉE 16 B.C.
NIMES, FRANCE

DURING JEFFERSON'S EUROPEAN TRAVELS HE SAT BEFORE THIS AUGUSTAN TEMPLE "LIKE A LOVER BEFORE HIS MISTRESS!"

VIRGINIA STATE CAPITOL RICHMOND, VIRGINIA

IN 1786 JEFFERSON DESIGNED THIS BUILDING USING MAISON CARRÉE AS A MODEL.

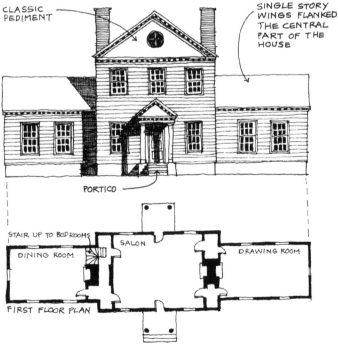

CLASSIC PEDIMENT

SINGLE STORY WINGS FLANKED THE CENTRAL PART OF THE HOUSE

PORTICO

STAIR UP TO BEDROOMS

DINING ROOM

SALON

DRAWING ROOM

FIRST FLOOR PLAN

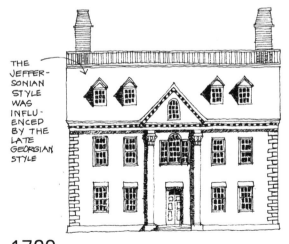

THE JEFFER-SONIAN STYLE WAS INFLU-ENCED BY THE LATE GEORGIAN STYLE

1760 LATE GEORGIAN STYLE HOUSE

1775 JEFFERSONIAN HOUSE, VIRGINIA
THOMAS JEFFERSON, PROBABLE ARCHITECT

Roman Revival Style, but its character in America was determined so much by Jefferson that we must call it Jeffersonian Classicism. His style originated in Virginia and remained primarily a southern style but was carried west in some rare instances.

The typical Jeffersonian building is red brick with a wooden portico painted white. Often there is a circular or semicircular window in the portico's pediment. The portico was designed to seem heavy and massive and always the central feature of a building—usually two stories in height with single- or two-story wings projecting on either side. Jefferson used these wings to break down the boxlike container of the Georgian house into a series of smaller boxes, each with specific functions. He obviously loved symmetry.

One of the simplest houses designed by Thomas Jefferson was known as Barboursville, built for Governor James Barbour of Virginia in 1817. The central two-story rooms of the house are flanked by two wings containing the study, sitting room, dining room, and bedrooms. Cooking was done in unattached buildings. The house had the usual fireplaces on the first floor but the upper rooms were heated by Franklin stoves—a wood- or coal-burning stove invented by Jefferson's friend, Benjamin Franklin.

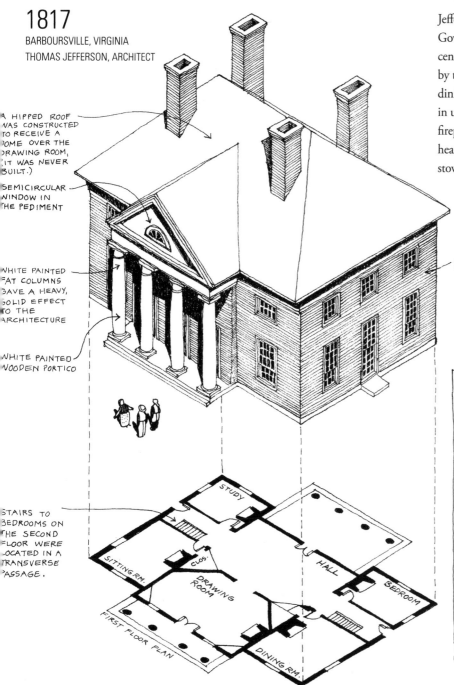

1817
BARBOURSVILLE, VIRGINIA
THOMAS JEFFERSON, ARCHITECT

A HIPPED ROOF WAS CONSTRUCTED TO RECEIVE A DOME OVER THE DRAWING ROOM, (IT WAS NEVER BUILT.)

SEMICIRCULAR WINDOW IN THE PEDIMENT

WHITE PAINTED FAT COLUMNS GAVE A HEAVY, SOLID EFFECT TO THE ARCHITECTURE

WHITE PAINTED WOODEN PORTICO

STAIRS TO BEDROOMS ON THE SECOND FLOOR WERE LOCATED IN A TRANSVERSE PASSAGE.

RED BRICK WALLS

STUDY

SITTING RM.

CLOS.

DRAWING ROOM

HALL

BEDROOM

DINING RM.

FIRST FLOOR PLAN

1 GEORGIAN HOUSE

2 3 PART JEFFERSONIAN COMPOSITION (COMMON)

3 5 PART JEFFERSONIAN COMPOSITION (RARE)

EVOLUTION OF JEFFERSONIAN HOUSE

Above and beyond utility, Jefferson felt that great architecture was a civilizing force. His advice to American tourists in Europe was, "Architecture is worth great attention. As we double our numbers every twenty years, we must double our houses…. Architecture is among the most important arts; and it is desirable to introduce taste into an art which shows so much…."

Thomas Jefferson's passionate involvement in the design, construction, and improvement of his own home, Monticello, began when he was twenty-four years old in 1767 and lasted fifty-nine years until his death. He was one of the first Americans to own a copy of Palladio's great work on architecture (not an English interpretation common during the Georgian Style) where he found designs for Italian villas that had a great effect on Monticello.

Jefferson's desire to have a flexible plan with privacy in most rooms was always modified by his desire to achieve classical symmetry. These two ambitions were realized through the use of a variety of devices invented by Jefferson. The central staircase, for example, was eliminated and replaced with two hallway stairs. He installed indoor privies on each floor, had self-winding clocks, wine lifts from the basement, and many other gadgets aimed at "modern" comforts.

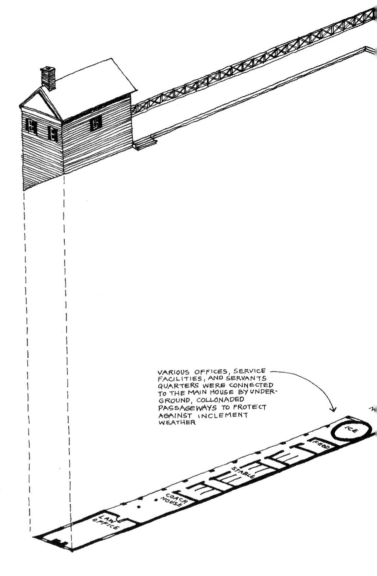

VARIOUS OFFICES, SERVICE FACILITIES, AND SERVANTS QUARTERS WERE CONNECTED TO THE MAIN HOUSE BY UNDERGROUND, COLLONADED PASSAGEWAYS TO PROTECT AGAINST INCLEMENT WEATHER

1826
MONTICELLO, VIRGINIA
THOMAS JEFFERSON, ARCHITECT

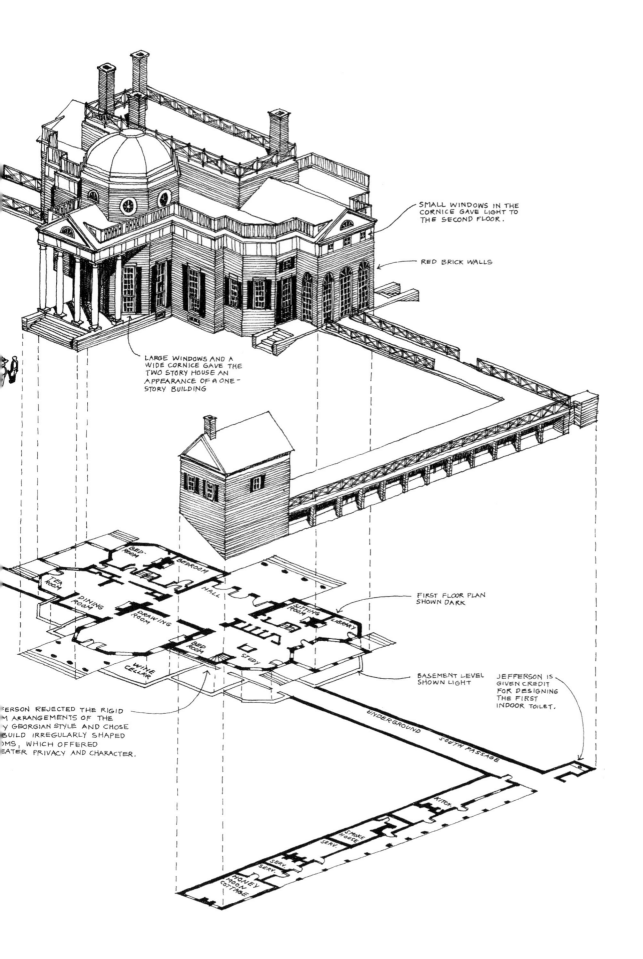

SMALL WINDOWS IN THE CORNICE GAVE LIGHT TO THE SECOND FLOOR.

RED BRICK WALLS

LARGE WINDOWS AND A WIDE CORNICE GAVE THE TWO STORY HOUSE AN APPEARANCE OF A ONE-STORY BUILDING

FIRST FLOOR PLAN SHOWN DARK

BASEMENT LEVEL SHOWN LIGHT

JEFFERSON IS GIVEN CREDIT FOR DESIGNING THE FIRST INDOOR TOILET.

...FERSON REJECTED THE RIGID ...M ARRANGEMENTS OF THE ...Y GEORGIAN STYLE AND CHOSE ...BUILD IRREGULARLY SHAPED ...OMS, WHICH OFFERED ...EATER PRIVACY AND CHARACTER.

TEA ROOM

DINING ROOM

DRAWING ROOM

WINE CELLAR

BED ROOM

BED ROOM

BEDROOM

HALL

STUDY

SITTING ROOM

LIBRARY

UNDERGROUND SOUTH PASSAGE

KITCH'

SMOKE HOUSE

SERV.

SERV.

SERV.

HONEY MOON COTTAGE

Adam

East
1800

The Adam Style is named after three Scottish-born brothers, Robert, James, and William, who had the biggest architectural practice in England during the years between 1760 and 1780. At one point, their firm had between 2,000 and 3,000 employees and controlled a number of businesses that supplied building materials. Their work replaced the "correct" British Palladian Style (Georgian) of the seventeenth and eighteenth centuries with a delicate classical mix virtually of their own making.

The eldest and most gifted brother, Robert Adam, had traveled extensively through Italy and Dalmatia during his youth, examining Roman ruins first-hand. He studied with French architect Charles-Louis Clerisseau, who was a good friend of Thomas Jefferson. In 1771, Robert, with his brother James, issued *The Works in Architecture of Robert and James Adam, Esquires*, a publication that led to widespread copies and modifications of their vast decorative vocabulary. It was this book that first brought the Adam Style to the attention of the American housebuilder.

The first American example of the Adam Style was the ceiling of George Washington's Mount Vernon (p. 82) dining room, built in 1775. To quote Robert Adam, "a beautiful variety of light mouldings, gracefully formed, delicately enriched and arranged with propriety and skill" replaced the more massive ornamentation previously used.

The Adam Style was championed in America by a Harvard-educated architect named Charles Bulfinch. He, like Thomas Jefferson, traveled in Europe to gain first-hand knowledge of his chosen profession. In fact, in 1785, Jefferson, who was then American minister to France, received Bulfinch in Paris and arranged many educational experiences for him. But, London and the neoclassic designs of the Adam Brothers impressed him most. Later, as his practice developed, he invented his own decorative and spatial vocabulary based on Adam influences. He was directly responsible for the design of Boston's Beacon Hill and Indian Wharf and many other important commissions, such as hospitals and prisons. In 1818 he replaced Thomas Jefferson's friend, architect Benjamin Latrobe, as the architect of the capitol, which was completed in 1828.

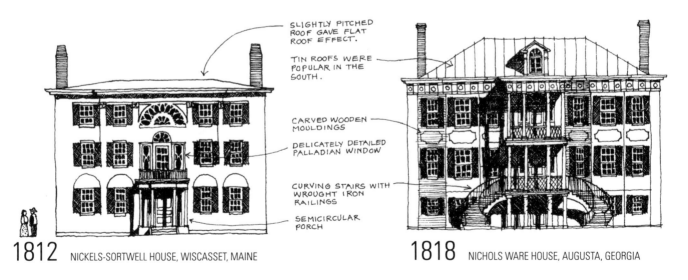

SLIGHTLY PITCHED ROOF GAVE FLAT ROOF EFFECT.

TIN ROOFS WERE POPULAR IN THE SOUTH.

CARVED WOODEN MOULDINGS

DELICATELY DETAILED PALLADIAN WINDOW

CURVING STAIRS WITH WROUGHT IRON RAILINGS

SEMICIRCULAR PORCH

1812 NICKELS-SORTWELL HOUSE, WISCASSET, MAINE

1818 NICHOLS WARE HOUSE, AUGUSTA, GEORGIA

Adam Style houses are always light and delicate and usually symmetrical. Porticoes and porches have widely spaced slender columns. Mouldings and other ornaments are delicate and geometrical. Windows are narrow with slender mullions. The general shape is boxlike with a semicircular porch or large portico over the centered front door. Curving steps with fancy wrought iron railings are popular in the South. Doorways often have semi-elliptical fanlights above and sidelights flanking the door. The Adam Style was primarily an Eastern Seaboard phenomenon. Beyond the Appalachian Mountains, the Greek Revival Style swept the area before the Adam Style had a chance to make even a modest debut.

PAINTED CARVED ORNAMENT

TALL BRICK CHIMNEYS TO DISPERSE SPARKS

DELICATE WOOD CARVED BALUSTRADE

WIDELY SPACED SLENDER WHITE COLUMNS

NARROW WINDOWS WITH SIDELIGHTS

FLUSH WOOD SIDING PAINTED GRAY TO GIVE THE ILLUSION OF STONE

SEMI-ELLIPTICAL FANLIGHT OVER DOOR

1804 BOSCOBEL, GARRISON, NEW YORK
STATES, MORRIS DYCKMAN, BUILDER

WOOD SHINGLE ROOF

FINELY DETAILED SEMI-ELLIPTICAL WINDOW IN PEDIMENT

CLASSIC CORNICE

DELICATE NARROW WINDOWS

PANELED SHUTTERS PAINTED WHITE

CEDAR CLAPBOARD SIDING PAINTED LIGHT YELLOW

BOXLIKE SHAPE WITH LARGE PORTICO

SLENDER WHITE COLUMNS

WROUGHT IRON RAILING

HIGH BRICK BASEMENT LEVEL

1810 SEABROOK PLANTATION, EDISTO ISLAND, SOUTH CAROLINA
WILLIAM SEABROOK, BUILDER

Regency

Countrywide
1815

The Regency Style was established in England at the turn of the century as the last in the evolution of Georgian Styles. It was a minor style in America but an important transition between the Adam Style and the Greek Revival. Its elegance, clean surfaces, geometric spaces, and classical detailing had a great deal of influence on the architecture of the South.

One of the most creative American architects using the Regency Style was William Jay. He designed many beautiful homes and several public buildings in and around Savannah, Georgia. He was influenced by the recent work of Sir John Soane, an English architect who was as concerned with the interior design of his buildings as he was the exterior. The imagination and variety of Jay's ideas shown in his Savannah houses represented the height of neoclassical town house design in America. He borrowed the orders of both Greece and Rome and adapted them to his own Adam Style vocabulary.

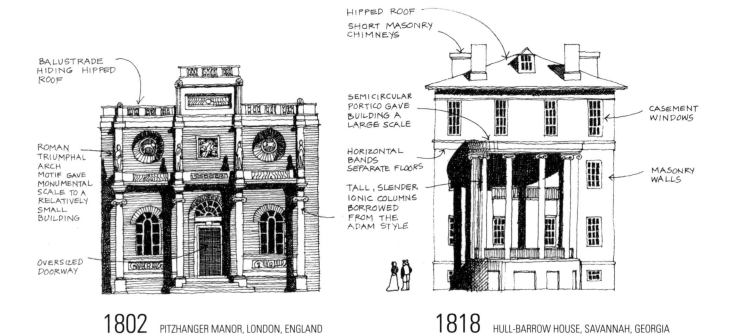

BALUSTRADE HIDING HIPPED ROOF

ROMAN TRIUMPHAL ARCH MOTIF GAVE MONUMENTAL SCALE TO A RELATIVELY SMALL BUILDING

OVERSIZED DOORWAY

HIPPED ROOF
SHORT MASONRY CHIMNEYS

SEMICIRCULAR PORTICO GAVE BUILDING A LARGE SCALE

HORIZONTAL BANDS SEPARATE FLOORS

TALL, SLENDER IONIC COLUMNS BORROWED FROM THE ADAM STYLE

CASEMENT WINDOWS

MASONRY WALLS

1802   PITZHANGER MANOR, LONDON, ENGLAND
JOHN SOANE, ARCHITECT

1818   HULL-BARROW HOUSE, SAVANNAH, GEORGIA
WILLIAM JAY, ARCHITECT

The Regency Style was similar to the Adam Style in its use of arched windows, smooth painted stuccoed wall surfaces, large windows, arched wall niches, and elliptical staircases. It corresponded to the Greek Revival Style in its plain surfaces, and simplicity, but differed in its slenderness, grace, and use of the Roman arch.

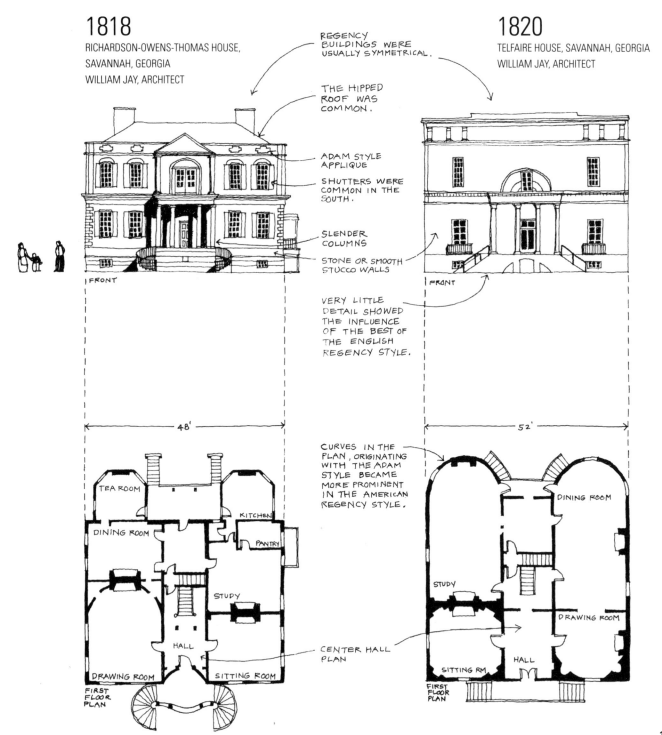

1818
RICHARDSON-OWENS-THOMAS HOUSE, SAVANNAH, GEORGIA
WILLIAM JAY, ARCHITECT

1820
TELFAIRE HOUSE, SAVANNAH, GEORGIA
WILLIAM JAY, ARCHITECT

REGENCY BUILDINGS WERE USUALLY SYMMETRICAL.

THE HIPPED ROOF WAS COMMON.

ADAM STYLE APPLIQUE

SHUTTERS WERE COMMON IN THE SOUTH.

SLENDER COLUMNS

STONE OR SMOOTH STUCCO WALLS

VERY LITTLE DETAIL SHOWED THE INFLUENCE OF THE BEST OF THE ENGLISH REGENCY STYLE.

FRONT

FRONT

48'

52'

CURVES IN THE PLAN, ORIGINATING WITH THE ADAM STYLE BECAME MORE PROMINENT IN THE AMERICAN REGENCY STYLE.

TEA ROOM

KITCHEN

DINING ROOM

PANTRY

STUDY

HALL

DRAWING ROOM

SITTING ROOM

FIRST FLOOR PLAN

DINING ROOM

STUDY

DRAWING ROOM

CENTER HALL PLAN

SITTING RM

HALL

FIRST FLOOR PLAN

Greek Revival

Countrywide 1820

The Greek Revival Style was one of the most popular and long-lived styles in America because it was thought to embody the ideals of democracy. America was eager to identify its new civic and political virtues with those of classical Greece. By 1830 practically every kind of building of any pretention, whether public or private, had adopted this new style.

The Greek Revival house ranged from the look of a windowed Greek temple to that of a simple Colonial house with a massive columned porch over the front door. Architects strictly copied the Greek orders when detailing a house and usually painted everything white to simulate the color of the Greek temple.

The first Greek Revival building in America was the Bank of Pennsylvania in Philadelphia designed by architect Benjamin Latrobe. But the style actually began with the mansions and public buildings of Washington, D.C. The style spread rapidly to adjacent areas; in part because of several American publications providing illustrated instructions for the new fashion in building. Baltimore, Richmond, Alexandria, Norfolk, and Petersburg all took up the style with great enthusiasm. Some of the more conservative southern cities clung to the Georgian and Federal styles, but by 1840, all had adopted the Greek Revival Style. As the style spread, each section of the country contributed its local flavor, dictated in most cases by climate, but sometimes by culture. The Moravians and Quakers in Winston-Salem built austerely simple houses with a Greek Revival Style porch attached to the front facade and protecting a delicately detailed front door—quite similar to an eighteenth century New England house. In South Carolina and Georgia, the dampness and heat led to Greek Revival houses with piazzas.

In this early part of the nineteenth century, most Greek Revival buildings were designed by architects. It was difficult, of course, to make a small wooden

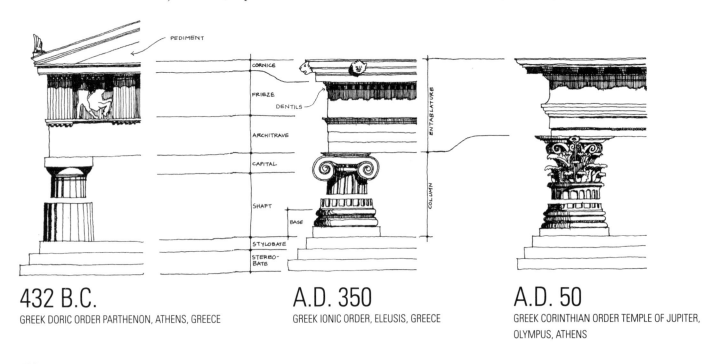

432 B.C.
GREEK DORIC ORDER PARTHENON, ATHENS, GREECE

A.D. 350
GREEK IONIC ORDER, ELEUSIS, GREECE

A.D. 50
GREEK CORINTHIAN ORDER TEMPLE OF JUPITER, OLYMPUS, ATHENS

house look like a large stone Greek temple. Builders and carpenters were unable to perform this task as well as an educated, practicing architect.

The Greek orders were columns with shafts, capitals, entablatures, and usually bases, decorated in one of the accepted modes of Doric, Ionic, and Corinthian. The Doric order probably originated in late 700 B.C. and was later developed by the Romans. It is distinguished from the Roman Doric order by the absence of a molded base holding up the column. The Ionic order began in Asia Minor in mid-600 B.C. and has a capital with larger volutes than the Roman. The Corinthian order was an Athenian invention in 500 B.C. and was subsequently copied by the Romans.

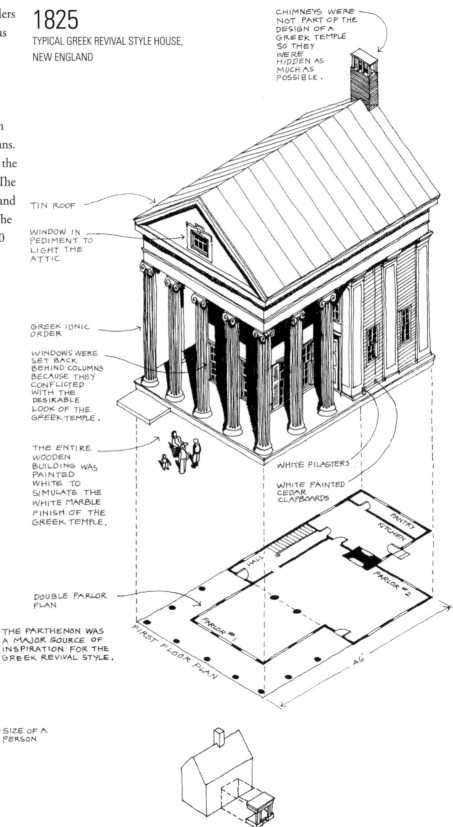

1825
TYPICAL GREEK REVIVAL STYLE HOUSE, NEW ENGLAND

CHIMNEYS WERE NOT PART OF THE DESIGN OF A GREEK TEMPLE SO THEY WERE HIDDEN AS MUCH AS POSSIBLE.

TIN ROOF

WINDOW IN PEDIMENT TO LIGHT THE ATTIC

GREEK IONIC ORDER

WINDOWS WERE SET BACK BEHIND COLUMNS BECAUSE THEY CONFLICTED WITH THE DESIRABLE LOOK OF THE GREEK TEMPLE.

THE ENTIRE WOODEN BUILDING WAS PAINTED WHITE TO SIMULATE THE WHITE MARBLE FINISH OF THE GREEK TEMPLE.

WHITE PILASTERS

WHITE PAINTED CEDAR CLAPBOARDS

DOUBLE PARLOR PLAN

FIRST FLOOR PLAN

PARLOR #1

PARLOR #2

HALL

PANTRY

KITCHEN

46

THE PARTHENON WAS A MAJOR SOURCE OF INSPIRATION FOR THE GREEK REVIVAL STYLE.

SIZE OF A PERSON

432 B.C.
PARTHENON, ATHENS, GREECE

AFTER 1830 MANY FARMHOUSES WERE CONVERTED TO THE GREEK REVIVAL STYLE BY ADDING A CLASSIC PORCH.

Few Greek Revival Style houses were built in New England before 1830. Occasionally a new traditional house would be given a Doric porch, but it took a long time to make the transition from a delicate Federal Style wood frame house to a building with classical monumentality. The early trend was to adapt a few timid Greek details to the house just to keep up with the fashion. When the style finally gained acceptance, it was found that the easiest way of converting the basic colonial house into a Greek temple was to turn the gable end to the street and redesign the front entrance into it. The gable was

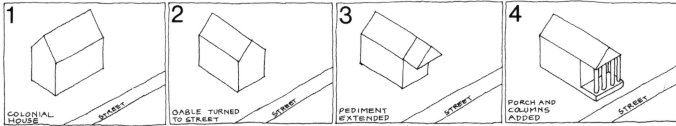

1 COLONIAL HOUSE / STREET
2 GABLE TURNED TO STREET / STREET
3 PEDIMENT EXTENDED / STREET
4 PORCH AND COLUMNS ADDED / STREET

CONVERTING A COLONIAL HOUSE DESIGN INTO A GREEK REVIVAL HOUSE DESIGN

1830
RURAL NEW ENGLAND GREEK REVIVAL HOUSE

1835
NEW ENGLAND GREEK REVIVAL TOWNHOUSE

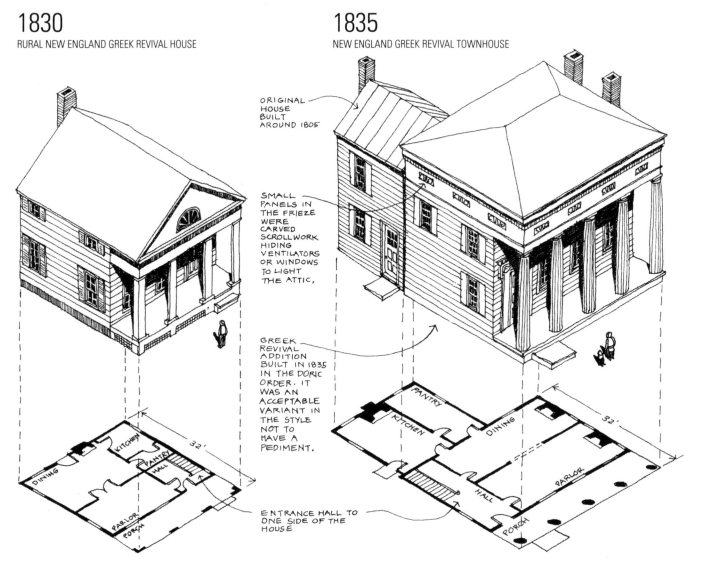

ORIGINAL HOUSE BUILT AROUND 1805

SMALL PANELS IN THE FRIEZE WERE CARVED SCROLLWORK HIDING VENTILATORS OR WINDOWS TO LIGHT THE ATTIC.

GREEK REVIVAL ADDITION BUILT IN 1835 IN THE DORIC ORDER. IT WAS AN ACCEPTABLE VARIANT IN THE STYLE NOT TO HAVE A PEDIMENT.

ENTRANCE HALL TO ONE SIDE OF THE HOUSE

made into an impressive pediment which either remained flat or was extended to rest on a row of columns. This scheme dictated a revolutionary new floor plan with an entrance hall on one side of the house and a single file of rooms on the opposite side.

1840 GREEK REVIVAL MIDWESTERN FARMHOUSE

1845 GREEK REVIVAL SOUTHERN PLANTATION HOUSE

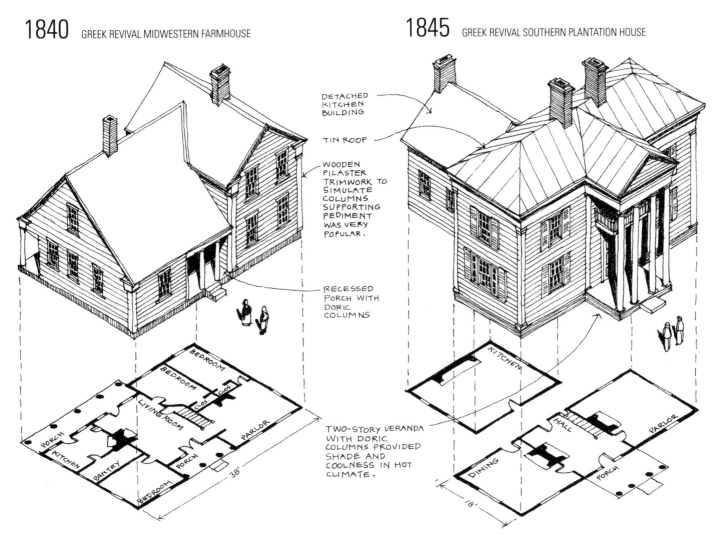

DETACHED KITCHEN BUILDING

TIN ROOF

WOODEN PILASTER TRIMWORK TO SIMULATE COLUMNS SUPPORTING PEDIMENT WAS VERY POPULAR.

RECESSED PORCH WITH DORIC COLUMNS

TWO-STORY VERANDA WITH DORIC COLUMNS PROVIDED SHADE AND COOLNESS IN HOT CLIMATE.

Before the Revolution, a few settlers and adventurers were beginning to head through the Cumberland Gap into Tennessee and down the Ohio River from Pittsburgh to Ohio, and what is now West Virginia, and Kentucky. By 1820 thousands of people were moving westward. Cities were being constructed and houses built. By 1840, settlers had pressed on into Michigan, Wisconsin, and Illinois and a building boom was on. In 1849, the California Gold Rush took the Greek Revival to the West Coast.

In New York, Illinois, and Michigan, a popular style was the two-story central block house, with porticoes and pediment and one-and-one-half story wings (an arrangement similar to Thomas Jefferson's three part composition shown on page 99). Ohio and Kentucky preferred simple houses with recessed porches, and the Deep South, particularly the plantation owners, preferred two-story verandas, a feature dictated by the climate.

Spanish Colonial

California 1825

California was originally settled in the late seventeenth century by Spanish and Mexican missionaries who set up small religious communities around tiny Baroque churches known as missions. These missions were established to convert the American Indians to Spanish Catholicism and to "civilize" them. Large Spanish and Mexican fortlike structures called presidios were built late in the eighteenth century to house soldiers responsible for protecting the mission chain and for administering the civil laws. There were over one hundred missions and only four presidios. They were located in what is now San Diego (1769), Monterey (1770), San Francisco (1776), and Santa Barbara (1782). In the 1780s, the California governor set up three civilian towns, known as puebloes, to encourage secular as well as religious colonization. They were not successful.

After the Mexican Revolution of 1821, the new government frowned upon the great holdings of the missions and encouraged private farming and stock raising by making huge land grants to individuals, families, and contractors. Large herds of cattle and sheep roamed inland ranges, and hides and tallow were traded from seaport towns with Yankee skippers who had sailed around the South American Horn. The presidio towns were experiencing great prosperity by 1840 and became centers of active social life.

The farmhouse was known as *casa de campo*, and its grounds a *hacienda* if devoted to livestock. A townhouse was called a *casa de pueblo*. Materials and methods of construction were basically the same as the missions and presidios—adobe, wood, and tile—but the detailing was simpler. Three wings were built to give shade and protection to a patio and garden. The fourth side, facing north, was open except for a six- to eight-foot-high

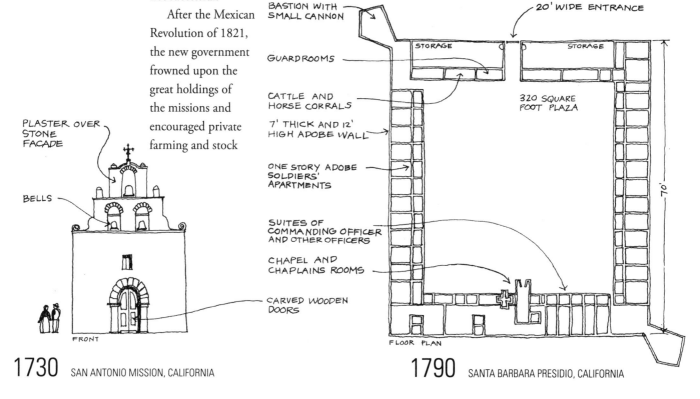

PLASTER OVER STONE FACADE

BELLS

CARVED WOODEN DOORS

FRONT

BASTION WITH SMALL CANNON

GUARDROOMS

CATTLE AND HORSE CORRALS

7' THICK AND 12' HIGH ADOBE WALL

ONE STORY ADOBE SOLDIERS' APARTMENTS

SUITES OF COMMANDING OFFICER AND OTHER OFFICERS

CHAPEL AND CHAPLAINS ROOMS

20' WIDE ENTRANCE

STORAGE

STORAGE

320 SQUARE FOOT PLAZA

70'

FLOOR PLAN

1730 SAN ANTONIO MISSION, CALIFORNIA

1790 SANTA BARBARA PRESIDIO, CALIFORNIA

wall. A veranda, known as a *corredor* was a roofed porch that embraced the patio inside the three wings. The *corredor* became a shady, cool lounging place adjacent to the patio that was much used for outdoor living. Every room in the house was planned so that it opened onto the *corredor*. A wine cellar was usually located in a basement, libraries were common, and gardens quite lavish, reflecting a sophisticated highly cultured society.

The Spanish Colonial Style was the forerunner of the California Ranch Style (p. 232). The house was built low to the ground within a one-story building to allow easy access in and out of the house without the hindrance of steps. Outdoor living was meshed with indoor living. The long porch or corridor connected all the rooms and served as an outdoor living room. Whether the house was built in town or on a ranch, the enclosed patio shut out cattle, sheep, and deer. It also provided relief from sun and wind.

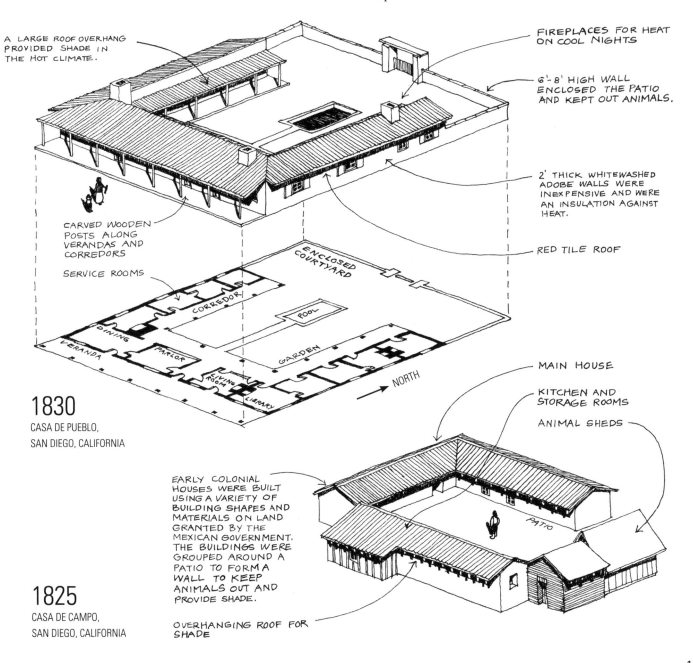

A LARGE ROOF OVERHANG PROVIDED SHADE IN THE HOT CLIMATE.

FIREPLACES FOR HEAT ON COOL NIGHTS

6'-8' HIGH WALL ENCLOSED THE PATIO AND KEPT OUT ANIMALS.

2' THICK WHITEWASHED ADOBE WALLS WERE INEXPENSIVE AND WERE AN INSULATION AGAINST HEAT.

RED TILE ROOF

CARVED WOODEN POSTS ALONG VERANDAS AND CORREDORS

SERVICE ROOMS

ENCLOSED COURTYARD

CORREDOR

DINING

POOL

PARLOR

VERANDA

LIVING ROOM

GARDEN

NORTH

LIBRARY

1830
CASA DE PUEBLO,
SAN DIEGO, CALIFORNIA

MAIN HOUSE

KITCHEN AND STORAGE ROOMS

ANIMAL SHEDS

EARLY COLONIAL HOUSES WERE BUILT USING A VARIETY OF BUILDING SHAPES AND MATERIALS ON LAND GRANTED BY THE MEXICAN GOVERNMENT. THE BUILDINGS WERE GROUPED AROUND A PATIO TO FORM A WALL TO KEEP ANIMALS OUT AND PROVIDE SHADE.

PATIO

1825
CASA DE CAMPO,
SAN DIEGO, CALIFORNIA

OVERHANGING ROOF FOR SHADE

Shaker

Northeast
1830

Of all the religious communities that began in America during the nineteenth century, the Shakers were the only one to produce a distinctive architectural style. Turning their backs on what they considered to be a corrupt world, they practiced a form of Christian communism in secluded agricultural settlements scattered around the Northeast. The Shakers maintained economic self-sufficiency by engaging in agriculture and light manufacturing. The quality of their products such as garden seeds, medicinal herbs, brooms, oval boxes, and baskets quickly gained them a worldwide reputation.

Shaker communities (usually four "families" of 30 to 100 individuals each) were based on a strict set of rules known as the Millennial Laws. Among other things, these rules prohibited "odd or fanciful styles of architecture." Each family lived in one large dwelling, which had its stylistic roots in the simple houses of New England. Their buildings were plain, well proportioned, and without embellishment. All of their structures, both inside and outside, reflected the lives of the Shaker people.

In the dwelling houses were bedrooms (or "retiring rooms"), kitchen, bake room, food storage room, and dining rooms. A large meeting room held the family for evening religious services and meetings. Each bedroom was large enough to accommodate from three to four single beds. Built-in chests of drawers held the belongings of those who occupied a room. Adjacent to each bedroom was a dressing room, which contained several wash-sinks with bowls and pitcher sets, towel racks, and peg boards.

The Shakers took elaborate precautions to minimize the mingling of the sexes since they regarded the sexual act as evil. The men (Brethren) and women (Sisters) had separate doorways to enter the dining room, separate dining tables, and separate stairs to ascend to their separate bedrooms.

Shaker chairs and benches epitomize Shaker simplicity and, despite all efforts to the contrary, Shaker beauty. They designed and built their furniture (and other objects as well) only to be functional. Designing beautiful objects for beauty's sake was forbidden by the Millennial Laws.

1830 SHAKER CHAIRS, RICHMOND, MASSACHUSETTS

PEGBOARDS ALONG WALLS WERE USED FOR HANGING CLOTHING AND SOME FURNITURE.

CHAIRS WERE HUNG ON PEGBOARD TO GET THEM OUT OF THE WAY FOR NEATNESS AND EASY CLEANING.

FURNITURE DESIGN WAS UTILITARIAN YET DELICATE.

1856 SPINDLED SETTEE, ENFIELD, NEW HAMPSHIRE

FURNITURE DESIGN WAS UTILITARIAN YET DELICATE.

1829
HOUSE OF THE WEST FAMILY OF
WATERVLIET COLONY, NEW YORK

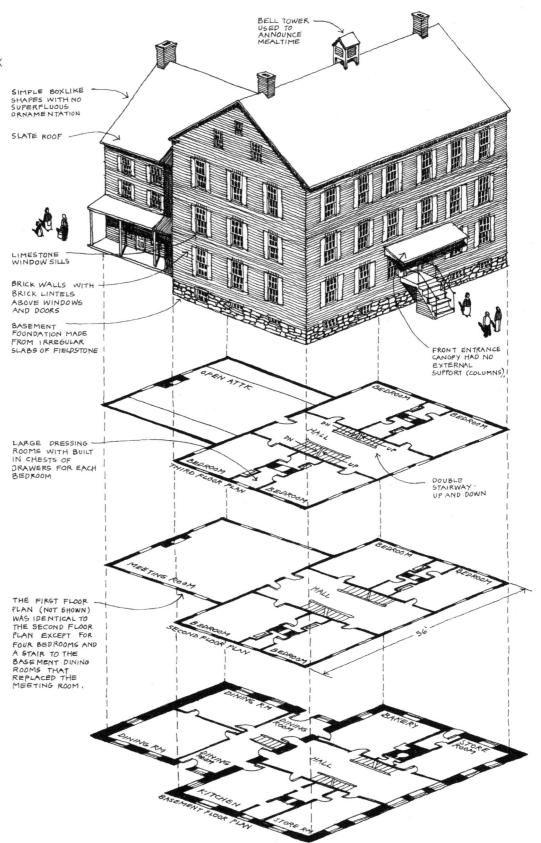

BELL TOWER
USED TO
ANNOUNCE
MEALTIME

SIMPLE BOXLIKE
SHAPES WITH NO
SUPERFLUOUS
ORNAMENTATION

SLATE ROOF

LIMESTONE
WINDOW SILLS

BRICK WALLS WITH
BRICK LINTELS
ABOVE WINDOWS
AND DOORS

BASEMENT
FOUNDATION MADE
FROM IRREGULAR
SLABS OF FIELDSTONE

FRONT ENTRANCE
CANOPY HAD NO
EXTERNAL
SUPPORT (COLUMNS)

LARGE DRESSING
ROOMS WITH BUILT
IN CHESTS OF
DRAWERS FOR EACH
BEDROOM

OPEN ATTIC

BEDROOM

BEDROOM

DN

HALL

UP

BEDROOM

THIRD FLOOR PLAN

BEDROOM

DOUBLE
STAIRWAY
UP AND DOWN

THE FIRST FLOOR
PLAN (NOT SHOWN)
WAS IDENTICAL TO
THE SECOND FLOOR
PLAN EXCEPT FOR
FOUR BEDROOMS AND
A STAIR TO THE
BASEMENT DINING
ROOMS THAT
REPLACED THE
MEETING ROOM.

MEETING ROOM

BEDROOM

HALL

BEDROOM

BEDROOM

SECOND FLOOR PLAN

BEDROOM

56'

DINING RM

DINING
ROOM

BAKERY

STORE
ROOM

DINING RM

DINING
ROOM

HALL

BASEMENT FLOOR PLAN

KITCHEN

STORE RM

Egyptian Revival

East & Midwest
1835

The Egyptian Revival Style was one of the many architectural styles that were temporarily popular in the 1830s when the influence of foreign architecture was at its peak. One of the country's most influential architects, Alexander Jackson Davis, recorded in his diary that he had planned buildings in fourteen different styles, including Etruscan, Greek, Oriental, Egyptian, and others, by 1845! In 1930, the *American Quarterly Review* devoted forty pages of one issue to Egyptian architecture sparking the beginning of the Egyptian Revival fad.

The first three Egyptian Revival Style buildings to appear in America were a Philadelphia prison, a Newark courthouse, and a New York City prison (later known as the Tombs). The style was chosen for its exoticism and for its imposing massiveness which inspired a sense of security. In the early 1830s, it became a popular style for cemetery entrances and along the Mississippi River, towns were named Cairo, Karnak, Memphis, and Thebes.

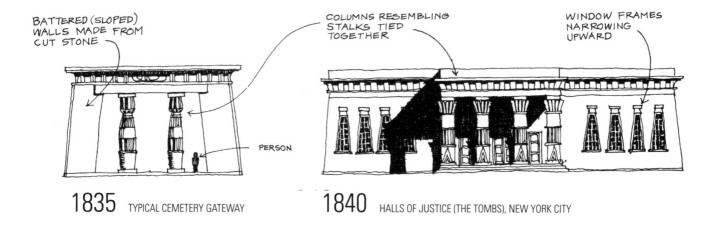

BATTERED (SLOPED) WALLS MADE FROM CUT STONE

COLUMNS RESEMBLING STALKS TIED TOGETHER

WINDOW FRAMES NARROWING UPWARD

PERSON

1835 TYPICAL CEMETERY GATEWAY

1840 HALLS OF JUSTICE (THE TOMBS), NEW YORK CITY

The Egyptian Revival Style is probably the easiest of all styles to identify. Every structure has at least one of the following features: (1) battered (sloped) walls; (2) window frames that narrow upward; and (3) columns with a pronounced bulge that sometimes resemble stalks tied together with horizontal bands below the capitals. Bulging columns were the only true Egyptian Revival feature found in these houses. Upward narrowing windows prohibited ventilation and battered walls did not function well on the inside.

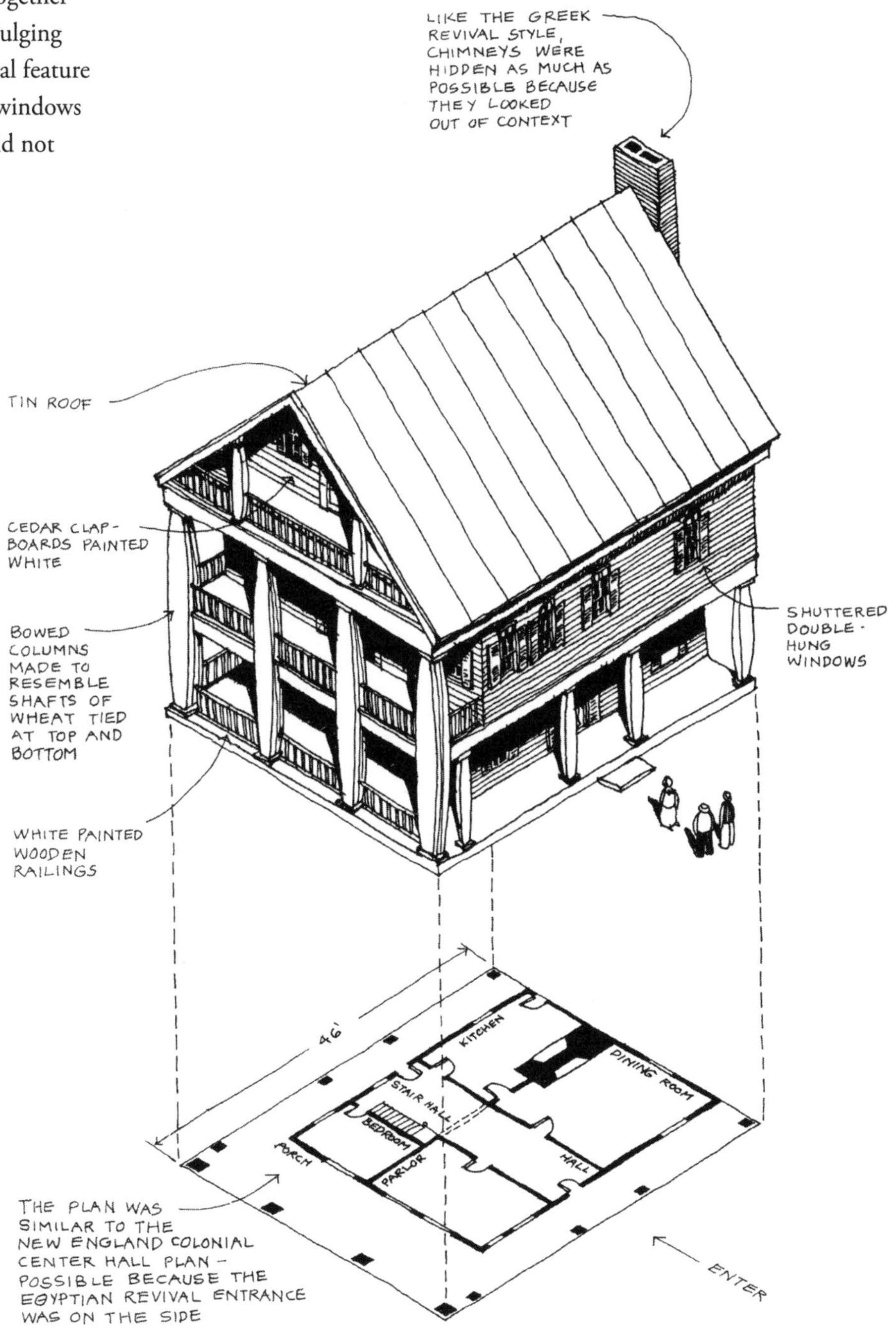

LIKE THE GREEK REVIVAL STYLE, CHIMNEYS WERE HIDDEN AS MUCH AS POSSIBLE BECAUSE THEY LOOKED OUT OF CONTEXT

TIN ROOF

CEDAR CLAP-BOARDS PAINTED WHITE

BOWED COLUMNS MADE TO RESEMBLE SHAFTS OF WHEAT TIED AT TOP AND BOTTOM

WHITE PAINTED WOODEN RAILINGS

SHUTTERED DOUBLE-HUNG WINDOWS

KITCHEN

DINING ROOM

STAIR HALL

BEDROOM

PORCH

PARLOR

HALL

4'6"

THE PLAN WAS SIMILAR TO THE NEW ENGLAND COLONIAL CENTER HALL PLAN - POSSIBLE BECAUSE THE EGYPTIAN REVIVAL ENTRANCE WAS ON THE SIDE

ENTER

1845 EGYPTIAN REVIVAL HOUSE, MASSACHUSETTS

Monterey

California 1835

Until the turn of the eighteenth century, the American Southwest had been settled by the Spanish and Mexicans moving northward from Mexico into California, Arizona, New Mexico, and Texas. The first American ship to arrive on the West Coast, the *Otter*, put in at Monterey, California, in 1796. It was soon followed by others and by 1820, Americans were arriving from the East, by sailing around the South American Horn, to homestead land. But it wasn't until the 1830s that Americans began to arrive in considerable numbers.

The arrival in 1832 of Thomas O. Larkin from Boston had an immediate impact on the evolution of the Monterey area. It quickly grew to become an enduring influence on the entire state. He opened the first retail and wholesale store, built Monterey's first wharf, founded the first nonmilitary hospital, brought the first American woman to live in Monterey, and became the father of the first "Yankee" child born in California. In 1835, he built a house for his family that created such a stir that a new style of domestic architecture evolved named after the city where he built, Monterey. Up until that time, the Spanish and Mexicans had built one-story rectangular tile-roofed adobes. Larkin, remembering his native New England architecture, built a two-story adobe house with a hipped roof and a two-story balcony at the front and sides! Neighbors who could afford it lost no time in following his example.

Soon the "Yankee" influence on the Monterey Style extended to almost every detail of the house. For example, neat little wooden interior staircases replaced exterior adobe stairs to balconies.

The Monterey Style and its one-story counterpart remained popular, and eventually they were a strong influence on the development of modern California architecture in the 1930s and 1940s.

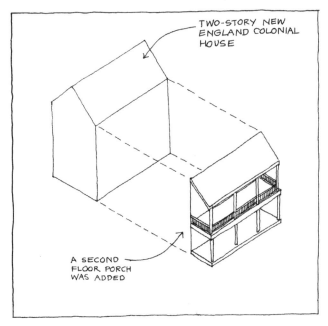

TWO-STORY NEW ENGLAND COLONIAL HOUSE

A SECOND FLOOR PORCH WAS ADDED

HOW THE MONTEREY STYLE BEGAN

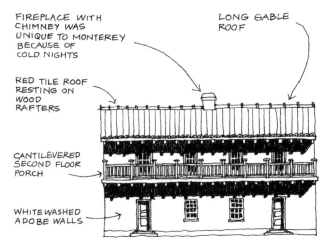

FIREPLACE WITH CHIMNEY WAS UNIQUE TO MONTEREY BECAUSE OF COLD NIGHTS

LONG GABLE ROOF

RED TILE ROOF RESTING ON WOOD RAFTERS

CANTILEVERED SECOND FLOOR PORCH

WHITEWASHED ADOBE WALLS

1840 TYPICAL EARLY MONTEREY HOUSE, MONTEREY, CALIFORNIA

The hipped roof built by Larkin puzzled his neighbors who preferred the simple long gable roof often used in the Spanish Colonial Style house. The Monterey house balcony was often cantilevered along the front of the house from the second floor, supporting an overhanging roof which provided shade to the entire front wall.

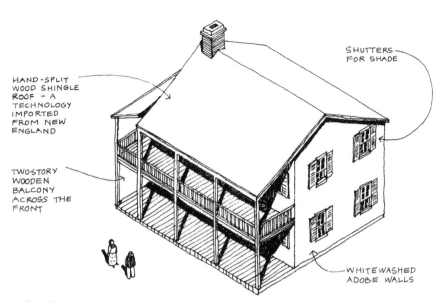

HAND-SPLIT WOOD SHINGLE ROOF - A TECHNOLOGY IMPORTED FROM NEW ENGLAND

SHUTTERS FOR SHADE

TWO-STORY WOODEN BALCONY ACROSS THE FRONT

WHITEWASHED ADOBE WALLS

1840 TYPICAL MONTEREY HOUSE, MONTEREY, CALIFORNIA

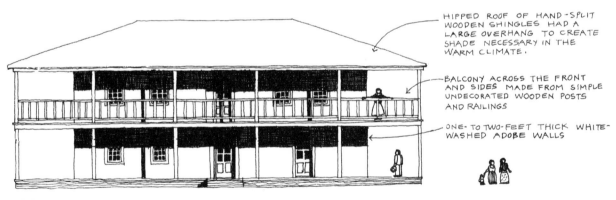

HIPPED ROOF OF HAND-SPLIT WOODEN SHINGLES HAD A LARGE OVERHANG TO CREATE SHADE NECESSARY IN THE WARM CLIMATE.

BALCONY ACROSS THE FRONT AND SIDES MADE FROM SIMPLE UNDECORATED WOODEN POSTS AND RAILINGS

ONE- TO TWO-FEET THICK WHITE-WASHED ADOBE WALLS

1835 THOMAS LARKIN RESIDENCE, MONTEREY, CALIFORNIA
THOMAS LARKIN, BUILDER

Shacks and Shanties

Countrywide 1840

Buildings in the Shacks and Shanties Style were small, temporary, crudely built and furnished dwellings made usually from tree limbs, old boards, and tar paper. They were built by traders, freighters, trappers, Indian agents, soldiers, explorers, miners, Mormons, travelers, railroaders, sportsmen, homesteaders, hunters, and people who could not afford a more substantial house. They have been built since the beginning of America as shelters to keep out the cold and rain, with no real style in mind. The designing of a shack or shanty requires the expertise of a woodsman rather than that of an architect; and the construction is better suited to the skill of an axeman than that of a carpenter. There are thousands of different designs for these structures, usually determined by available materials. (Many of the log cabins described on page 48 would fit into this category.)

Today, shacks and shanties are still being built. But, polyethylene sheeting has replaced tar paper, and lightweight tents have replaced the little tomahawk-made tree-branch shelters.

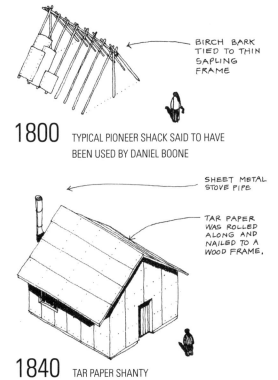

1800 TYPICAL PIONEER SHACK SAID TO HAVE BEEN USED BY DANIEL BOONE

BIRCH BARK TIED TO THIN SAPLING FRAME

SHEET METAL STOVE PIPE

TAR PAPER WAS ROLLED ALONG AND NAILED TO A WOOD FRAME.

1840 TAR PAPER SHANTY

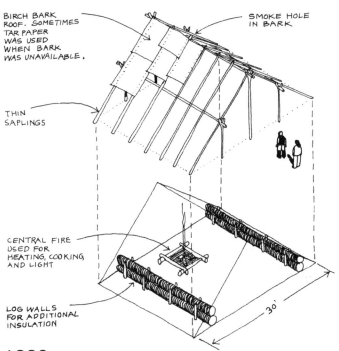

BIRCH BARK ROOF. SOMETIMES TAR PAPER WAS USED WHEN BARK WAS UNAVAILABLE.

SMOKE HOLE IN BARK

THIN SAPLINGS

CENTRAL FIRE USED FOR HEATING, COOKING AND LIGHT

LOG WALLS FOR ADDITIONAL INSULATION

30'

1920 BIRCH BARK SHACK, DESIGNED BY D.C. BEARD FOR USE IN TEMPORARY CAMPS

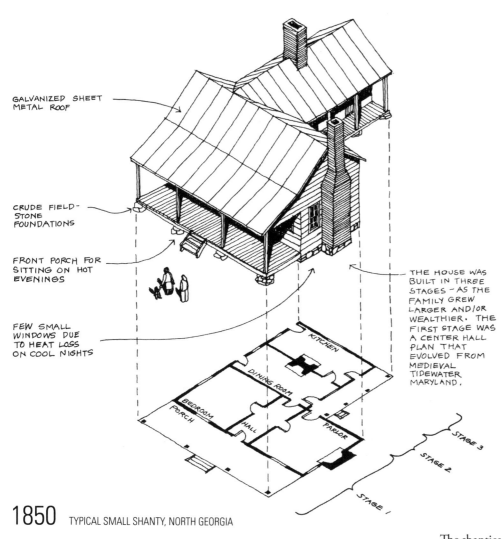

GALVANIZED SHEET METAL ROOF

CRUDE FIELD-STONE FOUNDATIONS

FRONT PORCH FOR SITTING ON HOT EVENINGS

FEW SMALL WINDOWS DUE TO HEAT LOSS ON COOL NIGHTS

KITCHEN

DINING ROOM

BEDROOM

PORCH

HALL

PARLOR

THE HOUSE WAS BUILT IN THREE STAGES — AS THE FAMILY GREW LARGER AND/OR WEALTHIER. THE FIRST STAGE WAS A CENTER HALL PLAN THAT EVOLVED FROM MEDIEVAL TIDEWATER MARYLAND.

STAGE 3

STAGE 2

STAGE 1

1850 TYPICAL SMALL SHANTY, NORTH GEORGIA

The shanties built by mountain folk, southern slaves, Midwestern pioneers, and western miners are included in this chapter because they were relatively crudely built and often thought of as temporary. Sometimes known as cabins, they have a weatherbeaten utilitarian style because they were partly constructed with such secondhand building parts as old boards, sheet metal, and doors.

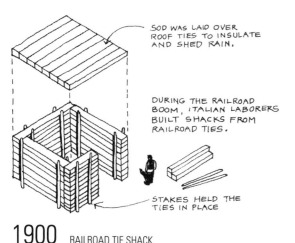

SOD WAS LAID OVER ROOF TIES TO INSULATE AND SHED RAIN.

DURING THE RAILROAD BOOM, ITALIAN LABORERS BUILT SHACKS FROM RAILROAD TIES.

STAKES HELD THE TIES IN PLACE

1900 RAILROAD TIE SHACK

Early Gothic Revival

East 1840

The Gothic Revival began in England in the early 1800s as a revolt against the rigidity of classic forms. It was championed in America by the architect Alexander Jackson Davis and his friend, landscape architect and writer, Andrew Jackson Downing. Both men had been heavily influenced by the work of John Ruskin and Augustus Welby Northmore Pugin, the Gothic Revival's principal English theorists. Downings's *Cottage Residences* in 1842 and

The Architecture of Country Houses in 1850 became best sellers and had a nationwide influence on the American Gothic movement.

By the 1840s, the popularity of the Greek Revival Style began to fade as it had already done in England. The most exciting and immediate change was the bursting forth of the plan from the regular and sometimes symmetrical forms of 175 years of housebuilding, into a building with a variety of odd

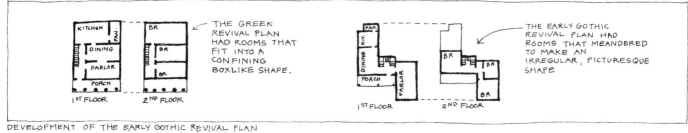

THE GREEK REVIVAL PLAN HAD ROOMS THAT FIT INTO A CONFINING BOXLIKE SHAPE.

THE EARLY GOTHIC REVIVAL PLAN HAD ROOMS THAT MEANDERED TO MAKE AN IRREGULAR, PICTURESQUE SHAPE

DEVELOPMENT OF THE EARLY GOTHIC REVIVAL PLAN

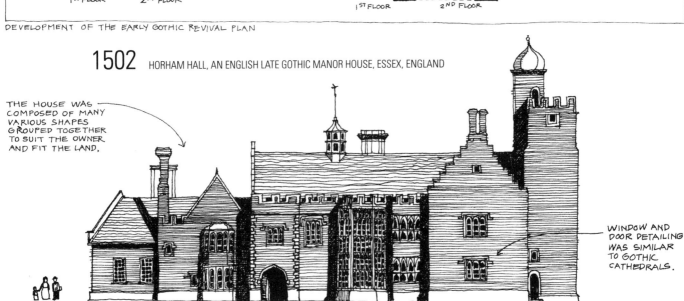

1502   HORHAM HALL, AN ENGLISH LATE GOTHIC MANOR HOUSE, ESSEX, ENGLAND

THE HOUSE WAS COMPOSED OF MANY VARIOUS SHAPES GROUPED TOGETHER TO SUIT THE OWNER AND FIT THE LAND.

WINDOW AND DOOR DETAILING WAS SIMILAR TO GOTHIC CATHEDRALS.

shapes. Designers of Greek Revival buildings had squeezed rooms into a surrounding form—usually a cube. Gothic Revival architects were allowing the plan to grow, naturally, from within, arriving at a final form that was based on the owner's needs and the lay of the land.

The first American Gothic Revival houses were built primarily of stone. Only the wealthy could afford these buildings since they required very highly skilled stone carvers. Soon, however, the costly Gothic Style was translated into wood. Narrow exposed lap siding gave little indication of a seam and stone tracery soon became wooden "gingerbread."

1850 JUSTIN SMITH MORRILL HOUSE, AN EARLY GOTHIC REVIVAL COTTAGE, VERMONT

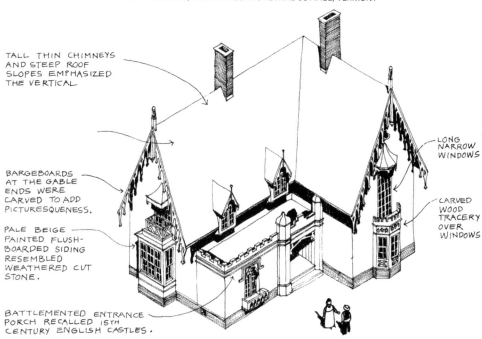

TALL THIN CHIMNEYS AND STEEP ROOF SLOPES EMPHASIZED THE VERTICAL

BARGEBOARDS AT THE GABLE ENDS WERE CARVED TO ADD PICTURESQUENESS.

PALE BEIGE PAINTED FLUSH-BOARDED SIDING RESEMBLED WEATHERED CUT STONE.

BATTLEMENTED ENTRANCE PORCH RECALLED 15TH CENTURY ENGLISH CASTLES.

LONG NARROW WINDOWS

CARVED WOOD TRACERY OVER WINDOWS

1840 LYNDHURST, AN AMERICAN EARLY GOTHIC REVIVAL MANSION, TARRYTOWN, NEW YORK
A.J. DAVIS, ARCHITECT

BATTLEMENT DETAILING

STONE PINNACLES

THE FIRST GOTHIC REVIVAL HOUSES BORROWED THEIR MASSING FROM 16TH AND 17TH CENTURY ENGLISH MANSIONS AND THEIR DETAILING FROM GOTHIC CATHEDRALS AND CASTLES.

FLUSH CUT STONE WALLS

121

By 1845 a radical new building method called balloon framing had evolved. A skeleton consisting of continuous, light, wooden members was constructed using inexpensive, machine-made nails. The light sticks of the structure were nailed together instead of notched and pegged as was the old post and beam frame. The method was so easy to learn, so inexpensive, so fast, and so strong that it caught on almost immediately. Some western cities were built seemingly overnight using this new method.

Many pattern books picked up on this new construction method and sometimes devoted an entire chapter to it. Below are framing plans for a small cottage as they might have appeared in a pattern book.

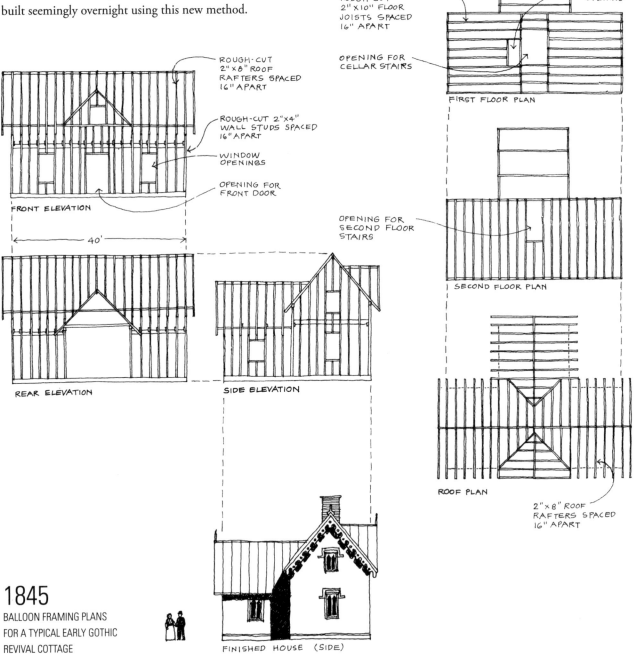

ROUGH-CUT 2" x 10" FLOOR JOISTS SPACED 16" APART

FIREPLACE FOUNDATION OPENING

OPENING FOR CELLAR STAIRS

FIRST FLOOR PLAN

ROUGH-CUT 2" x 8" ROOF RAFTERS SPACED 16" APART

ROUGH-CUT 2" x 4" WALL STUDS SPACED 16" APART

WINDOW OPENINGS

OPENING FOR FRONT DOOR

FRONT ELEVATION

40'

OPENING FOR SECOND FLOOR STAIRS

SECOND FLOOR PLAN

REAR ELEVATION

SIDE ELEVATION

ROOF PLAN

2" x 8" ROOF RAFTERS SPACED 16" APART

1845
BALLOON FRAMING PLANS FOR A TYPICAL EARLY GOTHIC REVIVAL COTTAGE

FINISHED HOUSE (SIDE)

In his influential book, *The Architecture of Country Houses*, A. J. Downing presented a series of house designs in various picturesque styles from which the reader could choose. Shown below is A. J. Davis's design for "a Cottage-Villa in a Rural Gothic Style." Note how simple and conservative the plan shape is—just a hint of irregularity. But the roof and ornamentation clearly show the beginnings of the new Gothic Revival Style, based on eleventh- to fifteenth-century English Gothic cathedrals and castles.

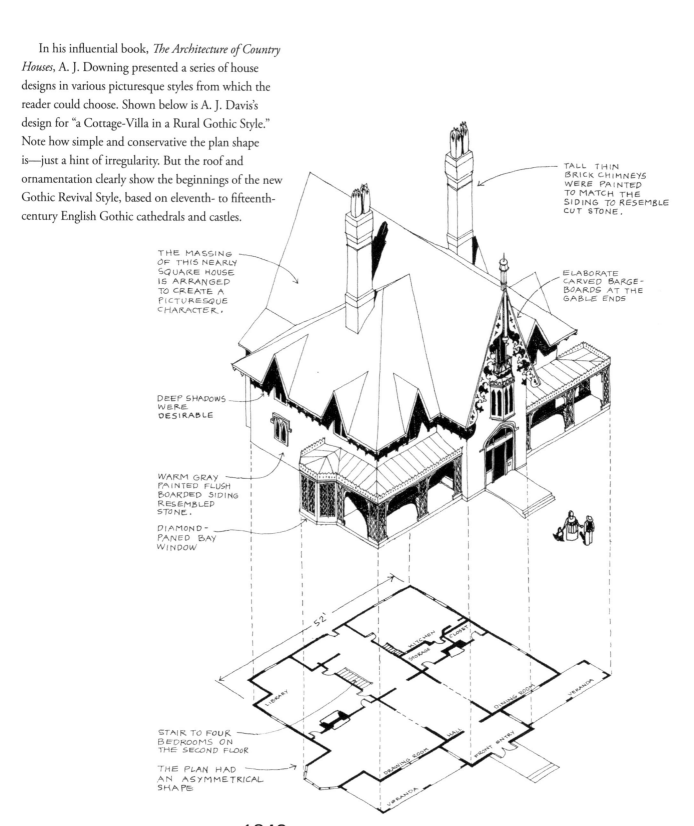

THE MASSING OF THIS NEARLY SQUARE HOUSE IS ARRANGED TO CREATE A PICTURESQUE CHARACTER.

TALL THIN BRICK CHIMNEYS WERE PAINTED TO MATCH THE SIDING TO RESEMBLE CUT STONE.

ELABORATE CARVED BARGE-BOARDS AT THE GABLE ENDS

DEEP SHADOWS WERE DESIRABLE

WARM GRAY PAINTED FLUSH BOARDED SIDING RESEMBLED STONE.

DIAMOND-PANED BAY WINDOW

STAIR TO FOUR BEDROOMS ON THE SECOND FLOOR

THE PLAN HAD AN ASYMMETRICAL SHAPE

52'

LIBRARY
KITCHEN
STORAGE
CLOSET
DINING ROOM
VERANDA
HALL
FRONT ENTRY
DRAWING ROOM
VERANDA

1846 WILLIAM ROTCH HOUSE, NEW BEDFORD, MASSACHUSETTS
A. J. DAVIS, ARCHITECT

Cottage

Countrywide 1845

The designs for cottages and farmhouses first portrayed by A. J. Downing in 1850 in *The Architecture of Country Houses* had a profound effect on the country. They were the beginning of a real vernacular domestic architecture that was to last a long time. His first two designs, the simplest, are shown on the opposite page.

Downing's houses were distinguished by steep roof slopes, balconies, porches, window gables, and deep shadows made by projecting roofs. He was after the ideal building—the house that suited the owner's needs and the land best. He saw the picturesque as a natural style that could provide "true, honest, and functional" architecture yet fit the landscape in a romantic way.

The Cottage Style borrowed from the Early Gothic Style but also created new rules soon to be followed by American housebuilders. The house was to be irregular like the forms of nature. It was to be nestled into the landscape to appear picturesque when viewed from various sites and also afford attractive views from its windows and porches. It was to be built of natural materials or painted tan, gray, or green to harmonize with the earth and its plants. It was the opposite of the symmetrical, hard-edged, white Greek Revival Style house designed to stand out in the landscape.

Many of the architects who contributed plans to Downing's books also produced pattern books of their own. Among them were A. J. Davis's *Rural Residences* (1837), Gervase Wheeler's *Rural Homes* (1851), and Calvert Vaux's *Villas and Cottages* (1857). They all emphasized the use of natural materials for building. The most significant of these was the utilization of board and batten siding for the exterior cladding of the house. This type of construction was welcomed by Downing as an honest and true replacement for painted flush-board siding meant to simulate cut stone. Board and batten siding also created strong vertical shadow lines totally in keeping with the Gothic Style. New tools like the steam-powered scroll saw and the development of the balloon frame made wooden construction inevitable. It was an obvious choice because of an endless supply of lumber, which was much less expensive and easier to work with than stone.

During the mid-nineteenth century, many house pattern books, inspired by Downing, provided the increasingly large middle class with detailed plans of highly affordable cottages. The building boom that occurred then was not only a product of the American economy but of the availability of a technologically sound, easy-to-build, inexpensive, comfortable dwelling.

WOOD SHINGLE ROOF

STONE WALLS

THATCHED ROOF

DIAMOND-PANED WINDOWS

BRICK CHIMNEY

1820 THREE ENGLISH COTTAGES IN THE PICTURESQUE STYLE, BLAIZE HAMLET, BRISTOL, ENGLAND, JOHN NASH, ARCHITECT

The Cottage Style is credited with giving birth to the American front porch. It provided a roof over the main entrance and a semiprivate place to sit and enjoy the outdoors while protected from the hot sun and inclement weather. It was usually covered with honeysuckle or some other flowering vine, which pleasantly scented warm summer evenings.

Downing, Davis, and many other American architects were greatly influenced by the English Picturesque Style. A few of the most characteristic houses from that period are sketched below. Notice the use of natural materials—rough in texture—and the irregularity of the massing and the overhanging roofs to produce deep shadows.

1850

A LABORER'S COTTAGE, DESIGN NUMBER ONE FROM
THE ARCHITECTURE OF COUNTRY HOUSES BY A. J. DOWNING

1850

A SMALL BRACKETED COTTAGE,
DESIGN NUMBER TWO FROM
THE ARCHITECTURE OF COUNTRY HOUSES
BY A. J. DOWNING

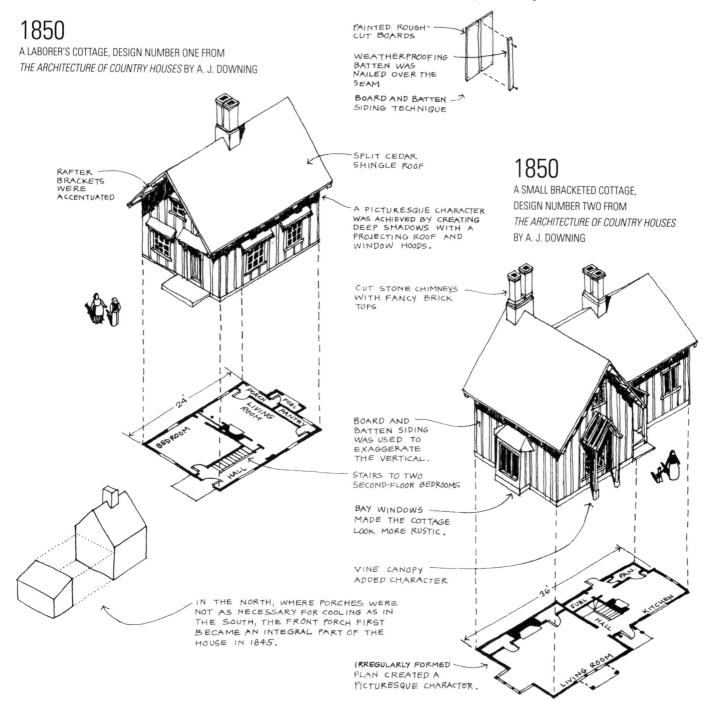

PAINTED ROUGH-CUT BOARDS

WEATHERPROOFING BATTEN WAS NAILED OVER THE SEAM

BOARD AND BATTEN SIDING TECHNIQUE

SPLIT CEDAR SHINGLE ROOF

RAFTER BRACKETS WERE ACCENTUATED

A PICTURESQUE CHARACTER WAS ACHIEVED BY CREATING DEEP SHADOWS WITH A PROJECTING ROOF AND WINDOW HOODS.

CUT STONE CHIMNEYS WITH FANCY BRICK TOPS

BOARD AND BATTEN SIDING WAS USED TO EXAGGERATE THE VERTICAL.

STAIRS TO TWO SECOND-FLOOR BEDROOMS

BAY WINDOWS MADE THE COTTAGE LOOK MORE RUSTIC.

VINE CANOPY ADDED CHARACTER

IN THE NORTH, WHERE PORCHES WERE NOT AS NECESSARY FOR COOLING AS IN THE SOUTH, THE FRONT PORCH FIRST BECAME AN INTEGRAL PART OF THE HOUSE IN 1845.

IRREGULARLY FORMED PLAN CREATED A PICTURESQUE CHARACTER.

24'

BEDROOM

LIVING ROOM

PORCH

PANTRY

FUEL

HALL

36'

FUEL

PAN

HALL

KITCHEN

LIVING ROOM

Carpenter Gothic

Countrywide 1850

The proliferation of house pattern books that began with the Cottage Style, the invention of powered saws for cutting wood, and the popularization of the new balloon frame gave the American carpenter the tools he needed. The result was a building phenomenon unique to this country. The strong carpentry tradition, the demand for quickly-built dwellings and the abundance of fine lumber combined to make a wooden Gothic, or Carpenter's Gothic, a natural development.

The Carpenter Gothic Style is characterized chiefly by its profusion of decorative sawn details (sometimes called "gingerbread"). The fact that most of these details were originally designed to be built of stone did not deter American carpenters from interpreting them into wood. Armed with a steam-powered scroll saw and a pattern book that provided floor plans, elevations, framing plans, and sometimes details, a carpenter with a small crew could build a relatively large, elaborate house in a matter of months.

In England, the Gothic Revival was blossoming because of craftsmen who had passed on techniques from generation to generation since the Middle Ages and because architects too, had become interested. In America, the Gothic Revival Style was inspired by such architects as Isthiel Town, A. J. Davis, and George E. Woodward and by local carpenters who copied the architects' designs from the pattern books. Davis was one of the few who worked on both levels—with wealthy clients and publishing plans. He has generally been given much of the credit, with A. J. Downing, for the direction of the early American Gothic movement, including the Cottage Style and the Carpenter Gothic Style.

Gingerbread Carpenter Gothic houses were being constructed all over the nation during the mid-nineteenth century. Some cities such as Cape May, New Jersey; Oak Bluffs, Martha's Vineyard, Massachusetts; and San Francisco became famous for the whimsical forms the decoration took on their buildings. They remain some of the finest examples of American craftsmanship.

1855
LAKE CITY, COLORADO

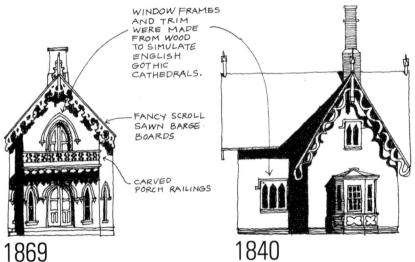

WINDOW FRAMES AND TRIM WERE MADE FROM WOOD TO SIMULATE ENGLISH GOTHIC CATHEDRALS.

FANCY SCROLL SAWN BARGE BOARDS

CARVED PORCH RAILINGS

1869
OAK BLUFFS, MARTHA'S VINEYARD, MASSACHUSETTS

1840
DAVID SIKES HOUSE, SUFFIELD, CONNECTICUT

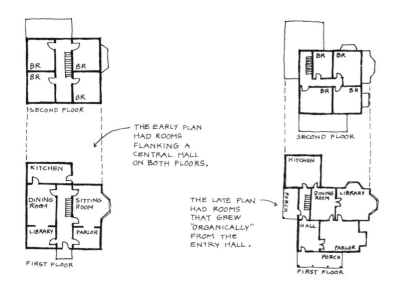

BR
BR
BR

SECOND FLOOR

KITCHEN

DINING ROOM

SITTING ROOM

LIBRARY

PARLOR

FIRST FLOOR

THE EARLY PLAN HAD ROOMS FLANKING A CENTRAL HALL ON BOTH FLOORS.

THE LATE PLAN HAD ROOMS THAT GREW "ORGANICALLY" FROM THE ENTRY HALL.

BR   BR

BR   BR

SECOND FLOOR

KITCHEN

PORCH

DINING ROOM

LIBRARY

HALL

PARLOR

PORCH

FIRST FLOOR

The typical early Carpenter Gothic Style house has a conservative, boxlike floor plan. It gained its picturesque distinction from the steep pitched gable roof and gingerbread ornamentation. As the style evolved, the plan became freer and more complex. As the house was being designed, rooms were allowed to expand or contract according to the owner's desires, resulting in an asymmetrical building.

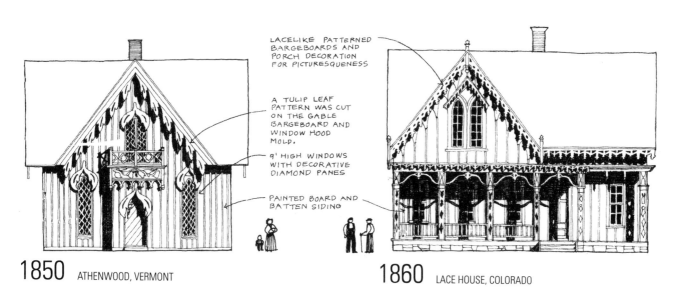

LACELIKE PATTERNED BARGEBOARDS AND PORCH DECORATION FOR PICTURESQUENESS

A TULIP LEAF PATTERN WAS CUT ON THE GABLE BARGEBOARD AND WINDOW HOOD MOLD.

9' HIGH WINDOWS WITH DECORATIVE DIAMOND PANES

PAINTED BOARD AND BATTEN SIDING

1850 ATHENWOOD, VERMONT

1860 LACE HOUSE, COLORADO

The invention of the steam-powered scroll saw made possible the various forms of ornamentation shown below. Carpenters found inspiration for their cut-outs in the shapes of nature.

THE BRACKET IS A DECORATIVE, RIGHT-ANGLE SUPPORT.

BRACKETS WERE SCROLL-SAWN FROM 1½" THICK SOFT WOOD.

BRACKETS

PORCH RAILINGS WERE DESIGNED IN AN INFINITE NUMBER OF PATTERNS, USING THE SCROLL SAW TO CUT HOLES, SLITS, AND SLOTS.

PORCH RAILINGS

THE POPULAR SUNSET/SUNRISE MOTIF WAS CUT FROM THIN WOOD STICKS THEN NAILED TO THE FACADE.

 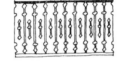 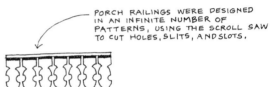

APPLIQUE

GREATER DELICACY IS ATTAINABLE SINCE THE DECORATION IS ATTACHED TO ITS BACKGROUND.

WOODEN SHINGLES WERE MASS PRODUCED FROM CEDAR IN DIFFERENT SHAPES, THEN NAILED TO THE WALL IN OVERLAPPING FASHION TO CREATE A VARIETY OF SHADOW PATTERNS.

 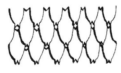 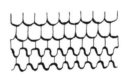

SHINGLES

OFTEN GABLE DECORATION WAS BUILT FROM STICKS INSTEAD OF SCROLL-SAWN ELEMENTS.

1½" THICK PLANED, SCROLL-SAWN, GABLE END BARGEBOARDS WERE THE MOST POPULAR KIND OF DECORATION.

GABLES

Because the Carpenter Gothic house had such a variety of shapes, it could be added to at anytime without diminishing its beauty. In most cases, as shown below, new construction increased the charm of the house.

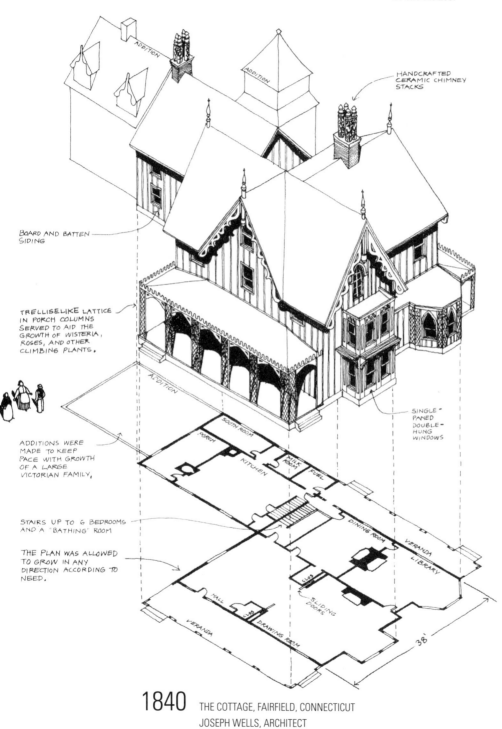

HANDCRAFTED
CERAMIC CHIMNEY
STACKS

BOARD AND BATTEN
SIDING

TRELLISELIKE LATTICE
IN PORCH COLUMNS
SERVED TO AID THE
GROWTH OF WISTERIA,
ROSES, AND OTHER
CLIMBING PLANTS.

SINGLE-
PANED
DOUBLE-
HUNG
WINDOWS

ADDITIONS WERE
MADE TO KEEP
PACE WITH GROWTH
OF A LARGE
VICTORIAN FAMILY.

STAIRS UP TO 6 BEDROOMS
AND A "BATHING" ROOM

THE PLAN WAS ALLOWED
TO GROW IN ANY
DIRECTION ACCORDING TO
NEED.

ADDITION
ADDITION
ADDITION

SOUTH ROOM
PORCH
KITCHEN
MILK ROOM
FUEL
DINING ROOM
VERANDA
LIBRARY
HALL
CLOS
SLIDING DOORS
VERANDA
DRAWING ROOM
38'

1840   THE COTTAGE, FAIRFIELD, CONNECTICUT
JOSEPH WELLS, ARCHITECT

Steamboat Gothic

Countrywide
1855

Steamboat Gothic was an elaborate form of Carpenter Gothic with an extreme amount of wooden ornamentation. It was also called Wedding Cake Gothic but a more appropriate title might be Flamboyant Carpenter Gothic or High Carpenter Gothic.

By 1855 some of the most fascinating Steamboat Gothic designs resulted from the remodeling of much earlier houses. The Gothic movement had become so popular that Greek Revival, Georgian, Federal, and even many of the early colonial styles were converted with the addition of overhanging roofs, porch trellises, fancy bargeboards, and a wide variety of window and door trims.

1860
CONVERSION OF A SEASIDE COTTAGE INTO
A STEAMBOAT GOTHIC STYLE HOUSE, NEW JERSEY

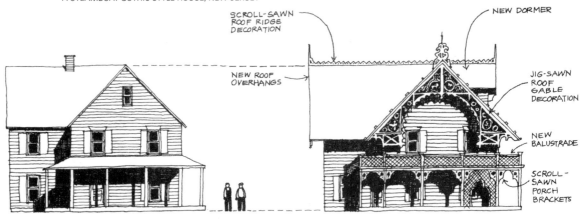

1850
THE DELTA QUEEN, MISSISSIPPI RIVER

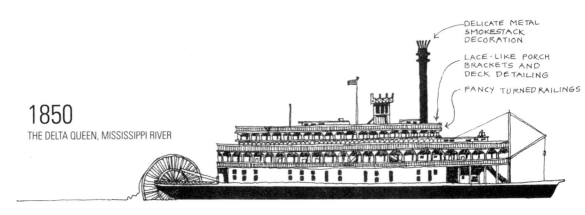

Steamboats, among the first structures to be "renovated," were decorated with wooden railings and columns turned on a power-driven lathe, scroll-sawn brackets, and other trimwork on decks and porches. Even such mechanical devices as smokestacks and water wheels were built with ornamentation.

Probably the most obvious example of the popularity of the Gothic Revival Style occurred in Kennebunkport, Maine, in 1854 when a perfectly proper red brick Federal house was given a "slipcover" conversion into a white painted castle-like house. The renovation, aptly called the Wedding Cake House, is shown below with all of its superfluous decoration borrowed from English cathedrals and castles.

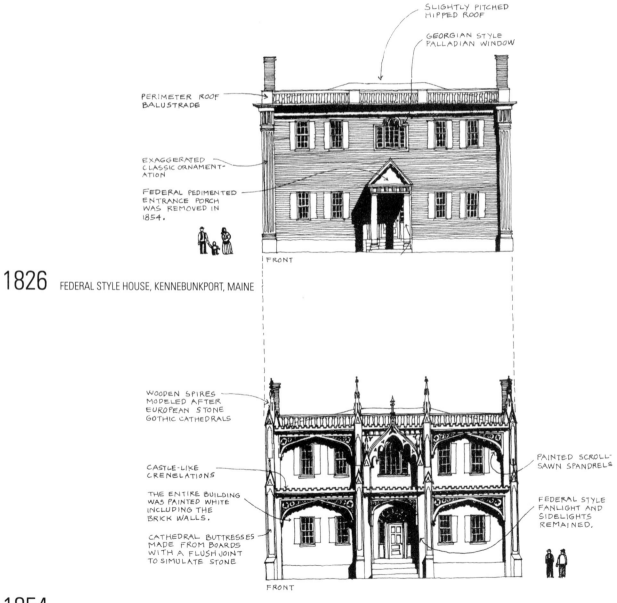

SLIGHTLY PITCHED HIPPED ROOF

GEORGIAN STYLE PALLADIAN WINDOW

PERIMETER ROOF BALUSTRADE

EXAGGERATED CLASSIC ORNAMENTATION

FEDERAL PEDIMENTED ENTRANCE PORCH WAS REMOVED IN 1854.

FRONT

1826 FEDERAL STYLE HOUSE, KENNEBUNKPORT, MAINE

WOODEN SPIRES MODELED AFTER EUROPEAN STONE GOTHIC CATHEDRALS

CASTLE-LIKE CRENELATIONS

THE ENTIRE BUILDING WAS PAINTED WHITE INCLUDING THE BRICK WALLS.

CATHEDRAL BUTTRESSES MADE FROM BOARDS WITH A FLUSH JOINT TO SIMULATE STONE

PAINTED SCROLL-SAWN SPANDRELS

FEDERAL STYLE FANLIGHT AND SIDELIGHTS REMAINED.

FRONT

1854 WEDDING CAKE HOUSE, KENNEBUNKPORT, MAINE

Italian Villa

Countrywide 1855

The asymmetrical Italian Villa Style became popular in England after 1800. It was inspired by the vernacular architecture of the Italian countryside. By the 1830s Italian villas were appearing, with equal popularity, in the company of Gothic and Greek residences in English design books.

The style began in America in 1837 when architect John Notman built an Italian villa for Bishop Doane in Burlington, New Jersey. In 1842 this house was published by A. J. Downing in *Treatise on the Theory and Practice of Landscape Gardening, Adapted to North America*. Downing further popularized the style by publishing many A. J. Davis designs for the Italian Villa Style in both *Cottage Residences* (1842) and *The Architecture of Country Houses* (1850). Downing recommended the style because "the irregularity in the masses of the edifice and the shape of the roof" rendered "the sky outline of a building in the style extremely picturesque." The style allowed exceptional freedom in planning in the design of a new house and in making an addition. The style was at once charming, attractive, and practical.

The Italian Villa Style was also known as Tuscan Revival, Hudson River Bracketed, Roman and Tuscan Villa, Lombard, Italian, Vitruvian, Etruscan, Suburban Greek, or Norman. A. J. Davis preferred to call it the American Style. It was by far the most influential style developed during the Victorian era. Almost all later American houses adapted some of its features. Since symmetry was undesirable, the rooms were grouped by function allowing an infinite number of irregularly shaped houses.

1845

VILLA IN THE ITALIAN STYLE
A. J. DAVIS, ARCHITECT
DESIGN #22 FROM *THE ARCHITECTURE OF COUNTRY HOUSES* BY A. J. DOWNING

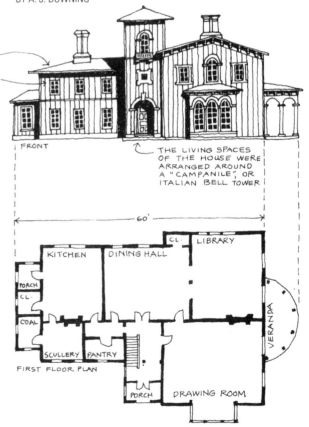

FLATTENED ROOF

WOODEN BOARD AND BATTEN SIDING

FRONT

THE LIVING SPACES OF THE HOUSE WERE ARRANGED AROUND A "CAMPANILE", OR ITALIAN BELL TOWER

60'

CL. LIBRARY
KITCHEN   DINING HALL
PORCH
CL.
COAL   VERANDA
SCULLERY PANTRY
FIRST FLOOR PLAN
PORCH   DRAWING ROOM

1800

VERNACULAR ITALIAN HOUSE, FLORENCE, ITALY

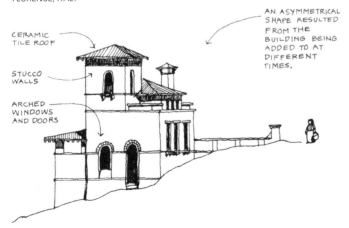

AN ASYMMETRICAL SHAPE RESULTED FROM THE BUILDING BEING ADDED TO AT DIFFERENT TIMES.

CERAMIC TILE ROOF

STUCCO WALLS

ARCHED WINDOWS AND DOORS

An asymmetrical Classic Style of architecture, unlike the formal Georgian and Greek Revival styles, emerged in the Italian Villa Style. Blocks of space were manipulated by designers until they arrived at a composition (usually irregular) that pleased the owner. Roofs were shallow, hipped, or gable, with large brackets under the eaves. Since the ideal Italian villa was one that closely resembled original Italian farmhouses, red ceramic tile was used on the roof and a smooth wall surface, such as stucco or painted brick, was built when economically possible. Otherwise, the picturesque board and batten siding was recommended.

1850

VILLA IN THE ITALIAN STYLE
DESIGN #6 FROM *COTTAGE RESIDENCES*
BY A. J. DOWNING

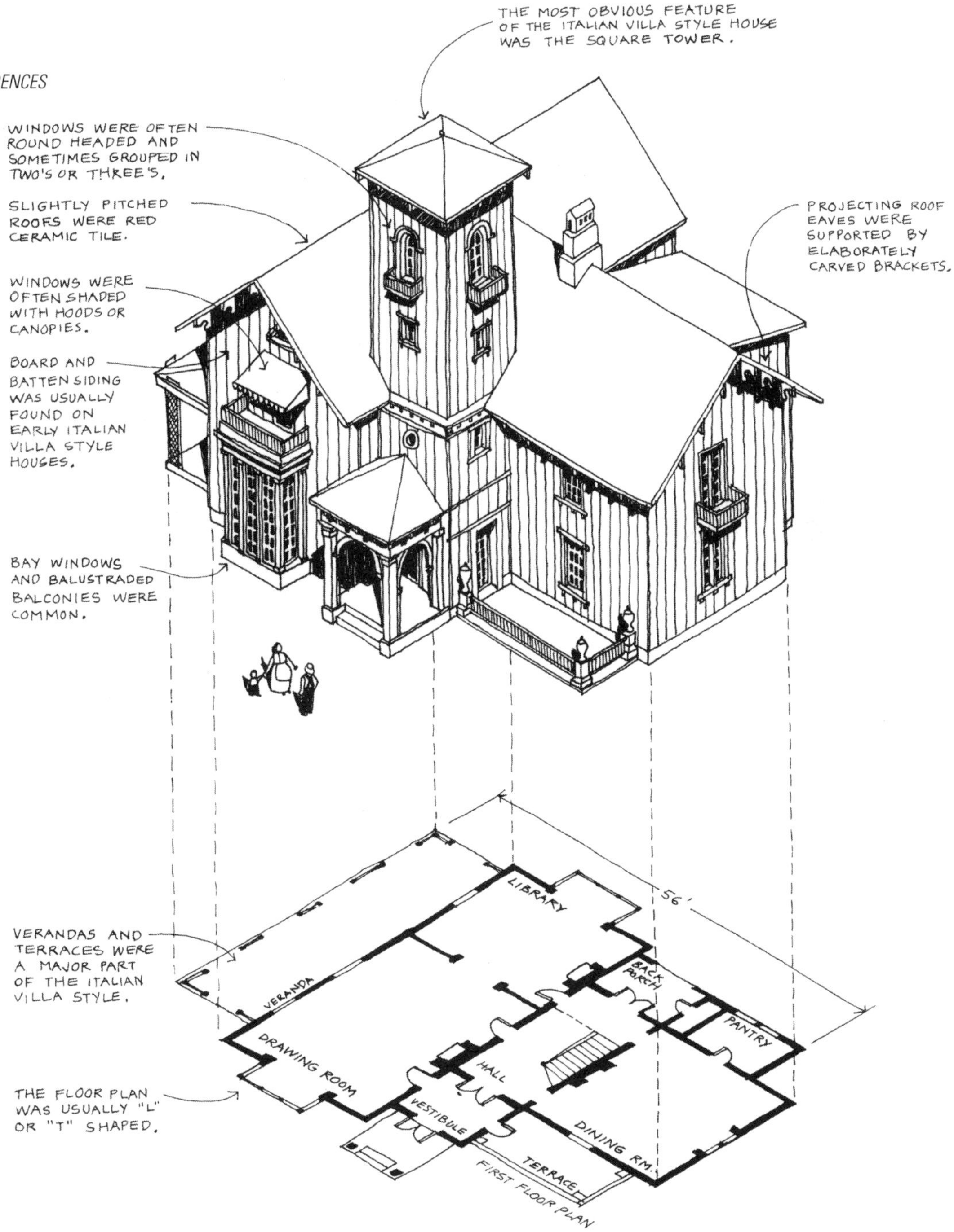

THE MOST OBVIOUS FEATURE OF THE ITALIAN VILLA STYLE HOUSE WAS THE SQUARE TOWER.

WINDOWS WERE OFTEN ROUND HEADED AND SOMETIMES GROUPED IN TWO'S OR THREE'S.

SLIGHTLY PITCHED ROOFS WERE RED CERAMIC TILE.

WINDOWS WERE OFTEN SHADED WITH HOODS OR CANOPIES.

BOARD AND BATTEN SIDING WAS USUALLY FOUND ON EARLY ITALIAN VILLA STYLE HOUSES.

BAY WINDOWS AND BALUSTRADED BALCONIES WERE COMMON.

PROJECTING ROOF EAVES WERE SUPPORTED BY ELABORATELY CARVED BRACKETS.

VERANDAS AND TERRACES WERE A MAJOR PART OF THE ITALIAN VILLA STYLE.

THE FLOOR PLAN WAS USUALLY "L" OR "T" SHAPED.

LIBRARY

56'

BACK PORCH

PANTRY

VERANDA

DRAWING ROOM

HALL

DINING RM.

VESTIBULE

TERRACE

FIRST FLOOR PLAN

Swiss Cottage

**Countrywide
1855**

In the mid-nineteenth century, the genuine Swiss cottage, or chalet, was perhaps the most appealing of wood-built house. The crudeness of its construction and its often wild and romantic site gave the Swiss Cottage Style a rustic, yet quaint aesthetic that became quite desirable in the northern part of America where snow fell.

The American version, of course, neither piled large stones on the roof nor gave up the first floor to cows. But the essential character was retained with the abundant use of galleries, balconies, large windows, and rough-cut lumber as a primary building material. Roofs were allowed to project widely around the building to create deep shadows, and stone was used in a raised foundation for further rustication. The finished exterior siding was made from one-inch wide, rough-cut boards nailed to a wooden underlayment so as to resemble the Swiss post and beam structure that was exposed on the outside of the building. (The American Swiss cottage was made in the usual balloon frame manner.) This created an architecture that has been called skinless, since the skeleton, or structure, is so apparent.

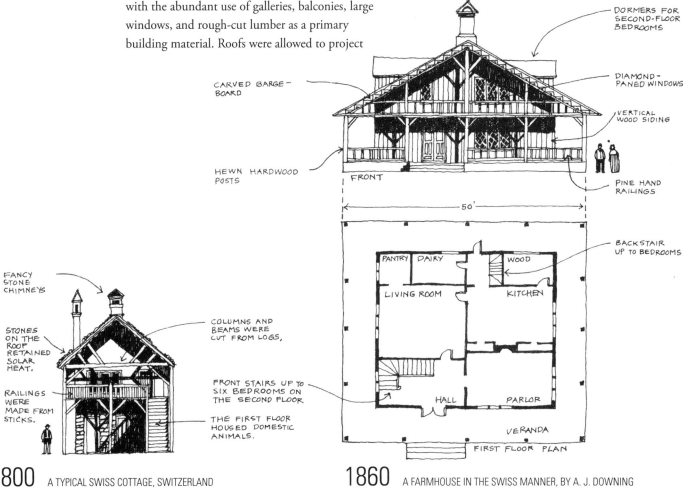

DORMERS FOR SECOND-FLOOR BEDROOMS

DIAMOND-PANED WINDOWS

VERTICAL WOOD SIDING

PINE HAND RAILINGS

CARVED BARGE-BOARD

HEWN HARDWOOD POSTS

FRONT

BACKSTAIR UP TO BEDROOMS

50'

FANCY STONE CHIMNEYS

STONES ON THE ROOF RETAINED SOLAR HEAT.

RAILINGS WERE MADE FROM STICKS.

COLUMNS AND BEAMS WERE CUT FROM LOGS.

FRONT STAIRS UP TO SIX BEDROOMS ON THE SECOND FLOOR

THE FIRST FLOOR HOUSED DOMESTIC ANIMALS.

PANTRY | DAIRY | WOOD

LIVING ROOM | KITCHEN

HALL | PARLOR

VERANDA

FIRST FLOOR PLAN

1800 A TYPICAL SWISS COTTAGE, SWITZERLAND

1860 A FARMHOUSE IN THE SWISS MANNER, BY A. J. DOWNING
IN *THE ARCHITECTURE OF COUNTRY HOUSES*

House design books, like A. J. Downing's *The Architecture of Country Houses*, published in 1850, stressed that the selection of the site for the American Swiss cottage was critical. The site was to be bold, mountainous if possible, on the side or bottom of a heavily wooded hill, or in a wild picturesque valley—or the spirit of the house would be lost.

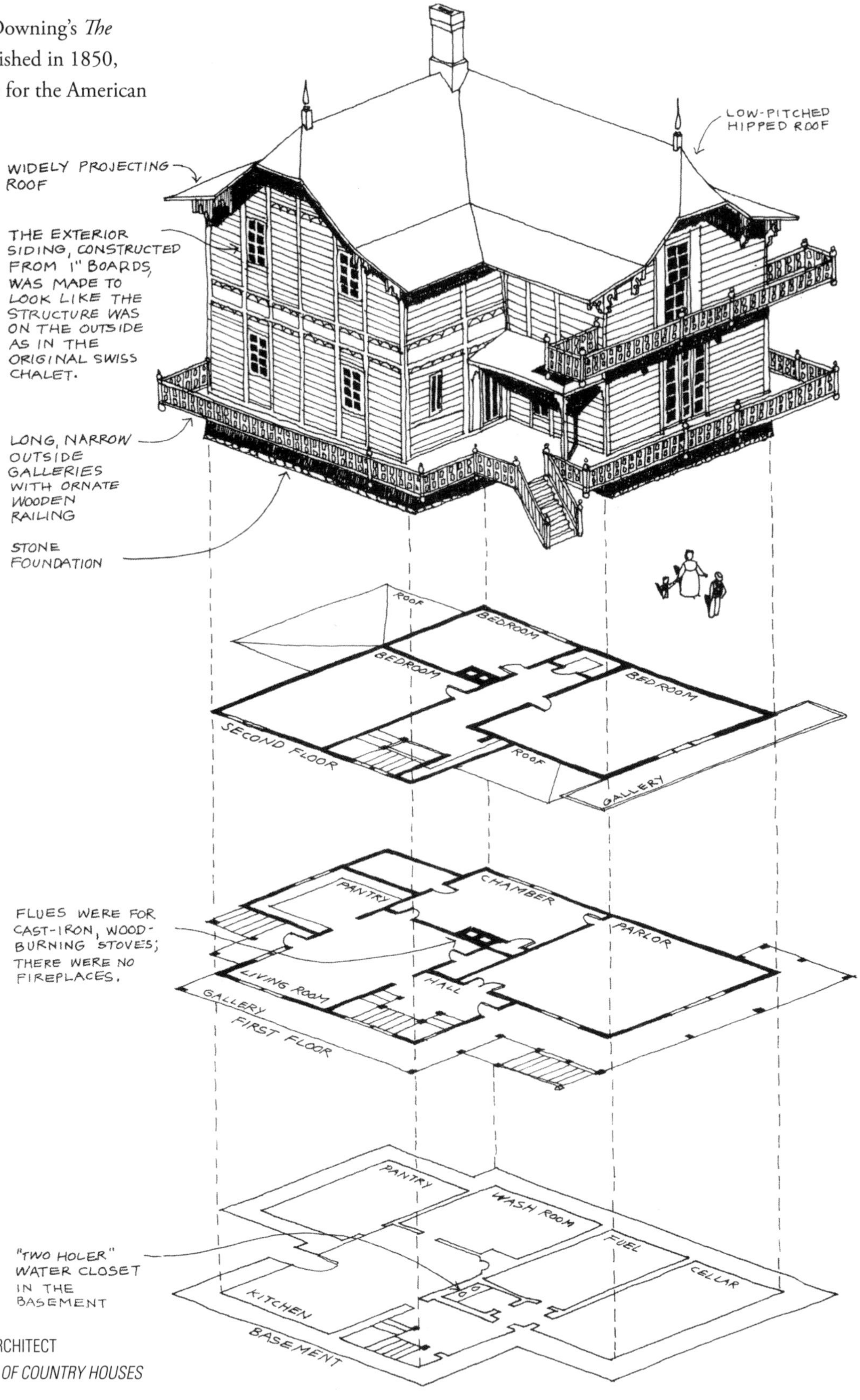

LOW-PITCHED HIPPED ROOF

WIDELY PROJECTING ROOF

THE EXTERIOR SIDING, CONSTRUCTED FROM 1" BOARDS, WAS MADE TO LOOK LIKE THE STRUCTURE WAS ON THE OUTSIDE AS IN THE ORIGINAL SWISS CHALET.

LONG, NARROW OUTSIDE GALLERIES WITH ORNATE WOODEN RAILING

STONE FOUNDATION

ROOF
BEDROOM
BEDROOM
BEDROOM
SECOND FLOOR
ROOF
GALLERY

FLUES WERE FOR CAST-IRON, WOOD-BURNING STOVES; THERE WERE NO FIREPLACES.

PANTRY
CHAMBER
LIVING ROOM
HALL
PARLOR
GALLERY
FIRST FLOOR

"TWO HOLER" WATER CLOSET IN THE BASEMENT

PANTRY
WASH ROOM
FUEL
CELLAR
KITCHEN
BASEMENT

1860

A SWISS COTTAGE, G. J. PENCHARD, ESQ. ARCHITECT
FROM A. J. DOWNING'S *THE ARCHITECTURE OF COUNTRY HOUSES*

Italianate

Countrywide
1855

Few American architects could afford to travel to Italy in the mid-nineteenth century so most of the Italian influence on American architecture came from English buildings and pattern books. Of the three styles of Italian houses that were built in America (the Italian Villa, p. 132), the Italianate, and the Urban Brownstone) the Italianate became the most popular.

The Italianate Style is a two- or three-story house that is boxlike, or cubic, in shape with very wide roof eaves supported by large brackets. The brackets are such a prominent feature that the style (along with the Italian Villa Style) was sometimes known as the Bracketed Style.

Around 1860 the use of cast-iron as a building material became very popular. The metal could be cast in any conceivable design and was used for everything from furniture to street lights. Foundry molds could be used over and over, thereby lowering costs. Cast-iron columns and facades were used primarily in commercial buildings, but houses throughout America employed a rich variety of designs on porches, balconies, railings, and fences. New Orleans is well known for its cast-iron ornamental tracery.

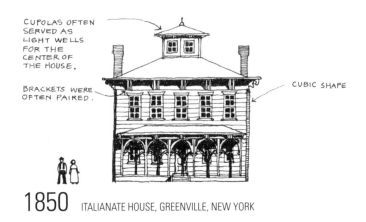

CUPOLAS OFTEN SERVED AS LIGHT WELLS FOR THE CENTER OF THE HOUSE.

BRACKETS WERE OFTEN PAIRED.

CUBIC SHAPE

1850 ITALIANATE HOUSE, GREENVILLE, NEW YORK

WIDOW'S WALK BALUSTRADE

CUBIC SHAPE

CENTRAL, ONE-BAY FRONT PORCHES WERE COMMON

CUPOLA SERV AS AN AIR VENT.

OUTHOUSES WERE OFTE BUILT IN THE ITALIANATE STYLE.

1855 ITALIANATE HOUSE, GEORGETOWN, COLORADO

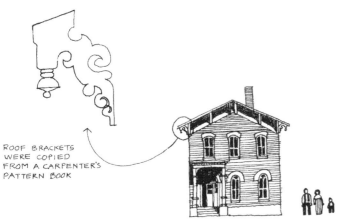

ROOF BRACKETS WERE COPIED FROM A CARPENTER'S PATTERN BOOK

1864 VERNACULAR ITALIANATE HOUSE, FREDONIA, NEW YORK

WIDE EAVES SUPPORTED BY LARGE BRACKETS

QUOINS WERE COMMON IN LATE ITALIANATE HOUSES.

1870 LATE ITALIANATE HOUSE, IONA, MICHIGAN

1864

TYPICAL ITALIANATE HOUSE
JOHN RIDDELL, ARCHITECT

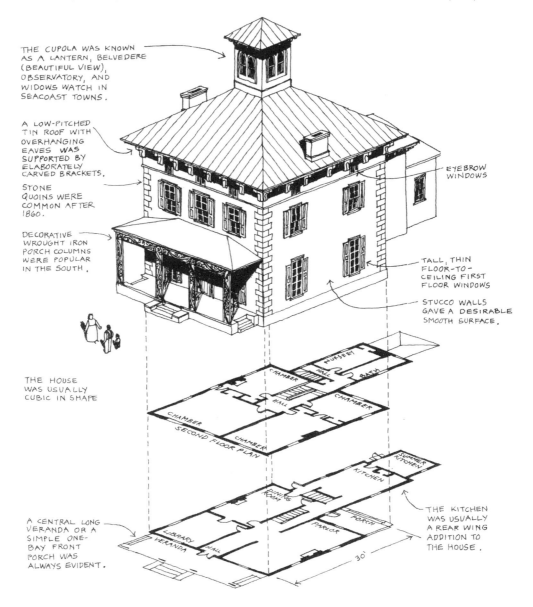

THE CUPOLA WAS KNOWN AS A LANTERN, BELVEDERE (BEAUTIFUL VIEW), OBSERVATORY, AND WIDOWS WATCH IN SEACOAST TOWNS.

A LOW-PITCHED TIN ROOF WITH OVERHANGING EAVES WAS SUPPORTED BY ELABORATELY CARVED BRACKETS.

STONE QUOINS WERE COMMON AFTER 1860.

DECORATIVE WROUGHT IRON PORCH COLUMNS WERE POPULAR IN THE SOUTH.

EYEBROW WINDOWS

TALL, THIN FLOOR-TO-CEILING FIRST FLOOR WINDOWS

STUCCO WALLS GAVE A DESIRABLE SMOOTH SURFACE.

THE HOUSE WAS USUALLY CUBIC IN SHAPE

NURSERY
HALL
BATH
CHAMBER
CHAMBER
HALL
CHAMBER
SECOND FLOOR PLAN
CHAMBER

SUMMER KITCHEN
KITCHEN
DINING ROOM
PORCH
LIBRARY
VERANDA
HALL
PARLOR
30'

A CENTRAL LONG VERANDA OR A SIMPLE ONE-BAY FRONT PORCH WAS ALWAYS EVIDENT.

THE KITCHEN WAS USUALLY A REAR WING ADDITION TO THE HOUSE.

Octagon

Countrywide 1860

There have been eight-sided buildings in many countries for thousands of years but the octagon house was the invention of an American, Orson Squire Fowler. He first published his octagon idea in his own *A Home for All, or the Gravel Wall and Octagon Mode of Building* in 1849. He argued that eight walls enclosed more space than four walls inscribed within the same circumference; that octagons received more daylight, were easier to heat and cool (through a central cupola); and that they saved steps and afforded better views.

Fowler also was among the first to incorporate into his houses hot and cold running water, filtered drinking water, dumbwaiters, speaking tubes, and indoor flush toilets. He built his own octagon house in Fishkill, New York, in 1850 with these modern conveniences.

A Home for All and other popular building manuals included instructions on how to construct octagons. Thousands were built throughout America, most of them around 1860, but the habit of living in a four-sided room was hard to break.

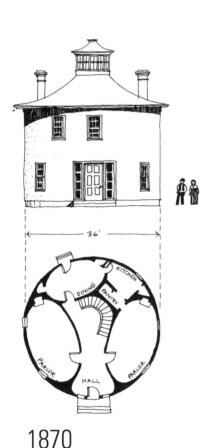

1870
ROUND HOUSE, MIDDLETOWN, RHODE ISLAND

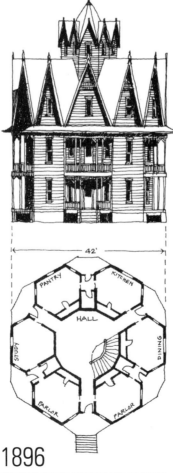

1896
HEXAGON HOUSE, MINERAL WELLS, TEXAS

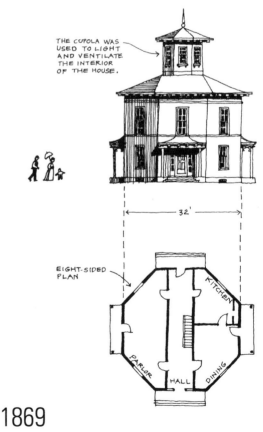

THE CUPOLA WAS USED TO LIGHT AND VENTILATE THE INTERIOR OF THE HOUSE.

EIGHT-SIDED PLAN

1869
TYPICAL OCTAGON HOUSE, FROM *THE AMERICAN COTTAGE BUILDER*

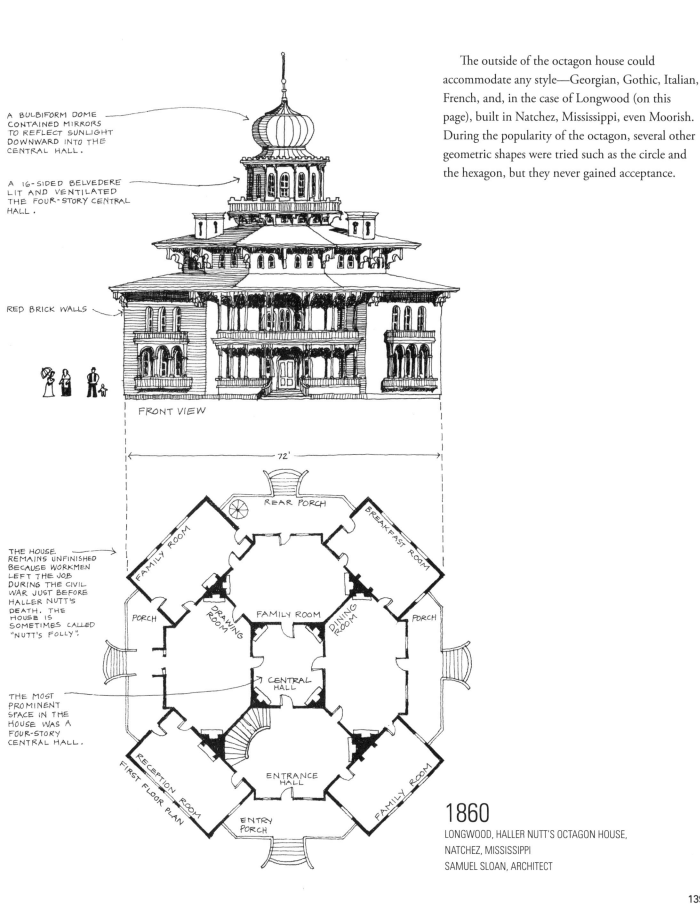

The outside of the octagon house could accommodate any style—Georgian, Gothic, Italian, French, and, in the case of Longwood (on this page), built in Natchez, Mississippi, even Moorish. During the popularity of the octagon, several other geometric shapes were tried such as the circle and the hexagon, but they never gained acceptance.

A BULBIFORM DOME CONTAINED MIRRORS TO REFLECT SUNLIGHT DOWNWARD INTO THE CENTRAL HALL.

A 16-SIDED BELVEDERE LIT AND VENTILATED THE FOUR-STORY CENTRAL HALL.

RED BRICK WALLS

FRONT VIEW

72'

THE HOUSE REMAINS UNFINISHED BECAUSE WORKMEN LEFT THE JOB DURING THE CIVIL WAR JUST BEFORE HALLER NUTT'S DEATH. THE HOUSE IS SOMETIMES CALLED "NUTT'S FOLLY".

THE MOST PROMINENT SPACE IN THE HOUSE WAS A FOUR-STORY CENTRAL HALL.

REAR PORCH

BREAKFAST ROOM

FAMILY ROOM

PORCH

DRAWING ROOM

FAMILY ROOM

DINING ROOM

PORCH

CENTRAL HALL

RECEPTION ROOM

FIRST FLOOR PLAN

ENTRANCE HALL

FAMILY ROOM

ENTRY PORCH

1860
LONGWOOD, HALLER NUTT'S OCTAGON HOUSE, NATCHEZ, MISSISSIPPI
SAMUEL SLOAN, ARCHITECT

False Front

Countrywide
1860

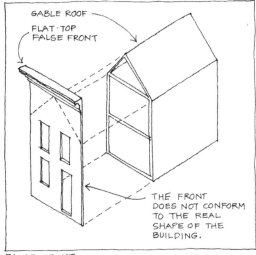

GABLE ROOF

FLAT·TOP
FALSE FRONT

THE FRONT
DOES NOT CONFORM
TO THE REAL
SHAPE OF THE
BUILDING.

FALSE FRONT

False front buildings first appeared in great numbers in the aftermath of the California Gold Rush of 1849. They were the result of small frontier town merchants attempting to make their simple shed and gable roof buildings appear larger, and more important, like the flat-roof buildings of eastern cities. The merchant wanted the casual shopper to see his sign (usually located on the false front), not the snow capped mountains behind his building. So the view was blocked and the false fronts dominated the street.

As the town's wealth increased, the use of the false front to create an urban atmosphere was no longer necessary. The false front, however, remained a significant commercial architectural form all over the country, in older, less prominent towns. The false front rarely was applied to residential architecture. The few houses on which they appeared were most often located on the main street and built to conform to the rest of the streetscape.

LINE OF
GABLE ROOF
BEHIND
THE FALSE
FACADE

POOL HALL

1860 FALSE-FRONTED MAIN STREET OF EUREKA, COLORADO

Many false fronts were reminiscent of the Jacobean Style, illustrated on page 62 and the early Dutch Colonial stepped gable façade, as shown on page 56. Some historians think that the False Front Style was based on the Dutch Colonial Style.

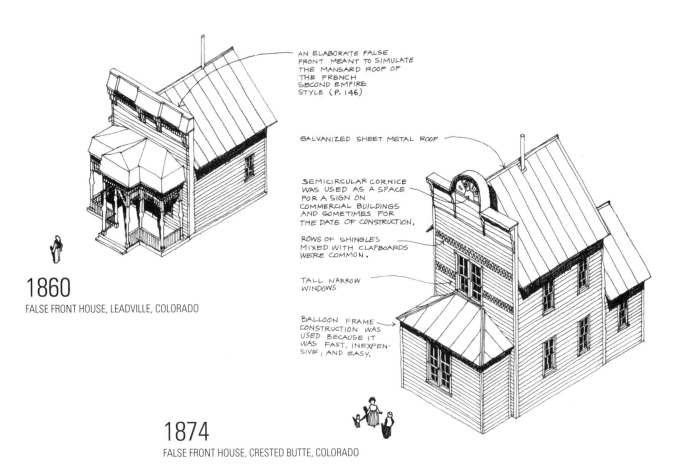

AN ELABORATE FALSE FRONT MEANT TO SIMULATE THE MANSARD ROOF OF THE FRENCH SECOND EMPIRE STYLE (P. 146)

GALVANIZED SHEET METAL ROOF

SEMICIRCULAR CORNICE WAS USED AS A SPACE FOR A SIGN ON COMMERCIAL BUILDINGS AND SOMETIMES FOR THE DATE OF CONSTRUCTION.

ROWS OF SHINGLES MIXED WITH CLAPBOARDS WERE COMMON.

TALL NARROW WINDOWS

BALLOON FRAME CONSTRUCTION WAS USED BECAUSE IT WAS FAST, INEXPENSIVE, AND EASY.

1860
FALSE FRONT HOUSE, LEADVILLE, COLORADO

1874
FALSE FRONT HOUSE, CRESTED BUTTE, COLORADO

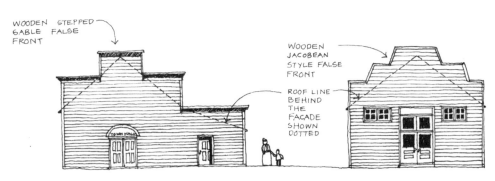

WOODEN STEPPED GABLE FALSE FRONT

WOODEN JACOBEAN STYLE FALSE FRONT

ROOF LINE BEHIND THE FACADE SHOWN DOTTED

1864 TOWN HALL, GENOA, NEVADA

Renaissance Revival

Countrywide 1860

The revival of the Italian palace of Renaissance Rome and Florence was initiated in England in 1829 by Charles Barry. It was brought to America in 1845 by architect John Notman with the construction of the Athenaeum in Philadelphia. Another early significant Renaissance Revival building was the A. T. Stewart store in New York City, designed by an Italian marble cutter named Ottavian Gori. This large five-story marble commercial palace created a sensation in its time. The Renaissance Revival Style was used for some federal buildings by architect Ammi B. Young in the 1850s—for example the Georgetown, Washington D.C., Custom House, shown on the next page.

The Renaissance Revival Style was quite academic and possessed neither the warmth nor the playful irregularity of Italian Villa and Italianate Styles. It proved an unpopular style for houses because it had to compete with the delightful picturesque Victorian styles of the mid-nineteenth century.

Buildings of the Renaissance Revival Style show a studied proper formalism. A tight cubic shape was made to contain closely spaced windows symmetrically placed on each side of a central door—as was done in sixteenth-century Italy. Projections or recessions in the main mass of the building were minimal. The Renaissance Revival buildings were constructed from finely cut ashlar stone that was accentuated, usually, with rusticated (rough-cut) quoins at the corners of the building. The design of the frames of the windows usually varied from floor to floor and the door was usually

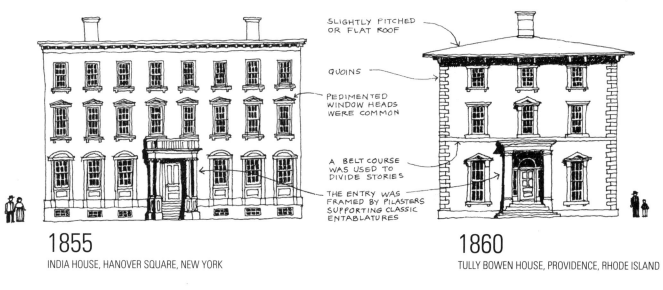

SLIGHTLY PITCHED OR FLAT ROOF

QUOINS

PEDIMENTED WINDOW HEADS WERE COMMON

A BELT COURSE WAS USED TO DIVIDE STORIES

THE ENTRY WAS FRAMED BY PILASTERS SUPPORTING CLASSIC ENTABLATURES

1855
INDIA HOUSE, HANOVER SQUARE, NEW YORK

1860
TULLY BOWEN HOUSE, PROVIDENCE, RHODE ISLAND

flanked by pediments supporting entablatures in the "correct" Italian Renaissance Style. The style promised "dignity" without the expense of columns or a complicated building facade. It could be given a certain richness, but it could never compete with the other Italian styles in this respect.

CARVED STONE CHIMNEYS

SLIGHTLY PITCHED SLATE ROOF

STONE BRACKETS

RUSTICATED QUOINS

WINDOWS FRAMED BY CARVED STONE PILASTERS SUPPORTING FULL ENTABLATURES

CUT STONE WALLS WITH SMOOTH FINISH

1896 THE BREAKERS, CORNELIUS VANDERBILT RESIDENCE, NEWPORT, RHODE ISLAND
RICHARD MORRIS HUNT, ARCHITECT

The Breakers, shown above, remains one of the most magnificent Renaissance Revival homes in America. It was modeled by architect Richard Morris Hunt after an Italian palace and built as a summer residence for Cornelius Vanderbilt in only two years by thousands of skilled European and American craftsmen.

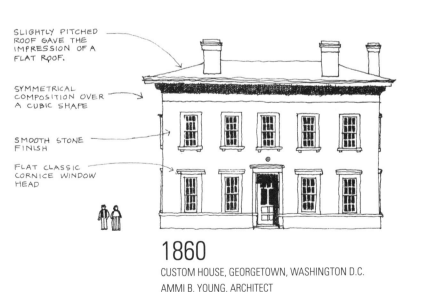

SLIGHTLY PITCHED ROOF GAVE THE IMPRESSION OF A FLAT ROOF.

SYMMETRICAL COMPOSITION OVER A CUBIC SHAPE

SMOOTH STONE FINISH

FLAT CLASSIC CORNICE WINDOW HEAD

1860
CUSTOM HOUSE, GEORGETOWN, WASHINGTON D.C.
AMMI B. YOUNG, ARCHITECT

Stick

East
1865

The sources for the Stick Style (a name given to the style by the architectural historian Vincent Scully) go back to A. J. Downing and the Cottage Style (p. 124) and the Swiss Cottage Style (p. 134) of the 1850s. Downing's insistence on "truthfulness" in wooden buildings had caused many architects and builders to begin to expose important balloon frame members on the facade of their structures.

By 1865 architects like Gervase Wheeler and Richard Morris Hunt were designing houses where (to quote Vincent Scully), "the skeleton becomes a total basketry of sticks and the house is a woven fabric, penetrated by the veranda voids of space which the structural members themselves define." Board and batten, vertical siding, horizontal clapboards, brackets, diagonal and "X" bracing, and sticklike porch posts and railings, were features used to create a unique, wooden stick-built character.

STEEP PITCHED GABLE ROOF

PROJECTING GABLE

1864
ST. LUKES EPISCOPAL CHURCH, METUCHEN, NEW JERSEY

MASSIVE GABLE TRIMWORK WAS THE MOST OBVIOUS FEATURE OF THE STICK STYLE.

A HORIZONTAL BAND OF VERTICAL BOARDING WAS COMMON.

1880
NATHAN PUTNAM HOUSE, FREDONIA, NEW YORK
ENOCH CURTIS, ARCHITECT

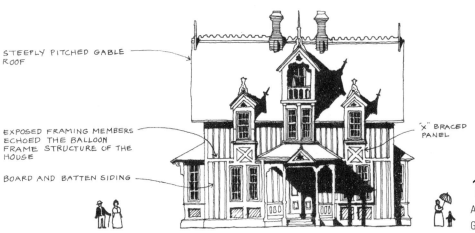

STEEPLY PITCHED GABLE ROOF

EXPOSED FRAMING MEMBERS ECHOED THE BALLOON FRAME STRUCTURE OF THE HOUSE

BOARD AND BATTEN SIDING

"X" BRACED PANEL

1868
A STICK STYLE HOUSE, DESIGN #6 FROM GEORGE WOODWARD'S *NATIONAL ARCHITECT*

Stick Style buildings have tall proportions with steep roofs, an asymmetrical silhouette and a complexion. Massive brackets usually support large roof projections. Verandas and porches are wide with their roofs supported by diagonally braced columns. The most noticeable characteristic of the Stick Style is diagonal "stick work" made to resemble half-timber construction or the exposed balloon frame.

One of the finest examples of the Stick Style is the Griswold house, built in Newport, Rhode Island, in 1862, shown below. It combined influences from the Medieval English Half-Timbered, Early Gothic Revival, Carpenter Gothic, and Swiss Cottage Styles. Its use of vertical, horizontal, and diagonal patterning articulated the light, new balloon framework that supported the house.

STEEPLY PITCHED GABLE ROOF

BRACKETED PURLINS

DIAGONAL "STICKS" WERE EXPOSED STRUCTURAL FRAMING MEMBERS.

HORIZONTAL INFILL SIDING

EXPOSED VERTICAL MEMBERS CALLED "STUDS"

PORCH ROOF RAFTERS WERE USUALLY EXPOSED.

PORCH RAILINGS WERE MADE FROM "STICKS".

1862
GRISWOLD HOUSE, NEWPORT, RHODE ISLAND
RICHARD MORRIS HUNT, ARCHITECT

Second Empire

Countrywide 1870

This style takes its name from the French Second Empire under the reign of Napoleon III (1852–1870). During this period Paris was renewed on a grand scale with wide boulevards and elegant new buildings. Paris became the world capital of art and fashion and attracted thousands of visitors with two successful international expositions in 1855 and 1867. French Second Empire Style buildings then began to rise in cities throughout the western world, but nowhere was the French impact stronger than in America.

From 1860 through 1875, the French Second Empire Style dominated both public and private construction in the United States. Americans were enamored of this "modern" and "fashionable" style. When the Second Empire was destroyed in the Franco-Prussian War (1870–1871), the cultural prestige of France also suffered a defeat and the popularity of the style died out.

The hallmark of the style was the mansard roof, named after its inventor, a seventeenth-century French architect named Francois Mansart. This roof style was especially popular because it allowed almost a full story of usable space to be included in what was normally wasted attic space, and at the same time it provided a stylish capping to a building. In some European cities, such as London, it was used to circumvent height restrictions. If a law barred buildings of more than four stories, a mansard roof provided a fifth rentable floor.

In America the mansard roof design was varied in several ways. It could be straight-sided, concave or convex arc, or a combination of concave and convex (a graceful "S" curve): At the top and bottom of the slope were strong, massive cornices or "French curbs," the lower resting on relatively small but bold brackets, the upper capped with cast-iron "cresting." On the

"WIDOWS WATCH" TOWER

THE MOST OBVIOUS FEATURE, THE MANSARD ROOF, GAVE ADDITIONAL SPACE TO THE ATTIC FLOOR

1864 EDWARD PENNIMAN HOUSE, EASTHAM, MASSACHUSETTS

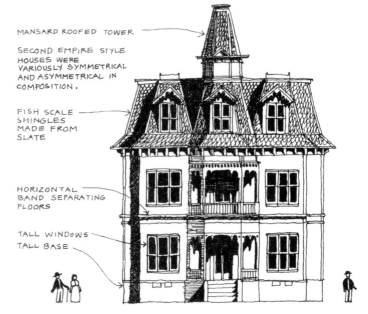

MANSARD ROOFED TOWER

SECOND EMPIRE STYLE HOUSES WERE VARIOUSLY SYMMETRICAL AND ASYMMETRICAL IN COMPOSITION.

FISH SCALE SHINGLES MADE FROM SLATE

HORIZONTAL BAND SEPARATING FLOORS

TALL WINDOWS TALL BASE

1886 RUFUS HERRICK DORN HOUSE, LOS ANGELES, CALIFORNIA
R. H. DORN, ARCHITECT

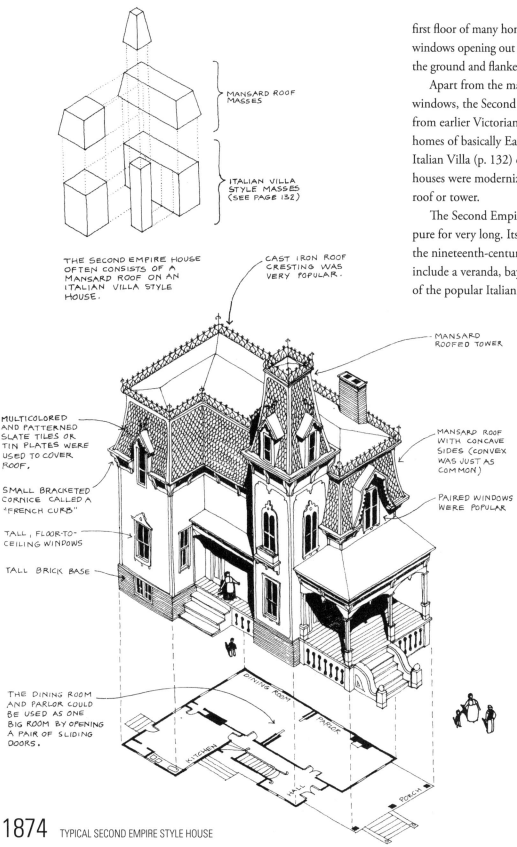

MANSARD ROOF MASSES

ITALIAN VILLA STYLE MASSES (SEE PAGE 132)

THE SECOND EMPIRE HOUSE OFTEN CONSISTS OF A MANSARD ROOF ON AN ITALIAN VILLA STYLE HOUSE.

CAST IRON ROOF CRESTING WAS VERY POPULAR.

MANSARD ROOFED TOWER

MULTICOLORED AND PATTERNED SLATE TILES OR TIN PLATES WERE USED TO COVER ROOF.

SMALL BRACKETED CORNICE CALLED A "FRENCH CURB"

TALL, FLOOR-TO-CEILING WINDOWS

TALL BRICK BASE

MANSARD ROOF WITH CONCAVE SIDES (CONVEX WAS JUST AS COMMON)

PAIRED WINDOWS WERE POPULAR

THE DINING ROOM AND PARLOR COULD BE USED AS ONE BIG ROOM BY OPENING A PAIR OF SLIDING DOORS.

DINING ROOM

PARLOR

KITCHEN

HALL

PORCH

1874 TYPICAL SECOND EMPIRE STYLE HOUSE

first floor of many homes were French, or casement, windows opening out like double doors, reaching to the ground and flanked by louvered shutters.

Apart from the mansard roof and French windows, the Second Empire house did not differ from earlier Victorian types, the mansard topped homes of basically Early Gothic Revival (p. 120) or Italian Villa (p. 132) design. Many pre-Victorian houses were modernized by adding a stylish mansard roof or tower.

The Second Empire Style did not remain pure for very long. Its formality often restricted the nineteenth-century lifestyle that had come to include a veranda, bay window, and light tower of the popular Italian Villa and Carpenter Gothic Styles. After 1874, the basic Second Empire Style house had become a composite of an Italian Villa with a mansard roof with Carpenter Gothic detailing around the windows, doors, and porches.

High Victorian Gothic

Countrywide 1875

It should be noted here that the term "Victorian" is commonly used to describe the group of architectural styles beginning with the Early Gothic Revival (1840) and ending with Eastlake (1880). The Victorian styles began in England under the reign of Queen Victoria and came to America in the late 1830s where they blossomed. They proved as adaptable to the needs of a new mining town as to the desires of the wealthy for a monumental house.

The Early Gothic Revival (p. 120) in America was inspired by English medieval architecture. The High Victorian Gothic Style is largely based on Gothic examples from Northern Italy. The style owed its popularity in Europe and America to *The Seven Lamps of Architecture* by John Ruskin, published in 1849. The book had such influence that the style is often called Ruskinian Gothic.

The Seven Lamps of Architecture proposed principles for the use of color on buildings (known as polychrome): It was not to be applied color like paint, it was to be an integral part of the materials used in construction. Hence the variety of stone work, bands of patterns of multicolored brick and slate. "Constructional coloration" or "permanent polychrome" were the terms used to describe it.

The High Victorian Gothic Style was employed primarily in the construction of such public buildings as libraries, municipal buildings, banks, and churches; but it did not have its effect on the character of houses built during the 1870s and 1880s. Materials of differing colors and textures created decorative bands highlighting corners, arches, and arcades. Ornamental pressed brick, carved stone, and slate tile were used to decorate flat wall and roof surfaces. Gable, porch, and eave trim was massive and strong.

STEEP PITCHED· GABLE DORMER

GABLE, PORCH, AND EAVE TRIM WAS MASSIVE AND STRONG, UNLIKE THE CARPENTER GOTHIC STYLE.

SMOOTH BOARD SIDING GAVE THE APPEARANCE OF STONE.

ROOFS WERE MADE FROM BANDS OF SLATE TILES OF DIFFERENT SHAPE AND COLOR.

SHORT COLUMNS

1880

CAMILLUS BAPTIST CHURCH, CAMILLUS, NEW YORK
ARCHIMEDES RUSSELL, ARCHITECT

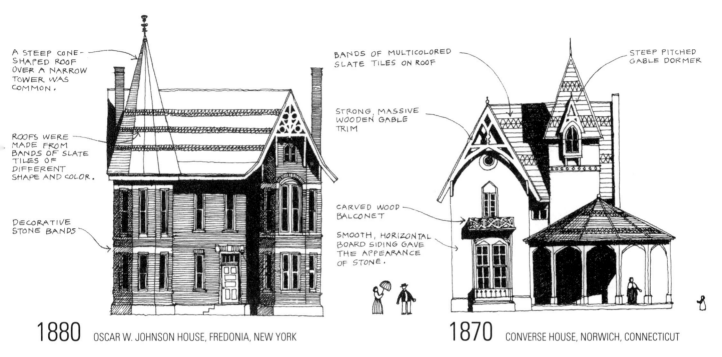

A STEEP CONE-
SHAPED ROOF
OVER A NARROW
TOWER WAS
COMMON.

ROOFS WERE
MADE FROM
BANDS OF SLATE
TILES OF
DIFFERENT
SHAPE AND COLOR.

DECORATIVE
STONE BANDS

BANDS OF MULTICOLORED
SLATE TILES ON ROOF

STRONG, MASSIVE
WOODEN GABLE
TRIM

CARVED WOOD
BALCONET

SMOOTH, HORIZONTAL
BOARD SIDING GAVE
THE APPEARANCE
OF STONE.

STEEP PITCHED
GABLE DORMER

1880 OSCAR W. JOHNSON HOUSE, FREDONIA, NEW YORK

1870 CONVERSE HOUSE, NORWICH, CONNECTICUT

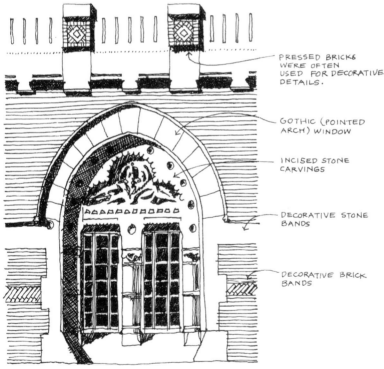

PRESSED BRICKS
WERE OFTEN
USED FOR DECORATIVE
DETAILS.

GOTHIC (POINTED
ARCH) WINDOW

INCISED STONE
CARVINGS

DECORATIVE STONE
BANDS

DECORATIVE BRICK
BANDS

COARSE STONE

1876
WINDOW OF THE PENNSYLVANIA ACADEMY OF FINE ARTS,
PHILADELPHIA, PENNSYLVANIA
FRANK FURNESS, ARCHITECT

Many historians feel that no buildings anywhere have ever had more character, in the Ruskinian sense, than those of architect Frank Furness. The High Victorian Gothic Style was at its best when various textured and colored bricks, stone, and slate could be patterned and carved into the exterior finish materials of a building. Furness was the American master of the High Victorian Gothic Style as shown here in his detailing of a window of the Pennsylvania Academy of Fine Arts.

Many High Victorian Gothic houses were attempts, by carpenters, at translating a masonry idiom into wood, as illustrated by the Converse House above. Thus, smooth board siding was used to give a stonelike appearance and heavy, massive trimwork on gables and porches was used to simulate carved stone.

Queen Anne

Countrywide 1880

The Queen Anne Style began in England with the early work of Richard Norman Shaw. The style harkened back to the simple, solid construction methods of the days of Queen Anne (150 years earlier) when craftsmanship was emphasized. America got its first look at the Queen Anne Style at the great Philadelphia Centennial of 1876 and it soon replaced the French Second Empire and Gothic Styles as the most popular of the times. Its chief competition, Romanesque, was constructed from stone and therefore was too expensive for most Americans. A wooden Queen Anne house could be erected inexpensively and quickly by any competent carpenter and his helper.

The Queen Anne house was the culmination of all the Victorian styles. It took the asymmetry of the Italian Villa Style (p. 132) as far as it would go—wings, porches, gables, and towers protruded in all directions. It borrowed the planning of the Early Gothic Revival Style (p. 120) which allowed the house to grow organically from the inside out. It found interesting ways to use Carpenter Gothic Style (p. 126) ornamentation. All wall and roof surfaces were given a colorful patterned texture as in the High Victorian Gothic Style (p. 148). Bricks were used as a base or foundation wall, horizontal clapboards were the normal cladding for the first floor, and often, half-timbering, as in the Stick Style (p. 144) was used on the attic gable. Several differently shaped shingle

ROUND, SQUARE, OR OCTAGONAL TOWERS WERE COMMON.

THE TOP SASH OF A WINDOW, SEEN THROUGH AN ARCH, WAS A COMMON QUEEN ANNE DETAIL.

STAINED GLASS WAS FREQUENTLY USED FOR HALL AND STAIRCASE WINDOWS.

1875
A TYPICAL QUEEN ANNE HOUSE, SAN FRANCISCO, CALIFORNIA

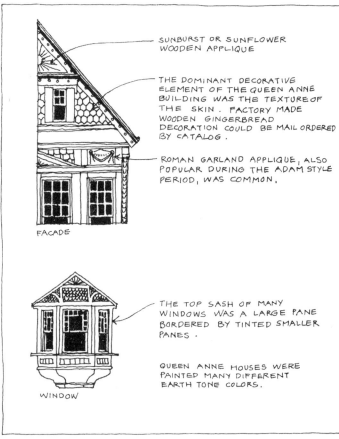

SUNBURST OR SUNFLOWER WOODEN APPLIQUE

THE DOMINANT DECORATIVE ELEMENT OF THE QUEEN ANNE BUILDING WAS THE TEXTURE OF THE SKIN. FACTORY MADE WOODEN GINGERBREAD DECORATION COULD BE MAIL ORDERED BY CATALOG.

ROMAN GARLAND APPLIQUE, ALSO POPULAR DURING THE ADAM STYLE PERIOD, WAS COMMON.

FACADE

THE TOP SASH OF MANY WINDOWS WAS A LARGE PANE BORDERED BY TINTED SMALLER PANES.

QUEEN ANNE HOUSES WERE PAINTED MANY DIFFERENT EARTH TONE COLORS.

WINDOW

EVERY SURFACE OF THE QUEEN ANNE HOUSE WAS TEXTURED OR APPLIQUED.

patterns were frequently used on house walls and roof surfaces. Carved, turned, and applique ornamentation could be found all over the building. Stylized sunburst or sunflower motifs were common applique on the attic gable. Ornate Eastlake (p. 154) turned posts were used as porch columns and railings. Classic Roman and Greek detailing was widely used. Swag and garland applique was common.

The first floor plan became much more open, allowing light and air into the rooms from all directions. Huge sliding doors opened up the rooms to each other, creating one large space, or smaller private rooms. This was made possible with the introduction of central heating. There was rarely more than one bathroom in the Queen Anne house. Even in 1880 indoor toilets were considered a luxury.

Queen Anne houses, with every conceivable type of trim, were built in towns across America during the late-nineteenth and early-twentieth centuries. There were practically no regional differences, because house designs were chosen from widely circulated pattern books. These pattern books, along with house plans, often gave plans for landscaping, interior design, and furniture style, allowing little for the imagination.

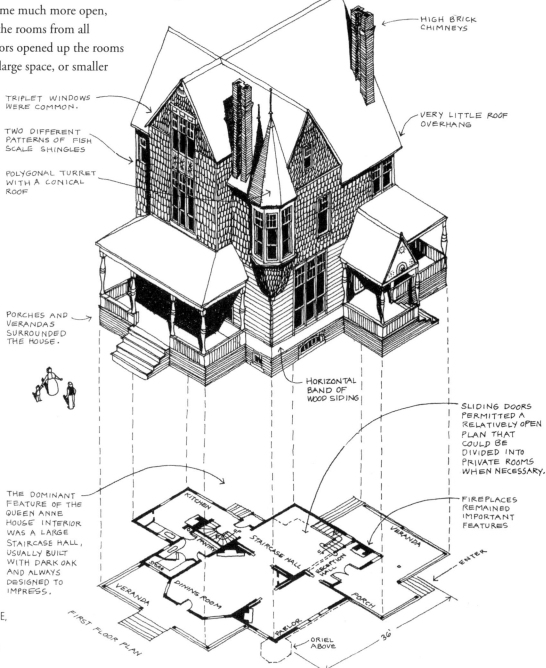

HIGH BRICK CHIMNEYS

VERY LITTLE ROOF OVERHANG

TRIPLET WINDOWS WERE COMMON.

TWO DIFFERENT PATTERNS OF FISH SCALE SHINGLES

POLYGONAL TURRET WITH A CONICAL ROOF

PORCHES AND VERANDAS SURROUNDED THE HOUSE.

HORIZONTAL BAND OF WOOD SIDING

SLIDING DOORS PERMITTED A RELATIVELY OPEN PLAN THAT COULD BE DIVIDED INTO PRIVATE ROOMS WHEN NECESSARY.

FIREPLACES REMAINED IMPORTANT FEATURES

THE DOMINANT FEATURE OF THE QUEEN ANNE HOUSE INTERIOR WAS A LARGE STAIRCASE HALL, USUALLY BUILT WITH DARK OAK AND ALWAYS DESIGNED TO IMPRESS.

KITCHEN

STAIRCASE HALL

RECEPTION HALL

VERANDA

ENTER

STORE

DINING ROOM

PORCH

VERANDA

PARLOR

ORIEL ABOVE

36'

FIRST FLOOR PLAN

1879

TYPICAL EARLY QUEEN ANNE HOUSE, SHORT HILLS, NEW JERSEY
LAMB AND WHEELER, ARCHITECTS

The Queen Anne Style borrowed many of its details from Islamic styles (Moorish or Turkish), with exotic results. Cusped arches, onion-shaped domes, and circular open kiosks are regularly found in Queen Anne buildings. Other exotic features, such as the oval and partial or full circular openings, were taken from the Orient.

Although it was popular for only twenty years, the impact of the Queen Anne Style on the American house-building scene was enormous: The rapid growth of the economy during the period of popularity resulted in the erection of hundreds of thousands of Queen Anne houses. The style represented a reaction to High Victorian "reality" and renewed interest in the picturesque.

1890
QUEEN ANNE HOUSE, CALVERT, TEXAS

METAL ROOF CRESTING

OCTAGONAL TOWER WITH DOMED ROOF

TALL ELABORATE BRICK CHIMNEY

SMALL PANES IN THE UPPER SASH WERE COMMON.

STRAIGHT TOP ARCHES OVER PORCHES WERE AS COMMON AS ROUND ARCHES, POINTED ARCHES WERE NEVER USED.

EXTRA LARGE WINDOWS

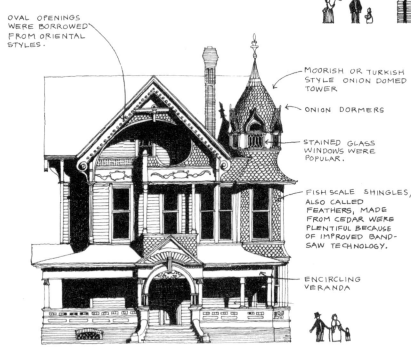

OVAL OPENINGS WERE BORROWED FROM ORIENTAL STYLES.

MOORISH OR TURKISH STYLE ONION DOMED TOWER

ONION DORMERS

STAINED GLASS WINDOWS WERE POPULAR.

FISH SCALE SHINGLES, ALSO CALLED FEATHERS, MADE FROM CEDAR WERE PLENTIFUL BECAUSE OF IMPROVED BAND-SAW TECHNOLOGY.

ENCIRCLING VERANDA

1884
FREDERICK MITCHELL HOUSE, LOS ANGELES, CALIFORNIA
ARCHITECT UNKNOWN

Late Queen Anne houses influenced and were influenced by the new Richardsonian Romanesque, Shingle, and Norman styles shown on pages 156 through 165. The example shown opposite combines features from these four major American styles. The result, as in many late nineteenth century houses, is hard to categorize.

1892

A LATE QUEEN ANNE HOUSE, DESIGN #420 FROM *MODERN HOUSES* BY R. W. SHOPPELL

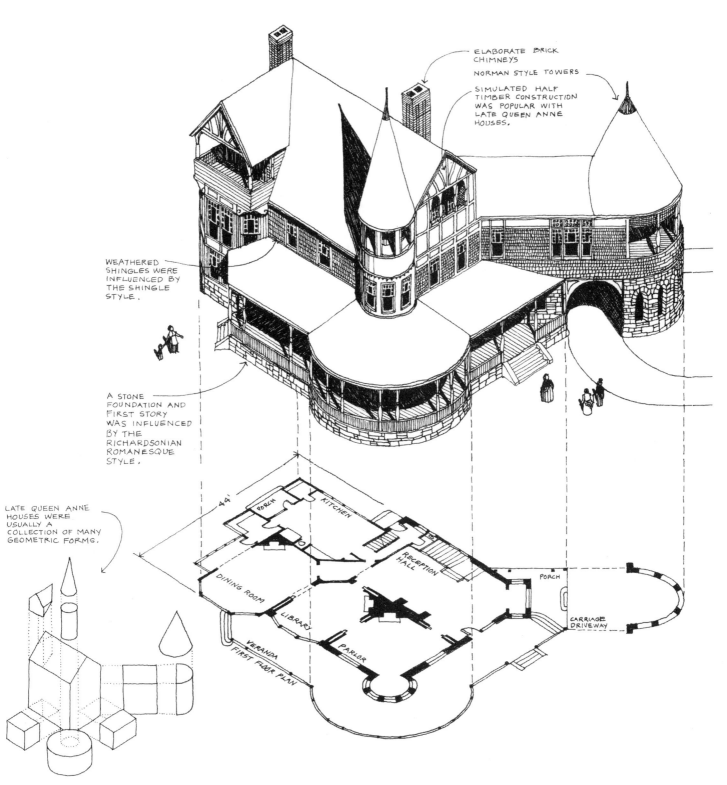

ELABORATE BRICK CHIMNEYS

NORMAN STYLE TOWERS

SIMULATED HALF TIMBER CONSTRUCTION WAS POPULAR WITH LATE QUEEN ANNE HOUSES.

WEATHERED SHINGLES WERE INFLUENCED BY THE SHINGLE STYLE.

A STONE FOUNDATION AND FIRST STORY WAS INFLUENCED BY THE RICHARDSONIAN ROMANESQUE STYLE.

LATE QUEEN ANNE HOUSES WERE USUALLY A COLLECTION OF MANY GEOMETRIC FORMS.

KITCHEN

PORCH

DINING ROOM

RECEPTION HALL

PORCH

LIBRARY

CARRIAGE DRIVEWAY

VERANDA

PARLOR

FIRST FLOOR PLAN

44'

Eastlake

Countrywide
1880

The Eastlake Style was simply a decorative style of ornamentation found on houses of various other Victorian styles, primarily the Queen Anne and Stick Styles. It is named after Charles L. Eastlake, an English architect who wrote *Hints on Household Taste*, published in 1868. The book was reprinted in America in 1872 and became so popular that it required six editions within eleven years.

In his book, Eastlake promotes a peculiar kind of furniture and interior decoration that was angular, notched and carved, and deliberately opposed to the curved shapes of French Baroque Revival Styles such as the Second Empire. Traditionally, furniture makers imitated architectural forms, but Eastlake reversed this process. Eastlake houses had architectural ornamentation that had copied the furniture inside the house.

American housebuilders found their own interpretations of the Eastlake Style, much to the displeasure of Eastlake himself. Porch posts, railings, and balustrades were characterized by a massive, oversized, and robust Eastlake quality; but over the years they became more curvelinear, more Baroque in style. This was a result not only of the independent minds of American architects and builders, but also of the need to have these members machine made—turned on a mechanical lathe.

Builders and architects, influenced by the Queen Anne Style, put no limits on the arrangement of forms or the amount of ornamentation on the exterior of the Eastlake house. Many of the pieces of the house had to be ordered by catalog and assembled at the housebuilding site, like a large piece of furniture.

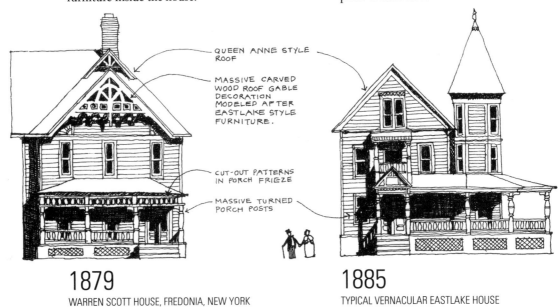

QUEEN ANNE STYLE ROOF

MASSIVE CARVED WOOD ROOF GABLE DECORATION MODELED AFTER EASTLAKE STYLE FURNITURE.

CUT-OUT PATTERNS IN PORCH FRIEZE

MASSIVE TURNED PORCH POSTS

1879
WARREN SCOTT HOUSE, FREDONIA, NEW YORK

1885
TYPICAL VERNACULAR EASTLAKE HOUSE

The most famous Victorian house in America is the William McKendrie Carson mansion in Eureka, California, shown below. Carson was the owner of redwood forests in northern California and was said to have used every kind of wood on the world market in the construction of his house. More than one hundred carpenters and other woodworkers worked on the hand-carved ornamentation for the eighteen-room Eastlake mansion for over two years.

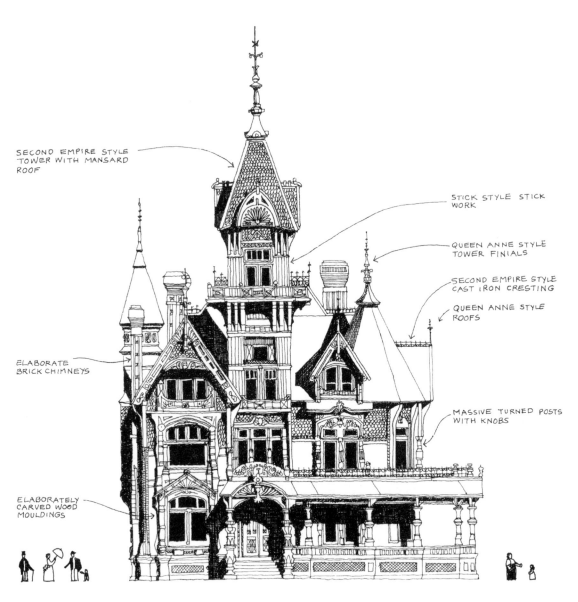

SECOND EMPIRE STYLE TOWER WITH MANSARD ROOF

STICK STYLE STICK WORK

QUEEN ANNE STYLE TOWER FINIALS

SECOND EMPIRE STYLE CAST IRON CRESTING

QUEEN ANNE STYLE ROOFS

ELABORATE BRICK CHIMNEYS

MASSIVE TURNED POSTS WITH KNOBS

ELABORATELY CARVED WOOD MOULDINGS

1885

WILLIAM McKENDRIE CARSON HOUSE, EUREKA, CALIFORNIA
SAMUEL AND JOSEPH NEWSOM, ARCHITECTS

Richardsonian Romanesque

Countrywide 1885

Richardsonian Romanesque houses, following the work of American architect Henry Hobson Richardson (1838–1886), are characterized by rock-faced masonry walls with heavily emphasized arches, lintels, and other structural features. A sense of weight, massiveness, and solidity were stressed, making a significant departure from the delicate, decorative detailing of the Queen Anne Style.

American architects had experimented with the Romanesque Style in the 1840s and 1850s based on the pre-Gothic architecture of Europe. (This style was used primarily for nonresidential buildings so it does not appear in this book.)

As interpreted by Richardson in the 1870s and 1880s, the Romanesque became a different, much bolder, uniquely American style. His buildings were heavier, more horizontal, and much rougher in texture. Robust columns, deep window reveals, cavernous door openings, and rough-cut ashlar stone construction were employed to emphasize weight.

H. H. Richardson is generally recognized as one of the three greatest American-born architects (along with Louis Sullivan and Frank Lloyd Wright). After graduating from Harvard in 1859 he became the second American architect (after Richard M. Hunt) to attend the Ecole des Beaux-Arts in Paris. After

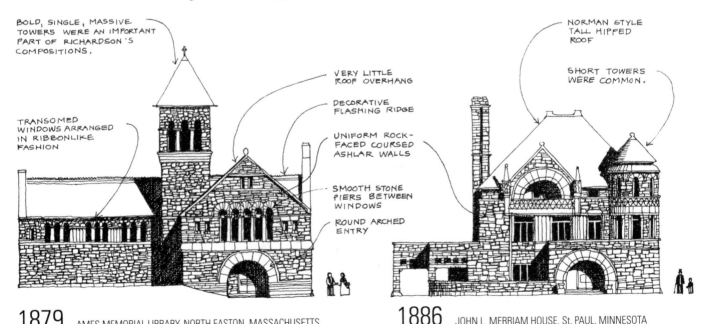

BOLD, SINGLE, MASSIVE TOWERS WERE AN IMPORTANT PART OF RICHARDSON'S COMPOSITIONS.

TRANSOMED WINDOWS ARRANGED IN RIBBONLIKE FASHION

VERY LITTLE ROOF OVERHANG

DECORATIVE FLASHING RIDGE

UNIFORM ROCK-FACED COURSED ASHLAR WALLS

SMOOTH STONE PIERS BETWEEN WINDOWS

ROUND ARCHED ENTRY

NORMAN STYLE TALL HIPPED ROOF

SHORT TOWERS WERE COMMON.

1879 AMES MEMORIAL LIBRARY, NORTH EASTON, MASSACHUSETTS
H. H. RICHARDSON, ARCHITECT

1886 JOHN L. MERRIAM HOUSE, St. PAUL, MINNESOTA
MOULD AND McNICHOL, ARCHITECTS

returning to America in 1865 he began a practice in New York City and in 1872 won the Trinity Church competition in Boston and with it, the commission to the building. The resulting design brought instant fame to Richardson and was the first influence on the change of the American concept of Romanesque to Richardsonian Romanesque.

By 1885, city halls, schools, railroad stations, county court houses, libraries, jails, and other public buildings were being built in the Richardsonian Romanesque Style all over the country. Richardson himself produced very few houses in his style but his work inspired many followers. His details such as broad round arches, squat chimneys and columns, and carved intertwining floral stone work found their way into the vocabulary of many local builders. The style was immensely popular though relatively short-lived.

1885

JOHN J. GLESSNER HOUSE, CHICAGO, ILLINOIS
H. H. RICHARDSON, ARCHITECT

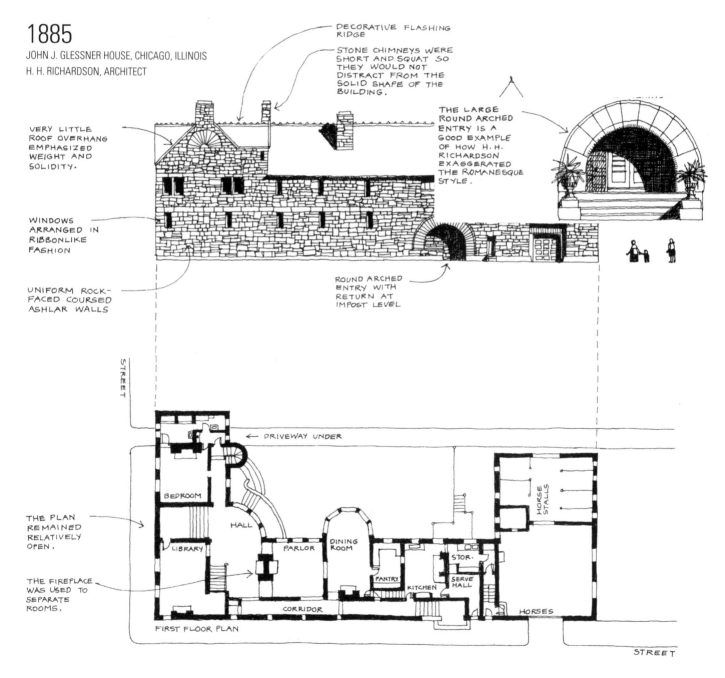

DECORATIVE FLASHING RIDGE

STONE CHIMNEYS WERE SHORT AND SQUAT SO THEY WOULD NOT DISTRACT FROM THE SOLID SHAPE OF THE BUILDING.

THE LARGE ROUND ARCHED ENTRY IS A GOOD EXAMPLE OF HOW H. H. RICHARDSON EXAGGERATED THE ROMANESQUE STYLE.

VERY LITTLE ROOF OVERHANG EMPHASIZED WEIGHT AND SOLIDITY.

WINDOWS ARRANGED IN RIBBONLIKE FASHION

UNIFORM ROCK-FACED COURSED ASHLAR WALLS

ROUND ARCHED ENTRY WITH RETURN AT IMPOST LEVEL

STREET

DRIVEWAY UNDER

BEDROOM

HALL

HORSE STALLS

THE PLAN REMAINED RELATIVELY OPEN.

LIBRARY

PARLOR

DINING ROOM

STOR.

THE FIREPLACE WAS USED TO SEPARATE ROOMS.

PANTRY

KITCHEN

SERVE HALL

CORRIDOR

HORSES

FIRST FLOOR PLAN

STREET

Norman

East
1885

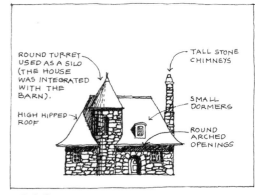

ROUND TURRET USED AS A SILO (THE HOUSE WAS INTEGRATED WITH THE BARN).

TALL STONE CHIMNEYS

HIGH HIPPED ROOF

SMALL DORMERS

ROUND ARCHED OPENINGS

1600

THE FRENCH, NORMAN COUNTRY HOME WAS THE PRIMARY INSPIRATION FOR THE AMERICAN NORMAN STYLE.

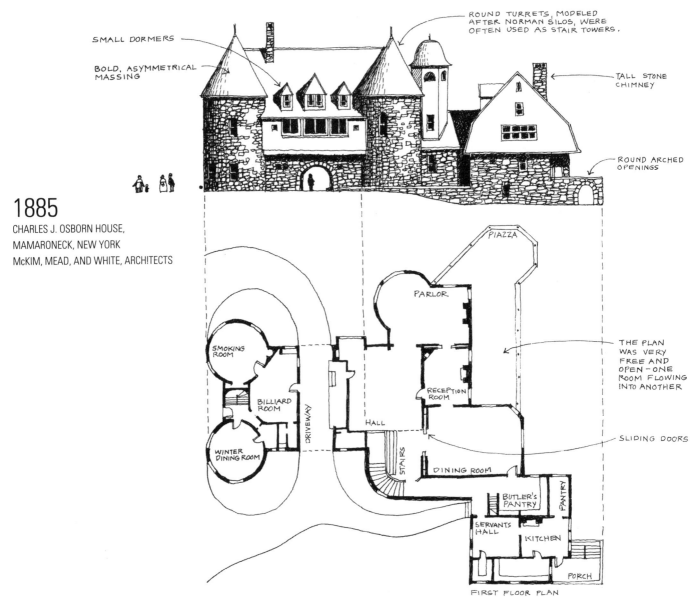

SMALL DORMERS

BOLD, ASYMMETRICAL MASSING

ROUND TURRETS, MODELED AFTER NORMAN SILOS, WERE OFTEN USED AS STAIR TOWERS.

TALL STONE CHIMNEY

ROUND ARCHED OPENINGS

1885

CHARLES J. OSBORN HOUSE,
MAMARONECK, NEW YORK
McKIM, MEAD, AND WHITE, ARCHITECTS

PIAZZA

PARLOR

SMOKING ROOM

BILLIARD ROOM

DRIVEWAY

WINTER DINING ROOM

RECEPTION ROOM

HALL

STAIRS

DINING ROOM

THE PLAN WAS VERY FREE AND OPEN — ONE ROOM FLOWING INTO ANOTHER

SLIDING DOORS

BUTLER'S PANTRY

PANTRY

SERVANTS HALL

KITCHEN

PORCH

FIRST FLOOR PLAN

The Norman Style was a minor movement based on the country house found in the Normandy area of France. Many historians have labeled it a transitional style linking the Queen Anne with the Shingle Style but it is more obviously a prediction of the Period Styles of the 1930s, shown on page 210.

By 1885 the popularity of the Queen Anne Style in particular was waning, as were all the Victorian styles in general. Architects interested in plainer, more simplified construction were returning to American colonial detailing and building styles. But, it was still important to keep the plan and the massing very free and organic. Building forms grew bolder, more massive, thicker, and heavier, and ornamentation virtually disappeared.

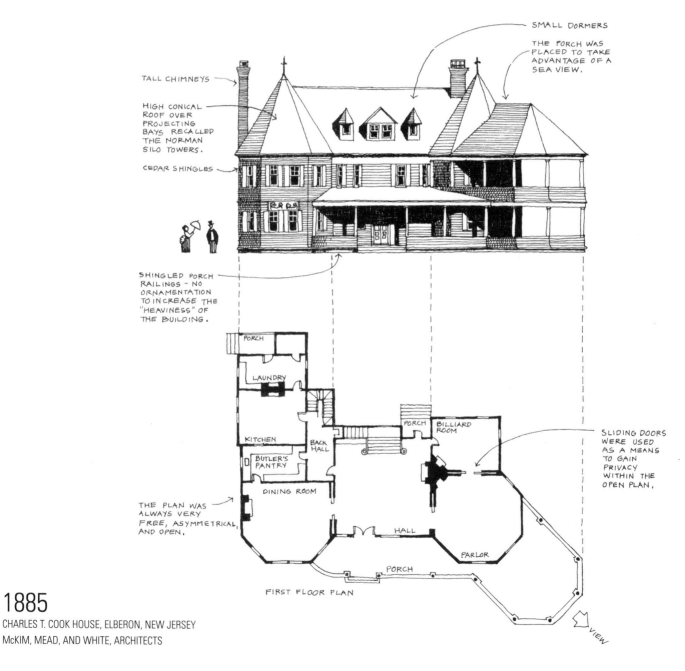

SMALL DORMERS

THE PORCH WAS PLACED TO TAKE ADVANTAGE OF A SEA VIEW.

TALL CHIMNEYS

HIGH CONICAL ROOF OVER PROJECTING BAYS RECALLED THE NORMAN SILO TOWERS.

CEDAR SHINGLES

SHINGLED PORCH RAILINGS - NO ORNAMENTATION TO INCREASE THE "HEAVINESS" OF THE BUILDING.

PORCH

LAUNDRY

KITCHEN

BUTLER'S PANTRY

BACK HALL

PORCH

BILLIARD ROOM

SLIDING DOORS WERE USED AS A MEANS TO GAIN PRIVACY WITHIN THE OPEN PLAN.

DINING ROOM

THE PLAN WAS ALWAYS VERY FREE, ASYMMETRICAL, AND OPEN.

HALL

PARLOR

PORCH

VIEW

FIRST FLOOR PLAN

1885

CHARLES T. COOK HOUSE, ELBERON, NEW JERSEY
McKIM, MEAD, AND WHITE, ARCHITECTS

Shingle

East Coast
1885

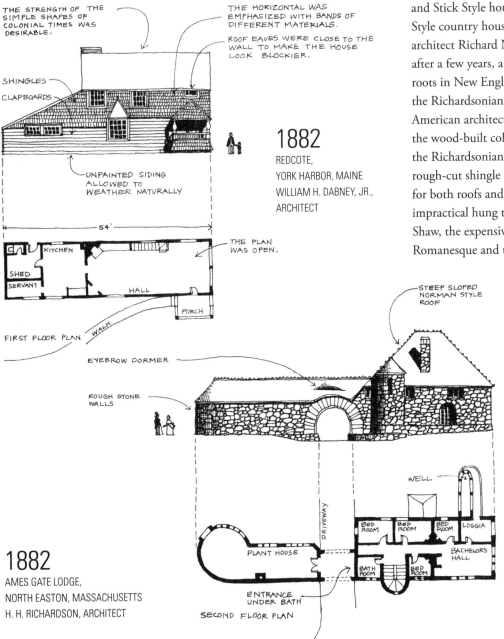

THE STRENGTH OF THE SIMPLE SHAPES OF COLONIAL TIMES WAS DESIRABLE.

THE HORIZONTAL WAS EMPHASIZED WITH BANDS OF DIFFERENT MATERIALS.

ROOF EAVES WERE CLOSE TO THE WALL TO MAKE THE HOUSE LOOK BLOCKIER.

SHINGLES
CLAPBOARDS

UNPAINTED SIDING ALLOWED TO WEATHER NATURALLY

54'

1882
REDCOTE,
YORK HARBOR, MAINE
WILLIAM H. DABNEY, JR.,
ARCHITECT

KITCHEN
SHED
SERVANT
HALL
PORCH

THE PLAN WAS OPEN.

FIRST FLOOR PLAN
WALK

EYEBROW DORMER

ROUGH STONE WALLS

STEEP SLOPED NORMAN STYLE ROOF

WELL

DRIVEWAY
PLANT HOUSE
BED ROOM
BED ROOM
BED ROOM
LOGGIA
BACHELOR'S HALL
BATH ROOM
BED ROOM

ENTRANCE UNDER BATH

SECOND FLOOR PLAN

1882
AMES GATE LODGE,
NORTH EASTON, MASSACHUSETTS
H. H. RICHARDSON, ARCHITECT

In the early 1880s, wealthy Americans sought comfortable, fashionable dwellings away from the cities for vacation retreats, primarily along the unspoiled Atlantic Coast. At first, Queen Anne and Stick Style houses, based on the Jacobean Style country houses popularized in England by architect Richard Norman Shaw, were built. But after a few years, a more American style, with its roots in New England Colonial architecture and the Richardsonian Romanesque Style, emerged. American architects began to recall the simplicity of the wood-built colonial houses and the strength of the Richardsonian Romanesque Style and used the rough-cut shingle as their primary cladding material for both roofs and walls. The shingle replaced the impractical hung tile of Jacobean buildings of Shaw, the expensive stone of the Richardsonian Romanesque and the decorative woodwork of the Queen Anne wall. The Shingle Style, so designated by architectural historian Vincent Scully, was popular for over a decade.

H. H. Richardson again became the preeminent spokesman for the Early Shingle Style. His translation of his own Richardsonian Romanesque stone house into a less expensive, more fashionable, shingle-clad house retained the strength and boldness of his earlier work. The rough-cut shingle, left to weather naturally, was perfectly compatible with the rubble stone, sometimes boulder size, he often used to lend a sense of

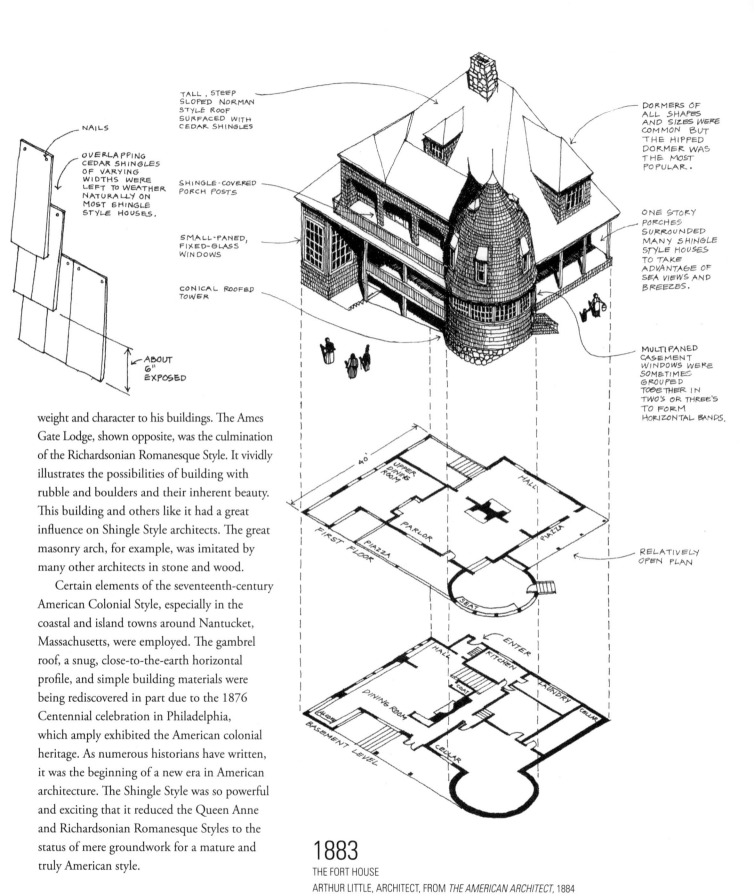

NAILS

OVERLAPPING CEDAR SHINGLES OF VARYING WIDTHS WERE LEFT TO WEATHER NATURALLY ON MOST SHINGLE STYLE HOUSES.

TALL, STEEP SLOPED NORMAN STYLE ROOF SURFACED WITH CEDAR SHINGLES

SHINGLE-COVERED PORCH POSTS

SMALL-PANED, FIXED-GLASS WINDOWS

CONICAL ROOFED TOWER

ABOUT 6" EXPOSED

DORMERS OF ALL SHAPES AND SIZES WERE COMMON BUT THE HIPPED DORMER WAS THE MOST POPULAR.

ONE STORY PORCHES SURROUNDED MANY SHINGLE STYLE HOUSES TO TAKE ADVANTAGE OF SEA VIEWS AND BREEZES.

MULTIPANED CASEMENT WINDOWS WERE SOMETIMES GROUPED TOGETHER IN TWO'S OR THREE'S TO FORM HORIZONTAL BANDS.

40'

UPPER DINING ROOM

HALL

PARLOR

FIRST FLOOR

PIAZZA

PIAZZA

SEAT

RELATIVELY OPEN PLAN

ENTER

KITCHEN

HALL

COAT

LAUNDRY

CELLAR

DINING ROOM

CLOS

BASEMENT LEVEL

CELLAR

weight and character to his buildings. The Ames Gate Lodge, shown opposite, was the culmination of the Richardsonian Romanesque Style. It vividly illustrates the possibilities of building with rubble and boulders and their inherent beauty. This building and others like it had a great influence on Shingle Style architects. The great masonry arch, for example, was imitated by many other architects in stone and wood.

Certain elements of the seventeenth-century American Colonial Style, especially in the coastal and island towns around Nantucket, Massachusetts, were employed. The gambrel roof, a snug, close-to-the-earth horizontal profile, and simple building materials were being rediscovered in part due to the 1876 Centennial celebration in Philadelphia, which amply exhibited the American colonial heritage. As numerous historians have written, it was the beginning of a new era in American architecture. The Shingle Style was so powerful and exciting that it reduced the Queen Anne and Richardsonian Romanesque Styles to the status of mere groundwork for a mature and truly American style.

1883

THE FORT HOUSE

ARTHUR LITTLE, ARCHITECT, FROM *THE AMERICAN ARCHITECT*, 1884

As eclectic as some of the larger seaside houses were, their overall conception and character remained true to the Shingle Style. Gambrels, porches, bays, and dormers were interwoven into a continuity of exterior and interior spaces. Entries were clearly defined, usually with over scaled openings like the Kragsyde arch below or the one-half beehive roof over the Grasshead entry on the opposite page. And, of course, the composition of forms was always covered with weathered brownish-gray shingles.

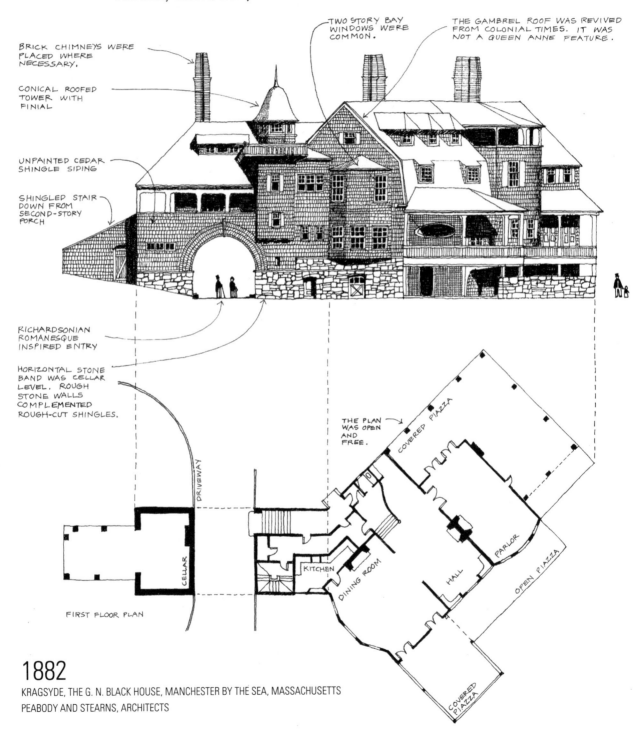

TWO STORY BAY WINDOWS WERE COMMON.

THE GAMBREL ROOF WAS REVIVED FROM COLONIAL TIMES. IT WAS NOT A QUEEN ANNE FEATURE.

BRICK CHIMNEYS WERE PLACED WHERE NECESSARY.

CONICAL ROOFED TOWER WITH FINIAL

UNPAINTED CEDAR SHINGLE SIDING

SHINGLED STAIR DOWN FROM SECOND-STORY PORCH

RICHARDSONIAN ROMANESQUE INSPIRED ENTRY

HORIZONTAL STONE BAND WAS CELLAR LEVEL. ROUGH STONE WALLS COMPLEMENTED ROUGH-CUT SHINGLES.

THE PLAN WAS OPEN AND FREE.

DRIVEWAY

CELLAR

KITCHEN

DINING ROOM

COVERED PIAZZA

HALL

PARLOR

OPEN PIAZZA

COVERED PIAZZA

FIRST FLOOR PLAN

1882

KRAGSYDE, THE G. N. BLACK HOUSE, MANCHESTER BY THE SEA, MASSACHUSETTS
PEABODY AND STEARNS, ARCHITECTS

The Shingle Style was a kind of Colonial Revival Style in which the frame was totally concealed, and walls and roof were perceived as a thin skin (of shingles) shaped by the enclosed living space. It was the opposite of the structuralism of the Stick Style (p. 144). It was a style that brought new freedom and openness into the planning of the American house. With central heating, even in cold regions, the interior was opened to provide a new sense of space. The hall was expanded into a large and informal living room and soon became the focal point of the activities of the house. The public spaces of the first floor revolved around a fireplace—an idea that Frank Lloyd Wright was to develop later.

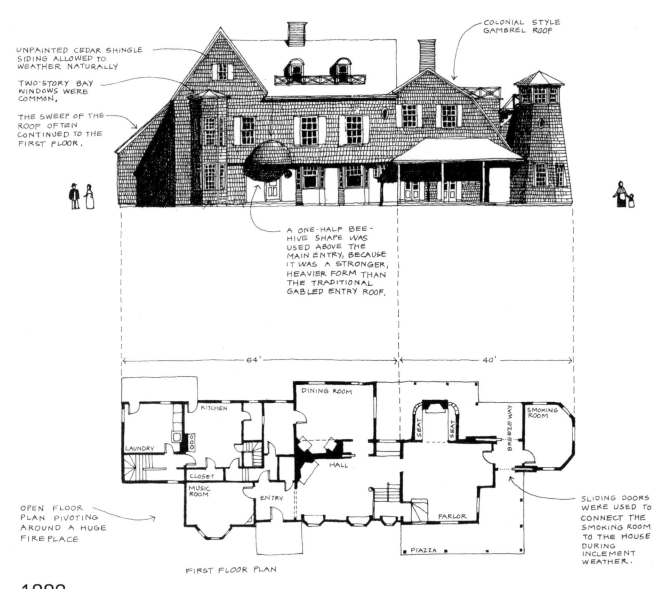

UNPAINTED CEDAR SHINGLE SIDING ALLOWED TO WEATHER NATURALLY

TWO-STORY BAY WINDOWS WERE COMMON.

THE SWEEP OF THE ROOF OFTEN CONTINUED TO THE FIRST FLOOR.

COLONIAL STYLE GAMBREL ROOF

A ONE-HALF BEE-HIVE SHAPE WAS USED ABOVE THE MAIN ENTRY, BECAUSE IT WAS A STRONGER, HEAVIER FORM THAN THE TRADITIONAL GABLED ENTRY ROOF.

64'   40'

KITCHEN
DINING ROOM
SMOKING ROOM
LAUNDRY
SEAT   SEAT
BREEZEWAY
CLOSET
HALL
MUSIC ROOM
ENTRY
PARLOR
PIAZZA

OPEN FLOOR PLAN PIVOTING AROUND A HUGE FIREPLACE

SLIDING DOORS WERE USED TO CONNECT THE SMOKING ROOM TO THE HOUSE DURING INCLEMENT WEATHER.

FIRST FLOOR PLAN

1882 GRASSHEAD, THE MR. AND MRS. JAMES LITTLE HOUSE, SWAMPSCOTT, MASSACHUSETTS
ARTHUR LITTLE, ARCHITECT

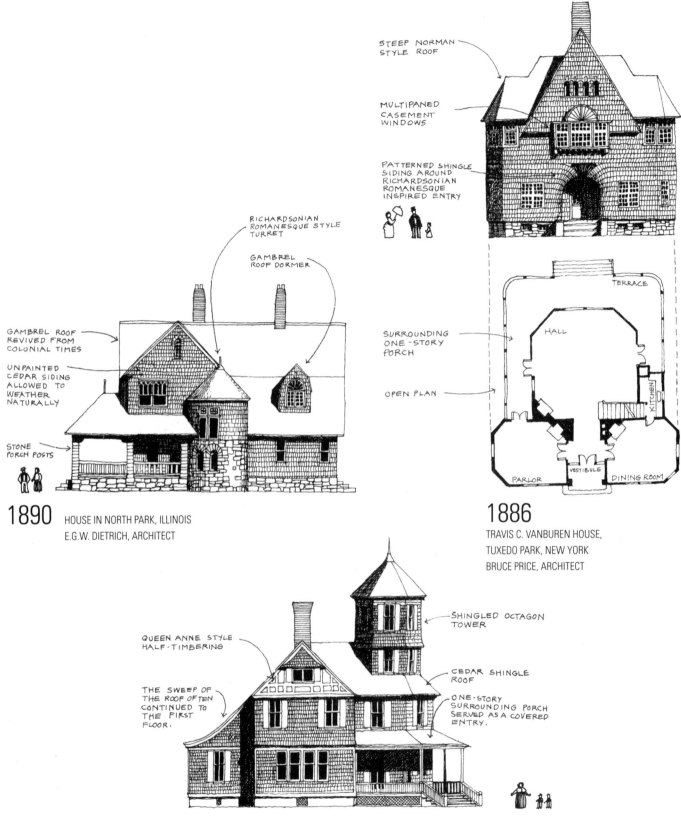

STEEP NORMAN
STYLE ROOF

MULTIPANED
CASEMENT
WINDOWS

PATTERNED SHINGLE
SIDING AROUND
RICHARDSONIAN
ROMANESQUE
INSPIRED ENTRY

TERRACE

HALL

KITCHEN

SURROUNDING
ONE-STORY
PORCH

OPEN PLAN

PARLOR

VESTIBULE

DINING ROOM

1886

TRAVIS C. VANBUREN HOUSE,
TUXEDO PARK, NEW YORK
BRUCE PRICE, ARCHITECT

RICHARDSONIAN
ROMANESQUE STYLE
TURRET

GAMBREL
ROOF DORMER

GAMBREL ROOF
REVIVED FROM
COLONIAL TIMES

UNPAINTED
CEDAR SIDING
ALLOWED TO
WEATHER
NATURALLY

STONE
PORCH POSTS

1890 HOUSE IN NORTH PARK, ILLINOIS
E.G.W. DIETRICH, ARCHITECT

QUEEN ANNE STYLE
HALF-TIMBERING

THE SWEEP OF
THE ROOF OFTEN
CONTINUED TO
THE FIRST
FLOOR.

SHINGLED OCTAGON
TOWER

CEDAR SHINGLE
ROOF

ONE-STORY
SURROUNDING PORCH
SERVED AS A COVERED
ENTRY.

1886 WARREN WESTON HOUSE, CHAPPAQUIDDICK ISLAND, MASSACHUSETTS

Many architectural firms worked in the Shingle Style in the 1880s. Some were conservative, basing their work heavily on the Queen Anne Style, as shown opposite, and others were more daring, expressing modern ideas with new forms, as shown below.

Some of America's best known architects, such as H. H. Richardson, the office of McKim, Mead, and White, William Ralph Emerson, and Bruce Price, were associated with the Shingle Style. Their work, culminating with the two examples shown on this page, was achieved in a relatively short time and was not only highly successful on its own terms, but also laid a firm foundation for later architectural accomplishments.

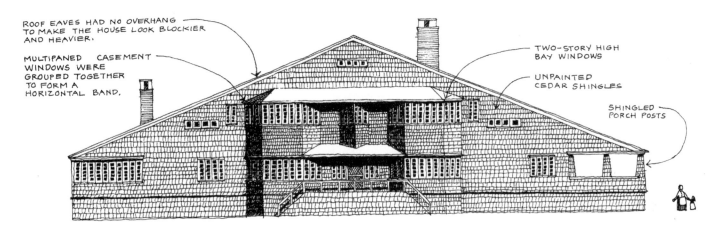

ROOF EAVES HAD NO OVERHANG TO MAKE THE HOUSE LOOK BLOCKIER AND HEAVIER.

MULTIPANED CASEMENT WINDOWS WERE GROUPED TOGETHER TO FORM A HORIZONTAL BAND.

TWO-STORY HIGH BAY WINDOWS

UNPAINTED CEDAR SHINGLES

SHINGLED PORCH POSTS

1887 W. G. LOW RESIDENCE, BRISTOL, RHODE ISLAND
McKIM, MEAD, AND WHITE, ARCHITECTS

Baled Hay and Sod

Nebraska 1890

Out on the Nebraska prairie, there were no trees, no stone, no fuel for firing bricks, nothing but flat, grassy land. Like the Indian who constructed lodges from the earth (p. 20), the pioneers turned to the materials furnished by the environment to build their homes. Wild grasses and domestic hays baled into large two-feet by two-feet by four-feet building blocks and sod bricks, cut from the soil (Nebraska marble) made substantial, well-insulated homes.

Early settlers lived in quickly built dugouts carved from small ravines or south-facing hills to gain heat from the sun and to shed the winter winds. The front of the dugout was usually walled with sod bricks into which a door and window were cut. When the family was able, they built a more substantial home of baled hay or sod.

Baling machines were introduced to Nebraska in the 1850s, and by 1890, settlers were using the hay bales as a construction material for houses and barns. Baled hay cost practically nothing, and building methods, as shown below, were so simple they were almost like using toy building blocks. It was not uncommon for a baled hay house or barn to be built in less than a week.

As might be expected, fire was a particular hazard to the baled hay house and extreme care had to be taken with cooking and heating, usually with cast-iron stoves. Another disadvantage of baled hay houses with unplastered walls (about half of those built) was that they made an excellent breeding ground for fleas.

The height of baled hay house construction was from 1900 to 1935, and the last baled hay house was built in 1939. The baled hay house never had the popularity of the sod house.

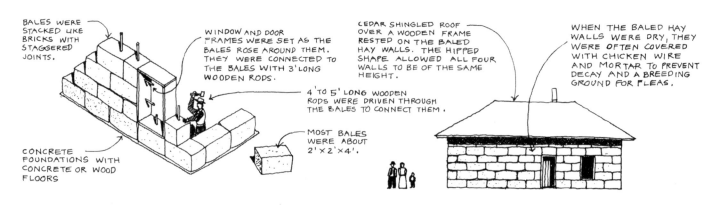

BALES WERE STACKED LIKE BRICKS WITH STAGGERED JOINTS.

WINDOW AND DOOR FRAMES WERE SET AS THE BALES ROSE AROUND THEM. THEY WERE CONNECTED TO THE BALES WITH 3' LONG WOODEN RODS.

CEDAR SHINGLED ROOF OVER A WOODEN FRAME RESTED ON THE BALED HAY WALLS. THE HIPPED SHAPE ALLOWED ALL FOUR WALLS TO BE OF THE SAME HEIGHT.

WHEN THE BALED HAY WALLS WERE DRY, THEY WERE OFTEN COVERED WITH CHICKEN WIRE AND MORTAR TO PREVENT DECAY AND A BREEDING GROUND FOR FLEAS.

4' TO 5' LONG WOODEN RODS WERE DRIVEN THROUGH THE BALES TO CONNECT THEM.

MOST BALES WERE ABOUT 2' X 2' X 4'.

CONCRETE FOUNDATIONS WITH CONCRETE OR WOOD FLOORS

BALED HAY BUILDING TECHNOLOGY, NEBRASKA

1905 SIMONTON PURDUM BALED HAY HOUSE, NEBRASKA

Houses made from sod bricks were known as Nebraska "soddies." The bricks were made from ground plowed into strips twelve to fourteen inches thick. These strips were cut into two-foot lengths and then placed lengthwise, with the green grass facing down, making a wall two-feet thick. With every few layers, the strips were placed crosswise to form an overlapping solid wall. When the desired height was reached, a huge cedar ridge pole and cedar rafters were placed on the top of the walls to support a willow brush matting and sod roof. Continuous leaking was a problem that was usually solved with strategically placed pans. The more affluent settlers built their soddies with a wood frame roof covered with sheeting boards and tar paper to support the sod. The tar paper stopped the leaking and the sod provided the necessary insulation. The window frames were often whitewashed in an attempt to control dirt and to reflect more light into the dark rooms. Bright plants in tin cans were set in the windows to brighten up the dank interior.

Soddies were warm in the winter and cool in the summer because of the excellent insulating qualities of the thick earth walls. Leaking, dirt, and bugs were the houses' worst problems, but they were able to resist the fierce Nebraska weather for an average life of seven years. After that, families were often able to afford to build a new wood frame structure. Although the era of soddy living came to an end around 1910, some sod houses still exist and are occupied in Nebraska.

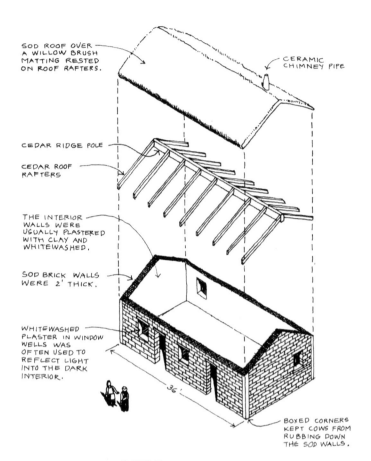

1890 TYPICAL SOD HOUSE CONSTRUCTION, NEBRASKA

SOD ROOF OVER A WILLOW BRUSH MATTING RESTED ON ROOF RAFTERS.

CERAMIC CHIMNEY PIPE

CEDAR RIDGE POLE

CEDAR ROOF RAFTERS

THE INTERIOR WALLS WERE USUALLY PLASTERED WITH CLAY AND WHITEWASHED.

SOD BRICK WALLS WERE 2' THICK.

WHITEWASHED PLASTER IN WINDOW WELLS WAS OFTEN USED TO REFLECT LIGHT INTO THE DARK INTERIOR.

BOXED CORNERS KEPT COWS FROM RUBBING DOWN THE SOD WALLS.

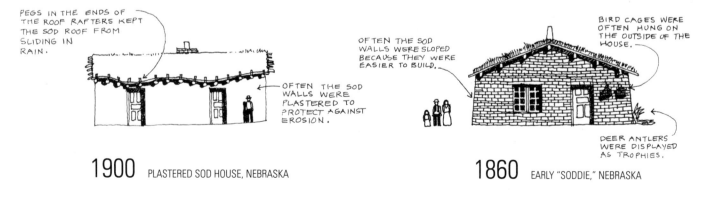

1900 PLASTERED SOD HOUSE, NEBRASKA

PEGS IN THE ENDS OF THE ROOF RAFTERS KEPT THE SOD ROOF FROM SLIDING IN RAIN.

OFTEN THE SOD WALLS WERE PLASTERED TO PROTECT AGAINST EROSION.

1860 EARLY "SODDIE," NEBRASKA

OFTEN THE SOD WALLS WERE SLOPED BECAUSE THEY WERE EASIER TO BUILD.

BIRD CAGES WERE OFTEN HUNG ON THE OUTSIDE OF THE HOUSE.

DEER ANTLERS WERE DISPLAYED AS TROPHIES.

Chateauesque

Countrywide
1890

The Chateauesque Style was based on the great French chateau built under the reign of Francis I between 1515 and 1547. The style, sometimes called the Francis I Style, originally borrowed forms from the Italian Renaissance and combined them with native French Gothic ideas.

Very wealthy Americans became enamored of the Chateauesque Style when pictures of the original French chateaus began appearing in architectural and home decorating journals in the 1880s. The style was championed by Richard Morris Hunt, the first American to study at the Ecole des Beaux-Arts in Paris. His eclecticism was most ambitious— the W. K. Vanderbilt house was described by Montgomery Schuyler as "an attempt to summarize in one building the history of a most active and fruitful century in the history of architecture which included the late Gothic of the fifteenth century and the early Renaissance of the sixteenth century."

1547 CHATEAU DE CHAMBORD, LOIRE DISTRICT, FRANCE
DOMENICO DA CORTONA, ARCHITECT

STEEPLY PITCHED ROOFS

TALL, ELABORATE CHIMNEYS

The successful mixing of these two styles was an achievement difficult for any but the most scholarly and sensitive of the architectural profession. The popular Queen Anne Style was a less hazardous undertaking and better suited to the average size house. A select few wealthy Americans, however, interested in building a house to impress, called on architects like Hunt in the East, Solon Spencer Beman in the Midwest, and Nicholas J. Clayton in the Southwest to build them such elaborate mansions.

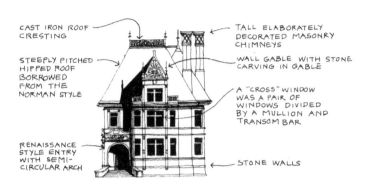

CAST IRON ROOF CRESTING

TALL ELABORATELY DECORATED MASONRY CHIMNEYS

STEEPLY PITCHED HIPPED ROOF BORROWED FROM THE NORMAN STYLE

WALL GABLE WITH STONE CARVING IN GABLE

A "CROSS" WINDOW WAS A PAIR OF WINDOWS DIVIDED BY A MULLION AND TRANSOM BAR

RENAISSANCE STYLE ENTRY WITH SEMI-CIRCULAR ARCH

STONE WALLS

1890 KIMBALL HOUSE, CHICAGO, ILLINOIS
SOLON SPENCER BEMAN, ARCHITECT

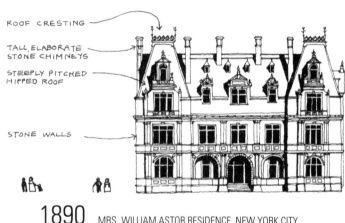

ROOF CRESTING

TALL, ELABORATE STONE CHIMNEYS

STEEPLY PITCHED HIPPED ROOF

STONE WALLS

1890 MRS. WILLIAM ASTOR RESIDENCE, NEW YORK CITY
RICHARD MORRIS HUNT, ARCHITECT

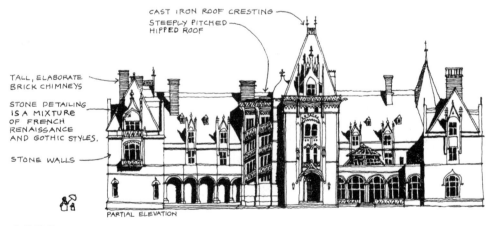

CAST IRON ROOF CRESTING
STEEPLY PITCHED HIPPED ROOF

TALL, ELABORATE BRICK CHIMNEYS

STONE DETAILING IS A MIXTURE OF FRENCH RENAISSANCE AND GOTHIC STYLES.

STONE WALLS

PARTIAL ELEVATION

1890 BILTMORE, GEORGE W. VANDERBILT RESIDENCE, ASHEVILLE, NORTH CAROLINA
RICHARD MORRIS HUNT, ARCHITECT

Georgian Revival

Countrywide
1895

The Georgian Revival Style house was an updated version of the original colonial Georgian house. It was a distinctive style, not a copy. It was generally larger than its original Colonial counterpart with many of the elements of the house oversized or exaggerated. Dormers and porches, for example, were much larger because of the need for increased space and the influence of the Queen Anne Style in which these forms became important features in the composition of the house. Historical details, such as an eighteenth-century swan's neck pediment, a Palladian window, Georgian Style classical wooden corner pilasters, Federal porch roofs, and Queen Anne multiupper sash window panes could be

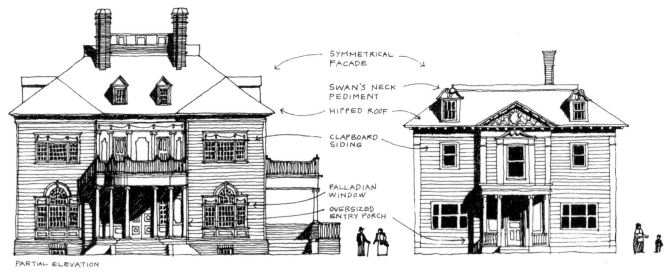

SYMMETRICAL FACADE

SWAN'S NECK PEDIMENT

HIPPED ROOF

CLAPBOARD SIDING

PALLADIAN WINDOW

OVERSIZED ENTRY PORCH

PARTIAL ELEVATION

1885
TAYLOR HOUSE, NEWPORT, RHODE ISLAND
McKIM, MEAD, AND WHITE, ARCHITECTS

1895
GEORGIAN REVIVAL HOUSE, MANCHESTER, NEW HAMPSHIRE

1915

A. W. FINLAY HOUSE, BROOKLINE, MASSACHUSETTS

C. T. McFARLAND, ARCHITECT

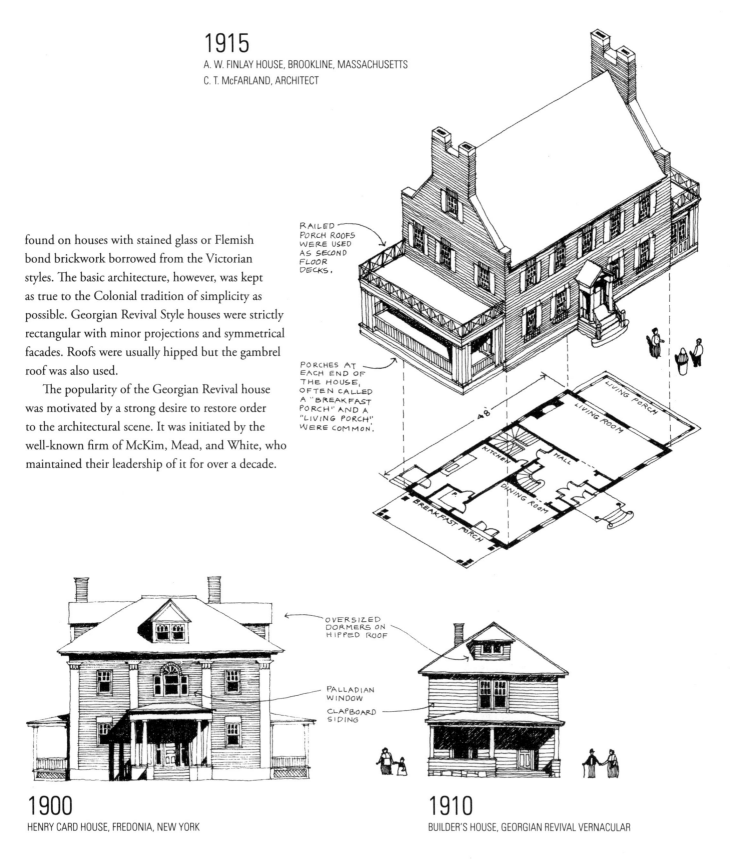

RAILED PORCH ROOFS WERE USED AS SECOND FLOOR DECKS.

PORCHES AT EACH END OF THE HOUSE, OFTEN CALLED A "BREAKFAST PORCH" AND A "LIVING PORCH" WERE COMMON.

found on houses with stained glass or Flemish bond brickwork borrowed from the Victorian styles. The basic architecture, however, was kept as true to the Colonial tradition of simplicity as possible. Georgian Revival Style houses were strictly rectangular with minor projections and symmetrical facades. Roofs were usually hipped but the gambrel roof was also used.

The popularity of the Georgian Revival house was motivated by a strong desire to restore order to the architectural scene. It was initiated by the well-known firm of McKim, Mead, and White, who maintained their leadership of it for over a decade.

OVERSIZED DORMERS ON HIPPED ROOF

PALLADIAN WINDOW

CLAPBOARD SIDING

1900

HENRY CARD HOUSE, FREDONIA, NEW YORK

1910

BUILDER'S HOUSE, GEORGIAN REVIVAL VERNACULAR

Mission

The Mission Style, also known as the Mission Revival Style, took the American Southwest, especially Southern California, by storm. It was the California counterpart of the Colonial Revival Style that later swept the East (p . 198). Both revivals were, to some degree, the result of disenchantment with prevailing late nineteenth-century architecture. But, most importantly, at last California had an architecture that was both original and traditional and not influenced by the eastern styles that had dominated the West since the Gold Rush.

The Mission Style had gained acceptance by 1885 but did not become popular until 1893 when the style was used for the California Building at the Columbian Exposition in Chicago. This was followed by the Manufacturers and Liberal Arts Building at the California Midwinter Fair in San Francisco in 1894. The architect for both buildings was A. Page Brown, one of the most successful Mission Style architects in the nineteenth century. However, the architect Lester S. Moore is generally given credit for first seeing and appreciating the possibilities of the Mission Style.

The basic simplicity of the Mission Style easily accommodated many different building technologies such as concrete, adobe, and stuccoed wood frame walls. Since the essential character of the style was expressed in bold, arched openings and large, unadorned expanses of plain whitewashed stuccoed surfaces, rather than in finely detailed craftsmanship, it could be either architect or contractor designed. Like the Craftsmen Style, and later the Bungalow Style, it became associated with the American Arts and Crafts movement, the primary emphasis of which was a return to the simple, the authentic, and the harmonious.

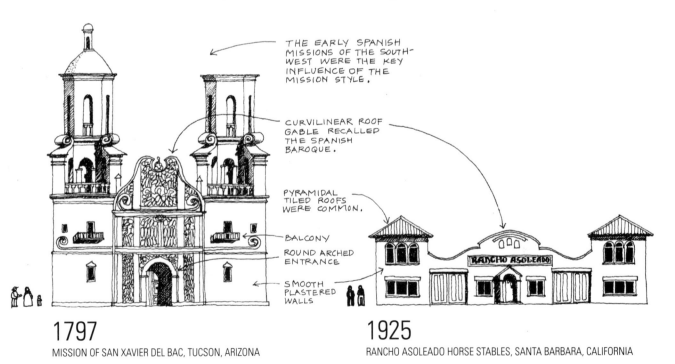

THE EARLY SPANISH MISSIONS OF THE SOUTH-WEST WERE THE KEY INFLUENCE OF THE MISSION STYLE.

CURVILINEAR ROOF GABLE RECALLED THE SPANISH BAROQUE.

PYRAMIDAL TILED ROOFS WERE COMMON.

BALCONY

ROUND ARCHED ENTRANCE

SMOOTH PLASTERED WALLS

1797
MISSION OF SAN XAVIER DEL BAC, TUCSON, ARIZONA

1925
RANCHO ASOLEADO HORSE STABLES, SANTA BARBARA, CALIFORNIA

By 1915 the Mission Style was being used for every conceivable building type from large hotels to motion picture studios. It was particularly popular in the construction of railroad stations in Nevada, New Mexico, Arizona, and California. Cities such as Riverside, California, remodeled their downtown in the Mission Style. Small towns, such as the wood false fronted town of Ojai, California, transformed their buildings into the calm, placid forms of the Mission Style. Whole new cities such as Planada, California, and Naples, California, were planned in the Mission Style.

One of the most creative American architects to use the style was Irving Gill. His early work (1907–1912), while quite blocky and simple, was obviously influenced by the traditional Mission Style. Later, his work became more "cubistic" and unrecognizably Mission (as shown in the Dodge House below), although he worked with the traditional Mission Style materials and detailing processes. His houses became known as stripped-down Mission Style, because of their austerity, and were quite influential in the initial development of the International Style (p. 214) in America in the 1930s.

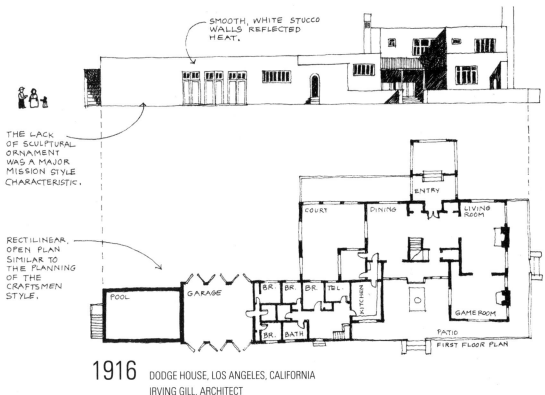

SMOOTH, WHITE STUCCO WALLS REFLECTED HEAT.

THE LACK OF SCULPTURAL ORNAMENT WAS A MAJOR MISSION STYLE CHARACTERISTIC.

RECTILINEAR, OPEN PLAN SIMILAR TO THE PLANNING OF THE CRAFTSMEN STYLE.

POOL   GARAGE

BR. BR. BR. TEL. KITCHEN   COURT   DINING   ENTRY   LIVING ROOM

BR. BATH   GAME ROOM

PATIO
FIRST FLOOR PLAN

1916   DODGE HOUSE, LOS ANGELES, CALIFORNIA
IRVING GILL, ARCHITECT

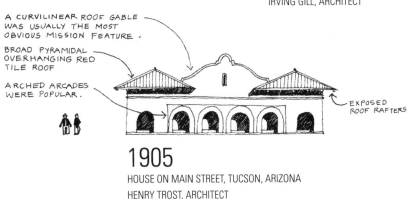

A CURVILINEAR ROOF GABLE WAS USUALLY THE MOST OBVIOUS MISSION FEATURE.

BROAD PYRAMIDAL OVERHANGING RED TILE ROOF

ARCHED ARCADES WERE POPULAR.

EXPOSED ROOF RAFTERS

1905
HOUSE ON MAIN STREET, TUCSON, ARIZONA
HENRY TROST, ARCHITECT

Tudor

Many early American settlers, including the Puritans and the first Germans (p. 70), brought the Half-Timbered Style with them to America. Their houses, however, quickly took on a different appearance than that of their European counterparts because of the harsh New England climate. The Tudor Style is the fourth in a series of six post-Victorian Revival Styles (including Norman, Chateauesque, Colonial Revival, Mission, and the Classic Revival Styles) that revive forms and methods of the past.

From 1890 through 1910 the style was known as Elizabethan because it was based on English cottages erected during the reign of Queen Elizabeth (1558–1603) and revived by English architect Richard Norman Shaw in the 1880s. When it began in America it was actually a Medieval Revival Style based on both the English Elizabethan and Jacobean Styles (to suggest both sources, many historians refer to the Tudor Style as "Jacobethan") adapted to the Queen Anne house. As it developed, it began to imitate the English historical style with greater accuracy and became known as the new English Tudor Style. By 1920 the preponderance of Tudor mansions gave rise to the term, "Stockbroker Tudor," and suburban builders were constructing smaller Tudor houses based on the English stone Cotswold cottage.

The most common exterior feature of the Tudor house is that of half-timbering. In this type of construction, the actual timber framework of the building is left exposed and the spaces between the timbers filled or "nogged" with brickwork and often covered with white stucco. This created a delineated building sometimes known as a "black and white house." Almost every suburban area in North America contains a Tudor neighborhood.

FRONT VIEW   SIDE VIEW

MASSIVE, ORNATE CHIMNEYS

EARLY TUDOR STYLE HOUSES WERE MADE WITH HALF TIMBERING ON A QUEEN ANNE STYLE HOUSE

1881 TUDOR DWELLING PUBLISHED IN ARCHITECTURAL DESIGNS AND DETAILS, A BUILDER'S PATTERN BOOK

1902 "COLLEGIATE GOTHIC" MANOR HOUSE, TYPICAL COLLEGE CAMPUS BUILDING

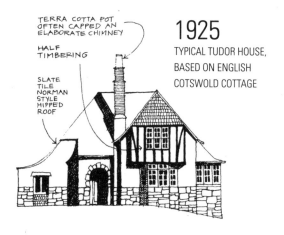

TERRA COTTA POT OFTEN CAPPED AN ELABORATE CHIMNEY

HALF TIMBERING

SLATE TILE NORMAN STYLE HIPPED ROOF

1925 TYPICAL TUDOR HOUSE, BASED ON ENGLISH COTSWOLD COTTAGE

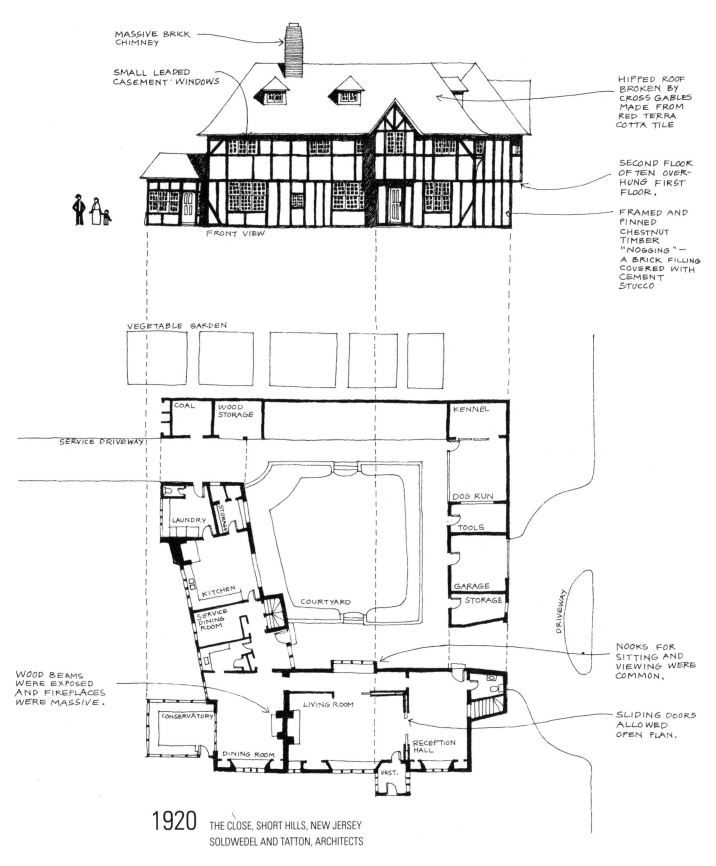

MASSIVE BRICK CHIMNEY

SMALL LEADED CASEMENT WINDOWS

HIPPED ROOF BROKEN BY CROSS GABLES MADE FROM RED TERRA COTTA TILE

SECOND FLOOR OFTEN OVER-HUNG FIRST FLOOR.

FRAMED AND PINNED CHESTNUT TIMBER "NOGGING" — A BRICK FILLING COVERED WITH CEMENT STUCCO

FRONT VIEW

VEGETABLE GARDEN

COAL

WOOD STORAGE

KENNEL

SERVICE DRIVEWAY

DOG RUN

LAUNDRY

STORAGE

TOOLS

KITCHEN

COURTYARD

GARAGE

STORAGE

DRIVEWAY

SERVICE DINING ROOM

NOOKS FOR SITTING AND VIEWING WERE COMMON.

WOOD BEAMS WERE EXPOSED AND FIREPLACES WERE MASSIVE.

LIVING ROOM

SLIDING DOORS ALLOWED OPEN PLAN.

CONSERVATORY

DINING ROOM

RECEPTION HALL

VEST.

1920 THE CLOSE, SHORT HILLS, NEW JERSEY
SOLDWEDEL AND TATTON, ARCHITECTS

Classic Revival

Countrywide
1905

The Beaux-Arts Style in America is seen most often in large public buildings, such as the one shown below. The style usually adhered to the principles set forth by the Ecoles des Beaux-Arts in Paris, where such American architects as Richard Morris Hunt, Louis Sullivan, H. H. Richardson, John Stewardson, and Bernard Maybeck were trained. All were influenced by the design principles of the Ecole, which emphasized the study of Greek and Roman structures, symmetrical composition, and elaborate watercolor wash renderings as presentation drawings. The monumentality of Beaux-Arts buildings, with heavy stone bases, grand stairways, medallions, grand arched openings, enriched mouldings, and free-standing statuary, gave way near the end of the nineteenth century to quieter, less dramatic forms. The result was a style more properly termed Classic Revival.

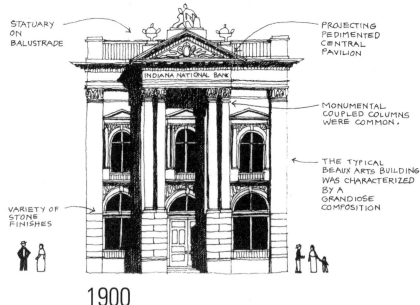

STATUARY ON BALUSTRADE

PROJECTING PEDIMENTED CENTRAL PAVILION

INDIANA NATIONAL BANK

MONUMENTAL COUPLED COLUMNS WERE COMMON.

THE TYPICAL BEAUX ARTS BUILDING WAS CHARACTERIZED BY A GRANDIOSE COMPOSITION

VARIETY OF STONE FINISHES

1900
INDIANA NATIONAL BANK BUILDING, INDIANAPOLIS, INDIANA

The more refined Classic Revival Style is found primarily in townhouses and country and resort villas built for the very wealthy. The style was based on the Greek, and to a lesser degree, the Roman architectural orders. It was characterized by a symmetrical arrangement of forms with a smooth or polished stone surface. Windows were large, and attic stories and parapet walls were popular. But, unlike the Beaux-Arts Style, the arch was not often used as Greek orders were preferred, and enriched mouldings and free-standing statuary was rare. The style was well suited to large suburban mansions but was also used after 1910 in many buildings of monumental size.

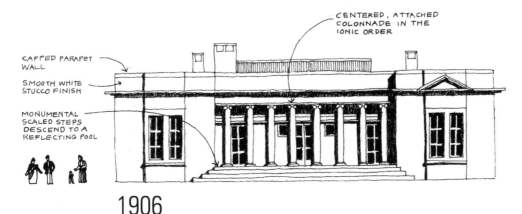

CENTERED, ATTACHED COLONNADE IN THE IONIC ORDER

CAPPED PARAPET WALL

SMOOTH WHITE STUCCO FINISH

MONUMENTAL SCALED STEPS DESCEND TO A REFLECTING POOL

1906

EL FUREIDIS, GILLISPIE HOUSE, SANTA BARBARA, CALIFORNIA
BERTRAM GOODHUE, ARCHITECT

In Southern California the Classic Revival Style sometimes had a Mediterranean flavor, suggested in such features as reflecting pools, smooth plaster surfaces, and overscaled windows. Often the style incorporated red tile roofs and arches giving it the appearance of being a transitional style between the Mission Revival and the Spanish Colonial Revival Styles. The large house shown above is an early twentieth-century classic interpretation of a Roman villa arranged around a central court.

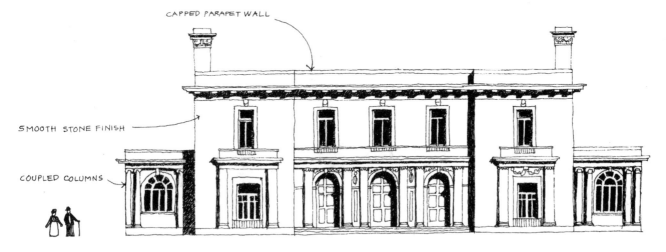

CAPPED PARAPET WALL

SMOOTH STONE FINISH

COUPLED COLUMNS

1914

TREMAINE-GALLAGHER HOUSE, CLEVELAND HEIGHTS, OHIO
F. W. STRIEBINGER, ARCHITECT

Craftsmen

California 1905

1901
THE ORCHARD, CHORLEYWOOD, HERTFORDSHIRE, ENGLAND
C. F. A. VOYSEY, ARCHITECT

The Craftsmen Style, also known as the Arts and Crafts Style, the Western Stick Style, and the Craft Movement Style, was based on the Arts and Crafts movement in Europe lead by English architect William Morris (1834–1896) and the English Arts and Crafts Exhibition Society formed in 1888. This society published articles and held exhibits extolling the virtues of handcrafted art and opposing the machine. The articles had a great influence on younger architects, especially in America where Frank Lloyd Wright, Bernard Maybeck, Gustave Stickley, and the Greene Brothers were beginning their illustrious careers. The Arts and Crafts movement took a stand against the English and German Functionalists who embraced the machine, and saw the French Art Nouveau group as decorators (although they shared decorative elements with the Art Nouveau, in that both styles were based on organic shapes). The machine aesthetic was regarded as impersonal and the solution was to design a house in which all the elements, inside and out, received artful attention.

The concern and care given to the details of Craftsmen Style houses gave rise to a planned "decor" with built-in furniture, stairways, windows, doorways, walls, ceilings, and floors, all constructed in the same carved and polished wooden aesthetic. Natural materials, such as redwood, tile, and stone and earth colors, were commonly employed. Craftsmen influences greatly affected small house design at the beginning of the twentieth century. The overall effect was a natural, warm, livable building.

THE WORK OF C.F.A. VOYSEY, A LEADER OF THE ENGLISH ARTS AND CRAFTS MOVEMENT, GREATLY INFLUENCED AMERICAN CRAFTSMEN STYLE ARCHITECTS.

MANY SMALL CRAFTSMEN HOUSES WERE INFLUENCED BY THE CALIFORNIA BUNGALOW.

GENTLY PITCHED GABLE ROOF OVER PROJECTING PURLINS

EXPOSED AND EXTENDED ROOF RAFTERS WERE ROUNDED AND POLISHED.

EXPOSED WOODEN PORCH STRUCTURE

1912
CONTRACTOR BUILT HOUSE, PUBLISHED IN
CRAFTSMEN MAGAZINE, SANTA BARBARA, CALIFORNIA

1908
GAMBLE HOUSE, PASADENA, CALIFORNIA
GREENE AND GREENE, ARCHITECTS

The most famous Craftsmen Style architects were Charles and Henry Greene who practiced along the California coast. They were best known for their "ultimate bungalows" such as the Pratt House shown below, built during the first decade of the twentieth century. They developed a style of residential wooden buildings based entirely on craftsmanship principles. They trained their workmen—most of them Japanese carpenters—to mortice and dowel the frames of their houses, made mainly from redwood. They fabricated most of their hardware, designed and leaded their own Art Nouveau-like windows, made decorative tile, and designed and built their own built-in and movable furniture.

The Greene Brothers' refusal to compromise their standards, combined with their unusually intense personal involvement in every facet of the design and construction process resulted in a beautiful architecture of natural materials that was used for inexpensive bungalows and vast estates. The Greenes brought dignity to the design of small houses and are given much of the credit for popularizing the Bungalow Style (p. 134) in the United States.

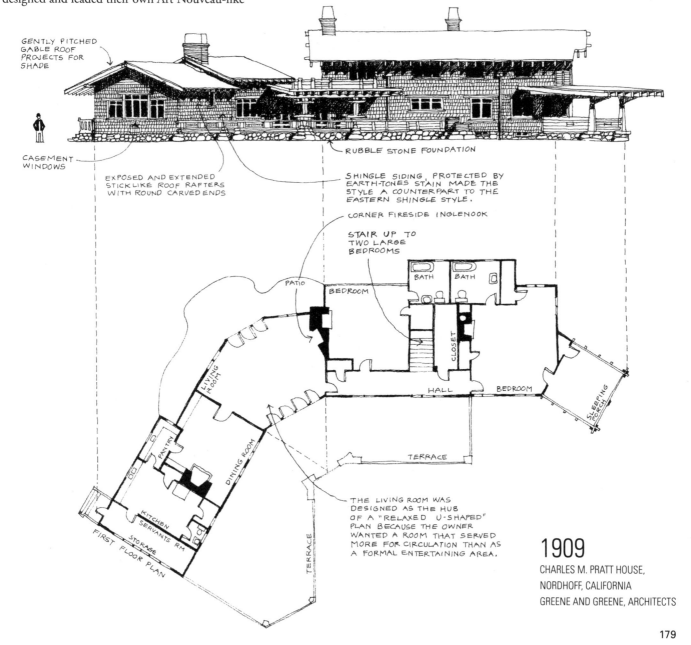

GENTLY PITCHED GABLE ROOF PROJECTS FOR SHADE

CASEMENT WINDOWS

EXPOSED AND EXTENDED STICKLIKE ROOF RAFTERS WITH ROUND CARVED ENDS

RUBBLE STONE FOUNDATION

SHINGLE SIDING, PROTECTED BY EARTH-TONES STAIN MADE THE STYLE A COUNTERPART TO THE EASTERN SHINGLE STYLE.

CORNER FIRESIDE INGLENOOK

STAIR UP TO TWO LARGE BEDROOMS

PATIO

BEDROOM

BATH

BATH

CLOSET

HALL

BEDROOM

SLEEPING PORCH

LIVING ROOM

TERRACE

PANTRY

DINING ROOM

KITCHEN

SERVANTS RM

STORAGE

FIRST FLOOR PLAN

TERRACE

THE LIVING ROOM WAS DESIGNED AS THE HUB OF A "RELAXED U-SHAPED" PLAN BECAUSE THE OWNER WANTED A ROOM THAT SERVED MORE FOR CIRCULATION THAN AS A FORMAL ENTERTAINING AREA.

1909

CHARLES M. PRATT HOUSE, NORDHOFF, CALIFORNIA
GREENE AND GREENE, ARCHITECTS

Wrightian

Midwest
1905

The architecture of Frank Lloyd Wright spanned several periods from 1893 to 1959 and gained an international reputation for him, unmatched by any other American architect. While he was acknowledged as the leader and spokesman for the Prairie Style (p. 194), his work was so unique and influential that it must be classified under its own heading.

Although he agreed in principle with Louis Sullivan's thesis that "Form follows function," at heart he was a romantic and his work seemed to follow more of a "Form follows aesthetic appeal" thesis. He was in sympathy with the Craftsmen Style (p. 178) particularly in terms of the attention given to such details as interior furnishings and the texture of materials. To him architecture had to be a living, organic thing. He deplored the readaptation of absolute forms in the revival styles of the 1910s and 1920s and the eclectic Period Styles (p. 210) in the 1930s. He advocated doing away with architectural libraries.

Every project was viewed by Wright as a fresh challenge. His theories on open planning, a flow throughout the building, and organic design were entirely original. He believed that if a project was located in a natural setting—prairie, mountains, meadow, desert—it should conform to that setting and enhance it. It should fulfill its function, primarily, but also have character, life, spirit, beauty, and create a vibrant environment. He thought most of our cities were ugly and inefficient and should be torn down.

— THE BLOCKS ARE THOUGHT TO BE RESPONSIBLE FOR THE POWERFUL GEOMETRY OF WRIGHT'S WORK.

1873
FROEBLE BLOCKS, PLACED IN HIS NURSERY BY HIS MOTHER, INSPIRED WRIGHT AS A CHILD

FLANKING WINGS

LOW PITCHED HIP ROOF WITH PROJECTING EAVES

RAISED CENTRAL BLOCK WAS AN ANCHOR TO THE REST OF THE FORMS OF THE HOUSE.

BRICK WALLS WITH STUCCO LEDGE

CONTINUOUS BANDS OF WINDOWS

1897
ROLLIN FURBECK HOUSE, OAK PARK, ILLINOIS
FRANK L. WRIGHT, ARCHITECT

1900
ROBERT ECKART HOUSE, RIVER FOREST, ILLINOIS
FRANK L. WRIGHT, ARCHITECT

During the years 1892 to 1910, Wright did his most important work, the influence of which reached many parts of the world. His Prairie houses (a name coined by Wright) gave birth to many new architectural ideas such as the strong accent given to the horizontal line, the cross-axis plan that pin-wheels away from a large central fireplace allowing flow from one room to another without doors or loss of privacy, rooms extending onto walled terraces making the house feel much larger than it really was, and bringing its inhabitant closer to the outdoors. These concepts greatly influenced European architects working toward a new architecture based on their love of the machine—later to be called the International Style.

In 1895, the editor of the *Ladies Home Journal*, Edward William Bok, began his own campaign to improve the "wretched" architecture of the small home in America. He published plans for houses costing from one to five thousand dollars and provided complete specifications for well-designed dwellings in a variety of styles. The campaign was a success. Magazine sales increased

and thousands of *Ladies Home Journal* houses were built in communities all over the country. Below is a submission by Frank Lloyd Wright, which was published in the *Ladies Home Journal* in 1901, costing just $5,800. It is interesting because it became an early model for his Prairie houses. Wright wrote of the design: "The plan disregards somewhat the economical limit in compact planning, to take advantage of light and air and prospect....The dining-room is so coupled with the living-room that one leads naturally into the other without destroying the privacy of either."

1900

"A SMALL HOUSE WITH LOTS OF ROOM IN IT"
FRANK LLOYD WRIGHT, ARCHITECT FOR THE *LADIES HOME JOURNAL*, 1900

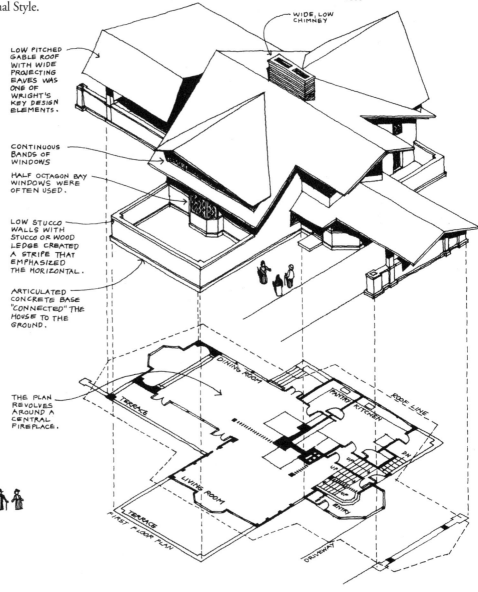

WIDE, LOW CHIMNEY

LOW PITCHED GABLE ROOF WITH WIDE PROJECTING EAVES WAS ONE OF WRIGHT'S KEY DESIGN ELEMENTS.

CONTINUOUS BANDS OF WINDOWS

HALF OCTAGON BAY WINDOWS WERE OFTEN USED.

LOW STUCCO WALLS WITH STUCCO OR WOOD LEDGE CREATED A STRIPE THAT EMPHASIZED THE HORIZONTAL.

ARTICULATED CONCRETE BASE "CONNECTED" THE HOUSE TO THE GROUND.

THE PLAN REVOLVES AROUND A CENTRAL FIREPLACE.

DINING ROOM · PANTRY · KITCHEN · ROOF LINE · TERRACE · LIVING ROOM · TERRACE · ENTRY · FIRST FLOOR PLAN · DRIVEWAY

WRIGHT'S EARLIEST WORK WAS INFLUENCED BY THE SHINGLE STYLE BUT HIS UNIQUE ABILITY TO SIMPLIFY SHAPES WAS ALREADY EVIDENT.

1889

FRANK LLOYD WRIGHT HOUSE, OAK PARK, ILLINOIS
FRANK L. WRIGHT, ARCHITECT

In a series of houses culminating in the Ward Willits house (shown below), Wright learned how to exploit the open cross-axial plan developed by Shingle Style architects, to break free and use his own combination of forms. He eliminated shingle siding, the gable roof, Palladian influences, and the chimney as a vertical design element. He allowed the plan to explode outward and used a Japanese influence interweaving of the interior. The Ward Willits house plan, published in Berlin in 1911, greatly influenced the development of the International Style (p. 214) in Europe by the Dutch De Stijl group, the German Mies Van der Rohe, and the French Le Corbusier.

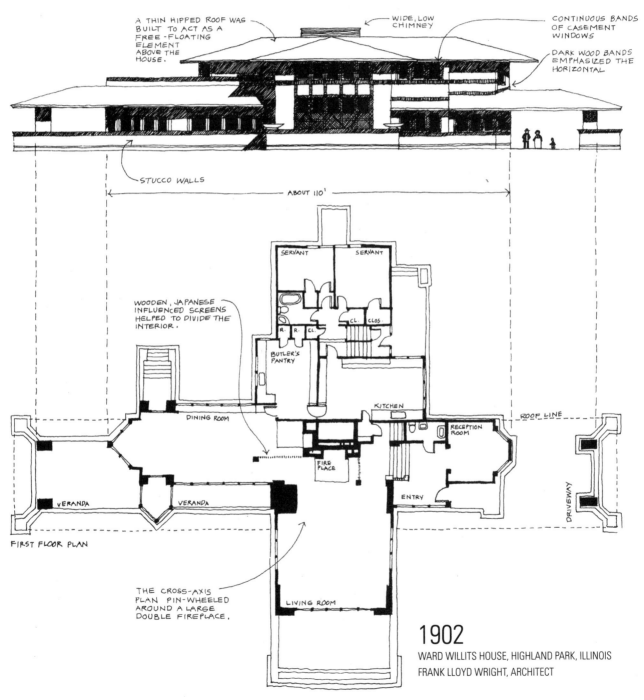

A THIN HIPPED ROOF WAS BUILT TO ACT AS A FREE-FLOATING ELEMENT ABOVE THE HOUSE.

WIDE, LOW CHIMNEY

CONTINUOUS BANDS OF CASEMENT WINDOWS

DARK WOOD BANDS EMPHASIZED THE HORIZONTAL

STUCCO WALLS

ABOUT 110'

WOODEN, JAPANESE INFLUENCED SCREENS HELPED TO DIVIDE THE INTERIOR.

SERVANT

SERVANT

CL. CLOS.

R. R. CL.

BUTLER'S PANTRY

KITCHEN

ROOF LINE

DINING ROOM

RECEPTION ROOM

FIRE PLACE

VERANDA

VERANDA

ENTRY

DRIVEWAY

FIRST FLOOR PLAN

THE CROSS-AXIS PLAN PIN-WHEELED AROUND A LARGE DOUBLE FIREPLACE.

LIVING ROOM

1902
WARD WILLITS HOUSE, HIGHLAND PARK, ILLINOIS
FRANK LLOYD WRIGHT, ARCHITECT

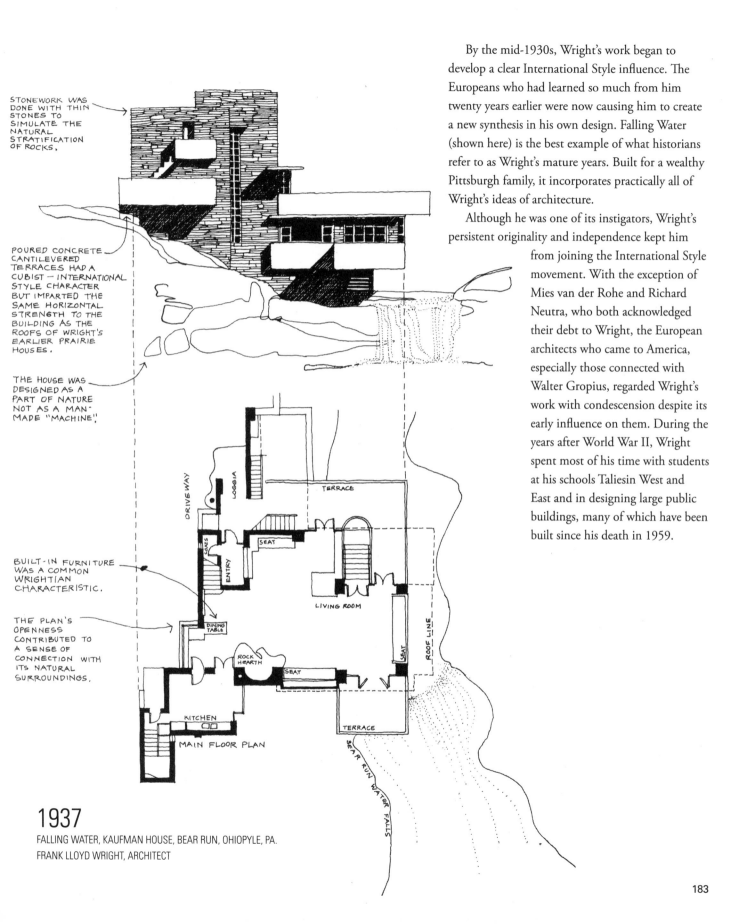

STONEWORK WAS DONE WITH THIN STONES TO SIMULATE THE NATURAL STRATIFICATION OF ROCKS.

POURED CONCRETE CANTILEVERED TERRACES HAD A CUBIST — INTERNATIONAL STYLE CHARACTER BUT IMPARTED THE SAME HORIZONTAL STRENGTH TO THE BUILDING AS THE ROOFS OF WRIGHT'S EARLIER PRAIRIE HOUSES.

THE HOUSE WAS DESIGNED AS A PART OF NATURE NOT AS A MAN-MADE "MACHINE".

BUILT-IN FURNITURE WAS A COMMON WRIGHTIAN CHARACTERISTIC.

THE PLAN'S OPENNESS CONTRIBUTED TO A SENSE OF CONNECTION WITH ITS NATURAL SURROUNDINGS.

DRIVE WAY
LOGGIA
TERRACE
COATS
SEAT
ENTRY
LIVING ROOM
ROOF LINE
DINING TABLE
ROCK HEARTH
SEAT
SEAT
KITCHEN
TERRACE
MAIN FLOOR PLAN
BEAR RUN WATER FALLS

1937
FALLING WATER, KAUFMAN HOUSE, BEAR RUN, OHIOPYLE, PA.
FRANK LLOYD WRIGHT, ARCHITECT

By the mid-1930s, Wright's work began to develop a clear International Style influence. The Europeans who had learned so much from him twenty years earlier were now causing him to create a new synthesis in his own design. Falling Water (shown here) is the best example of what historians refer to as Wright's mature years. Built for a wealthy Pittsburgh family, it incorporates practically all of Wright's ideas of architecture.

Although he was one of its instigators, Wright's persistent originality and independence kept him from joining the International Style movement. With the exception of Mies van der Rohe and Richard Neutra, who both acknowledged their debt to Wright, the European architects who came to America, especially those connected with Walter Gropius, regarded Wright's work with condescension despite its early influence on them. During the years after World War II, Wright spent most of his time with students at his schools Taliesin West and East and in designing large public buildings, many of which have been built since his death in 1959.

Bungalow

Countrywide 1910

The Bungalow Style was an outgrowth of many influences—the Craftsmen Style, Japanese architecture derived from new tea houses built in this country and from photographs and travel in Japan, the low adobe dwellings of the Spanish Colonial Style of the Southwest, the open informal planning of the Eastern Shingle Style, shacklike rural cottages, the Swiss chalet, and barn and log cabin construction. Bungalows, built throughout the country primarily from 1890 to 1920, were loosely described as any cottagelike dwelling, informal in plan, elevation, and detail. They answered a widespread need for simpler residences brought on by economic setbacks of the 1890s. The bungalow began in California, evolving from the Craftsmen heritage, and quickly spread to other parts of the country where it was adapted to a multitude of different styles. Despite these variations, the bungalow had certain basic characteristics. Its lines were low and simple with wide projecting roofs. It had at most two stories, but usually one, large porches (verandas), and was made with materials that suggested a kind of coziness. The bungalow was sometimes defined as "the least house for the most money," and indeed, although low cost materials were

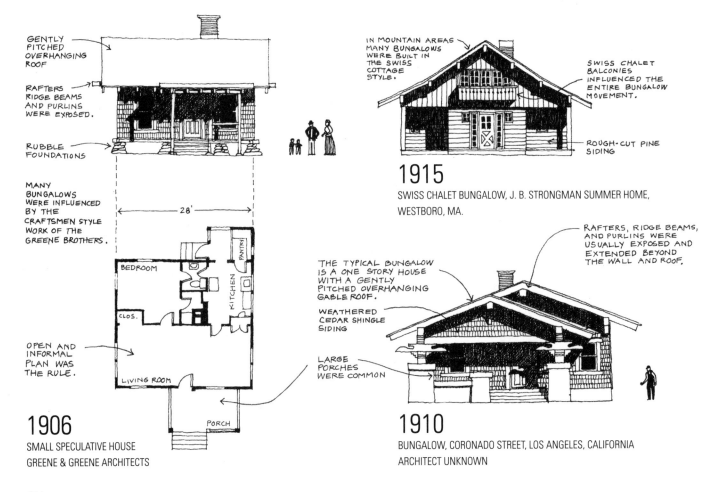

GENTLY PITCHED OVERHANGING ROOF

RAFTERS RIDGE BEAMS AND PURLINS WERE EXPOSED.

RUBBLE FOUNDATIONS

MANY BUNGALOWS WERE INFLUENCED BY THE CRAFTSMEN STYLE WORK OF THE GREENE BROTHERS.

28'

BEDROOM

PANTRY

KITCHEN

CLOS.

OPEN AND INFORMAL PLAN WAS THE RULE.

LIVING ROOM

PORCH

1906
SMALL SPECULATIVE HOUSE
GREENE & GREENE ARCHITECTS

IN MOUNTAIN AREAS MANY BUNGALOWS WERE BUILT IN THE SWISS COTTAGE STYLE.

SWISS CHALET BALCONIES INFLUENCED THE ENTIRE BUNGALOW MOVEMENT.

ROUGH-CUT PINE SIDING

1915
SWISS CHALET BUNGALOW, J. B. STRONGMAN SUMMER HOME, WESTBORO, MA.

RAFTERS, RIDGE BEAMS, AND PURLINS WERE USUALLY EXPOSED AND EXTENDED BEYOND THE WALL AND ROOF.

THE TYPICAL BUNGALOW IS A ONE STORY HOUSE WITH A GENTLY PITCHED OVERHANGING GABLE ROOF.

WEATHERED CEDAR SHINGLE SIDING

LARGE PORCHES WERE COMMON

1910
BUNGALOW, CORONADO STREET, LOS ANGELES, CALIFORNIA
ARCHITECT UNKNOWN

emphasized the bungalow was not inexpensive. It depended on costly foundations, wall, and roof areas because of the spread-out first floor.

The Bungalow Style was so popular after 1905 that it became the first style to be built in quantity by the contractor-builder. By 1910, throughout all of California and most other parts of the country, street after street was lined with differently styled bungalows built for speculative sale. Plan books and monthly journals made it possible for any contractor or future homeowner in any part of the country to erect a bungalow. So, despite its lofty aspirations and exotic antecedants, the Bungalow Style ended up sloppily imitated in thousands of tacky boxes. It has come to represent both the best and the worst in American architecture.

Just as the Cottage Style is given credit for popularizing the front porch, the Bungalow Style is given credit for introducing the front stoop to the American house. The stoop became a distinctive part of the architecture of the suburban bungalow by providing a semipublic transition place between the front porch and the connecting walkway to the sidewalk and the street. The stoop was a place to sit and talk, for children to play, or to simply pause before entering the privacy of the porch or house.

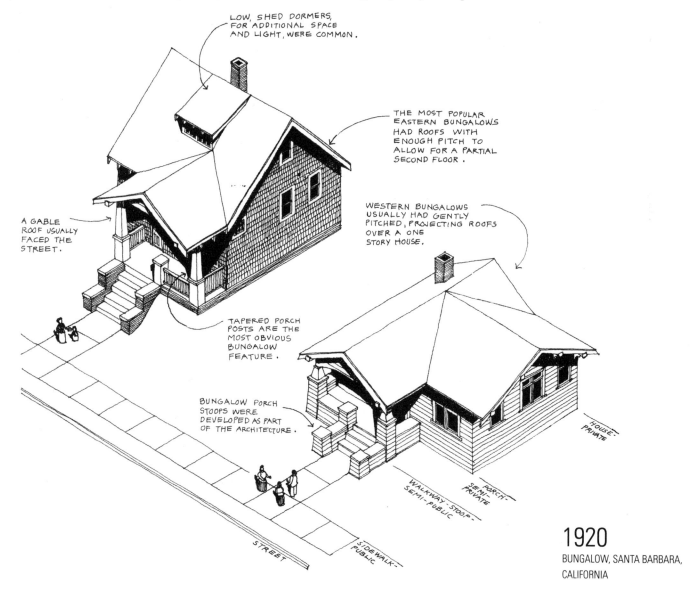

LOW, SHED DORMERS, FOR ADDITIONAL SPACE AND LIGHT, WERE COMMON.

THE MOST POPULAR EASTERN BUNGALOWS HAD ROOFS WITH ENOUGH PITCH TO ALLOW FOR A PARTIAL SECOND FLOOR.

WESTERN BUNGALOWS USUALLY HAD GENTLY PITCHED, PROJECTING ROOFS OVER A ONE STORY HOUSE.

A GABLE ROOF USUALLY FACED THE STREET.

TAPERED PORCH POSTS ARE THE MOST OBVIOUS BUNGALOW FEATURE.

BUNGALOW PORCH STOOPS WERE DEVELOPED AS PART OF THE ARCHITECTURE.

HOUSE - PRIVATE

PORCH - SEMI-PRIVATE

WALKWAY-STOOP - SEMI-PUBLIC

STREET

SIDEWALK - PUBLIC

1920
BUNGALOW, SANTA BARBARA, CALIFORNIA

It would be almost impossible to list all of the variations of the Bungalow Style. Each geographical area seemed to adapt it to a favorite cottagelike style. The Chicago area used the Prairie Style as its source, California used the Craftsmen and Spanish Colonial Styles, the Catskill and Adirondack Mountain areas in the East developed its own picturesque Camp Building Style, and so on. Several of these and a few other distinctive Bungalow styles are discussed on the next four pages.

The term "Bungalow" (from the Hindustani word "Bangla" meaning low house for travelers with surrounding porches) was used in America to describe any modest, low-slung, picturesque cottage. Shown below are two of the more distinctive bungalow types: The Chicago bungalow, based on the Prairie Style of the Midwest, and the Spanish Colonial Revival bungalow being built in the Southwest during the height of the Spanish Colonial Revival (p. 208). Both these bungalows, while adapting to vastly differing regional styles, conveyed a feeling of coziness and one-story livability.

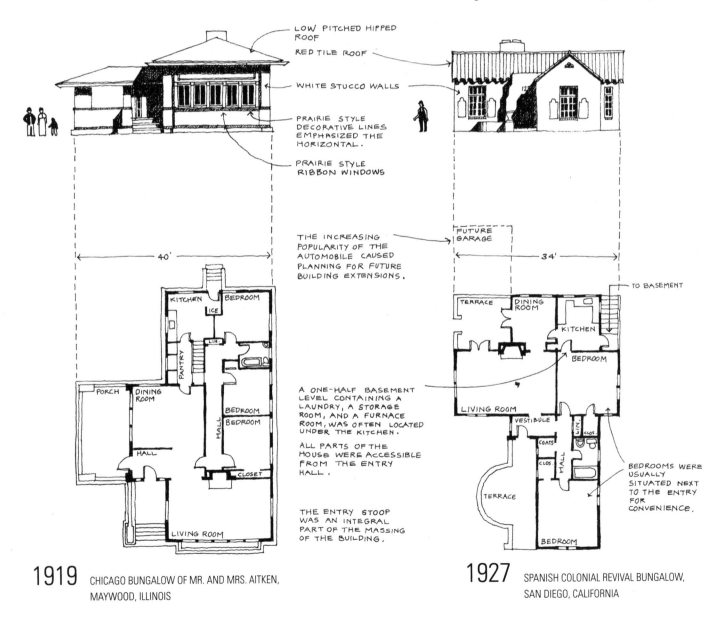

LOW PITCHED HIPPED ROOF

RED TILE ROOF

WHITE STUCCO WALLS

PRAIRIE STYLE DECORATIVE LINES EMPHASIZED THE HORIZONTAL.

PRAIRIE STYLE RIBBON WINDOWS

THE INCREASING POPULARITY OF THE AUTOMOBILE CAUSED PLANNING FOR FUTURE BUILDING EXTENSIONS.

A ONE-HALF BASEMENT LEVEL CONTAINING A LAUNDRY, A STORAGE ROOM, AND A FURNACE ROOM, WAS OFTEN LOCATED UNDER THE KITCHEN.

ALL PARTS OF THE HOUSE WERE ACCESSIBLE FROM THE ENTRY HALL.

THE ENTRY STOOP WAS AN INTEGRAL PART OF THE MASSING OF THE BUILDING.

BEDROOMS WERE USUALLY SITUATED NEXT TO THE ENTRY FOR CONVENIENCE.

1919 CHICAGO BUNGALOW OF MR. AND MRS. AITKEN, MAYWOOD, ILLINOIS

1927 SPANISH COLONIAL REVIVAL BUNGALOW, SAN DIEGO, CALIFORNIA

The Patio Bungalow Style, found primarily in Southern California, was an offshoot of the Craftsmen Style but based its plan on the Spanish Colonial Style (p. 110). The inner court, or patio, provided a cool outdoor living area with plants, fountains, and pools.

The first patio bungalows copied the Spanish Colonial plans by either encircling the patio with the house or enclosing the patio with a wall. Later patio bungalows placed the patio on the front or rear of the plan, depending on the constraints of the site.

Below are plans of two common patio bungalows: The "H" shaped central living room plan and the "0" shaped patio-encircling plan. The single-story "H" shaped plan inspired the development of "wings"; the bedroom wing was quiet and private while the dining/kitchen wing was used for noisy, more public activities. The "0" shaped plan had rooms grouped around a central patio to provide shade and private outdoor living space.

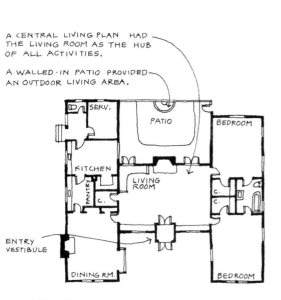

A CENTRAL LIVING PLAN HAD THE LIVING ROOM AS THE HUB OF ALL ACTIVITIES.

A WALLED-IN PATIO PROVIDED AN OUTDOOR LIVING AREA.

1914 FRANCIS W. WILSON, PATIO BUNGALOW, CALIFORNIA
F. W. WILSON, ARCHITECT

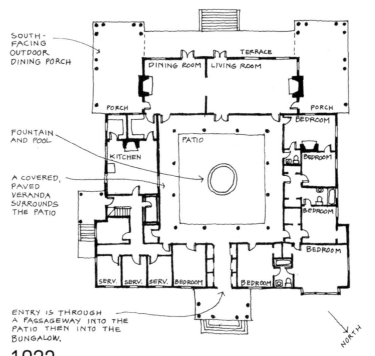

SOUTH-FACING OUTDOOR DINING PORCH

FOUNTAIN AND POOL

A COVERED, PAVED VERANDA SURROUNDS THE PATIO

ENTRY IS THROUGH A PASSAGEWAY INTO THE PATIO THEN INTO THE BUNGALOW.

1923 JAMES M. CODMAN, PATIO BUNGALOW, WARSHAM, MASSACHUSETTS
GUY LOWELL, ARCHITECT

California had many shacklike bungalows intended for temporary use. The Southern California tent bungalow had hinged wall panels made from canvas stretched over frames designed to cool the house quickly in the warm climate. It was an excellent outdoor sleeping room when so arranged. The temporary bungalow was used as a residence for many people moving into the area until they found a more substantial home.

All along the Atlantic Coast are seashore towns with hundreds of bungalows designed primarily as a place to sleep, since more resort activities occur outdoors away from the house. These seacoast bungalows were usually long and narrow to give each room cross ventilation and light. They borrowed much of their style from New England colonial architecture.

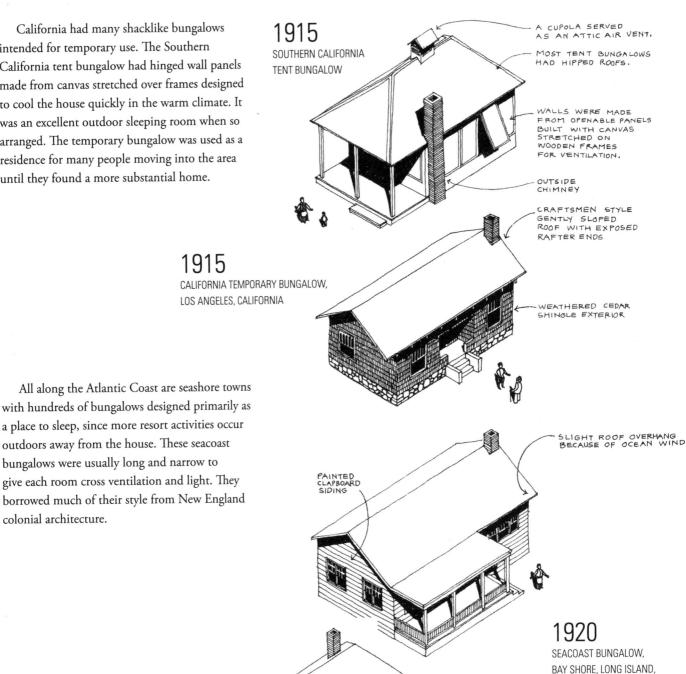

1915
SOUTHERN CALIFORNIA
TENT BUNGALOW

A CUPOLA SERVED AS AN ATTIC AIR VENT.

MOST TENT BUNGALOWS HAD HIPPED ROOFS.

WALLS WERE MADE FROM OPENABLE PANELS BUILT WITH CANVAS STRETCHED ON WOODEN FRAMES FOR VENTILATION.

OUTSIDE CHIMNEY

1915
CALIFORNIA TEMPORARY BUNGALOW,
LOS ANGELES, CALIFORNIA

CRAFTSMEN STYLE GENTLY SLOPED ROOF WITH EXPOSED RAFTER ENDS

WEATHERED CEDAR SHINGLE EXTERIOR

SLIGHT ROOF OVERHANG BECAUSE OF OCEAN WIND

PAINTED CLAPBOARD SIDING

1920
SEACOAST BUNGALOW,
BAY SHORE, LONG ISLAND,
NEW YORK

EACH ROOM HAD ONE WINDOW FOR LIGHT AND VENTILATION.

1923
SEACOAST BUNGALOW,
MANASQUAN, NEW JERSEY

SCREENED OR GLAZED FRONT PORCH

Bungalows in the Camp and Picturesque Lodge Styles located primarily in the Adirondack, Catskill, and Pocono Mountain areas of the East are of an endless variety. There are so many examples that it would be impossible to classify them. All of them, however, used rough natural materials, such as fieldstone, logs, rough-cut pine, and split cedar shingles, and were based on the Craftsmen and Swiss Chalet Styles, popular in all the mountain retreats of the country.

The two examples shown here are taken from the Catskill Mountain region: The Sadler bungalow was built in the Camp Style, popular in little communities that were summertime retreats for New York area children. The Ralph Whitehead residence is part of Byrdcliffe, a beautiful community built by artists and craftspeople for themselves in Woodstock, New York, in the Picturesque Style between 1902 and 1910. Both buildings illustrate growth by accretion (beginning with a small cabin and adding rooms as necessary) and each has a thin projecting roof line that gives it a light, cardboard quality.

1906
RALPH WHITEHEAD RESIDENCE, BYRDCLIFFE, WOODSTOCK, NEW YORK

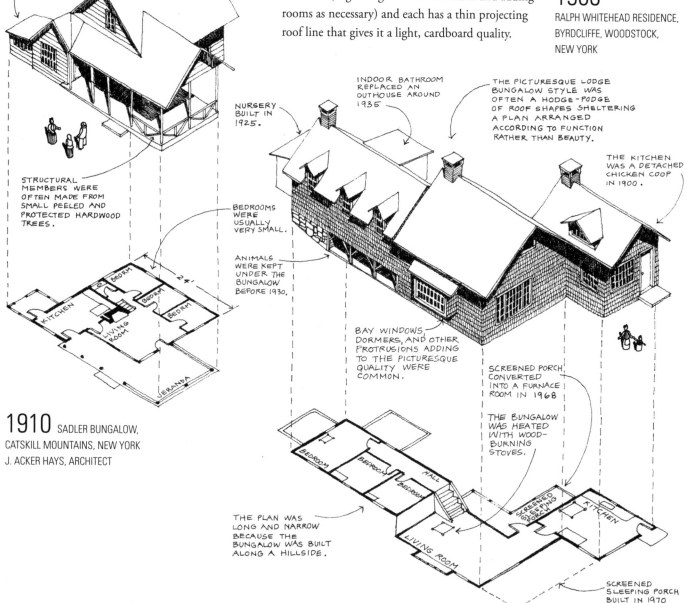

THROUGH THE YEARS SHEDS WERE BUILT ONTO THE MAIN STRUCTURE WHEN NECESSARY.

STRUCTURAL MEMBERS WERE OFTEN MADE FROM SMALL PEELED AND PROTECTED HARDWOOD TREES.

NURSERY BUILT IN 1925.

INDOOR BATHROOM REPLACED AN OUTHOUSE AROUND 1935

THE PICTURESQUE LODGE BUNGALOW STYLE WAS OFTEN A HODGE-PODGE OF ROOF SHAPES SHELTERING A PLAN ARRANGED ACCORDING TO FUNCTION RATHER THAN BEAUTY.

THE KITCHEN WAS A DETACHED CHICKEN COOP IN 1900.

BEDROOMS WERE USUALLY VERY SMALL.

ANIMALS WERE KEPT UNDER THE BUNGALOW BEFORE 1930.

BAY WINDOWS, DORMERS, AND OTHER PROTRUSIONS ADDING TO THE PICTURESQUE QUALITY WERE COMMON.

SCREENED PORCH CONVERTED INTO A FURNACE ROOM IN 1968

THE BUNGALOW WAS HEATED WITH WOOD-BURNING STOVES.

1910 SADLER BUNGALOW,
CATSKILL MOUNTAINS, NEW YORK
J. ACKER HAYS, ARCHITECT

KITCHEN
BEDRM
BEDRM
BEDRM
LIVING ROOM
VERANDA

BEDROOM
BEDROOM
BEDRM
HALL
LIVING ROOM
SCREENED SLEEPING PORCH
KITCHEN

THE PLAN WAS LONG AND NARROW BECAUSE THE BUNGALOW WAS BUILT ALONG A HILLSIDE.

SCREENED SLEEPING PORCH BUILT IN 1970

Bay Region

San Francisco
1910, 1930, 1960

Since the turn of the century, architects working in the San Francisco Bay area have been building houses that are modest, straightforward, and distinctive. Rather than give in to their own creative needs or their clients social aspirations, these architects designed houses that were simply a place to relax, a welcome retreat.

The Bay Region Style is a continuing idiom, but there were three important periods when it influenced the nation. In 1910 houses by Bay Area architects were characterized by a natural redwood shingled veneer and exposed interior structural members inspired by the Craftsmen, Swiss Chalet, and Eastern Shingle Styles. In 1930 the International Style influenced low, single-story buildings with large expanses of glass that incorporated local vernacular building techniques to create the unique California "ranch" house. In the 1960s, extremely innovative architects synthesized the previous two traditions using redwood shingles and other natural materials to create rustic, woodsy buildings inspired by California sheds and barns.

FIRST BAY REGION STYLE

The houses of the Eastern Shingle Style with their large living areas and wide openings between rooms, when mixed with the Craftsmen, Swiss Chalet, some Queen Anne, and Art Nouveau Styles with a Japanese influence in detailing, formed the basis of the work of early practitioners in the San Francisco Bay region. Late works of Charles and Henry Greene, Bernard Maybeck, and the early

work of Ernest Coxhead and Willis Polk gave to the architecture of this region a reputation for being wildly expressionistic and creative.

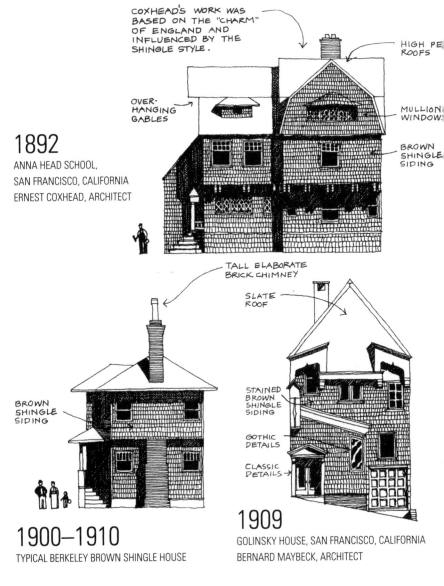

COXHEAD'S WORK WAS BASED ON THE "CHARM" OF ENGLAND AND INFLUENCED BY THE SHINGLE STYLE.

OVER-HANGING GABLES

HIGH PE ROOFS

MULLION WINDOW

BROWN SHINGLE SIDING

1892
ANNA HEAD SCHOOL, SAN FRANCISCO, CALIFORNIA
ERNEST COXHEAD, ARCHITECT

BROWN SHINGLE SIDING

TALL ELABORATE BRICK CHIMNEY

SLATE ROOF

STAINED BROWN SHINGLE SIDING

GOTHIC DETAILS

CLASSIC DETAILS

1900–1910
TYPICAL BERKELEY BROWN SHINGLE HOUSE

1909
GOLINSKY HOUSE, SAN FRANCISCO, CALIFORNIA
BERNARD MAYBECK, ARCHITECT

SECOND BAY REGION STYLE

The Second Bay Region Style was a unique combination of the "Less is More" dictum of the International Style and the woodsy local rural Bay Region vernacular architecture of ranches, barns, and low-cost homes. In essence, it was a bridge between the lively Maybeckian First Bay Region Style and the austere International Style.

Local vernacular techniques such as redwood board and batten siding (sometimes without the batten and sometimes whitewashed), exposed interior roof structure, interior redwood paneling, and low pitched roofs were mixed with International Style influences such as flat roofs, simple cubistic forms, large expanses of glass, and open plans. The resulting structure came to be well-known as the California house or the California Ranch Style house (p. 232). It was popular all over the nation from the 1940s to the 1960s.

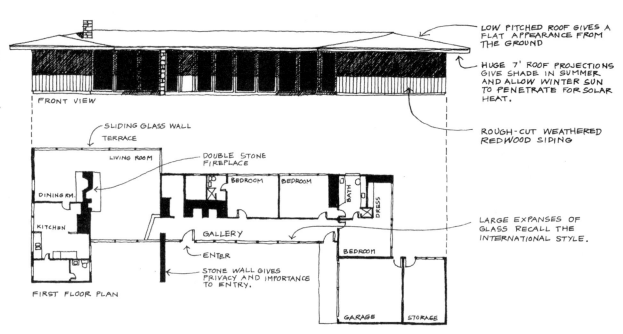

1949
TAMALPAIS HOUSE, MARIN COUNTY, CALIFORNIA
ALBERT H. HILL, ARCHITECT

FRONT VIEW

LOW PITCHED ROOF GIVES A FLAT APPEARANCE FROM THE GROUND

HUGE 7' ROOF PROJECTIONS GIVE SHADE IN SUMMER AND ALLOW WINTER SUN TO PENETRATE FOR SOLAR HEAT.

ROUGH-CUT WEATHERED REDWOOD SIDING

SLIDING GLASS WALL
TERRACE
LIVING ROOM
DOUBLE STONE FIREPLACE
DINING RM.
KITCHEN
BEDROOM
BEDROOM
BATH
DRESS
GALLERY
ENTER
BEDROOM
STONE WALL GIVES PRIVACY AND IMPORTANCE TO ENTRY.
GARAGE
STORAGE
FIRST FLOOR PLAN

LARGE EXPANSES OF GLASS RECALL THE INTERNATIONAL STYLE.

California architect Cliff May has been given credit by most historians for the development of the California Ranch Style but William Wurster and his circle of colleagues are generally recognized as the designers who conceived and popularized the Second Bay Region Style.

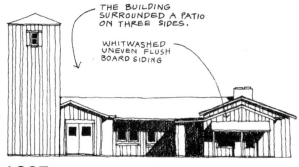

THE BUILDING SURROUNDED A PATIO ON THREE SIDES.

WHITWASHED UNEVEN FLUSH BOARD SIDING

1927
GREGORY RANCH HOUSE, SANTA CRUZ MOUNTAINS, CALIFORNIA
WILLIAM W. WURSTER, ARCHITECT

BY 1940 THE CUBIST SHAPES POPULAR WITH INTERNATIONAL STYLE ARCHITECTS WERE STRONG INFLUENCES IN THE BAY AREA.

LARGE EXPANSES OF GLASS

REDWOOD SIDED CHIMNEYS

REDWOOD HORIZONTAL SIDING LEFT TO WEATHER NATURALLY

1941
STEVENS HOUSE, SAN FRANCISCO, CALIFORNIA
WURSTER, BERNARDI AND EMMONS ARCHITECTS

THIRD BAY REGION STYLE

Houses in the Bay Region Style continued to be built through the 1950s. Architects designed houses that ran the gamut from traditional to rustic, from the low boxy ranch to the high, vertical hillside house. But there always was a strong tendency to emulate the earlier Bay Region traditions. By the early 1960s architects Charles Moore and his office of Moore, Lyndon, Turnbull, and Whitaker and Joseph Esherick and his office of Esherick, Homsey, and Dodge became key figures in the revitalization of the Bay Region Style. They exploited the ordinary, the vernacular of their day, primarily barns and sheds settled into the nearby farmland, just as Maybeck, Coxhead, and Wurster had in theirs.

Bay Region architects preferred plain wood siding, industrial fixtures, exposed roof framing, and other vernacular materials to those which fell under the category of "high design." In northern California the Bay Region Style gave birth to the popular California Rustic Style and to thousands of ski houses in the northeastern woods. It was a key inspiration for the New Shingle Style illustrated on page 288.

In their book, *The Place of Houses*, Charles Moore and Gerald Allen present three interesting ways to conceptualize a house design. Most Bay Region houses were designed using one or more of these methods (see opposite).

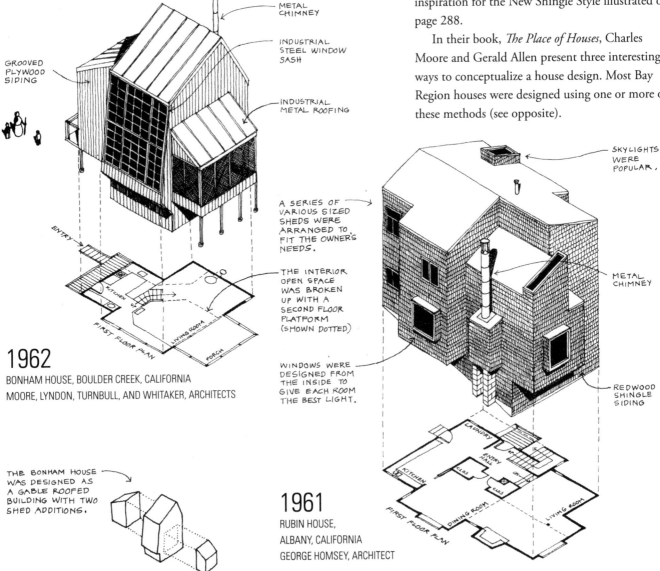

METAL CHIMNEY

INDUSTRIAL STEEL WINDOW SASH

INDUSTRIAL METAL ROOFING

GROOVED PLYWOOD SIDING

ENTRY

KITCHEN

LIVING ROOM

PORCH

FIRST FLOOR PLAN

A SERIES OF VARIOUS SIZED SHEDS WERE ARRANGED TO FIT THE OWNER'S NEEDS.

THE INTERIOR OPEN SPACE WAS BROKEN UP WITH A SECOND FLOOR PLATFORM (SHOWN DOTTED)

WINDOWS WERE DESIGNED FROM THE INSIDE TO GIVE EACH ROOM THE BEST LIGHT.

SKYLIGHTS WERE POPULAR.

METAL CHIMNEY

REDWOOD SHINGLE SIDING

LAUNDRY

ENTRY HALL

KITCHEN

CLOS

CLOS

DINING ROOM

LIVING ROOM

FIRST FLOOR PLAN

1962
BONHAM HOUSE, BOULDER CREEK, CALIFORNIA
MOORE, LYNDON, TURNBULL, AND WHITAKER, ARCHITECTS

THE BONHAM HOUSE WAS DESIGNED AS A GABLE ROOFED BUILDING WITH TWO SHED ADDITIONS.

1961
RUBIN HOUSE,
ALBANY, CALIFORNIA
GEORGE HOMSEY, ARCHITECT

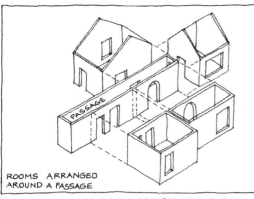

ROOMS ARRANGED
AROUND A PASSAGE

1 VARIOUS SHAPED ROOMS ARE PLACED NEXT TO A CONNECTING PASSAGEWAY.

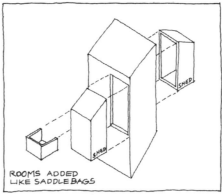

ROOMS ADDED
LIKE SADDLEBAGS

2 SHEDS ARE "HUNG" ON THE MAIN STRUCTURE LIKE SADDLEBAGS ON A HORSE.

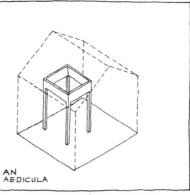

AN
AEDICULA

3 AN AEDICULA (FOUR COLUMNS SUPPORTING FOUR BEAMS), AN OPEN SPACE FRAME, IS USED TO CREATE A SYMBOLIC CENTER IN THE MIDST OF THE SPECIFIC DEMANDS OF THE HOUSEHOLD.

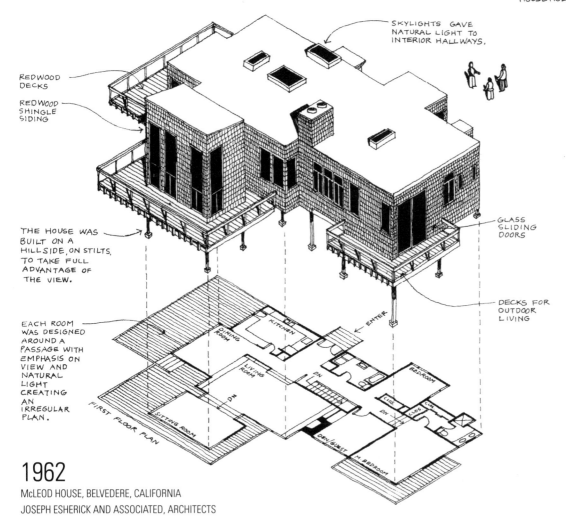

SKYLIGHTS GAVE NATURAL LIGHT TO INTERIOR HALLWAYS.

REDWOOD DECKS

REDWOOD SHINGLE SIDING

THE HOUSE WAS BUILT ON A HILLSIDE, ON STILTS, TO TAKE FULL ADVANTAGE OF THE VIEW.

EACH ROOM WAS DESIGNED AROUND A PASSAGE WITH EMPHASIS ON VIEW AND NATURAL LIGHT CREATING AN IRREGULAR PLAN.

GLASS SLIDING DOORS

DECKS FOR OUTDOOR LIVING

FIRST FLOOR PLAN

KITCHEN
DINING ROOM
LIVING ROOM
SITTING ROOM
ENTER
BEDROOM
DEN/GUEST
M. BEDROOM

1962

McLEOD HOUSE, BELVEDERE, CALIFORNIA

JOSEPH ESHERICK AND ASSOCIATED, ARCHITECTS

Prairie

Midwest
1915

Prairie Style architects, working in the prairies of the Midwest, primarily around suburban Chicago and rural Minnesota, Iowa, and Wisconsin, have created some of the most original, influential American architecture. They explored new ways of relating buildings to the land, used undecorated natural materials, and, most importantly, invented new concepts of interior space. Prairie Style influences came from the strength of the Shingle Style, the commercial architecture of Chicago, and the English Arts and Crafts movement. The Prairie Style had a great effect on the European International Style in the 1920s and later, the American International Style (p. 214).

The Prairie Style began in Chicago around 1897 with a group of architects whose goal was the development of a new American architecture especially suited to the Midwest, forming an office at Steinway Hall. A disciple of architect Louis Sullivan (world famous for his writing and commercial architecture), Frank Lloyd Wright, was the first among the group to move toward an original

architecture and soon leadership passed to him. He has written, "We of the Middle West are living on the prairie. The prairie has a beauty of its own and we should recognize and accentuate this natural beauty, its quiet level. Hence, gently sloping roofs, low proportions, quiet sky lines, suppressed heavy-set chimneys and sheltering overhangs, low terraces and out-reaching walls sequestering private gardens."

The center of Prairie Style activity moved from Steinway Hall to Wright's studio in Oak Park in 1899. There he trained several young architects, among them Walter Burley Griffin and Walter Drummond. Other well-known Prairie Style architects, such as George Elmslie and William Steele, worked for Louis Sullivan; while William Purcell, George Maher, and Robert Spencer worked for other architects before opening their own offices. These men formed the main body of architects that constituted what became known as the Prairie School.

Shown below are two houses that were typical early influences of Prairie Style architects.

LOW PITCHED HIPPED ROOF WITH WIDE PROJECTING EAVES CREATED A LOW-TO-THE-GROUND HORIZONTAL LOOK.

STUCCO FINISH OVER A WOOD FRAME OR BRICK STRUCTURE

1900
"A SOUTHERN FARMHOUSE," ROBERT SPENCER, ARCHITECT
PUBLISHED IN 1901 BY THE *LADIES HOME JOURNAL*

A CONTINUOUS BAND OF CASEMENT WINDOWS KNOWN AS RIBBON WINDOWS

1902
NETTIE F. McCORMICK HOUSE, LAKE FOREST, ILLINOIS
LOUIS SULLIVAN AND GEORGE C. ELMSLIE, ARCHITECTS

The Prairie Style encompasses the period from 1900 until 1919, but it reached its height in 1915. By then Frank Lloyd Wright had mastered the style. His most famous Prairie Style design, the Robie House, is shown below. This house, like most of his work (p. 180) uses a centrally located fireplace as a divider of space and as the focal point of the building. The fireplace incorporates an entry stair and separates the living room, dining room, and entry. Wright was a genius at arranging rooms so as to create highly efficient interior space.

Other Prairie Style architects greatly contributed to the style but the quality of Wright's work was so powerful that he is generally given credit for its beginnings. But, Wright himself was influenced by Walter Burley Griffin's split level vertical organization of the plan and his use of poured concrete and concrete blocks in residential architecture. William Drummond is responsible for the use of precise geometric forms, the right angle, and the slab roof. Purcell and Elmslie employed a technique that juxtaposed smooth surface with sharp-edged voids in their late white stucco work.

Historical interest in the Prairie Style has fluctuated greatly over the years. The style was recognized early and enjoyed national publicity until about the time of World War I when rising interest in technology and the machine age caused it to be all but forgotten. It experienced something of a revival in the 1950s when it became the basis for the split level and ranch house. More recently, in the 1960s, it had an influence on California Bay architecture and the New Shingle Style in the East.

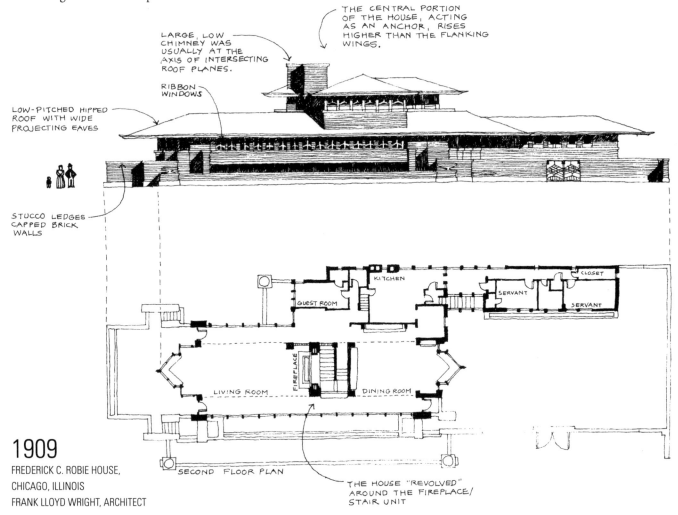

THE CENTRAL PORTION OF THE HOUSE, ACTING AS AN ANCHOR, RISES HIGHER THAN THE FLANKING WINGS.

LARGE, LOW CHIMNEY WAS USUALLY AT THE AXIS OF INTERSECTING ROOF PLANES.

RIBBON WINDOWS

LOW-PITCHED HIPPED ROOF WITH WIDE PROJECTING EAVES

STUCCO LEDGES CAPPED BRICK WALLS

GUEST ROOM

KITCHEN

CLOSET

SERVANT

SERVANT

FIREPLACE

LIVING ROOM

DINING ROOM

SECOND FLOOR PLAN

THE HOUSE "REVOLVED" AROUND THE FIREPLACE/ STAIR UNIT

1909

FREDERICK C. ROBIE HOUSE,
CHICAGO, ILLINOIS
FRANK LLOYD WRIGHT, ARCHITECT

Pueblo Revival

Southwest
1920

The Pueblo Revival Style takes its name from the prototypical adobe, flat-roofed puebloes built by the Hopi and Pueblo Indians (p. 22) in New Mexico and northern Arizona. It was introduced in California by Boston architect A. C. Schweinfurth with a hotel at Montalvo in 1894. Later, he designed a number of buildings, including the Hearst ranch at Pleasanton, in the style. By 1915, in New Mexico and Arizona, the Pueblo Revival Style became popular for hotels, college campus buildings, churches, and other public buildings. It was seen as the marriage of an archeological and modern spirit.

The Pueblo Revival house, like the original pueblo dwelling, is characterized by massive looking battered walls with rounded corners. Roofs are always flat and usually have parapet walls. The most recognizable element of the style is the projecting rounded roof beam known as a "viga." Second- and third-story levels are usually stepped and terraced to resemble the Indian habitats. When not built of adobe, Pueblo Revival Style buildings try to look as though they were. Walls are always plastered when they are not adobe and are always given a heavy rounded look.

The style is also known as the Southwest Indian Revival, the Hopi, and Pueblo Indian Styles.

PARAPET WALL WITH WATER SPOUTS CALLED CANALES

FLAT ROOF

VIGAS

WHITE PAINTED ADOBE OR STUCCO WALLS

BATTERED WALLS

1700
LAGUNA CHURCH AND PUEBLO, NEAR ALBUQUERQUE, NEW MEXICO

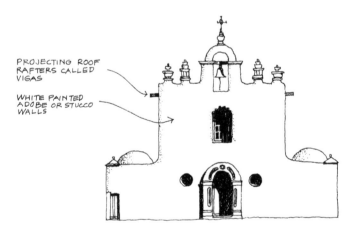

PROJECTING ROOF RAFTERS CALLED VIGAS

WHITE PAINTED ADOBE OR STUCCO WALLS

1935
OUR LADY OF MT. CARMEL CHURCH, EAST VALLEY, MONTECITO, CALIFORNIA
ROSS MONTGOMERY AND WILLIAM MULLARY, ARCHITECTS

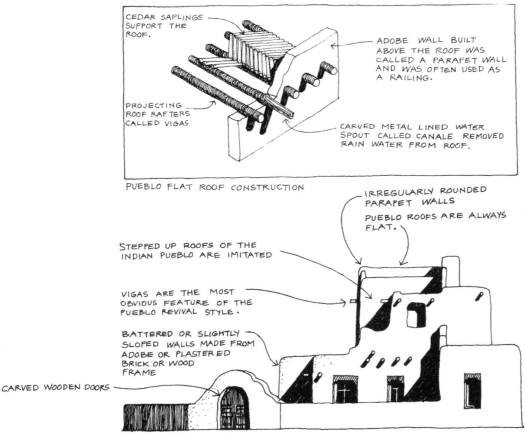

CEDAR SAPLINGS SUPPORT THE ROOF.

ADOBE WALL BUILT ABOVE THE ROOF WAS CALLED A PARAPET WALL AND WAS OFTEN USED AS A RAILING.

PROJECTING ROOF RAFTERS CALLED VIGAS

CARVED METAL LINED WATER SPOUT CALLED CANALE REMOVED RAIN WATER FROM ROOF.

PUEBLO FLAT ROOF CONSTRUCTION

IRREGULARLY ROUNDED PARAPET WALLS

PUEBLO ROOFS ARE ALWAYS FLAT.

STEPPED UP ROOFS OF THE INDIAN PUEBLO ARE IMITATED

VIGAS ARE THE MOST OBVIOUS FEATURE OF THE PUEBLO REVIVAL STYLE.

BATTERED OR SLIGHTLY SLOPED WALLS MADE FROM ADOBE OR PLASTERED BRICK OR WOOD FRAME

CARVED WOODEN DOORS

1930 ZIMMERMAN HOUSE, ALBUQUERQUE, NEW MEXICO
W. MILES BRITTELLE, ARCHITECT

Pueblo Revival Style architecture mixed with Spanish Colonial Revival forms (p. 208) was very popular with developers in Los Angeles and other southern California cities in the 1920s. It became a true vernacular style, primarily used for small stucco houses with little embellishment.

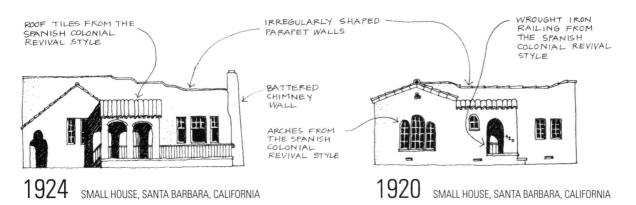

ROOF TILES FROM THE SPANISH COLONIAL REVIVAL STYLE

IRREGULARLY SHAPED PARAPET WALLS

WROUGHT IRON RAILING FROM THE SPANISH COLONIAL REVIVAL STYLE

BATTERED CHIMNEY WALL

ARCHES FROM THE SPANISH COLONIAL REVIVAL STYLE

1924 SMALL HOUSE, SANTA BARBARA, CALIFORNIA

1920 SMALL HOUSE, SANTA BARBARA, CALIFORNIA

Colonial Revival

Countrywide
1925

The years from 1920 to 1929 witnessed an extraordinary prosperity among a large part of America's growing population. New housing was in demand to an unprecedented degree, resulting in a building boom that inspired houses to be built in more different styles than during the mid- to late-nineteenth century. The perfection of the automobile, the improvement in highways, and the ease of communication between city and country caused growth along the edges of all of America's densely populated areas. In short, suburbia mushroomed with a variety of housing styles.

The traditional Colonial styles, because they evoked memories of America's past, or because they had a certain old-world charm that was in harmony with the older architecture of the neighborhood, became most popular. A wide variety of styles based on the Cape Cod Style evolved, including many developed by the prefabrication industry. The Cape Cod quickly became the most popular housing style in America.

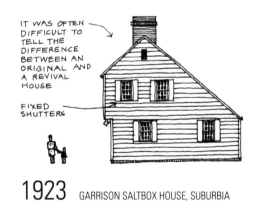

IT WAS OFTEN DIFFICULT TO TELL THE DIFFERENCE BETWEEN AN ORIGINAL AND A REVIVAL HOUSE

FIXED SHUTTERS

1923   GARRISON SALTBOX HOUSE, SUBURBIA

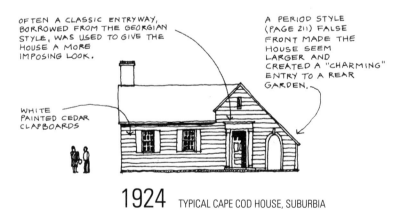

OFTEN A CLASSIC ENTRYWAY, BORROWED FROM THE GEORGIAN STYLE, WAS USED TO GIVE THE HOUSE A MORE IMPOSING LOOK.

A PERIOD STYLE (PAGE 211) FALSE FRONT MADE THE HOUSE SEEM LARGER AND CREATED A "CHARMING" ENTRY TO A REAR GARDEN.

WHITE PAINTED CEDAR CLAPBOARDS

1924   TYPICAL CAPE COD HOUSE, SUBURBIA

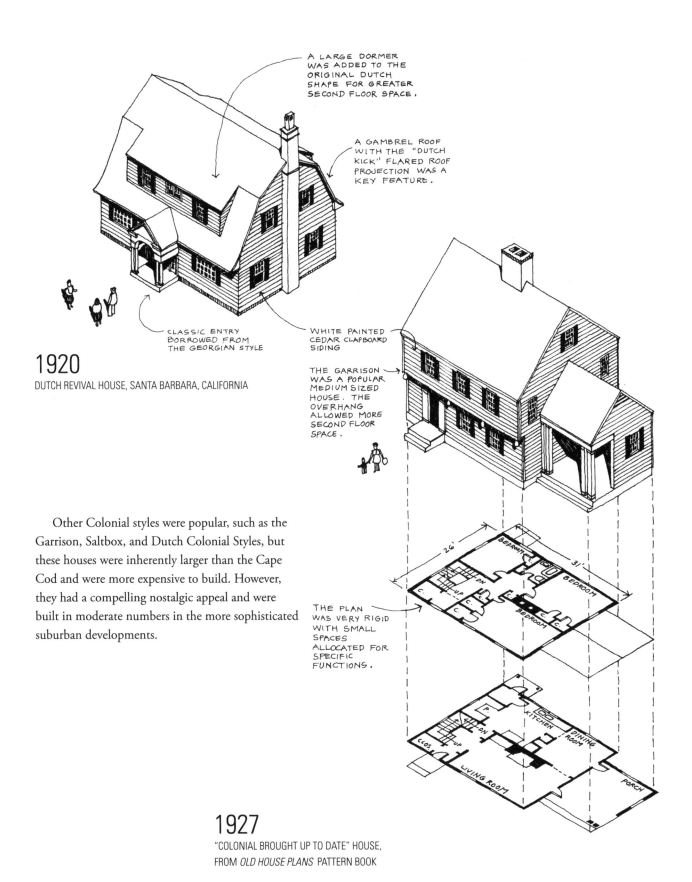

A LARGE DORMER WAS ADDED TO THE ORIGINAL DUTCH SHAPE FOR GREATER SECOND FLOOR SPACE.

A GAMBREL ROOF WITH THE "DUTCH KICK" FLARED ROOF PROJECTION WAS A KEY FEATURE.

CLASSIC ENTRY BORROWED FROM THE GEORGIAN STYLE

WHITE PAINTED CEDAR CLAPBOARD SIDING

1920
DUTCH REVIVAL HOUSE, SANTA BARBARA, CALIFORNIA

THE GARRISON WAS A POPULAR MEDIUM SIZED HOUSE. THE OVERHANG ALLOWED MORE SECOND FLOOR SPACE.

Other Colonial styles were popular, such as the Garrison, Saltbox, and Dutch Colonial Styles, but these houses were inherently larger than the Cape Cod and were more expensive to build. However, they had a compelling nostalgic appeal and were built in moderate numbers in the more sophisticated suburban developments.

THE PLAN WAS VERY RIGID WITH SMALL SPACES ALLOCATED FOR SPECIFIC FUNCTIONS.

1927
"COLONIAL BROUGHT UP TO DATE" HOUSE,
FROM *OLD HOUSE PLANS* PATTERN BOOK

Fantasy

Countrywide 1925

There have been many houses built in America that are so original, so strange, or imaginative that they defy categorization. They could be called "bizarre," "fantastic," or even "eccentric," but "fantasy" is the term that seems to best describe such buildings. They are, after all, attempts by their designers to realize their dreams—extraordinary dreams of transforming visionary images into nontraditional architecture.

There are two types of Fantasy Style houses: The first is called prefigured because it is a building that is made from a preconceived shape without regard to interior functioning. Some architects call this designing from the outside-in. A good example is the Margate City Elephant House shown on the opposite page. The interior room layout and circulation patterns had to conform to the exterior shape. The second type of fantasy house, the opposite of prefigured, is called *evolutionary* because it is a building whose shape evolves from the layout of the spaces within. The house is designed from the inside-out with little regard to its exterior look. Good examples of this style are the work of sculptor-artist-builders Clarence Schmidt of Woodstock, New York, and Art Beal of West Cambria Pines, California. Their work comes out of a personal vision, and appears as a kind of rambling dreamlike, pop sculpture.

Robert Venturi, Denise Scott Brown, and Steven Izenour, in their book *Learning from Las Vegas*, devised two interesting categories of highway architecture that are applicable here: The *duck* and the *decorated shed*.

THE DUCK IS A SYMBOL ATTRACTING CARS FROM THE HIGHWAY.

THE DECORATED SHED IS A BUILDING DECORATED WITH SIGNS THAT ATTRACT CARS FROM THE HIGHWAY.

The duck is obviously a prefigured shape designed from the outside without regard to interior functioning. The decorated shed is a conventional, but conspicuously ornamented building. Both buildings are designed to attract speeding cars from highways—the duck presents the viewer with a whimsical symbol of the activity within and the shed has had ornamental signs applied to it for the same purpose. Many American houses have been built as ducks (a prefigured shape designed for exterior visual impact) and others as decorated sheds (a conventional house with an applied style).

HOT DOG STAND

DRIVE-IN RESTAURANT

ICE CREAM PARLOR

SNACK BAR

1925–1940 PREFIGURED ARCHITECTURE AT ITS BEST, FOUR LUNCH AND REFRESHMENT STANDS, LOS ANGELES, CALIFORNIA

Probably the finest example of Prefigured Fantasy Style house architecture in America is the Elephant House built by James V. Lafferty in 1883 in Margate City, New Jersey. Lafferty built a three-story, 122-foot high elephant hotel on Coney Island around the same time but it burned in 1896. Lafferty argued that the elephant shape was ideal for human habitation because, "the elevation of the body permits the circulation of air beneath it and removes it from the dampness and moisture of the ground…. Furthermore, the body is exposed to light and air on all sides, wherefore it provides a healthy and suitable place of occupancy for invalids and others."

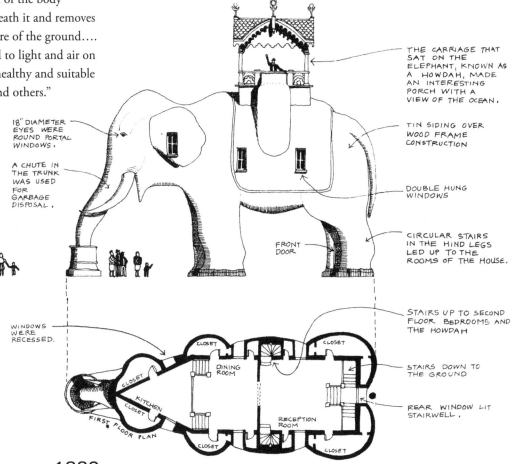

THE CARRIAGE THAT SAT ON THE ELEPHANT, KNOWN AS A HOWDAH, MADE AN INTERESTING PORCH WITH A VIEW OF THE OCEAN.

18" DIAMETER EYES WERE ROUND PORTAL WINDOWS.

A CHUTE IN THE TRUNK WAS USED FOR GARBAGE DISPOSAL.

TIN SIDING OVER WOOD FRAME CONSTRUCTION

DOUBLE HUNG WINDOWS

FRONT DOOR

CIRCULAR STAIRS IN THE HIND LEGS LED UP TO THE ROOMS OF THE HOUSE.

WINDOWS WERE RECESSED.

STAIRS UP TO SECOND FLOOR BEDROOMS AND THE HOWDAH

STAIRS DOWN TO THE GROUND

REAR WINDOW LIT STAIRWELL.

CLOSET — DINING ROOM — KITCHEN — FIRST FLOOR PLAN — RECEPTION ROOM — CLOSET

1882 ELEPHANT HOUSE, MARGATE CITY, NEW JERSEY
JAMES V. LAFFERTY, ARCHITECT

1927
TEAPOT HOUSE, TACOMA, WASHINGTON

1940
MOTHER GOOSE HOUSE, HAZARD, KENTUCKY

1948
SHOE HOUSE, HALLAM, PENNSYLVANIA

Shown below and on the opposite page are two dreamlike houses designed and built by their owners. Mercer's Castle, formally known as Fonthill, was built primarily of reinforced concrete and decorative tile by Dr. Henry Mercer, an amateur architect, with a large crew skilled in the use of concrete. Mercer designed as he built (he built by eye—without a level), using a large model to precheck his work. He began with a small 1742 woodframe farmhouse (where he and his crew lived during construction) and expanded room by room.

The house is a good example of the Additive or Evolutionary Fantasy Style, although the exterior facade has been somewhat formalized by Mercer's eclectic shapes recalled from his travels abroad. The plan, however, is a maze of rooms, interconnecting staircases, and passageways that remind one of the settings in *Dr. Caligari's Cabinet*. The exterior is even stranger because of the austerity of the gray reinforced concrete walls and the configuration of exotic, nostalgic facade and roof shapes.

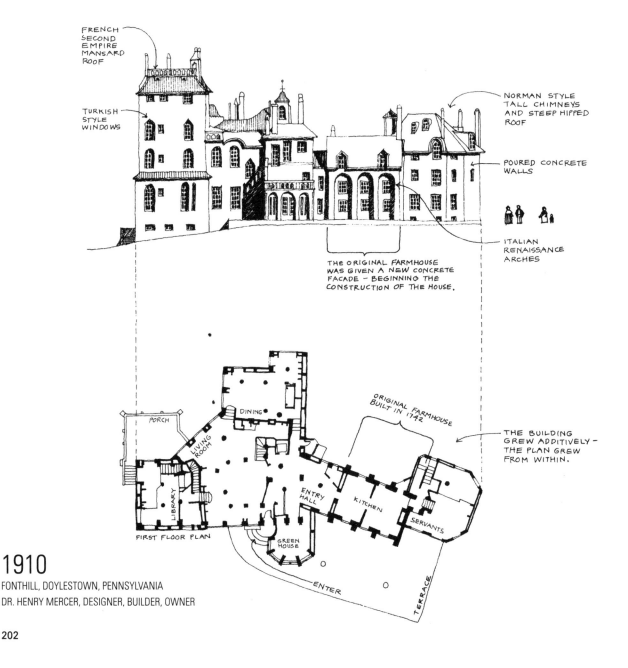

FRENCH SECOND EMPIRE MANSARD ROOF

TURKISH STYLE WINDOWS

NORMAN STYLE TALL CHIMNEYS AND STEEP HIPPED ROOF

POURED CONCRETE WALLS

ITALIAN RENAISSANCE ARCHES

THE ORIGINAL FARMHOUSE WAS GIVEN A NEW CONCRETE FACADE – BEGINNING THE CONSTRUCTION OF THE HOUSE.

ORIGINAL FARMHOUSE BUILT IN 1742

THE BUILDING GREW ADDITIVELY – THE PLAN GREW FROM WITHIN.

PORCH

DINING

LIVING ROOM

LIBRARY

ENTRY HALL

KITCHEN

SERVANTS

GREEN HOUSE

FIRST FLOOR PLAN

ENTER

TERRACE

1910

FONTHILL, DOYLESTOWN, PENNSYLVANIA
DR. HENRY MERCER, DESIGNER, BUILDER, OWNER

Shown below is the house of architect Bruce Goff. It is a prefigured stone spiral enclosing a series of "living pods" (designated activity areas such as sleeping, eating, etc.) with a large mast that supports the roof with cables. The spiral is so large that it allowed the interior to evolve into an arrangement of spaces that suited the owners. Although the spiral is prefigured, the interior is evolutionary.

1957
BRUCE GOFF RESIDENCE, NORMAN, OKLAHOMA
BRUCE GOFF, ARCHITECT, BUILDER, OWNER

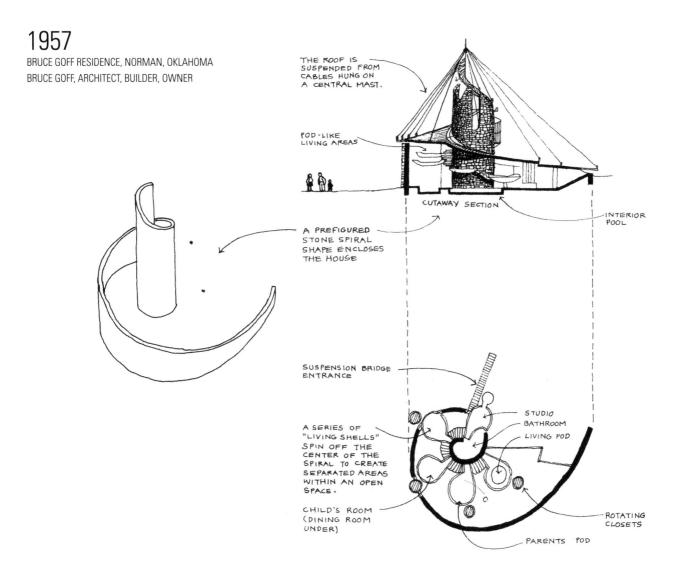

THE ROOF IS SUSPENDED FROM CABLES HUNG ON A CENTRAL MAST.

POD-LIKE LIVING AREAS

CUTAWAY SECTION

INTERIOR POOL

A PREFIGURED STONE SPIRAL SHAPE ENCLOSES THE HOUSE

SUSPENSION BRIDGE ENTRANCE

A SERIES OF "LIVING SHELLS" SPIN OFF THE CENTER OF THE SPIRAL TO CREATE SEPARATED AREAS WITHIN AN OPEN SPACE.

CHILD'S ROOM (DINING ROOM UNDER)

STUDIO
BATHROOM
LIVING POD

ROTATING CLOSETS

PARENTS POD

Two of the best examples of the evolutionary style house were the homes of Art Beal, shown below, and Clarence Schmidt, shown on the opposite page.

Art Beal (alias Doctor Tinkerpaws or Captain Nitwit) built his house additively, from within, on the side of a 250-foot high cliff in Cambria Pines, California. It took him forty-five years to build and it was constructed primarily with found materials such as beer cans, tires, car wheels, pots and pans, and scrap lumber. Beal says of his house, "In 1927 I created my first one-room shack. But that wasn't enough. I put up another and another and another."

STONE FROM THE HILLSIDE WAS USED FOR ARCHED WALLS.

WORKSHOP WING

RAILINGS WERE MADE FROM DISCARDED WATER PIPES.

ENTRY FROM STREET LEVEL

1927–1972 ART BEAL RESIDENCE, CAMBRIA PINES, CALIFORNIA
ART BEAL, BUILDER, OWNER

The home of Clarence Schmidt, a retired mason of Woodstock, New York, was a seven-story, multi-roomed, labyrinthian complex that was built on a hillside over a period of eighteen years beginning in 1949. Schmidt started with a one-room cabin and added to it in all directions, applying found materials, primarily wood windows and scrap siding, to a wood skeletal scaffolding. The principal living space in his ever expanding house always centered on the original cabin even though it was completely enclosed. Most of the thirty-five or more rooms were spaces used by Schmidt to experiment with his art, for which he put together found objects like plastic flowers, mirrors, aluminum foil, plastic dolls, Christmas lights, and discarded furniture pieces to create strange outdoor sculpture gardens and terraces that in turn became an integral part of this house. The house unfortunately was burned to the ground in 1967, nine years before Schmidt's death.

THE HOUSE WAS BUILT AS A SERIES OF TIERS WITH INTERCONNECTING BALCONIES, RAMPS, AND WALKWAYS.

DIFFERENT TYPES OF WINDOWS WERE ATTACHED TO A SCAFFOLDLIKE WOOD FRAME ALLOWING THE HOUSE TO EXPAND.

ENTRY FROM THE HILLTOP

STONEWORK PROVIDED A FOUNDATION FOR THE HOUSE AND WALLS FOR A TERRACE.

1949–1967 CLARENCE SCHMIDT RESIDENCE, WOODSTOCK, NEW YORK
CLARENCE SCHMIDT, BUILDER, OWNER

This page and the opposite page show two houses designed by Oklahoma architect Bruce Goff that can only be termed Fantasy, although they both were realistic, though unbuilt, projects. Like most of Goff's work, both houses are designed within a prefigured shape requiring an interesting structural solution. The Nicol House, a scheme never shown to its client because of its high cost, used laminated wood beams to span its relatively large distance. The Abrahams House, approved for construction by the client but not the lending agencies, used sprayed gas-concrete over a thin steel structure to create smooth spherical forms.

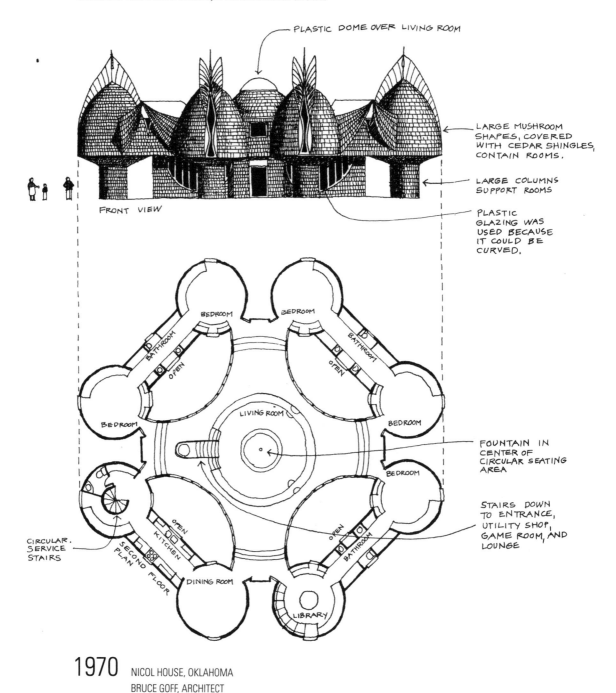

PLASTIC DOME OVER LIVING ROOM

FRONT VIEW

LARGE MUSHROOM SHAPES, COVERED WITH CEDAR SHINGLES, CONTAIN ROOMS.

LARGE COLUMNS SUPPORT ROOMS

PLASTIC GLAZING WAS USED BECAUSE IT COULD BE CURVED.

BEDROOM

BEDROOM

BATHROOM

OPEN

BATHROOM

OPEN

BEDROOM

BEDROOM

LIVING ROOM

BEDROOM

FOUNTAIN IN CENTER OF CIRCULAR SEATING AREA

STAIRS DOWN TO ENTRANCE, UTILITY SHOP, GAME ROOM, AND LOUNGE

OPEN

KITCHEN

OPEN

BATHROOM

CIRCULAR SERVICE STAIRS

SECOND FLOOR PLAN

DINING ROOM

LIBRARY

1970 NICOL HOUSE, OKLAHOMA
BRUCE GOFF, ARCHITECT

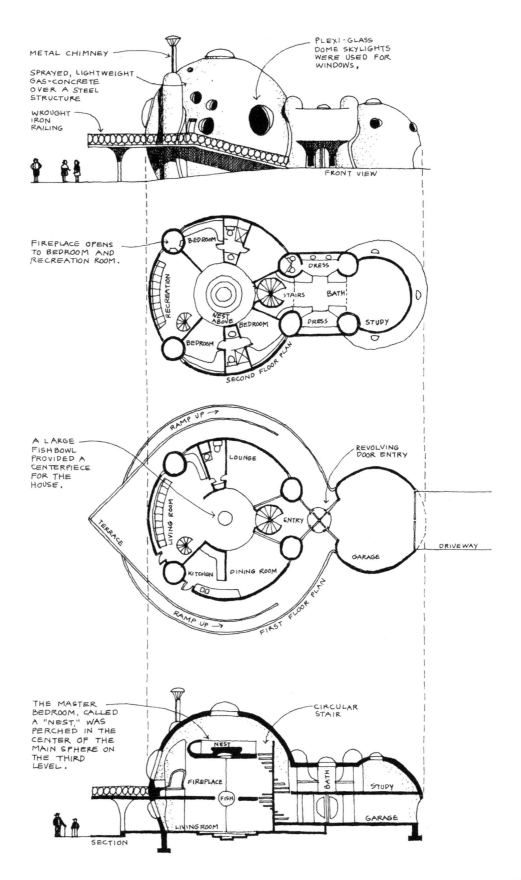

METAL CHIMNEY

SPRAYED, LIGHTWEIGHT GAS-CONCRETE OVER A STEEL STRUCTURE

WROUGHT IRON RAILING

PLEXI-GLASS DOME SKYLIGHTS WERE USED FOR WINDOWS.

FRONT VIEW

FIREPLACE OPENS TO BEDROOM AND RECREATION ROOM.

BEDROOM

DRESS

RECREATION

STAIRS BATH

NEST ABOVE

BEDROOM

DRESS STUDY

BEDROOM

SECOND FLOOR PLAN

A LARGE FISHBOWL PROVIDED A CENTERPIECE FOR THE HOUSE.

RAMP UP →

LOUNGE

REVOLVING DOOR ENTRY

TERRACE

LIVING ROOM

ENTRY

KITCHEN

DINING ROOM

GARAGE

DRIVEWAY

RAMP UP →

FIRST FLOOR PLAN

THE MASTER BEDROOM, CALLED A "NEST," WAS PERCHED IN THE CENTER OF THE MAIN SPHERE ON THE THIRD LEVEL.

CIRCULAR STAIR

NEST

FIREPLACE

BATH

STUDY

FISH

1967
ABRAHAMS HOUSE, OKLAHOMA
BRUCE GOFF, ARCHITECT

LIVING ROOM

GARAGE

SECTION

Spanish Colonial Revival

Southwest and Florida
1925

The Spanish Colonial Revival Style is a mixture of styles derived from the Mediterranean world, unified by the use of arches, courtyards, plain white wall surfaces, and red tile roofs. Architects were inspired by many sources: the adobe and Spanish Colonial buildings of southern California, late Moorish architecture, medieval Spanish church architecture, the Baroque architecture of Colonial Spain and Portugal, and the Pueblo and Mission styles.

The Spanish Colonial Revival Style began to gain acceptance with the popularity of Spanish Colonial buildings in the 1915 San Diego Exposition. Further impetus came from designers who sought wider sources for this "Spanish Renaissance." The style became popular in areas with a Hispanic past: Southern California, New Mexico, southern Arizona, Texas, and Florida. It lasted from 1915 to 1940, but around 1925, it became a craze. Models such as mission churches, California Ranch Style houses, and Mexican Baroque forts were used for the design of all sorts of public buildings as well as single family homes. The style was essentially a continuation of the Mission Style (p. 172) which initiated the Spanish Revival movement.

The leading practitioner of the Spanish Colonial Revival movement was the architect of the buildings at the San Diego Exposition, Bertram Goodhue. He was one of southern California's leading architects and was the author of a book on Spanish Colonial architecture in Mexico. His designs were among the first to earn the new classification, Spanish Colonial Revival.

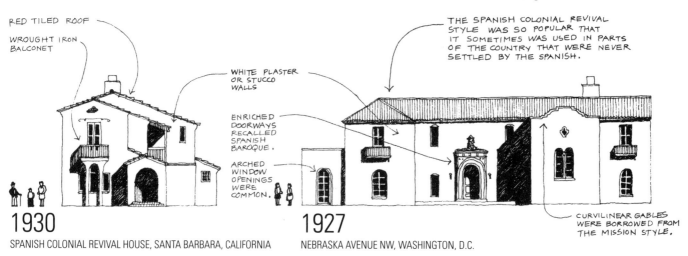

RED TILED ROOF

WROUGHT IRON BALCONET

WHITE PLASTER OR STUCCO WALLS

ENRICHED DOORWAYS RECALLED SPANISH BAROQUE.

ARCHED WINDOW OPENINGS WERE COMMON.

THE SPANISH COLONIAL REVIVAL STYLE WAS SO POPULAR THAT IT SOMETIMES WAS USED IN PARTS OF THE COUNTRY THAT WERE NEVER SETTLED BY THE SPANISH.

CURVILINEAR GABLES WERE BORROWED FROM THE MISSION STYLE.

1930
SPANISH COLONIAL REVIVAL HOUSE, SANTA BARBARA, CALIFORNIA

1927
NEBRASKA AVENUE NW, WASHINGTON, D.C.

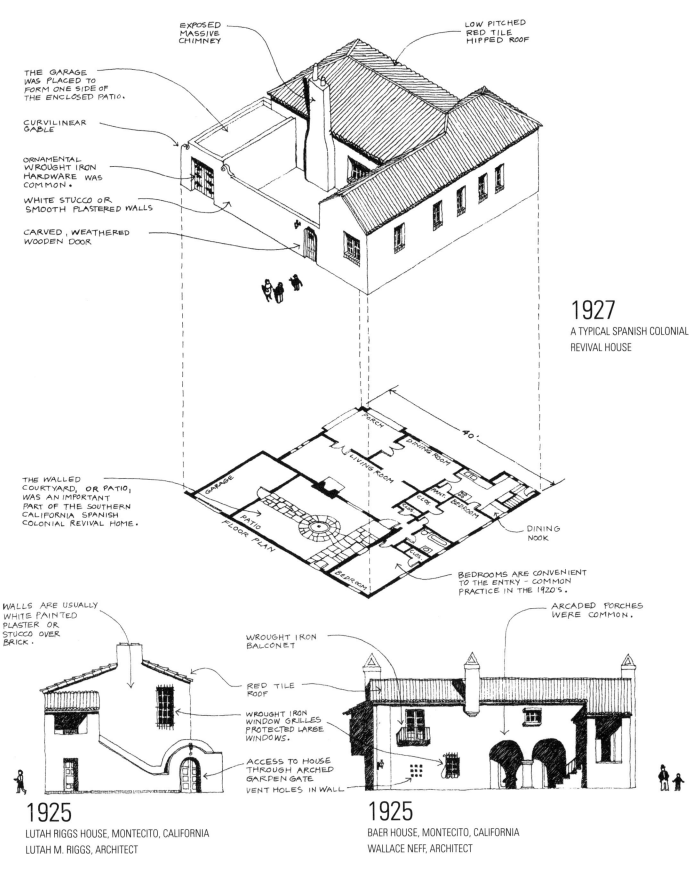

EXPOSED MASSIVE CHIMNEY

LOW PITCHED RED TILE HIPPED ROOF

THE GARAGE WAS PLACED TO FORM ONE SIDE OF THE ENCLOSED PATIO.

CURVILINEAR GABLE

ORNAMENTAL WROUGHT IRON HARDWARE WAS COMMON.

WHITE STUCCO OR SMOOTH PLASTERED WALLS

CARVED, WEATHERED WOODEN DOOR

1927
A TYPICAL SPANISH COLONIAL REVIVAL HOUSE

THE WALLED COURTYARD, OR PATIO, WAS AN IMPORTANT PART OF THE SOUTHERN CALIFORNIA SPANISH COLONIAL REVIVAL HOME.

PORCH

DINING ROOM

LIVING ROOM

40'

GARAGE

PATIO

FLOOR PLAN

CLOS.

PMNT.

BEDROOM

CLOS.

DINING NOOK

BEDROOM

BEDROOMS ARE CONVENIENT TO THE ENTRY - COMMON PRACTICE IN THE 1920'S.

WALLS ARE USUALLY WHITE PAINTED PLASTER OR STUCCO OVER BRICK.

ARCADED PORCHES WERE COMMON.

WROUGHT IRON BALCONET

RED TILE ROOF

WROUGHT IRON WINDOW GRILLES PROTECTED LARGE WINDOWS.

ACCESS TO HOUSE THROUGH ARCHED GARDEN GATE

VENT HOLES IN WALL

1925
LUTAH RIGGS HOUSE, MONTECITO, CALIFORNIA
LUTAH M. RIGGS, ARCHITECT

1925
BAER HOUSE, MONTECITO, CALIFORNIA
WALLACE NEFF, ARCHITECT

Period

Countrywide 1930

The years between World War I and the start of the Great Depression saw yet another revival of the picturesque house. It was called the "era of the Period house." Period Style buildings were convincing copies of older styles designed by conservative architects who looked to styles of proven worth and popular appeal for solutions to the current problems of house design. The variety of Period houses was endless. Architects who could build the most accurate replica of an Old-World house without compromising the client's desires for modern utility were in great demand. The styles of medieval English and French cottages were by far the most popular, but Georgian, Italian, Spanish, and American Colonial designs were also imitated.

In the early 1930s, as the International Style (p. 214) gained strength in America, Period Styles began to lose their popularity. Critics claimed it was "novelty for novelty's sake," and a feeble substitute for the original. Period architects, however, saw no reason why their structures should not be considered modern architecture at its best. H. H. Mencken suggested: "If I were building a house tomorrow it would certainly not follow the lines of a dynamo or a steam shovel....To say that the florid chicken coops of Le Corbusier and company are closer to nature than the houses of the eighteenth century is as absurd as to say that tar paper shacks behind the railroad tracks are closer to nature."

Fairy tale houses, such as the Hansel and Gretel cottage (opposite page), gave owners an intimate, romantic dollhouse quality. Arched entryways, and many different exterior surface textures were used to create stylish houses built by speculators by the millions in modest suburban neighborhoods throughout the country.

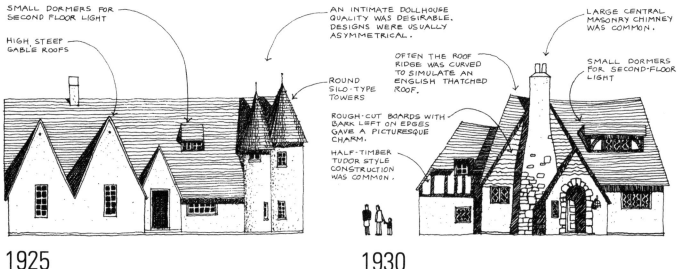

SMALL DORMERS FOR SECOND FLOOR LIGHT

HIGH STEEP GABLE ROOFS

AN INTIMATE DOLLHOUSE QUALITY WAS DESIRABLE. DESIGNS WERE USUALLY ASYMMETRICAL.

ROUND SILO-TYPE TOWERS

LARGE CENTRAL MASONRY CHIMNEY WAS COMMON.

OFTEN THE ROOF RIDGE WAS CURVED TO SIMULATE AN ENGLISH THATCHED ROOF.

SMALL DORMERS FOR SECOND-FLOOR LIGHT

ROUGH-CUT BOARDS WITH BARK LEFT ON EDGES GAVE A PICTURESQUE CHARM.

HALF-TIMBER TUDOR STYLE CONSTRUCTION WAS COMMON.

1925

TYPICAL PERIOD HOUSE BASED ON 16TH CENTURY FRENCH FARMHOUSE, MONTECITO, CALIFORNIA
PIERPONT DAVIS, ARCHITECT

1930

TYPICAL PERIOD HOUSE, BASED ON THE ENGLISH COTSWOLD COTTAGE

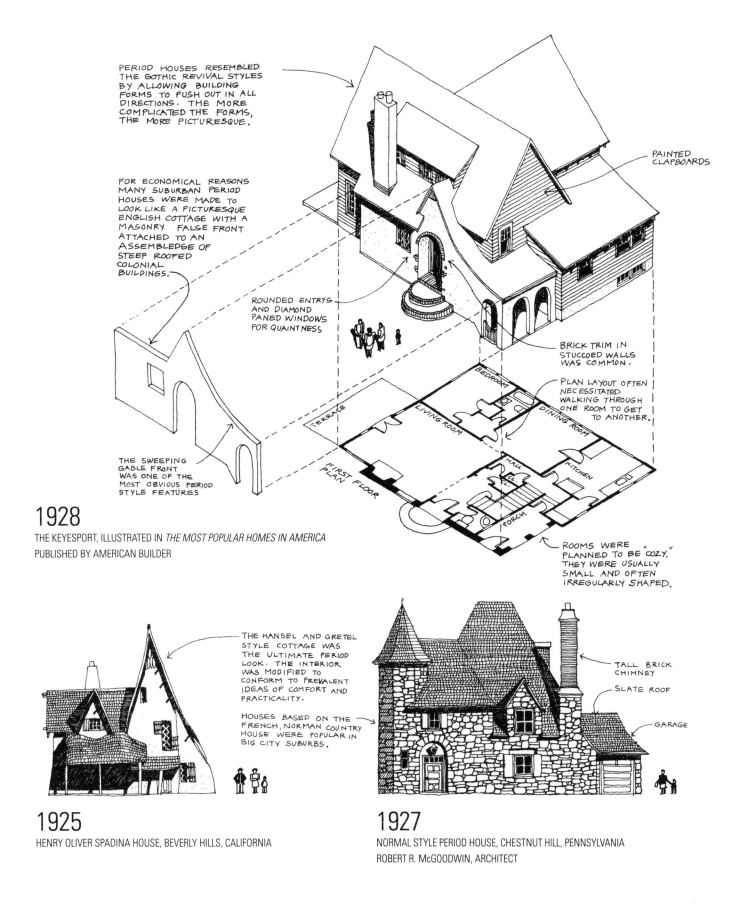

PERIOD HOUSES RESEMBLED THE GOTHIC REVIVAL STYLES BY ALLOWING BUILDING FORMS TO PUSH OUT IN ALL DIRECTIONS. THE MORE COMPLICATED THE FORMS, THE MORE PICTURESQUE.

PAINTED CLAPBOARDS

FOR ECONOMICAL REASONS MANY SUBURBAN PERIOD HOUSES WERE MADE TO LOOK LIKE A PICTURESQUE ENGLISH COTTAGE WITH A MASONRY FALSE FRONT ATTACHED TO AN ASSEMBLEDGE OF STEEP ROOFED COLONIAL BUILDINGS.

ROUNDED ENTRYS AND DIAMOND PANED WINDOWS FOR QUAINTNESS

BRICK TRIM IN STUCCOED WALLS WAS COMMON.

PLAN LAYOUT OFTEN NECESSITATED WALKING THROUGH ONE ROOM TO GET TO ANOTHER.

THE SWEEPING GABLE FRONT WAS ONE OF THE MOST OBVIOUS PERIOD STYLE FEATURES

TERRACE

BEDROOM

LIVING ROOM

DINING ROOM

FIRST FLOOR PLAN

HALL

CL.

KITCHEN

PORCH

ROOMS WERE PLANNED TO BE "COZY." THEY WERE USUALLY SMALL AND OFTEN IRREGULARLY SHAPED.

1928

THE KEYESPORT, ILLUSTRATED IN *THE MOST POPULAR HOMES IN AMERICA*
PUBLISHED BY AMERICAN BUILDER

THE HANSEL AND GRETEL STYLE COTTAGE WAS THE ULTIMATE PERIOD LOOK. THE INTERIOR WAS MODIFIED TO CONFORM TO PREVALENT IDEAS OF COMFORT AND PRACTICALITY.

HOUSES BASED ON THE FRENCH, NORMAN COUNTRY HOUSE WERE POPULAR IN BIG CITY SUBURBS.

TALL BRICK CHIMNEY

SLATE ROOF

GARAGE

1925

HENRY OLIVER SPADINA HOUSE, BEVERLY HILLS, CALIFORNIA

1927

NORMAL STYLE PERIOD HOUSE, CHESTNUT HILL, PENNSYLVANIA
ROBERT R. McGOODWIN, ARCHITECT

In the mid-1930s, *Pencil Points* magazine held regular house design competitions, usually sponsored by a building materials manufacturer. Houses shown on this and the opposite page were awarded a "mention" in 1934 and 1935 competitions, losing out to houses designed in the International or Art Moderne Styles that were quickly gaining popularity.

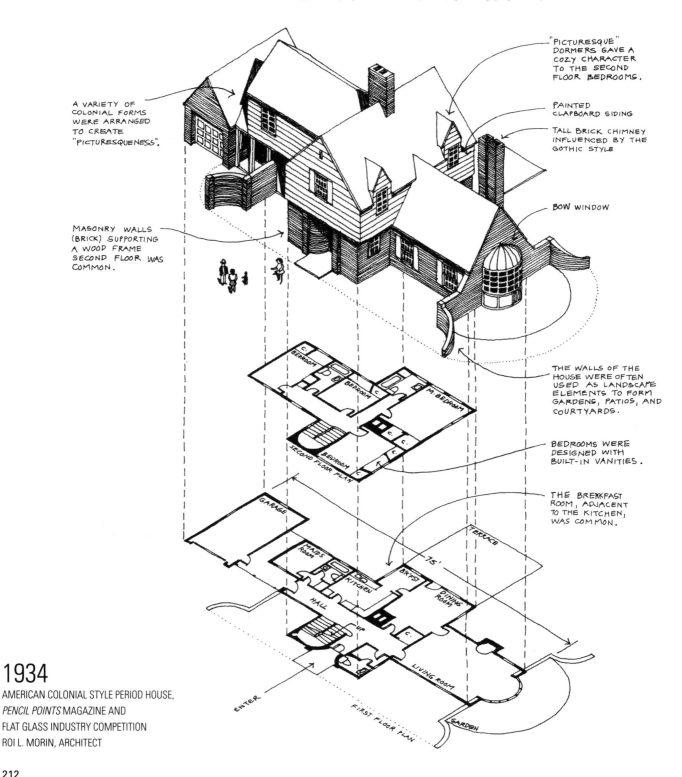

"PICTURESQUE" DORMERS GAVE A COZY CHARACTER TO THE SECOND FLOOR BEDROOMS.

A VARIETY OF COLONIAL FORMS WERE ARRANGED TO CREATE "PICTURESQUENESS".

PAINTED CLAPBOARD SIDING

TALL BRICK CHIMNEY INFLUENCED BY THE GOTHIC STYLE

BOW WINDOW

MASONRY WALLS (BRICK) SUPPORTING A WOOD FRAME SECOND FLOOR WAS COMMON.

THE WALLS OF THE HOUSE WERE OFTEN USED AS LANDSCAPE ELEMENTS TO FORM GARDENS, PATIOS, AND COURTYARDS.

BEDROOMS WERE DESIGNED WITH BUILT-IN VANITIES.

THE BREAKFAST ROOM, ADJACENT TO THE KITCHEN, WAS COMMON.

BEDROOM
BEDROOM
M. BEDROOM
BEDROOM
SECOND FLOOR PLAN

GARAGE
MAID'S ROOM
KITCHEN
BK'F'ST
TERRACE
DINING ROOM
HALL
UP
LIVING ROOM
ENTER
FIRST FLOOR PLAN
GARDEN

1934
AMERICAN COLONIAL STYLE PERIOD HOUSE,
PENCIL POINTS MAGAZINE AND
FLAT GLASS INDUSTRY COMPETITION
ROI L. MORIN, ARCHITECT

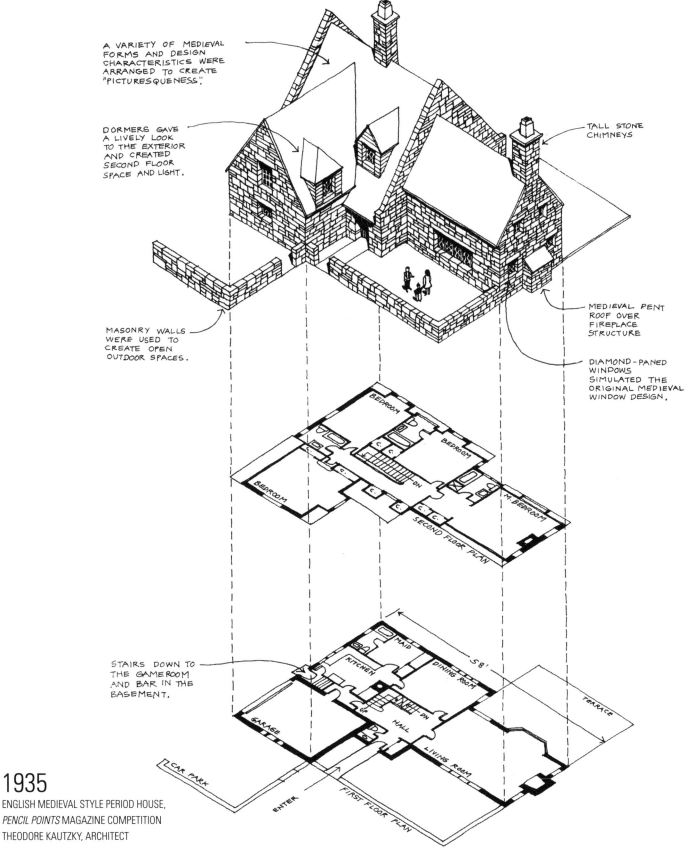

A VARIETY OF MEDIEVAL FORMS AND DESIGN CHARACTERISTICS WERE ARRANGED TO CREATE "PICTURESQUENESS".

DORMERS GAVE A LIVELY LOOK TO THE EXTERIOR AND CREATED SECOND FLOOR SPACE AND LIGHT.

TALL STONE CHIMNEYS

MASONRY WALLS WERE USED TO CREATE OPEN OUTDOOR SPACES.

MEDIEVAL PENT ROOF OVER FIREPLACE STRUCTURE

DIAMOND-PANED WINDOWS SIMULATED THE ORIGINAL MEDIEVAL WINDOW DESIGN.

BEDROOM

BEDROOM

BEDROOM

M. BEDROOM

SECOND FLOOR PLAN

STAIRS DOWN TO THE GAMEROOM AND BAR IN THE BASEMENT.

MAID

DINING ROOM

58'

KITCHEN

TERRACE

GARAGE

UP

HALL

DN

LIVING ROOM

CAR PARK

ENTER

FIRST FLOOR PLAN

1935
ENGLISH MEDIEVAL STYLE PERIOD HOUSE,
PENCIL POINTS MAGAZINE COMPETITION
THEODORE KAUTZKY, ARCHITECT

International

Countrywide
1930

Early in 1932, the Museum of Modern Art in New York City exhibited its first architectural show entitled "Modern Architecture." It was intended to prove that the stylistic confusion of the preceding forty years was about to come to an end. Photographs and drawings of works by architects practicing in fifteen different countries were grouped under the title "International Style." The name became a household word.

In Europe, the International Style began in close association with two movements in painting: Expressionism in Germany—a revolt against Impressionism—and Neoplasticism in Holland with the painter Mondriaan reducing his compositions to related rectangles, lines, and primary colors in relation to black and white. European International Style architects such as Walter Gropius working with the Bauhaus School in Germany, Le Corbusier whose practice was beginning in France, and the German Mies van der Rohe (p. 236) were the early masters. They created a style based on modern engineering principles and materials. Concrete, glass, and steel were the primary materials and the unadorned, utilitarian factory was the resulting aesthetic.

The International Style developed as a vigorously functional, stark, unadorned style that was based on open flexible planning. The International Style architect thought of his creation as a skeleton enclosed by a thin light skin. He thought in terms of volume—spaces enclosed by surfaces—and not in terms of mass and solidity. He designed his surfaces accordingly, eliminating moldings and making his doors and windows flush with the surface. The Villa Savoie by the French master Le Corbusier (shown below) is internationally known to students of architecture as one of the world's best examples of the International Style.

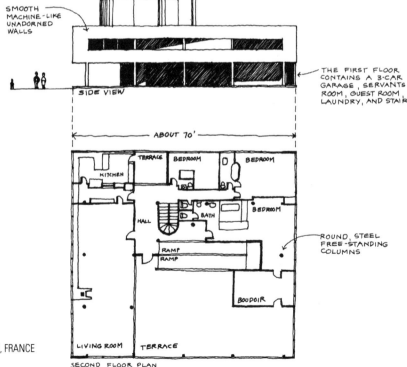

SMOOTH MACHINE-LIKE UNADORNED WALLS

SIDE VIEW

THE FIRST FLOOR CONTAINS A 3-CAR GARAGE, SERVANTS ROOM, GUEST ROOM, LAUNDRY, AND STAIR

ABOUT 70'

TERRACE   BEDROOM   BEDROOM

KITCHEN

BEDROOM

HALL   BATH

ROUND, STEEL FREE-STANDING COLUMNS

RAMP
RAMP

BOUDOIR

LIVING ROOM   TERRACE

SECOND FLOOR PLAN

1930
VILLA SAVOYE, POISSY-SUR-SEINE, FRANCE
LE CORBUSIER, ARCHITECT

Many European-born architects, such as Viennese architects Rudolph Schindler and Richard Neutra and German born Marcel Breuer and Mies van der Rohe, immigrated to America and gained international reputations. Schindler and Nuetra worked in southern California where radical innovation and experimentation in rapidly expanding Los Angeles was praised. Also, the Mission Style and the work of Irving Gill (p. 172) had paved the way for an open, unadorned style. Breuer became the head of the influential office named The Architect's Collaborative (TAC) in Boston. Mies set up practice in Chicago, where his glass and thin steel skeleton buildings became famous. American International Style architects were also always influenced by the work of Le Corbusier and the Finn, Alvar Aalto, as it was published in architectural journals.

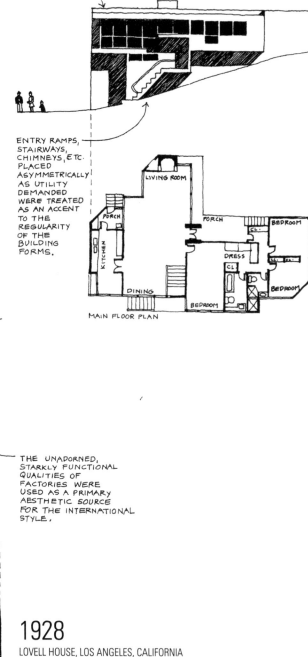

1933

OLIVER HOUSE, LOS ANGELES, CALIFORNIA
RUDOLPH SCHINDLER, ARCHITECT

FLAT ROOF

ENTRY RAMPS, STAIRWAYS, CHIMNEYS, ETC. PLACED ASYMMETRICALLY AS UTILITY DEMANDED WERE TREATED AS AN ACCENT TO THE REGULARITY OF THE BUILDING FORMS.

LIVING ROOM
PORCH
KITCHEN
BEDROOM
DRESS
CL
PORCH
CL
DINING
BEDROOM
BEDROOM

MAIN FLOOR PLAN

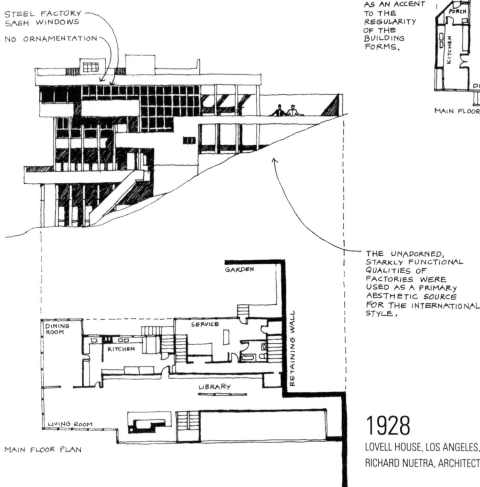

STEEL FACTORY SASH WINDOWS

NO ORNAMENTATION

THE UNADORNED, STARKLY FUNCTIONAL QUALITIES OF FACTORIES WERE USED AS A PRIMARY AESTHETIC SOURCE FOR THE INTERNATIONAL STYLE.

GARDEN

DINING ROOM
KITCHEN
SERVICE
RETAINING WALL
LIBRARY
LIVING ROOM

MAIN FLOOR PLAN

1928

LOVELL HOUSE, LOS ANGELES, CALIFORNIA
RICHARD NUETRA, ARCHITECT

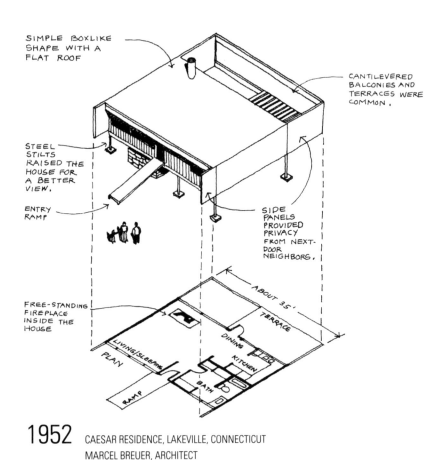

SIMPLE BOXLIKE SHAPE WITH A FLAT ROOF

CANTILEVERED BALCONIES AND TERRACES WERE COMMON.

STEEL STILTS RAISED THE HOUSE FOR A BETTER VIEW.

ENTRY RAMP

SIDE PANELS PROVIDED PRIVACY FROM NEXT-DOOR NEIGHBORS.

FREE-STANDING FIREPLACE INSIDE THE HOUSE

ABOUT 35'

TERRACE

DINING

LIVING/SLEEPING

PLAN

KITCHEN

BATH

RAMP

1952 CAESAR RESIDENCE, LAKEVILLE, CONNECTICUT
MARCEL BREUER, ARCHITECT

Before World War I, modern architecture was the creation of a few great individuals. Since the war, the International Style grew throughout Europe and America, not as an invention of one person but as a coordinated effort by many architects. After 1922, the International Style did not change fundamentally. Based as it was on modern engineering and utilitarian design practices it spread to all parts of the world. In America it has remained a popular and influential style since its beginnings. Revival International Style houses are discussed beginning on page 296.

Second generation American International Style architects like Paul Rudolph and Eliot Noyes who studied with Gropius and Breuer at Harvard believed that climatic site differences were good reason to stress regional characteristics in building. By the early 1950s, these architects and others like them were designing houses using International Style rules, set down by their mentors twenty-five years earlier, but building with materials more indigenous to the site. The example shown opposite, no longer a white stucco box, incorporates native fieldstone for exterior walls with a cedar roof fascia board—natural materials influenced by the rugged character of the site.

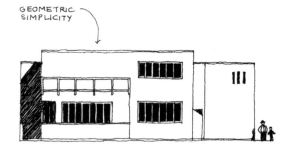

GEOMETRIC SIMPLICITY

1927
LEWIN HOUSE,
BERLIN, GERMANY
WALTER GROPIUS, ARCHITECT

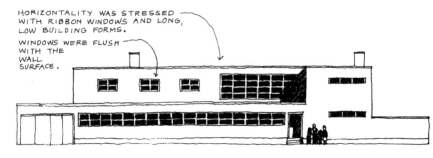

HORIZONTALITY WAS STRESSED WITH RIBBON WINDOWS AND LONG, LOW BUILDING FORMS.

WINDOWS WERE FLUSH WITH THE WALL SURFACE.

1935
#64 OLD CHURCH ST.,
LONDON, ENGLAND
MENDELSOHN AND CHERMAYEFF, ARCHITECTS

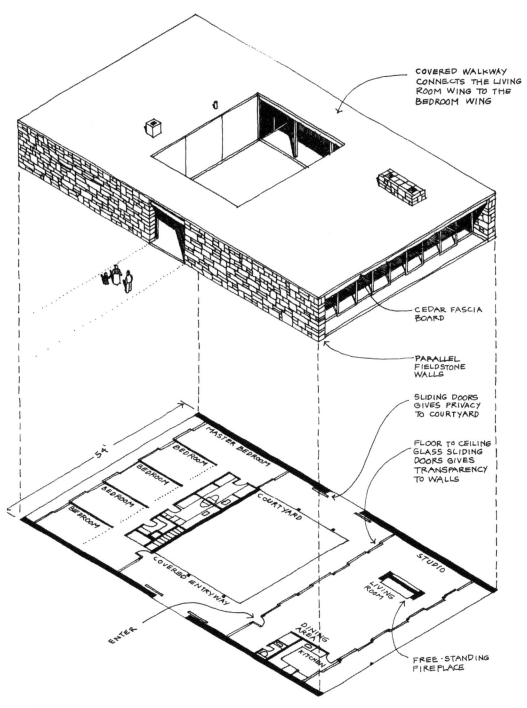

COVERED WALKWAY CONNECTS THE LIVING ROOM WING TO THE BEDROOM WING

CEDAR FASCIA BOARD

PARALLEL FIELDSTONE WALLS

SLIDING DOORS GIVES PRIVACY TO COURTYARD

FLOOR TO CEILING GLASS SLIDING DOORS GIVES TRANSPARENCY TO WALLS

MASTER BEDROOM

BEDROOM

BEDROOM

BEDROOM

BEDROOM

54'

COURTYARD

STUDIO

COVERED ENTRYWAY

LIVING ROOM

ENTER

DINING AREA

KITCHEN

FREE-STANDING FIREPLACE

1954 ELIOT NOYES HOUSE, NEW CANAAN, CONNECTICUT
ELIOT NOYES, ARCHITECT

Art Moderne

Countrywide 1935

Art Moderne, sometimes called Moderne, Modernistic, or Depression Modern, was a style that consciously strove for an architectural expression to compliment the machine age. It was a unique American style although it was part of the International Style movement, it borrowed from the French Art Nouveau, and was somewhat influenced by Art Deco. In a five-year period beginning around 1932, it changed the shape of virtually everything in the American home including the home itself.

The Art Moderne Style is often confused with the Art Deco Style, a style embraced by the tastemakers of Paris that became a fashionable fad in America by the end of the 1920s. It was a style of decoration, primarily hard edge and angular, and lent itself well to some public buildings, such as movie theaters, hotels, and office building facades and lobbies. It enjoyed a short-lived vogue as applied decoration to jewelry, cigarette lighters, ash trays, and the like but never became a popular domestic architectural style.

Art Moderne was inspired by America's love affair with machines—the airplane, the car, the train, and the toaster. It was a new machine art: honest, simple, and above all, functional. Houses were streamlined like every other machine with rounded corners, flat roofs, horizontal bands of windows, and smooth walls with no ornamentation. Curved window glass, used to wrap around corners, stainless steel window and door trim, and thin sunshade roofs over southern windows were popular Art Moderne details.

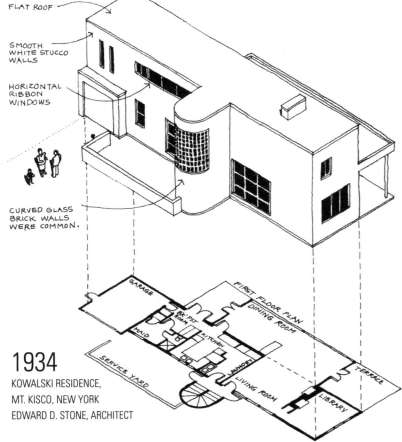

FLAT ROOF

SMOOTH WHITE STUCCO WALLS

HORIZONTAL RIBBON WINDOWS

CURVED GLASS BRICK WALLS WERE COMMON.

GARAGE

BK'FST ROOM

MAID

KITCHEN

LAUNDRY

FIRST FLOOR PLAN

DINING ROOM

SERVICE YARD

LIVING ROOM

LIBRARY

TERRACE

1934
KOWALSKI RESIDENCE, MT. KISCO, NEW YORK
EDWARD D. STONE, ARCHITECT

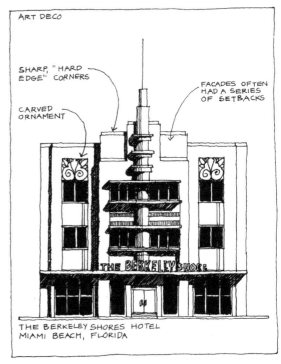

ART DECO

SHARP, "HARD EDGE" CORNERS

CARVED ORNAMENT

FACADES OFTEN HAD A SERIES OF SETBACKS

THE BERKELEY SHORE

THE BERKELEY SHORES HOTEL MIAMI BEACH, FLORIDA

ART DECO WAS A RARELY USED STYLE FOR HOUSES

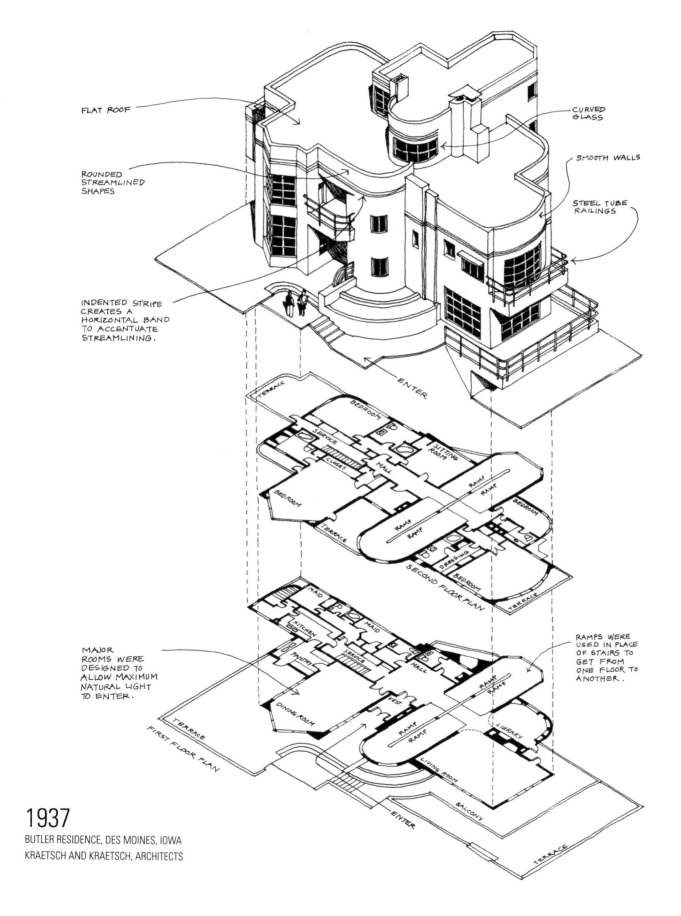

FLAT ROOF

CURVED GLASS

ROUNDED STREAMLINED SHAPES

SMOOTH WALLS

STEEL TUBE RAILINGS

INDENTED STRIPE CREATES A HORIZONTAL BAND TO ACCENTUATE STREAMLINING.

ENTER

TERRACE

BEDROOM

SERVICE

SITTING ROOM

CLOSET

HALL

BEDROOM

RAMP

RAMP

BEDROOM

RAMP

RAMP

TERRACE

DRESSING

BEDROOM

SECOND FLOOR PLAN

TERRACE

MAID

MAID

KITCHEN

RAMPS WERE USED IN PLACE OF STAIRS TO GET FROM ONE FLOOR TO ANOTHER.

PANTRY

SERVICE

HALL

RAMP

RAMP

MAJOR ROOMS WERE DESIGNED TO ALLOW MAXIMUM NATURAL LIGHT TO ENTER.

DINING ROOM

VEST

RAMP

RAMP

LIBRARY

TERRACE

FIRST FLOOR PLAN

LIVING ROOM

ENTER

BALCONY

TERRACE

1937
BUTLER RESIDENCE, DES MOINES, IOWA
KRAETSCH AND KRAETSCH, ARCHITECTS

Northwestern

Puget Sound Region
1945

The Northwestern Style was developed by Ellsworth Storey working primarily in the Seattle, Washington, region just after the turn of the century. He was a native Chicagoan where he was influenced by the work of Louis Sullivan and Frank Lloyd Wright and the buildings of the World's Columbian Exposition held in Chicago in 1893. After graduating from the University of Illinois he traveled through Europe and was intrigued by the vernacular domestic architecture of Switzerland and Austria.

In 1903 Storey set up an architectural practice in Seattle and built several cottages and other small public buildings. His work was not "discovered" until after World War II when it became relatively

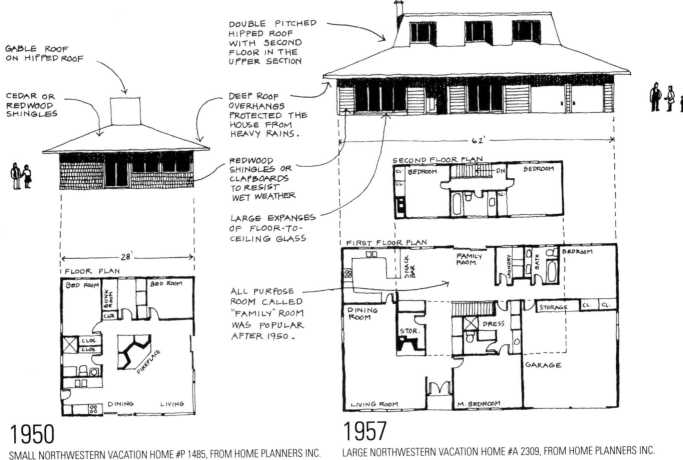

GABLE ROOF ON HIPPED ROOF

CEDAR OR REDWOOD SHINGLES

DOUBLE PITCHED HIPPED ROOF WITH SECOND FLOOR IN THE UPPER SECTION

DEEP ROOF OVERHANGS PROTECTED THE HOUSE FROM HEAVY RAINS.

REDWOOD SHINGLES OR CLAPBOARDS TO RESIST WET WEATHER

LARGE EXPANSES OF FLOOR-TO-CEILING GLASS

ALL PURPOSE ROOM CALLED "FAMILY" ROOM WAS POPULAR AFTER 1950.

1950
SMALL NORTHWESTERN VACATION HOME #P 1485, FROM HOME PLANNERS INC.
VACATION HOMES, RICHARD POLLMAN, DESIGNER

1957
LARGE NORTHWESTERN VACATION HOME #A 2309, FROM HOME PLANNERS INC.
VACATION HOMES, RICHARD POLLMAN, DESIGNER

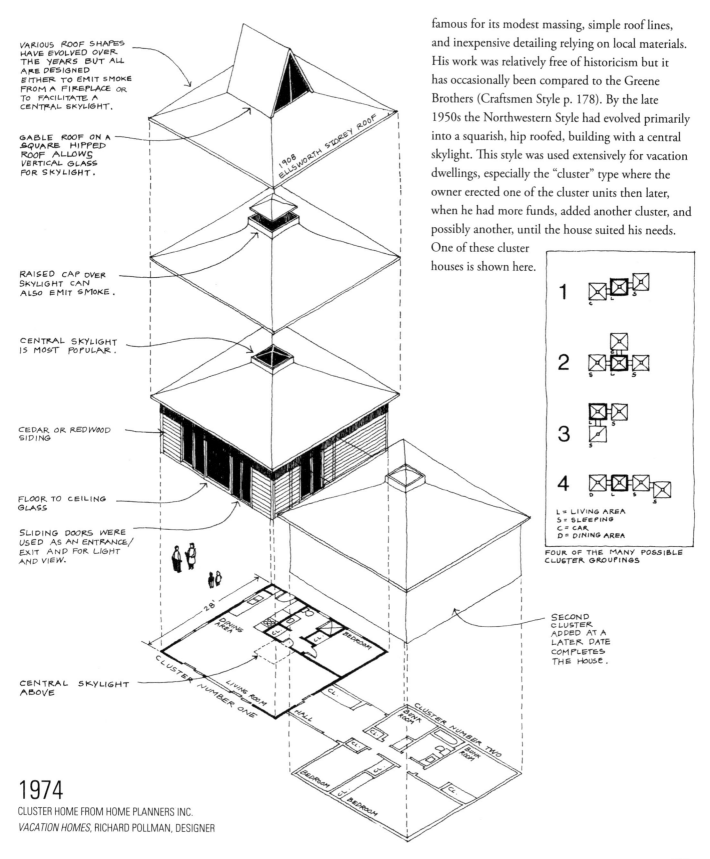

VARIOUS ROOF SHAPES HAVE EVOLVED OVER THE YEARS BUT ALL ARE DESIGNED EITHER TO EMIT SMOKE FROM A FIREPLACE OR TO FACILITATE A CENTRAL SKYLIGHT.

GABLE ROOF ON A SQUARE HIPPED ROOF ALLOWS VERTICAL GLASS FOR SKYLIGHT.

1908 ELLSWORTH STOREY ROOF

RAISED CAP OVER SKYLIGHT CAN ALSO EMIT SMOKE.

CENTRAL SKYLIGHT IS MOST POPULAR.

CEDAR OR REDWOOD SIDING

FLOOR TO CEILING GLASS

SLIDING DOORS WERE USED AS AN ENTRANCE/EXIT AND FOR LIGHT AND VIEW.

CENTRAL SKYLIGHT ABOVE

28'

CLUSTER NUMBER ONE

DINING AREA

LIVING ROOM

HALL

BEDROOM

CL.

CLUSTER NUMBER TWO

BUNK ROOM

BUNK ROOM

BEDROOM

BEDROOM

CL.

SECOND CLUSTER ADDED AT A LATER DATE COMPLETES THE HOUSE.

famous for its modest massing, simple roof lines, and inexpensive detailing relying on local materials. His work was relatively free of historicism but it has occasionally been compared to the Greene Brothers (Craftsmen Style p. 178). By the late 1950s the Northwestern Style had evolved primarily into a squarish, hip roofed, building with a central skylight. This style was used extensively for vacation dwellings, especially the "cluster" type where the owner erected one of the cluster units then later, when he had more funds, added another cluster, and possibly another, until the house suited his needs. One of these cluster houses is shown here.

1

2

3

4

L = LIVING AREA
S = SLEEPING
C = CAR
D = DINING AREA

FOUR OF THE MANY POSSIBLE CLUSTER GROUPINGS

1974

CLUSTER HOME FROM HOME PLANNERS INC.
VACATION HOMES, RICHARD POLLMAN, DESIGNER

Rammed Earth

**South
1945**

The Rammed Earth Style is based on the technology of building walls from moist earth. It is an ancient, inexpensive construction method rarely used in America because it requires hard, relatively skilled, labor and special soil conditions. But in a dry hot climate with sandy clay soil, the rammed earth house, when properly built, becomes a quick form of adobe with all the advantages of the early American Indian dwelling.

Architect Tom Hibben, with his experiments in 1936 in Gardendale, Alabama, has been given most of the credit for introducing to America the construction technique of the Rammed Earth Style (sometimes called by its French name, *Pisé de terre*). His successful building complex convinced a very skeptical public that the rammed earth technique could be used to make strong, relatively impervious walls for houses. A 1945 Federal Public Housing Authority report describes the Hibben buildings as being in excellent condition with the occupants highly pleased. The walls did not "sweat," and in the summer the houses were surprisingly cool.

The walls of the rammed earth house are made from stockpiled soil (laboratory checked periodically for moisture content) poured into heavy wooden forms and tamped, or "rammed," into a monolithic continuous wall as shown below. Then windows, doors, and roof are added. A good rammed earth wall is one that has been tamped until it is packed to its maximum density. At this point, after curing (drying) the wall is strong. A well-made rammed earth wall is one of the most durable earth walls that can be made. Some have lasted for centuries.

1936
RAMMED EARTH TECHNOLOGY

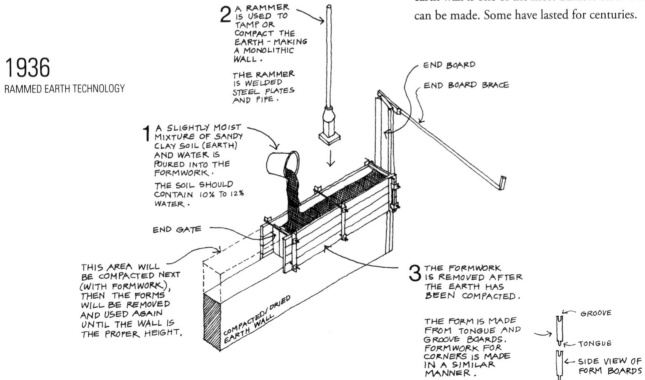

2 A RAMMER IS USED TO TAMP OR COMPACT THE EARTH – MAKING A MONOLITHIC WALL.

THE RAMMER IS WELDED STEEL PLATES AND PIPE.

END BOARD

END BOARD BRACE

1 A SLIGHTLY MOIST MIXTURE OF SANDY CLAY SOIL (EARTH) AND WATER IS POURED INTO THE FORMWORK.

THE SOIL SHOULD CONTAIN 10% TO 12% WATER.

END GATE

THIS AREA WILL BE COMPACTED NEXT (WITH FORMWORK), THEN THE FORMS WILL BE REMOVED AND USED AGAIN UNTIL THE WALL IS THE PROPER HEIGHT.

COMPACTED/DRIED EARTH WALL

3 THE FORMWORK IS REMOVED AFTER THE EARTH HAS BEEN COMPACTED.

THE FORM IS MADE FROM TONGUE AND GROOVE BOARDS. FORMWORK FOR CORNERS IS MADE IN A SIMILAR MANNER.

GROOVE

TONGUE

SIDE VIEW OF FORM BOARDS

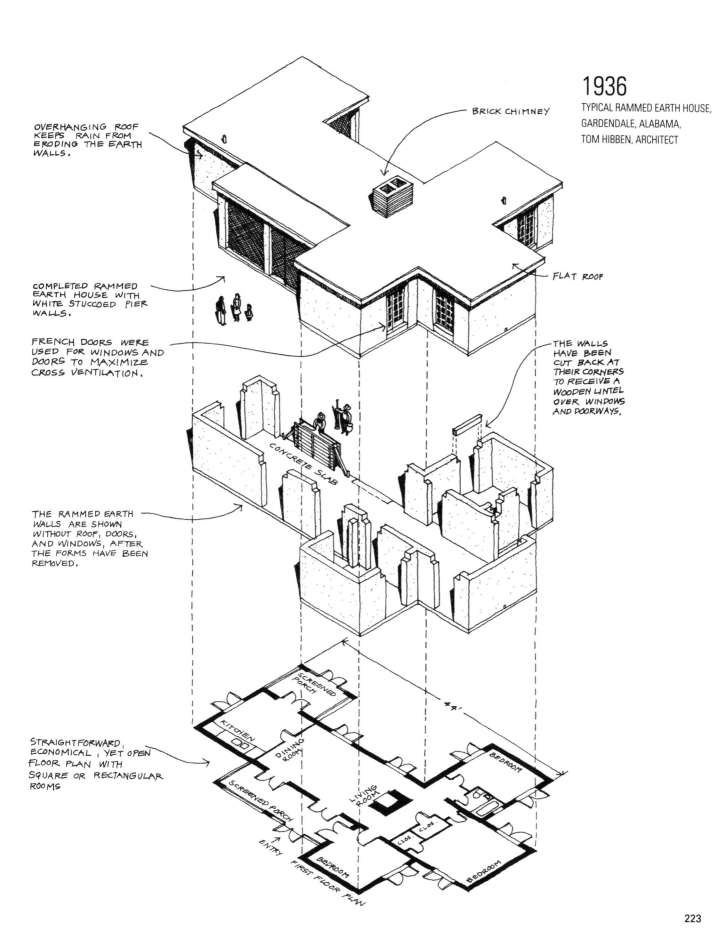

OVERHANGING ROOF KEEPS RAIN FROM ERODING THE EARTH WALLS.

BRICK CHIMNEY

1936
TYPICAL RAMMED EARTH HOUSE,
GARDENDALE, ALABAMA,
TOM HIBBEN, ARCHITECT

COMPLETED RAMMED EARTH HOUSE WITH WHITE STUCCOED PIER WALLS.

FRENCH DOORS WERE USED FOR WINDOWS AND DOORS TO MAXIMIZE CROSS VENTILATION.

FLAT ROOF

THE WALLS HAVE BEEN CUT BACK AT THEIR CORNERS TO RECEIVE A WOODEN LINTEL OVER WINDOWS AND DOORWAYS.

CONCRETE SLAB

THE RAMMED EARTH WALLS ARE SHOWN WITHOUT ROOF, DOORS, AND WINDOWS, AFTER THE FORMS HAVE BEEN REMOVED.

STRAIGHTFORWARD, ECONOMICAL, YET OPEN FLOOR PLAN WITH SQUARE OR RECTANGULAR ROOMS

SCREENED PORCH

KITCHEN

DINING ROOM

BEDROOM

SCREENED PORCH

LIVING ROOM

CLOS. CLOS.

ENTRY

FIRST FLOOR PLAN

BEDROOM

BEDROOM

42'

Quonset Hut

Countrywide 1945

The Quonset hut is the most famous of the mass-produced, mass-distributed, prefabricated buildings. The familiar steel tunnel structure was developed during World War II as quick-built housing for Allied soldiers and quickly found its way into the postwar housing market.

The Quonset consists of structural steel "I" shaped ribs to which corrugated metal skins are fastened so as to assemble a huge metal shell. There are no structural obstructions, like columns, inside which makes for planning flexibility. The Quonset shell is available nationally, through local dealers who also assemble the parts after which the owner completes the inside of the shell. Since the Quonset is mass-produced it is one of the least expensive structures available in America. It takes about four person-days to assemble a 1000-square-foot Quonset.

Like the tipi, the longhouse, and the geodesic dome, the roof and walls of the Quonset hut are the same material. This is advantageous as far as leaking and cost are concerned, but it does create an unusable space where the roof/walls meet the floor. The basic Quonset hut, like a tunnel, will allow light to enter only at its ends, but creative engineering work by architectural firms, such as Campbell and Wong of California, has inspired many ways to gain natural light through the sides of the Quonset.

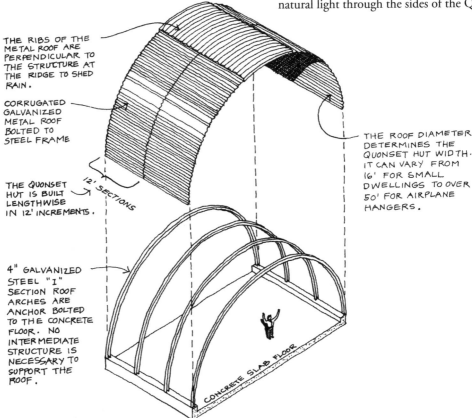

THE RIBS OF THE METAL ROOF ARE PERPENDICULAR TO THE STRUCTURE AT THE RIDGE TO SHED RAIN.

CORRUGATED GALVANIZED METAL ROOF BOLTED TO STEEL FRAME

THE QUONSET HUT IS BUILT LENGTHWISE IN 12' INCREMENTS.

12' SECTIONS

THE ROOF DIAMETER DETERMINES THE QUONSET HUT WIDTH. IT CAN VARY FROM 16' FOR SMALL DWELLINGS TO OVER 50' FOR AIRPLANE HANGERS.

4" GALVANIZED STEEL "I" SECTION ROOF ARCHES ARE ANCHOR BOLTED TO THE CONCRETE FLOOR. NO INTERMEDIATE STRUCTURE IS NECESSARY TO SUPPORT THE ROOF.

CONCRETE SLAB FLOOR

PRINCIPAL PARTS OF TYPICAL QUONSET HUT

1947 QUONSET HOUSE, FALLEN LEAF LAKE, CALIFORNIA
CAMPBELL AND WONG, ARCHITECTS

The utilitarian form of the Quonset hut has been converted into handsome, comfortable, well-lit homes by architects and engineers interested in industrialized buildings. Shown here are two such houses.

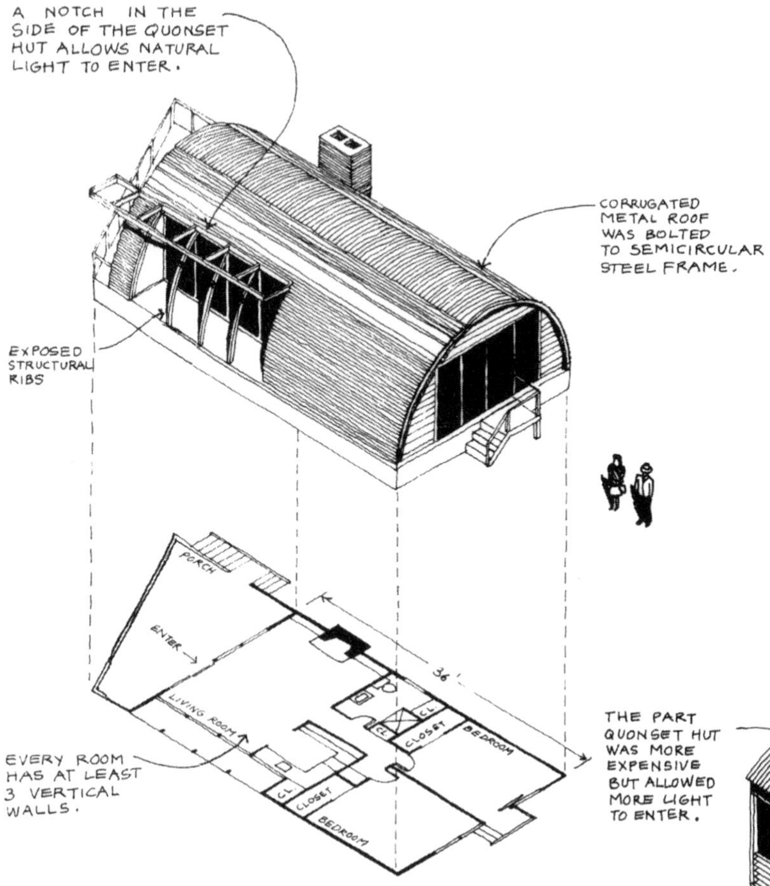
A NOTCH IN THE SIDE OF THE QUONSET HUT ALLOWS NATURAL LIGHT TO ENTER.
CORRUGATED METAL ROOF WAS BOLTED TO SEMICIRCULAR STEEL FRAME.
EXPOSED STRUCTURAL RIBS
PORCH
ENTER
36'
LIVING ROOM
CL
CLOSET
BEDROOM
EVERY ROOM HAS AT LEAST 3 VERTICAL WALLS.

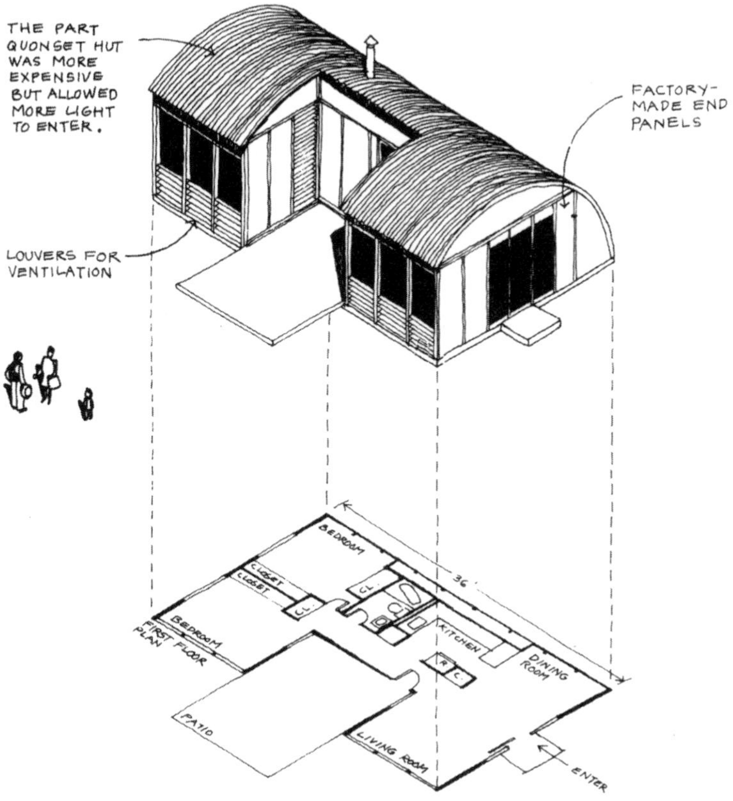
THE PART QUONSET HUT WAS MORE EXPENSIVE BUT ALLOWED MORE LIGHT TO ENTER.
FACTORY-MADE END PANELS
LOUVERS FOR VENTILATION
BEDROOM
CLOSET
CL
36'
KITCHEN
DINING ROOM
FIRST FLOOR PLAN
PATIO
LIVING ROOM
ENTER

1947 TYPICAL "PART" QUONSET HUT

Mobile Home

Countrywide 1950

The mobile home in America is closely related to the automobile. Both are factory-made, wheeled vehicles that are sold by dealers who showcase typical models on a lot. The mobile home had its beginnings in the 1930s when it was known simply as a travel trailer. Trailers became popular in the 1940s and then, in the 1950s and 1960s as the industry moved to create low-cost houses, sales skyrocketed. By 1970 almost 60 percent of the single-family, nonfarm house starts were mobile homes.

Today, there are several kinds of mobile homes. The first is the trailer, a small wheeled housing unit that hitches onto the back of a car or truck. This vehicle is used for vacations and other outings where shelter and cooking facilities are desired. The second is the recreational vehicle, a motorized housing unit

that became popular in the late 1960s. This vehicle is also used for vacations and other recreational trips. The third is the mobile home, a house designed to be shipped, on its own wheels, to its building site (usually a mobile home park) where it hooks up to pre-installed utilities and becomes, more or less, a permanent home.

The Mobile Home Style, at first, was influenced by the designers of cars—streamlined for their traveling conditions. The leaders in this field were the Airstream Corporation who adapted the special lightweight construction techniques used by the aircraft industry to trailer construction. As mobile homes evolved through the years into more permanent structures, they became less streamlined and more permanent looking. In their attempt to look like "normal" houses they have gained a wide variety of synthetic

1935
MERCURY TRAILER DISTRIBUTING COMPANY INC.

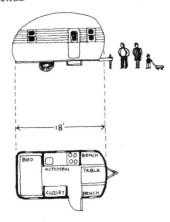

STREAMLINED FOR FREQUENT TRAVEL

18'

A SMALL TRAVEL TRAILER DESIGNED TO PROVIDE TEMPORARY SHELTER AND COOKING FACILITIES FOR VACATIONS AND WEEKEND OUTINGS

1950
SILVER STREAK TRAILER CO.

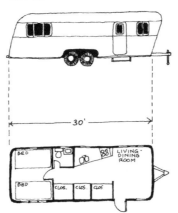

SEMISTREAMLINED FOR ONCE-A-YEAR TRAVEL

30'

A LARGE TRAVEL TRAILER DESIGNED AS A COMPLETE HOME AWAY FROM HOME

1965
PATHFINDER INCORPORATED

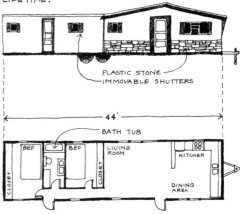

BOX-LIKE TO SIMULATE A PERMANENT HOUSE. DESIGNED TO TRAVEL 2 OR 3 TIMES IN ITS LIFETIME.

PLASTIC STONE
IMMOVABLE SHUTTERS

44'

BATH TUB

A MEDIUM SIZED MOBILE HOME DESIGNED AS A COMPLETE STATIONARY HOME

exterior finishes and even developed slightly pitched roofs. With aluminum siding that looks like wood clapboards, plastic brick and stone, and a large list of accessories that can be purchased by mail (shown below) the distinctive style of the mobile home has moved quickly toward the more permanent, non-architect designed, vernacular of the Contractor Modern Style (p. 252).

Once a mobile home is purchased and is firmly set into its site, the owner often embellishes it with small luxuries, like porch awnings and retractable TV antennas, available through mail-order catalogs. The customized mobile home, like the customized 1950s car, is a reflection of the owner's character and individuality.

Mobile homes are available in a wide range of lengths and several widths. The standard units are rectangles between twelve and fourteen feet wide (dictated by highway laws) and forty to eighty feet long.

1953 TOUR-A-HOME MANUFACTURING CORPORATION, MOBILE HOME WITH ACCESSORIES

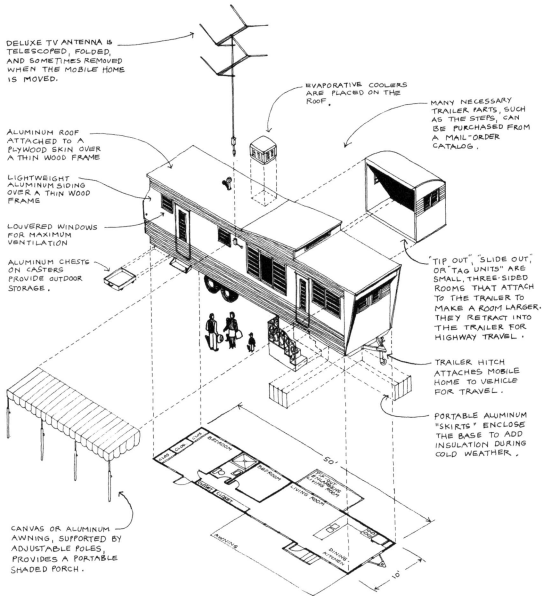

DELUXE TV ANTENNA IS TELESCOPED, FOLDED, AND SOMETIMES REMOVED WHEN THE MOBILE HOME IS MOVED.

EVAPORATIVE COOLERS ARE PLACED ON THE ROOF.

MANY NECESSARY TRAILER PARTS, SUCH AS THE STEPS, CAN BE PURCHASED FROM A MAIL-ORDER CATALOG.

ALUMINUM ROOF ATTACHED TO A PLYWOOD SKIN OVER A THIN WOOD FRAME

LIGHTWEIGHT ALUMINUM SIDING OVER A THIN WOOD FRAME

LOUVERED WINDOWS FOR MAXIMUM VENTILATION

ALUMINUM CHESTS ON CASTERS PROVIDE OUTDOOR STORAGE.

"TIP OUT", "SLIDE OUT", OR "TAG UNITS" ARE SMALL, THREE-SIDED ROOMS THAT ATTACH TO THE TRAILER TO MAKE A ROOM LARGER. THEY RETRACT INTO THE TRAILER FOR HIGHWAY TRAVEL.

TRAILER HITCH ATTACHES MOBILE HOME TO VEHICLE FOR TRAVEL.

PORTABLE ALUMINUM "SKIRTS" ENCLOSE THE BASE TO ADD INSULATION DURING COLD WEATHER.

CANVAS OR ALUMINUM AWNING, SUPPORTED BY ADJUSTABLE POLES, PROVIDES A PORTABLE SHADED PORCH.

There are approximately 400 manufacturers of mobile homes and about 1,000 manufacturers of recreational vehicles in America. While the mobile home industry has remained stable, the recreational vehicle industry is, of course, dependent on the availability and cost of fuel. Recreational vehicles are designed to be as light as possible yet the best of them gets poor gas mileage. Assuming that the American gas situation stays the same, perhaps the recreational vehicle will go the same route as the original 1930 travel trailer and slowly become more permanent. One such development is the recycling of old buses and used vans into "rolling homes" inspired by the "hippie" culture of the 1960s. These mobile homes get only four to six miles-per-gallon but provide adequate shelter without the cost of land or foundations.

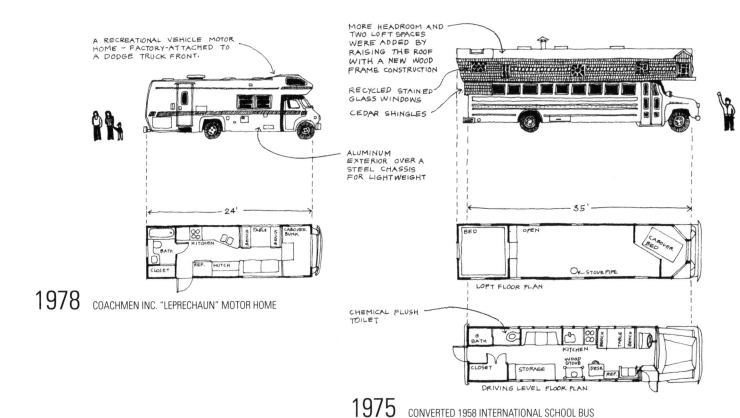

A RECREATIONAL VEHICLE MOTOR HOME – FACTORY-ATTACHED TO A DODGE TRUCK FRONT.

ALUMINUM EXTERIOR OVER A STEEL CHASSIS FOR LIGHTWEIGHT

24'

BATH KITCHEN BENCH TABLE BENCH CABOVER BUNK

CLOSET REF. HUTCH

1978 COACHMEN INC. "LEPRECHAUN" MOTOR HOME

MORE HEADROOM AND TWO LOFT SPACES WERE ADDED BY RAISING THE ROOF WITH A NEW WOOD FRAME CONSTRUCTION

RECYCLED STAINED GLASS WINDOWS

CEDAR SHINGLES

35'

BED OPEN CABOVER BED

LOFT FLOOR PLAN STOVE PIPE

CHEMICAL FLUSH TOILET

BATH KITCHEN BENCH TABLE BENCH

CLOSET STORAGE WOOD STOVE DESK REF.

DRIVING LEVEL FLOOR PLAN

1975 CONVERTED 1958 INTERNATIONAL SCHOOL BUS

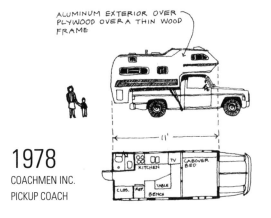

ALUMINUM EXTERIOR OVER PLYWOOD OVER A THIN WOOD FRAME

11'

KITCHEN TV CABOVER BED

CLOS. REF. TABLE BENCH

1978 COACHMEN INC. PICKUP COACH

In the mid-1970s, a small factory-fabricated house was specially made to fit American made one-half-ton pickup trucks. This unit became quite popular because it could be installed in a matter of minutes without complicated trailer hitches, was easier to drive, and got better gas mileage than trailers.

Two of the more innovative developments of the mobile home industry in the 1960s were the camping trailer and the Volkswagen camping bus. The former is a unique shelter with two double beds and ample cooking and dining facilities that folds out of a three-feet-high aluminum trailer. The latter is the familiar VW bus that contains factory-installed cooking equipment and sleeping facilities. The VW camper gets 25 miles-per-gallon and the low-profiled camping trailer could get the same when hooked up to a car that gets good mileage.

As mentioned earlier, the leader in trailer design through the years has been the Airstream Corporation. They have created a lightweight, aerodynamic design using aircraft-type construction (aluminum sheeting riveted to an aluminum cage) that has inspired industrial designers and trailer buffs alike. Below are examples of Airstream's small and medium-sized models.

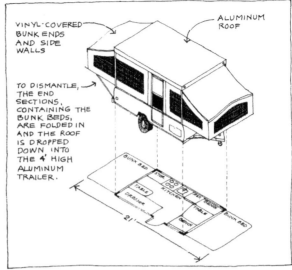

1978
COACHMEN INC.
"SUN CLASSIC" CAMPING T

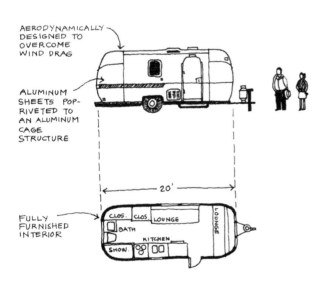

1978
VOLKSWAGEN CAMPER BUS

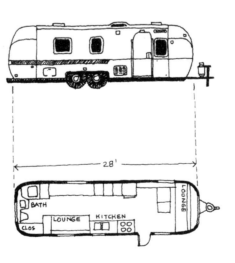

1980
AIRSTREAM "MINUET" TRAILER

1980
AIRSTREAM "ARGOSY" TRAILER

In an effort to become more like a conventional home, mobile home units have been doubled up to create a twenty-foot-wide home known in the industry as a double wide. This home consists of two ten-foot-wide units (the width is dictated by highway safety laws) brought to the site separately and joined there.

Double wides were the inspiration for factory built modular housing discussed on page 280. The only difference between the two is that the mobile homes have wheels and are designed to be moved while modular homes are considered permanent.

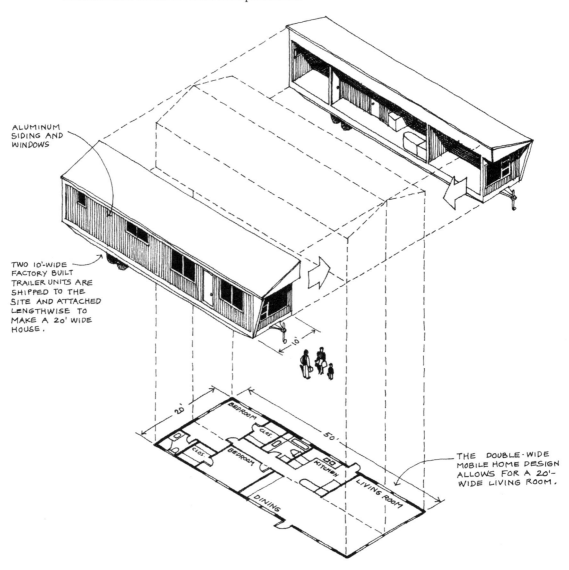

ALUMINUM SIDING AND WINDOWS

TWO 10'-WIDE FACTORY BUILT TRAILER UNITS ARE SHIPPED TO THE SITE AND ATTACHED LENGTHWISE TO MAKE A 20' WIDE HOUSE.

THE DOUBLE-WIDE MOBILE HOME DESIGN ALLOWS FOR A 20'-WIDE LIVING ROOM.

BEDROOM   CLOS.   BEDROOM   CLOS.   KITCHEN   LIVING ROOM   DINING

10'   20'   50'

1965   DOUBLE-WIDE MOBILE HOME, KIT MANUFACTURING CO. INC.

The mobile home industry has had a bad image because of its lack of structural regulations. Quality ranges from the tacky pink-and-turquoise-trimmed aluminum-sided metal box to the more recent natural wood-clad modular structures. In an attempt to avoid the "trailer look," architects, in the late 1960s, began to treat the trailer unit as a building component. One of the first examples of this idea was the "courtyard house" by architect James Hill, shown below. This house has many of the advantages of the one-story California ranch house (p. 232) at much less cost.

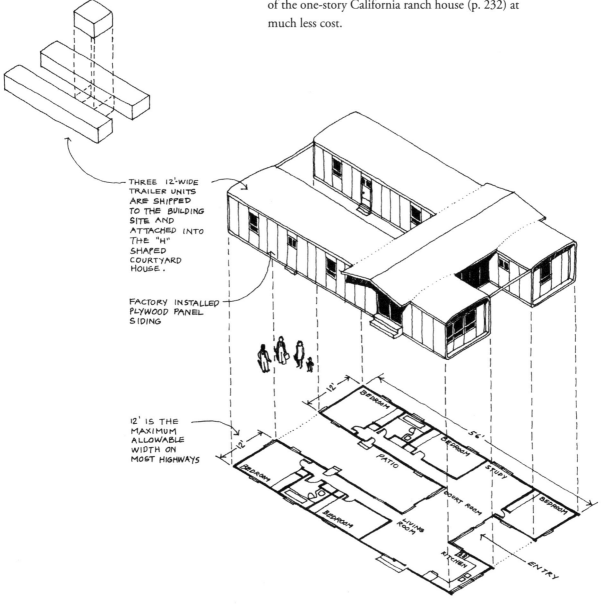

THREE 12'-WIDE TRAILER UNITS ARE SHIPPED TO THE BUILDING SITE AND ATTACHED INTO THE "H" SHAPED COURTYARD HOUSE.

FACTORY INSTALLED PLYWOOD PANEL SIDING

12' IS THE MAXIMUM ALLOWABLE WIDTH ON MOST HIGHWAYS

1964 MOBILE HOME "COURTYARD HOUSE," JAMES HILL, ARCHITECT, HOUSE OF ARCHITECTURE, INC.

California Ranch

Countrywide 1950

The California Ranch Style, also known as the Texas Ranch or Western Ranch Style, was created during the Spanish Colonial period in the American Southwest in the 1830s (p. 110). It was revived by California Bay Region architects in the 1930s (p. 191). It embraces the Spanish Colonial, Spanish Colonial Revival (p. 208), Second Bay Region, and Contractor Modern Styles (p. 252).

In the 1950s almost any one-story, close-to-the-ground, rambling house was called a California ranch house. Having the ability to move freely about the house, without steps, into large private porches and patios from almost every room was living the "good life."

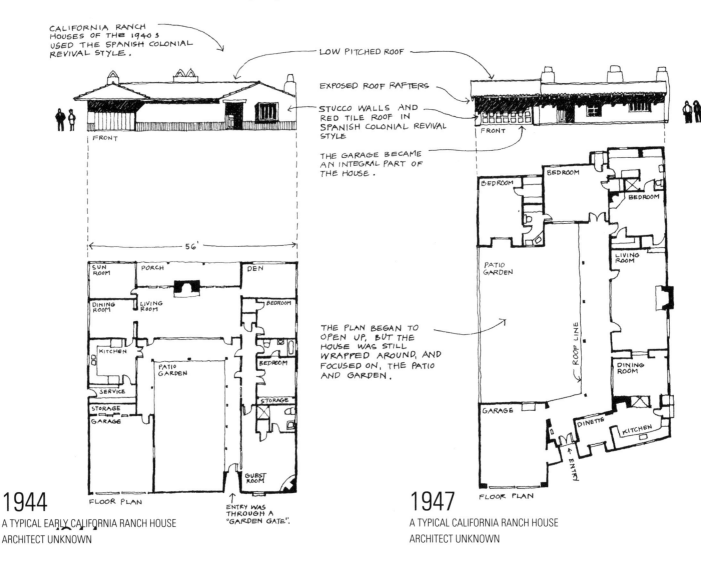

CALIFORNIA RANCH HOUSES OF THE 1940s USED THE SPANISH COLONIAL REVIVAL STYLE.

LOW PITCHED ROOF

EXPOSED ROOF RAFTERS

STUCCO WALLS AND RED TILE ROOF IN SPANISH COLONIAL REVIVAL STYLE

THE GARAGE BECAME AN INTEGRAL PART OF THE HOUSE.

THE PLAN BEGAN TO OPEN UP, BUT THE HOUSE WAS STILL WRAPPED AROUND, AND FOCUSED ON, THE PATIO AND GARDEN.

FRONT

56'

SUN ROOM · PORCH · DEN · DINING ROOM · LIVING ROOM · BEDROOM · KITCHEN · PATIO GARDEN · BEDROOM · SERVICE · STORAGE · STORAGE · GARAGE · GUEST ROOM

FLOOR PLAN

ENTRY WAS THROUGH A "GARDEN GATE".

FRONT

BEDROOM · BEDROOM · BEDROOM · PATIO GARDEN · LIVING ROOM · ROOF LINE · DINING ROOM · GARAGE · DINETTE · KITCHEN · ENTRY

FLOOR PLAN

1944
A TYPICAL EARLY CALIFORNIA RANCH HOUSE
ARCHITECT UNKNOWN

1947
A TYPICAL CALIFORNIA RANCH HOUSE
ARCHITECT UNKNOWN

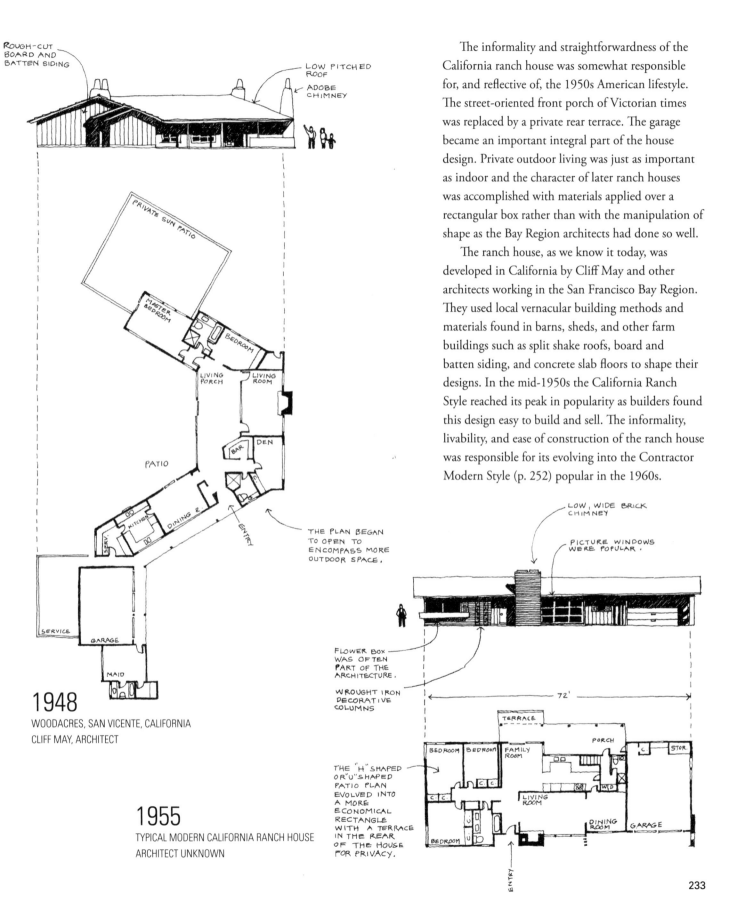

The informality and straightforwardness of the California ranch house was somewhat responsible for, and reflective of, the 1950s American lifestyle. The street-oriented front porch of Victorian times was replaced by a private rear terrace. The garage became an important integral part of the house design. Private outdoor living was just as important as indoor and the character of later ranch houses was accomplished with materials applied over a rectangular box rather than with the manipulation of shape as the Bay Region architects had done so well.

The ranch house, as we know it today, was developed in California by Cliff May and other architects working in the San Francisco Bay Region. They used local vernacular building methods and materials found in barns, sheds, and other farm buildings such as split shake roofs, board and batten siding, and concrete slab floors to shape their designs. In the mid-1950s the California Ranch Style reached its peak in popularity as builders found this design easy to build and sell. The informality, livability, and ease of construction of the ranch house was responsible for its evolving into the Contractor Modern Style (p. 252) popular in the 1960s.

ROUGH-CUT BOARD AND BATTEN SIDING

LOW PITCHED ROOF

ADOBE CHIMNEY

PRIVATE SUN PATIO

MASTER BEDROOM

BEDROOM

LIVING PORCH

LIVING ROOM

BAR   DEN

PATIO

ENTRY

THE PLAN BEGAN TO OPEN TO ENCOMPASS MORE OUTDOOR SPACE.

SERV.   KITCHEN   DINING R.

SERVICE

GARAGE

MAID

1948

WOODACRES, SAN VICENTE, CALIFORNIA
CLIFF MAY, ARCHITECT

1955

TYPICAL MODERN CALIFORNIA RANCH HOUSE
ARCHITECT UNKNOWN

LOW, WIDE BRICK CHIMNEY

PICTURE WINDOWS WERE POPULAR.

FLOWER BOX WAS OFTEN PART OF THE ARCHITECTURE.

WROUGHT IRON DECORATIVE COLUMNS

THE "H" SHAPED OR "U" SHAPED PATIO PLAN EVOLVED INTO A MORE ECONOMICAL RECTANGLE WITH A TERRACE IN THE REAR OF THE HOUSE FOR PRIVACY.

72'

TERRACE

PORCH

BEDROOM   BEDROOM   FAMILY ROOM

C   STOR.

LIVING ROOM

W D

DINING ROOM   GARAGE

BEDROOM

ENTRY

POST AND BEAM CONSTRUCTION

Post and beam construction, also known as plank and beam construction, consists of large framing members (posts, beams, and planks), which are spaced farther apart than the conventional, more popular platform frame construction shown on page 260. Post and beam construction is similar to mill construction methods used in heavy timber buildings throughout America, and is the popular method for framing the California Ranch Style house because of the distinctive architectural effect achieved by exposing the ceiling beams and the underside of the roof planks.

Below are a series of seven simplified steps showing how post and beam construction works.

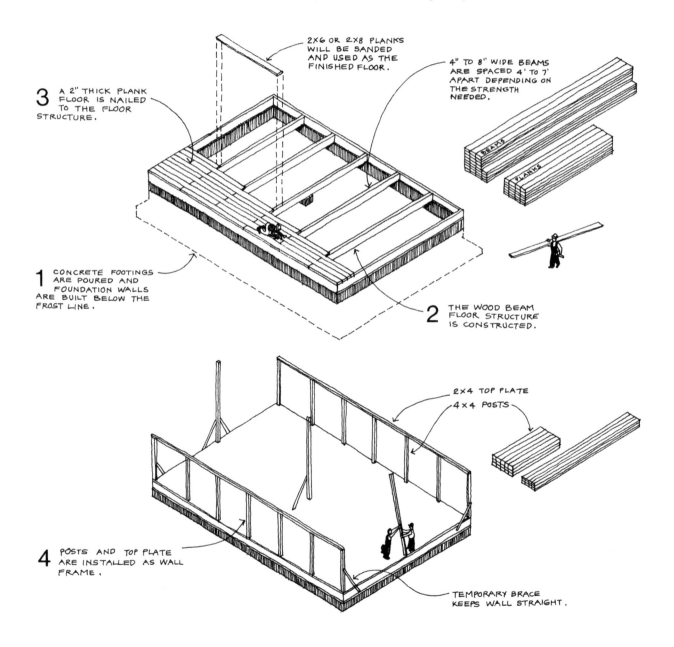

2X6 OR 2X8 PLANKS WILL BE SANDED AND USED AS THE FINISHED FLOOR.

4" TO 8" WIDE BEAMS ARE SPACED 4' TO 7' APART DEPENDING ON THE STRENGTH NEEDED.

BEAMS

PLANKS

3 A 2" THICK PLANK FLOOR IS NAILED TO THE FLOOR STRUCTURE.

1 CONCRETE FOOTINGS ARE POURED AND FOUNDATION WALLS ARE BUILT BELOW THE FROST LINE.

2 THE WOOD BEAM FLOOR STRUCTURE IS CONSTRUCTED.

2X4 TOP PLATE
4X4 POSTS

4 POSTS AND TOP PLATE ARE INSTALLED AS WALL FRAME.

TEMPORARY BRACE KEEPS WALL STRAIGHT.

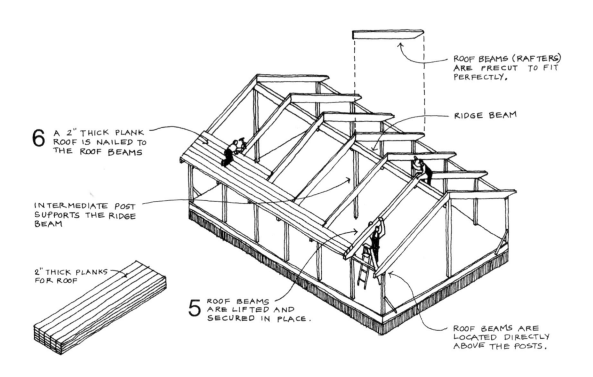

ROOF BEAMS (RAFTERS) ARE PRECUT TO FIT PERFECTLY.

RIDGE BEAM

6 A 2" THICK PLANK ROOF IS NAILED TO THE ROOF BEAMS

INTERMEDIATE POST SUPPORTS THE RIDGE BEAM

2" THICK PLANKS FOR ROOF

5 ROOF BEAMS ARE LIFTED AND SECURED IN PLACE.

ROOF BEAMS ARE LOCATED DIRECTLY ABOVE THE POSTS.

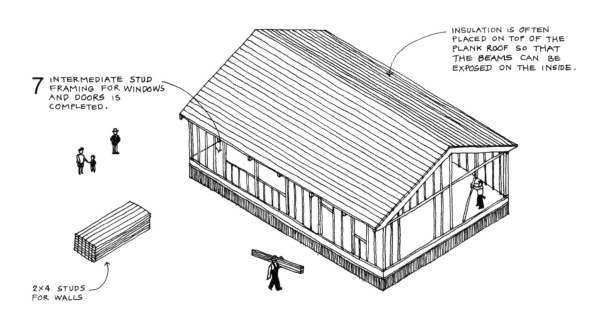

INSULATION IS OFTEN PLACED ON TOP OF THE PLANK ROOF SO THAT THE BEAMS CAN BE EXPOSED ON THE INSIDE.

7 INTERMEDIATE STUD FRAMING FOR WINDOWS AND DOORS IS COMPLETED.

2×4 STUDS FOR WALLS

Miesian

Countrywide
1950

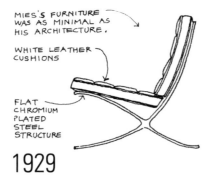

MIES'S FURNITURE WAS AS MINIMAL AS HIS ARCHITECTURE.

WHITE LEATHER CUSHIONS

FLAT CHROMIUM PLATED STEEL STRUCTURE

1929

BARCELONA CHAIR, DESIGNED BY
MIES VAN DER ROHE FOR THE GERMAN PAVILION,
INTERNATIONAL EXPOSITION, BARCELONA, SPAIN

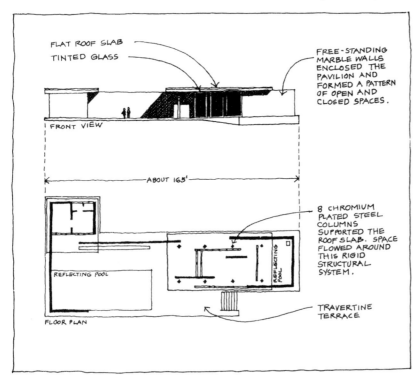

FLAT ROOF SLAB
TINTED GLASS

FREE-STANDING MARBLE WALLS ENCLOSED THE PAVILION AND FORMED A PATTERN OF OPEN AND CLOSED SPACES.

FRONT VIEW

ABOUT 165'

REFLECTING POOL

8 CHROMIUM PLATED STEEL COLUMNS SUPPORTED THE ROOF SLAB. SPACE FLOWED AROUND THIS RIGID STRUCTURAL SYSTEM.

REFLECTING POOL

TRAVERTINE TERRACE

FLOOR PLAN

1929 GERMAN PAVILION, INTERNATIONAL EXPOSITION, BARCELONA, SPAIN
MIES VAN DER ROHE, ARCHITECT

When Ludwig Mies van der Rohe migrated from Germany to America in 1938 he was considered one of the three leaders of the International Style, along with Le Corbusier and Walter Gropius. His German Pavilion at the 1929 International Exposition in Barcelona, Spain (commonly referred to as the Barcelona Pavilion), was the best example of his unique early work. He was a master at placing screen walls within glass-enclosed space giving the impression of space beyond, while providing privacy (without doors) to the required areas of the building. The Barcelona Pavilion had no other function than to represent Germany so Mies (as he was most often called) was allowed maximum freedom. The resulting design was a synthesis of his previous work and architectural ideas. It had enormous influence with architects around the world.

Mies and his followers exploited the freedom of planning that skeleton construction allows. (The walls have no structural duties.) In his American work Mies treated the steel frame as a discipline comparable in many respects with that of the classical orders, where expressiveness was achieved through the refinement of proportion and detail. He differed from most International Style architects by designing spaces in his buildings that were open and could be used for many different functions.

Mies's style was particularly suited to America because it was inspired to some degree by American technology. By 1958, he had demonstrated its adaptability in a variety of different buildings from the Farnsworth House in Plano, Illinois (opposite page), to the campus buildings of the Illinois Institute of Technology, the twin towers at 860 Lake Shore Drive in Chicago, and the Seagram Building in New York City, designed with Philip Johnson. The Miesian Style has been very influential in the design of large city office buildings but, due to the expense of steel construction, the style has had only a limited popularity in American domestic architecture.

Mies is known as the father of the austere, modern glass box. The two most famous American glass box houses, the Farnsworth House (called "a quantity of air caught between a floor and a roof" by Mies himself), and a house designed by Philip Johnson for himself, are excellent examples of the Miesian Style. In both houses, everything seems to float because there is so much open space with so little structure holding up the roof. Critics would say that the style is sterile and critically inefficient energywise due to heat loss through all the glass. The owners would answer that the spiritual value of making the outdoors such a major part of the living environment far outweighs energy cost.

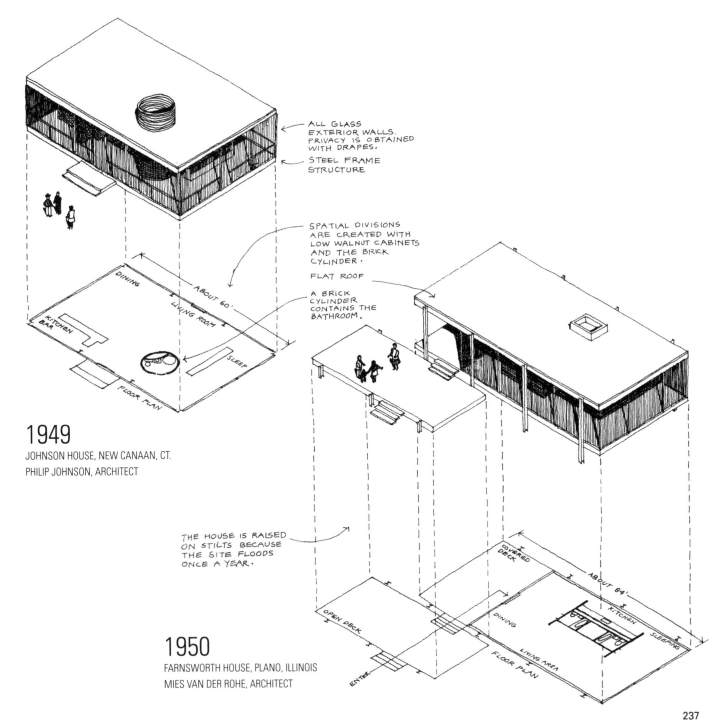

ALL GLASS EXTERIOR WALLS. PRIVACY IS OBTAINED WITH DRAPES.

STEEL FRAME STRUCTURE

SPATIAL DIVISIONS ARE CREATED WITH LOW WALNUT CABINETS AND THE BRICK CYLINDER.

FLAT ROOF

A BRICK CYLINDER CONTAINS THE BATHROOM.

DINING

LIVING ROOM

ABOUT 60'

KITCHEN BAR

SLEEP

FLOOR PLAN

1949
JOHNSON HOUSE, NEW CANAAN, CT.
PHILIP JOHNSON, ARCHITECT

THE HOUSE IS RAISED ON STILTS BECAUSE THE SITE FLOODS ONCE A YEAR.

1950
FARNSWORTH HOUSE, PLANO, ILLINOIS
MIES VAN DER ROHE, ARCHITECT

COVERED DECK

ABOUT 84'

KITCHEN

SLEEPING

OPEN DECK

DINING

LIVING AREA

FLOOR PLAN

ENTER

Craig Ellwood, a southern California architect, gained quite a bit of notoriety in the 1950s and 1960s with his work in the Miesian Style. His houses grew from his interest in architecture evolving from structure. He used "skin and bones," low-cost, industrialized materials and techniques to create work that has been called an abstraction of the Japanese. He developed his ideas apart from Mies van der Rohe but by the late 1950s his work was as important to the Miesian Style as Mies himself.

Below and on the opposite page are two of Ellwood's best houses. Both symmetrical, steel-framed, flat-roofed elegant boxlike shapes, they are designed for two drastically different sites and budgets.

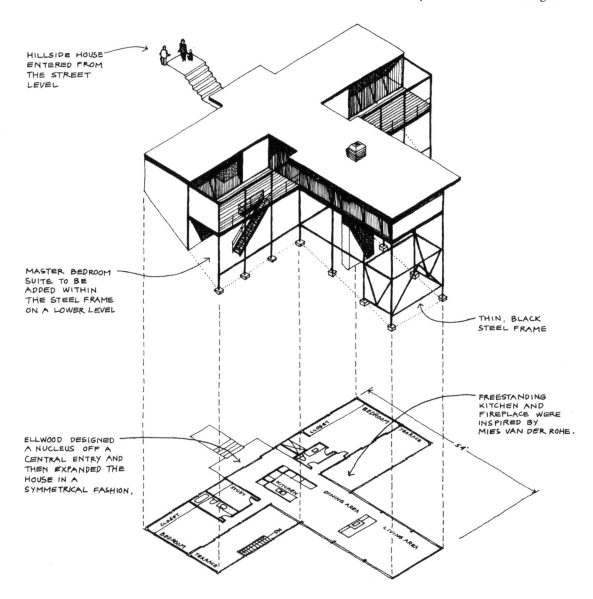

HILLSIDE HOUSE ENTERED FROM THE STREET LEVEL

MASTER BEDROOM SUITE TO BE ADDED WITHIN THE STEEL FRAME ON A LOWER LEVEL

THIN, BLACK STEEL FRAME

FREESTANDING KITCHEN AND FIREPLACE WERE INSPIRED BY MIES VAN DER ROHE.

ELLWOOD DESIGNED A NUCLEUS OFF A CENTRAL ENTRY AND THEN EXPANDED THE HOUSE IN A SYMMETRICAL FASHION.

CLOSET
BEDROOM
TERRACE
54'
STUDY
KITCHEN
DINING AREA
CLOSET
BEDROOM
TERRACE
DN
LIVING AREA

1957 SMITH HOUSE, CRESTWOOD HILLS, WEST LOS ANGELES, CALIFORNIA
CRAIG ELLWOOD, ARCHITECT

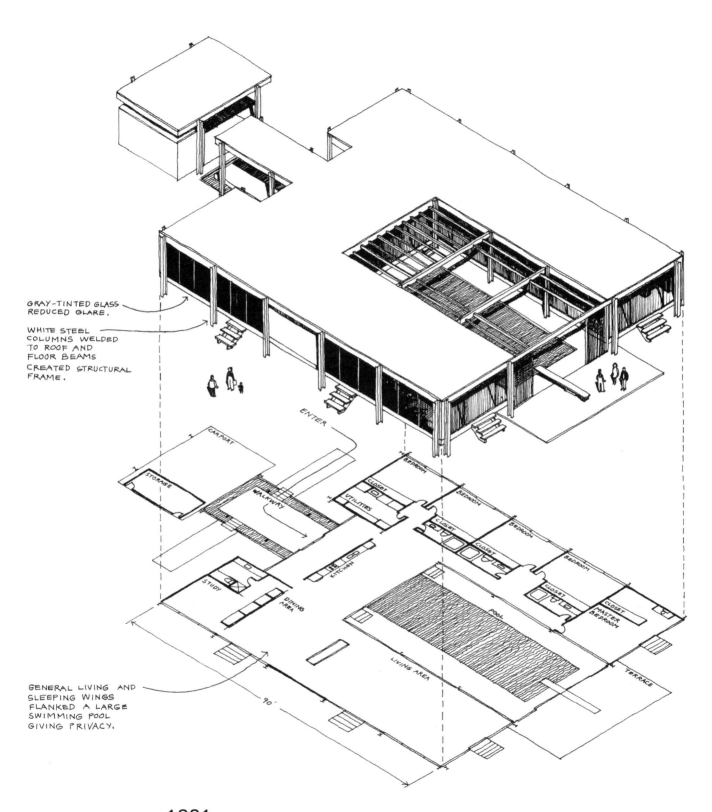

GRAY-TINTED GLASS REDUCED GLARE.

WHITE STEEL COLUMNS WELDED TO ROOF AND FLOOR BEAMS CREATED STRUCTURAL FRAME.

ENTER

CARPORT

STORAGE

WALKWAY

UTILITIES

BEDROOM

CLOSET

CLOSET

BEDROOM

CLOSET

BEDROOM

KITCHEN

STUDY

DINING AREA

CLOSET

CLOSET

BEDROOM

CLOSET

MASTER BEDROOM

POOL

LIVING AREA

CLOSET

TERRACE

GENERAL LIVING AND SLEEPING WINGS FLANKED A LARGE SWIMMING POOL GIVING PRIVACY.

90'

1961 DAPHNE HOUSE, HILLSBOROUGH, CALIFORNIA
CRAIG ELLWOOD, ARCHITECT

239

Prefabricated

Countrywide 1950

A prefabricated home is one built by precutting and pre-assembly in a factory of some or all parts of the house. Walls, floors, and ceiling/roofs are usually made in sections, or panels, some as large as eight feet by twenty-four feet, with both exterior and interior finish work completed in the factory. Large structural members are cut to size and made ready to join into a frame. Kitchens, bathrooms, and closet units are built like cars on an assembly line complete with plumbing and electrical work ready for hook-up at the site. These parts (shown below) are then shipped by rail or truck to a building site for erection on a previously prepared foundation.

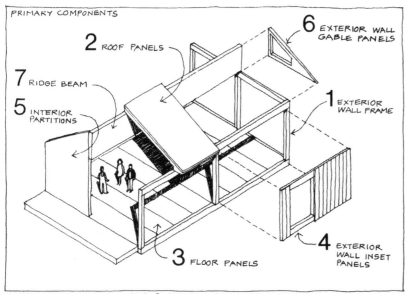

PRIMARY COMPONENTS

2 ROOF PANELS
6 EXTERIOR WALL GABLE PANELS
7 RIDGE BEAM
5 INTERIOR PARTITIONS
1 EXTERIOR WALL FRAME
3 FLOOR PANELS
4 EXTERIOR WALL INSET PANELS

ELEVEN BASIC FACTORY-MADE PARTS TO A PREFABRICATED HOUSE

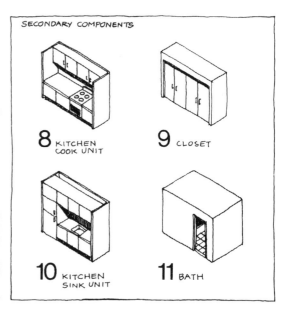

SECONDARY COMPONENTS

8 KITCHEN COOK UNIT
9 CLOSET
10 KITCHEN SINK UNIT
11 BATH

THE FIRST PREFABRICATED HOUSES LOOKED LIKE THIS.

IN 1905 SEARS, ROEBUCK & COMPANY BEGAN TO SELL PREFABRICATED HOUSES IN A VARIETY OF STYLES THROUGH THEIR MAIL ORDER CATALOG. THE NEW OWNER WOULD CHOOSE A HOUSE FROM THE CATALOG AND SEARS WOULD SHIP PRECUT PARTS TO THE BUILDING SITE FOR A LOCAL CONTRACTOR TO ERECT.

FROM 1927 TO 1944 R. BUCKMINSTER FULLER DESIGNED A SERIES OF LIGHTWEIGHT METAL HOUSES WITH VARIOUS INGENIOUS TECHNICAL ADVANCEMENTS, SUCH AS AN AUTOMATIC LAUNDRY AND SELF-CONTAINED WASTE DISPOSAL UNIT.

THE COMPLETE HOUSE WAS CONSTRUCTED FROM LIGHTWEIGHT, FACTORY-MADE, METAL COMPONENTS. NO PART WEIGHED OVER 10 POUNDS ALLOWING ERECTION OF THE HOUSE BY ONE PERSON.

VENTILATOR

ENTRY

1912
SEARS, ROEBUCK & CO. CATALOG HOUSE, DANBURY, CONNECTICUT

1944
DYMAXION DWELLING MACHINE, WICHITA, KANSAS
R. BUCKMINSTER FULLER, ARCHITECT

As early as 1905, new home buyers could choose a house from a catalog (Sears, Roebuck and Co. was one of the first with its *Book of Modern Homes and Building Plans*) and have precut and marked building materials shipped to the local train station where they were met by horse drawn vehicles for transportation to, and erection on, a prepared foundation at the building site. As time passed, Henry Ford's assembly line inspired a factory-built housebuilding technique, and by 1938, prefab companies were producing the parts that made American history as panelized, pre-engineered or precut houses.

When the factory-made house parts are unloaded, the manufacturer's obligation to the customer is often concluded and local on-site workers are usually hired to complete the dwelling. Many prefabricated houses fit together in a matter of days like a large toy with ingenious connectors for panels and structural members. The Butler House shown here is typical of the panelized houses of the 1940s.

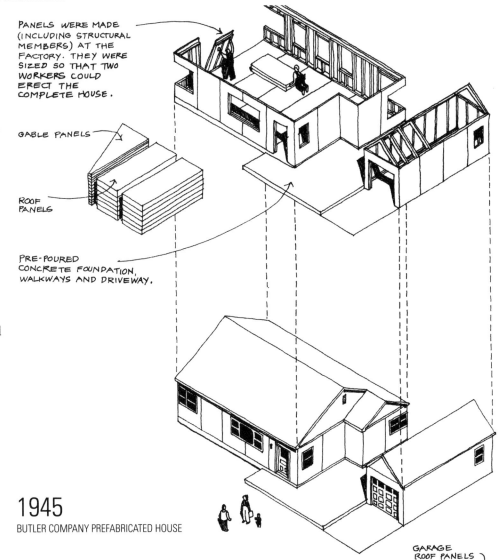

PANELS WERE MADE (INCLUDING STRUCTURAL MEMBERS) AT THE FACTORY. THEY WERE SIZED SO THAT TWO WORKERS COULD ERECT THE COMPLETE HOUSE.

GABLE PANELS

ROOF PANELS

PRE-POURED CONCRETE FOUNDATION, WALKWAYS AND DRIVEWAY.

1945
BUTLER COMPANY PREFABRICATED HOUSE

GARAGE ROOF PANELS

PRECUT ROOF RAFTERS

THIS ART MODERNE STYLE HOUSE WAS DESIGNED AS A COLLECTION OF PREFABRICATED PARTS MADE IN SPECIALIZED FACTORIES ALL OVER AMERICA. THE CUSTOMER ORDERED THE HOUSE FROM GENERAL HOUSES, INC., WHO NOTIFIED THE FACTORIES WHERE TO SHIP THEIR PARTS.

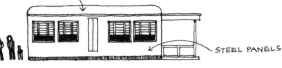

STEEL PANELS

1933
GENERAL HOUSES INC., PREFABRICATED HOUSE, HOWARD T. FISHER, COORDINATOR

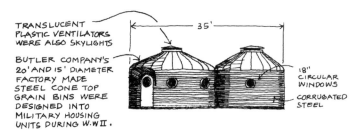

TRANSLUCENT PLASTIC VENTILATORS WERE ALSO SKYLIGHTS

BUTLER COMPANY'S 20' AND 15' DIAMETER FACTORY MADE STEEL CONE TOP GRAIN BINS WERE DESIGNED INTO MILITARY HOUSING UNITS DURING W.W II.

35'

18" CIRCULAR WINDOWS

CORRUGATED STEEL

1941
TWIN CYLINDER DYMAXION DEPLOYMENT UNIT (D.D.U.)
R. BUCKMINSTER FULLER, DESIGNER

The Great Depression of the 1930s, the cessation of housebuilding during World War II, and a high marriage and birth rate during and immediately after the war were the principal causes of the enormous housing shortage of the late 1940s. It was estimated in 1946 that three million houses would have to be built over the next five years just to keep the situation from worsening.

The prefabrication industry was slow in gaining public acceptance and in refining its building technology so that it could produce a competitive low-cost product. But by 1950 a large list of companies using a wide variety of assembly-line techniques were providing America with a significant portion of its much needed single-family dwellings. William Levitt, the most prolific housebuilder in American history, built over 6,000 houses in his Levittowns on Long Island, New York, and in Pennsylvania in 1949 and 1950.

THE LOW PRICE OF $2,950 ($350 DOWN AND $21/MO.) PROVED TO BE A KEY ADVANTAGE OF EARLY PRE-FABRICATED HOMES.

PLYWOOD PANELS

1938 "MIRACLE HOME," GUNNISON HOMES, INC., OHIO RIVER VALLEY

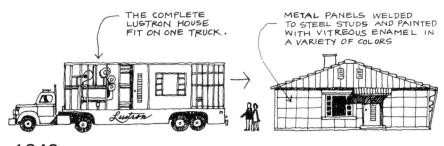

THE COMPLETE LUSTRON HOUSE FIT ON ONE TRUCK.

METAL PANELS WELDED TO STEEL STUDS AND PAINTED WITH VITREOUS ENAMEL IN A VARIETY OF COLORS

1943 METAL PREFABRICATED HOME, LUSTRON CORPORATION

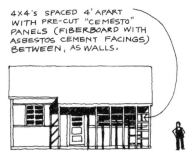

4X4'S SPACED 4' APART WITH PRE-CUT "CEMESTO" PANELS (FIBERBOARD WITH ASBESTOS CEMENT FACINGS) BETWEEN, AS WALLS.

1944

THE CELOTEX "CEMESTO HOUSE," DESIGNED BY THE JOHN B. PIERCE FOUNDATION, NEW JERSEY

WOODFRAMED PANELS COVERED WITH SHINGLES OR STUCCO AT THE BUILDING SITE

STUCCO

1947

PREFABRICATED HOME, KAISER COMMUNITY HOMES, LOS ANGELES, CALIFORNIA

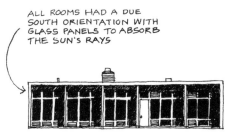

ALL ROOMS HAD A DUE SOUTH ORIENTATION WITH GLASS PANELS TO ABSORB THE SUN'S RAYS

1947

FIRST SOLAR HOUSE, GREEN'S READY-BUILT SOLAR HOUSE, GEORGE KECK, DESIGNER

LOW-COST DWELLING ($5,300) MADE FROM PLYWOOD PANELS

1948

"THRIFT HOUSE," NATIONAL HOUSES INC., INDIANA

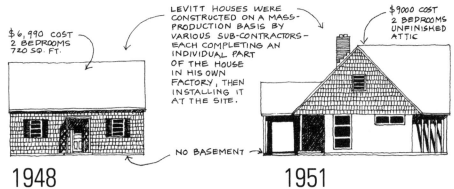

$6,990 COST 2 BEDROOMS 720 SQ. FT.

LEVITT HOUSES WERE CONSTRUCTED ON A MASS-PRODUCTION BASIS BY VARIOUS SUB-CONTRACTORS— EACH COMPLETING AN INDIVIDUAL PART OF THE HOUSE IN HIS OWN FACTORY, THEN INSTALLING IT AT THE SITE.

$9000 COST 2 BEDROOMS UNFINISHED ATTIC

NO BASEMENT

1948

CAPE COD HOUSE, LEVITT AND SONS, LEVITTOWN, LONG ISLAND AND PENNSYLVANIA

1951

RANCH HOUSE, LEVITT AND SONS LEVITTOWN, LONG ISLAND AND PENNSYLVANIA

By the mid-1970s the prefabrication industry had moved into the vacation or second-home market, and was selling factory built homes that were called kit-built houses. The process of buying, selling, and building was basically unchanged but the high construction standards met by most of the 150 companies specializing in kit homes had dramatically changed the reputation of the industry for the better. Today the types of kits available range from log cabins, geodesic domes, traditional colonial and solar designs, to the basic Contractor Modern or California Ranch Style house.

All prefabricated housebuilding companies advertise in newspapers and magazines having the interested reader send for a catalog that usually illustrates building techniques, models available, cost and financing, and the owner's on-site responsibilities. Many kit home purchasers are saving 15 to 20 percent of the overall cost of the home by doing most of the erecting themselves.

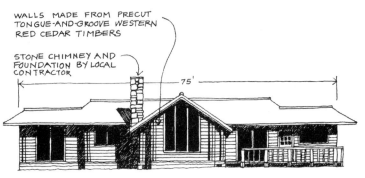

WALLS MADE FROM PRECUT TONGUE-AND-GROOVE WESTERN RED CEDAR TIMBERS

STONE CHIMNEY AND FOUNDATION BY LOCAL CONTRACTOR

75'

1976 "ARISTOCRAT 11," PAN ADOBE CO.

MANY NEW COMPANIES ARE PREFABRICATING A BARN-LIKE FRAME, LIKE THIS BRACED, RED OAK, POST-AND-BEAM STRUCTURE, THAT REQUIRE EXTENSIVE LOCAL CARPENTRY BEFORE COMPLETION.

40'

1977 "MULLIGAN FRAME," DAVID HOWARD, INC.

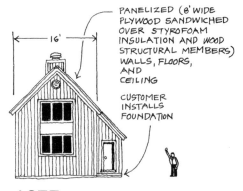

PANELIZED (8' WIDE PLYWOOD SANDWICHED OVER STYROFOAM INSULATION AND WOOD STRUCTURAL MEMBERS) WALLS, FLOORS, AND CEILING

CUSTOMER INSTALLS FOUNDATION

16'

1977 N 38, GREEN MOUNTAIN HOMES

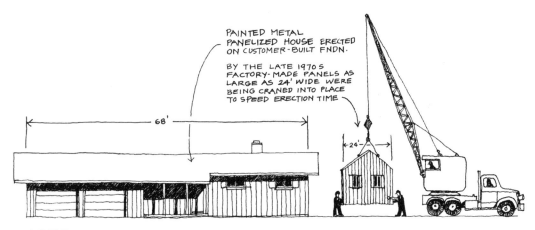

PAINTED METAL
PANELIZED HOUSE ERECTED
ON CUSTOMER-BUILT FNDN.

BY THE LATE 1970S
FACTORY-MADE PANELS AS
LARGE AS 24' WIDE WERE
BEING CRANED INTO PLACE
TO SPEED ERECTION TIME

68'

24'

1978 IMPERIAL SERIES DESIGN #200-C24, WAUSAU HOMES INC.

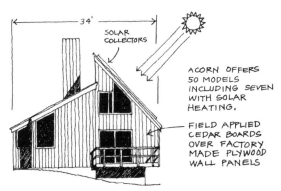

34'

SOLAR
COLLECTORS

ACORN OFFERS
50 MODELS
INCLUDING SEVEN
WITH SOLAR
HEATING.

FIELD APPLIED
CEDAR BOARDS
OVER FACTORY
MADE PLYWOOD
WALL PANELS

1980 SOLAR SERIES #SS1100, ACORN STRUCTURES, INC.

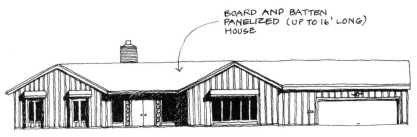

BOARD AND BATTEN
PANELIZED (UP TO 16' LONG)
HOUSE

1980 "CITATION" PREFABRICATED RANCH STYLE HOUSE, PEASE CO.

High Tech

Countrywide 1955

After the Great Depression of the 1930s, and World War II, America began to build houses in great numbers. There were a few designers who thought we should capitalize on our new knowledge of industrialized building materials and erect houses whose major parts had been factory-made. Architects working primarily in southern California had been greatly influenced by factories, barracks, airplane shelters, and other industrialized buildings. They were enchanted with a belief in the flexibility, economy, and beauty of interchangeable, prefabricated building parts.

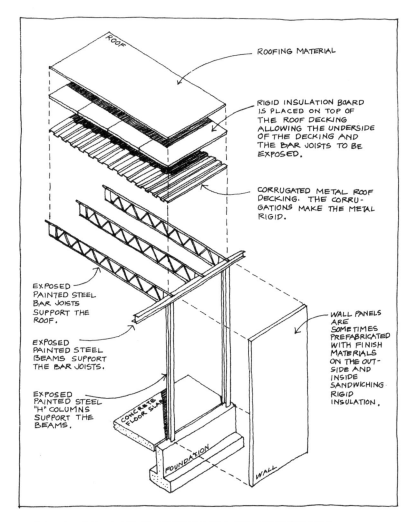

KEY PARTS USED IN THE CONSTRUCTION OF A HIGH TECH BUILDING

This idea, of course was not new. Mies van der Rohe and Craig Ellwood had done much work in pioneering light steel construction (p. 236). The Aluminaire House built in 1931 (above) was one of the many "modern" houses designed with factory-made components to be shipped and erected at the building site. So, the High Tech (short for Technology) Style could be considered a revival of the Miesian Style.

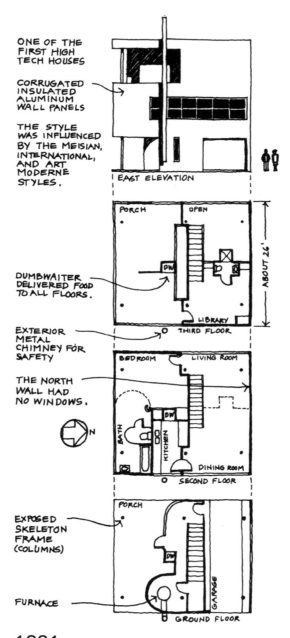

ONE OF THE FIRST HIGH TECH HOUSES

CORRUGATED INSULATED ALUMINUM WALL PANELS

THE STYLE WAS INFLUENCED BY THE MEISIAN, INTERNATIONAL, AND ART MODERNE STYLES.

EAST ELEVATION

PORCH   OPEN

DUMBWAITER DELIVERED FOOD TO ALL FLOORS.

ABOUT 26'

DW

LIBRARY

EXTERIOR METAL CHIMNEY FOR SAFETY

THIRD FLOOR

BEDROOM   LIVING ROOM

THE NORTH WALL HAD NO WINDOWS.

N

BATH

DW

KITCHEN

DINING ROOM

SECOND FLOOR

PORCH

EXPOSED SKELETON FRAME (COLUMNS)

DW

GARAGE

FURNACE

GROUND FLOOR

1931
ALUMINAIRE HOUSE SYOSSET, LONG ISLAND, NEW YORK
A.L. KOCHER AND ALBERT FREY, ARCHITECTS

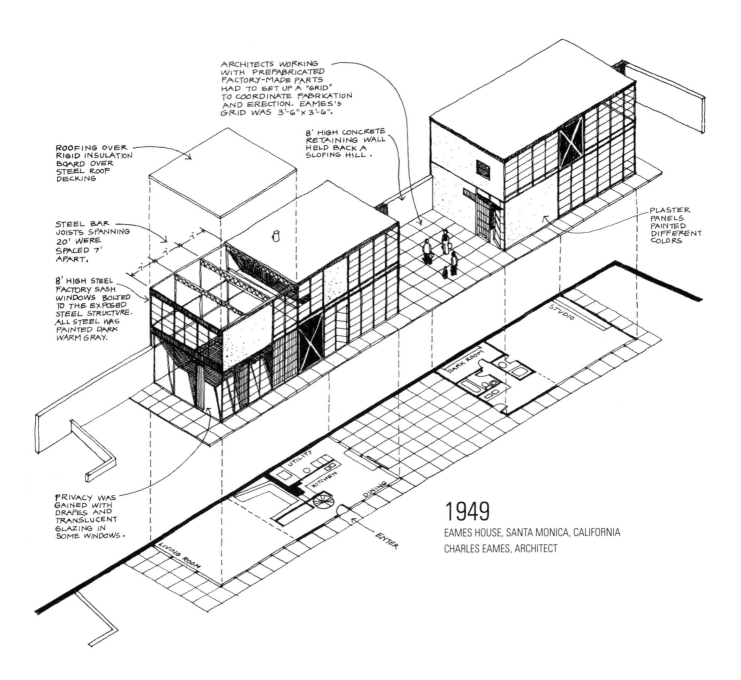

ARCHITECTS WORKING WITH PREFABRICATED FACTORY-MADE PARTS HAD TO SET UP A "GRID" TO COORDINATE FABRICATION AND ERECTION. EAMES'S GRID WAS 3'-6" x 3'-6".

ROOFING OVER RIGID INSULATION BOARD OVER STEEL ROOF DECKING

8' HIGH CONCRETE RETAINING WALL HELD BACK A SLOPING HILL.

STEEL BAR JOISTS SPANNING 20' WERE SPACED 7' APART.

PLASTER PANELS PAINTED DIFFERENT COLORS

8' HIGH STEEL FACTORY SASH WINDOWS BOLTED TO THE EXPOSED STEEL STRUCTURE. ALL STEEL WAS PAINTED DARK WARM GRAY.

STUDIO

DARK ROOM

PRIVACY WAS GAINED WITH DRAPES AND TRANSLUCENT GLAZING IN SOME WINDOWS.

UTILITY

KITCHEN

DINING

ENTER

LIVING ROOM

1949
EAMES HOUSE, SANTA MONICA, CALIFORNIA
CHARLES EAMES, ARCHITECT

248

But, while Mies tediously detailed all of his parts so that they had to be custom factory-made, High Tech designers used more readily available inexpensive off-the-shelf factory-made parts for their buildings. America's most influential High Tech example is the Eames House (above) designed by Charles Eames for his wife and himself in Santa Monica, California. This house received national attention when it was featured in *Art and Architecture* magazine's Case Study house program in 1949. The High Tech Style is still extremely popular with many designers.

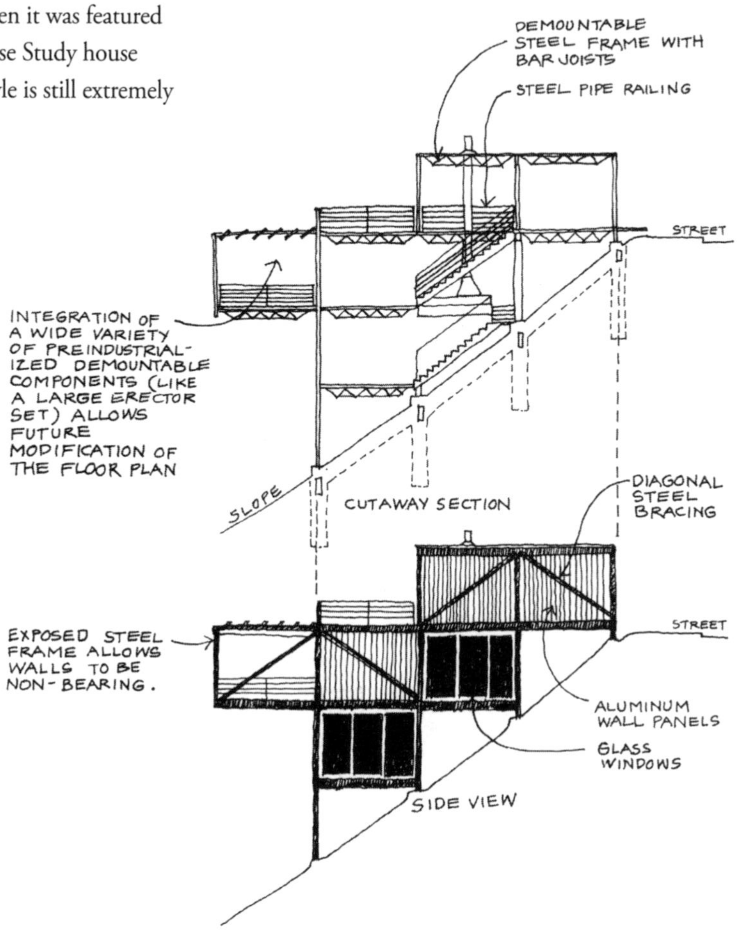

DEMOUNTABLE STEEL FRAME WITH BAR JOISTS

STEEL PIPE RAILING

STREET

INTEGRATION OF A WIDE VARIETY OF PREINDUSTRIAL-IZED DEMOUNTABLE COMPONENTS (LIKE A LARGE ERECTOR SET) ALLOWS FUTURE MODIFICATION OF THE FLOOR PLAN

SLOPE

CUTAWAY SECTION

DIAGONAL STEEL BRACING

EXPOSED STEEL FRAME ALLOWS WALLS TO BE NON-BEARING.

STREET

ALUMINUM WALL PANELS

GLASS WINDOWS

SIDE VIEW

1977
T.E.S.T. HOUSE, BEVERLY HILLS, CALIFORNIA
HELMUT SCHULITZ, ARCHITECT

Roof Architectur

Countrywide 1955

During the mid-1950s the International Style reached its height of popularity in America. The many basic principles set by the older European modernists had remained but experimentation with the style soon led to the breaking of one rule after another.

The roof seemed to be the first part of the house open for innovation. Inspired by a wide variety of new materials and structural systems developed during World War II, designers produced startling new roof forms that greatly enriched the interior of the house, but in some instances gave a world's fair appearance to the exterior. The International Style principle of "beauty through technology" was redefined.

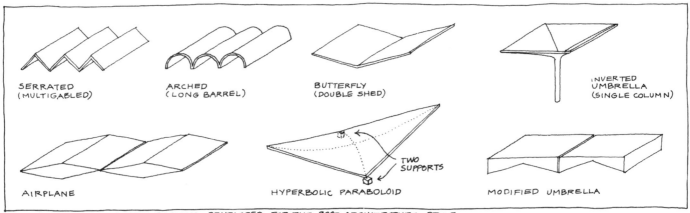

SERRATED (MULTIGABLED)

ARCHED (LONG BARREL)

BUTTERFLY (DOUBLE SHED)

INVERTED UMBRELLA (SINGLE COLUMN)

AIRPLANE

HYPERBOLIC PARABOLOID — TWO SUPPORTS

MODIFIED UMBRELLA

A FEW OF THE MANY ROOF DESIGNS DEVELOPED FOR THE ROOF ARCHITECTURE STYLE

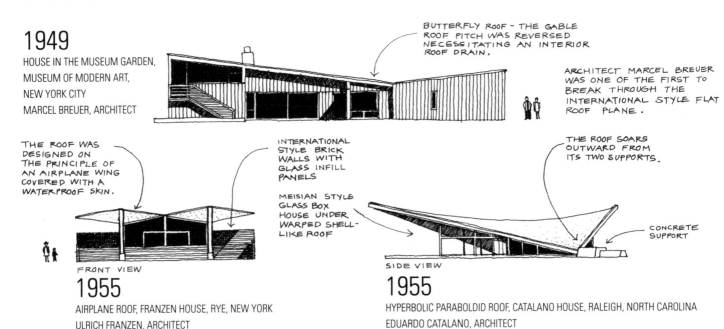

1949
HOUSE IN THE MUSEUM GARDEN,
MUSEUM OF MODERN ART,
NEW YORK CITY
MARCEL BREUER, ARCHITECT

BUTTERFLY ROOF – THE GABLE ROOF PITCH WAS REVERSED NECESSITATING AN INTERIOR ROOF DRAIN.

ARCHITECT MARCEL BREUER WAS ONE OF THE FIRST TO BREAK THROUGH THE INTERNATIONAL STYLE FLAT ROOF PLANE.

THE ROOF WAS DESIGNED ON THE PRINCIPLE OF AN AIRPLANE WING COVERED WITH A WATERPROOF SKIN.

INTERNATIONAL STYLE BRICK WALLS WITH GLASS INFILL PANELS

MEISIAN STYLE GLASS BOX HOUSE UNDER WARPED SHELL-LIKE ROOF

THE ROOF SOARS OUTWARD FROM ITS TWO SUPPORTS.

CONCRETE SUPPORT

FRONT VIEW

SIDE VIEW

1955
AIRPLANE ROOF, FRANZEN HOUSE, RYE, NEW YORK
ULRICH FRANZEN, ARCHITECT

1955
HYPERBOLIC PARABOLDID ROOF, CATALANO HOUSE, RALEIGH, NORTH CAROLINA
EDUARDO CATALANO, ARCHITECT

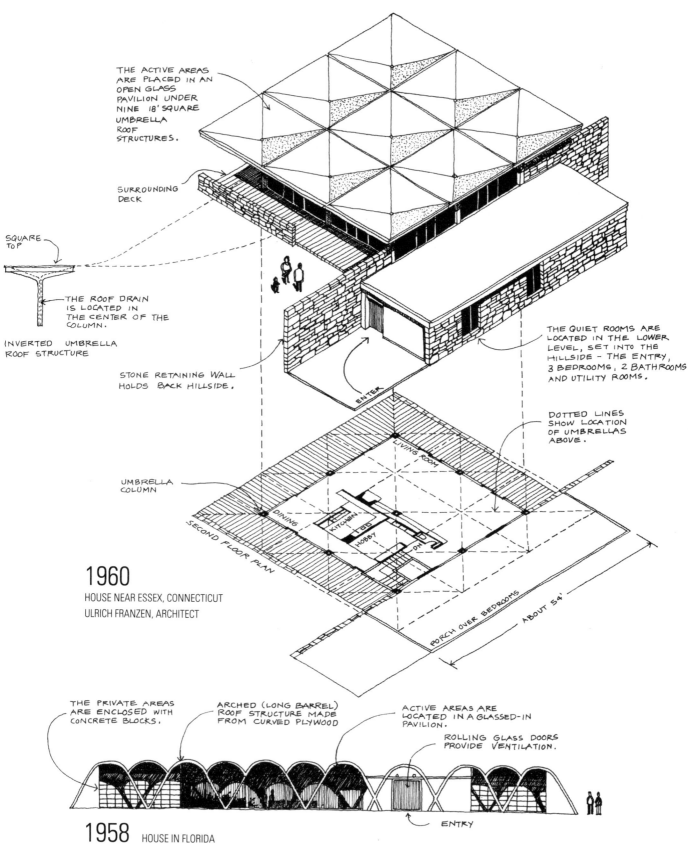

THE ACTIVE AREAS ARE PLACED IN AN OPEN GLASS PAVILION UNDER NINE 18' SQUARE UMBRELLA ROOF STRUCTURES.

SURROUNDING DECK

SQUARE TOP

THE ROOF DRAIN IS LOCATED IN THE CENTER OF THE COLUMN.

INVERTED UMBRELLA ROOF STRUCTURE

STONE RETAINING WALL HOLDS BACK HILLSIDE.

ENTER

THE QUIET ROOMS ARE LOCATED IN THE LOWER LEVEL, SET INTO THE HILLSIDE - THE ENTRY, 3 BEDROOMS, 2 BATHROOMS AND UTILITY ROOMS.

DOTTED LINES SHOW LOCATION OF UMBRELLAS ABOVE.

UMBRELLA COLUMN

SECOND FLOOR PLAN

LIVING ROOM

DINING

KITCHEN

HOBBY

PORCH OVER BEDROOMS

ABOUT 54'

1960
HOUSE NEAR ESSEX, CONNECTICUT
ULRICH FRANZEN, ARCHITECT

THE PRIVATE AREAS ARE ENCLOSED WITH CONCRETE BLOCKS.

ARCHED (LONG BARREL) ROOF STRUCTURE MADE FROM CURVED PLYWOOD

ACTIVE AREAS ARE LOCATED IN A GLASSED-IN PAVILION.

ROLLING GLASS DOORS PROVIDE VENTILATION.

ENTRY

1958 HOUSE IN FLORIDA
PAUL RUDOLPH, ARCHITECT

A-Frame

Countrywide
1955

The A-Frame has been the traditional vacation home or second home for many Americans since World War II. It gets its name from the "A"-shaped structural system that allows the elimination of the two side walls of the house. The result is an inexpensive building with only four surfaces: two end walls and the gable roof.

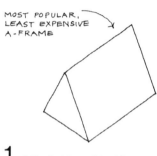

MOST POPULAR, LEAST EXPENSIVE A-FRAME

1 STANDARD A-FRAME

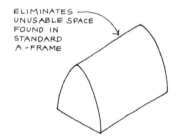

ELIMINATES UNUSABLE SPACE FOUND IN STANDARD A-FRAME

2 ARCHED (GOTHIC) A-FRAME

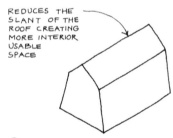

REDUCES THE SLANT OF THE ROOF CREATING MORE INTERIOR USABLE SPACE

3 GAMBREL ROOF A-FRAME

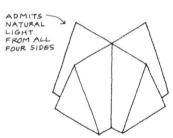

ADMITS NATURAL LIGHT FROM ALL FOUR SIDES

4 DOUBLE STANDARD A-FRAME

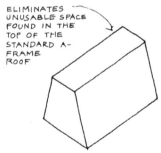

ELIMINATES UNUSABLE SPACE FOUND IN THE TOP OF THE STANDARD A-FRAME ROOF

5 FLAT TOP A-FRAME

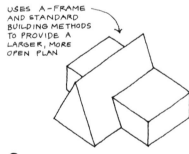

USES A-FRAME AND STANDARD BUILDING METHODS TO PROVIDE A LARGER, MORE OPEN PLAN

6 A-FRAME WITH WINGS

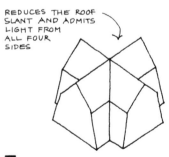

REDUCES THE ROOF SLANT AND ADMITS LIGHT FROM ALL FOUR SIDES

7 DOUBLE GAMBREL ROOF A-FRAME

SEVEN DIFFERENT KINDS OF A-FRAMES

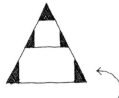

A KEY DISADVANTAGE OF THE A-FRAME IS THE UNUSABLE SPACE IN THE CORNERS OF THE TRIANGLE (SHOWN SHADED)

The disadvantages of this style of house are the space lost in the top and corners of the steep slanting roof, and the amount of natural light entering only from the ends is usually insufficient. The advantages are, of course, the low cost and the rustic, woodsy Swiss Chalet aesthetic.

Opposite are several configurations of the basic A-Frame Style, illustrating the versatility of the structure.

The basic A-Frame is usually located in vacation areas in the mountains, on the ocean, or near a lake. The house can be built relatively inexpensively because of the unique structural system (the triangle is independently strong) and because siding must be purchased only for the two end walls and they are primarily glass.

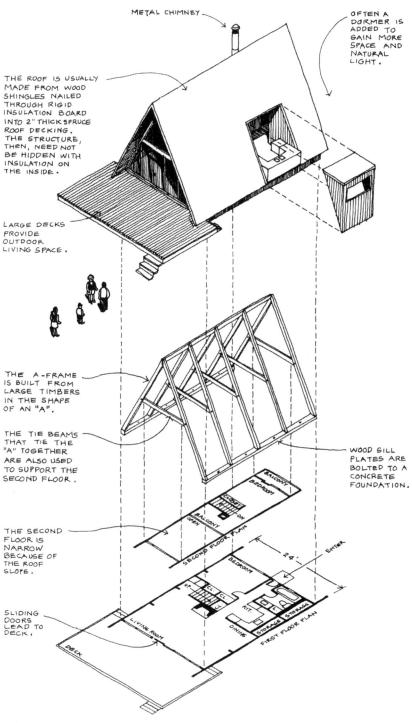

METAL CHIMNEY

OFTEN A DORMER IS ADDED TO GAIN MORE SPACE AND NATURAL LIGHT.

THE ROOF IS USUALLY MADE FROM WOOD SHINGLES NAILED THROUGH RIGID INSULATION BOARD INTO 2" THICK SPRUCE ROOF DECKING. THE STRUCTURE, THEN, NEED NOT BE HIDDEN WITH INSULATION ON THE INSIDE.

LARGE DECKS PROVIDE OUTDOOR LIVING SPACE.

THE A-FRAME IS BUILT FROM LARGE TIMBERS IN THE SHAPE OF AN "A".

THE TIE BEAMS THAT TIE THE "A" TOGETHER ARE ALSO USED TO SUPPORT THE SECOND FLOOR.

WOOD SILL PLATES ARE BOLTED TO A CONCRETE FOUNDATION.

THE SECOND FLOOR IS NARROW BECAUSE OF THE ROOF SLOPE.

SLIDING DOORS LEAD TO DECK.

SECOND FLOOR PLAN
BALCONY
BEDROOM
CLOSET
OPEN

FIRST FLOOR PLAN
ENTER
24'
BEDROOM
LIVING ROOM
DINING
STORAGE
KIT.
DECK

1960 BASIC A-FRAME HOUSE

Contractor Moderr

Countrywide
1955

The Contractor Modern Style has been called the true twentieth-century vernacular mode. Its compactness and simplicity and its use of many stylistic features dictated by the experience of builders and contractors made it the most commonly used style for the thousands of subdivision ranch houses being constructed all over America.

Wright's influence was found primarily on the exterior: the long, low profile, the gently sloped low-cable roof covering both house and garage, the combination of several materials (usually in horizontal stripes), and the use of bands of windows

(called ribbon windows). The contractor used Wright's ideas but built expediently with factory-made, often synthetic, materials, such as imitation plastic stone, pressed fiber imitation wood siding, and metal shutters and siding.

The Contractor Modern Style has been called the true twentieth century vernacular mode. Its compactness and simplicity and its use of many stylistic features dictated by the experience of builders and contractors made it the most commonly used style for the thousands of subdivision ranch houses being constructed all over America.

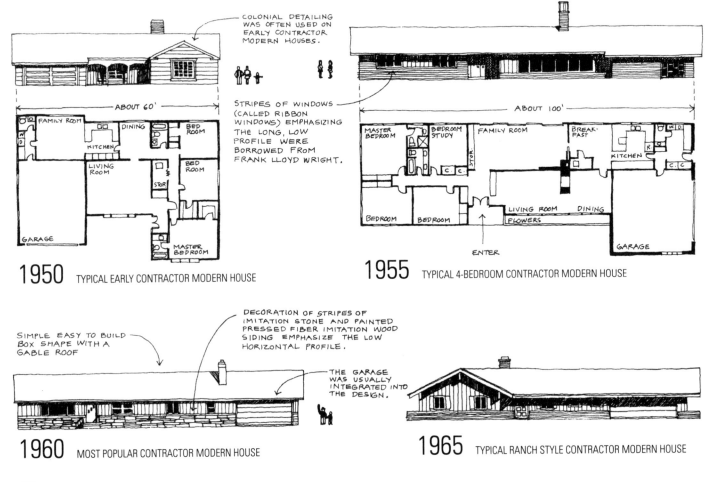

COLONIAL DETAILING WAS OFTEN USED ON EARLY CONTRACTOR MODERN HOUSES.

STRIPES OF WINDOWS (CALLED RIBBON WINDOWS) EMPHASIZING THE LONG, LOW PROFILE WERE BORROWED FROM FRANK LLOYD WRIGHT.

1950 TYPICAL EARLY CONTRACTOR MODERN HOUSE

1955 TYPICAL 4-BEDROOM CONTRACTOR MODERN HOUSE

SIMPLE EASY TO BUILD BOX SHAPE WITH A GABLE ROOF

DECORATION OF STRIPES OF IMITATION STONE AND PAINTED PRESSED FIBER IMITATION WOOD SIDING EMPHASIZE THE LOW HORIZONTAL PROFILE.

THE GARAGE WAS USUALLY INTEGRATED INTO THE DESIGN.

1960 MOST POPULAR CONTRACTOR MODERN HOUSE

1965 TYPICAL RANCH STYLE CONTRACTOR MODERN HOUSE

From 1948 until 1955, American homes were being built at the rate of one million per year in the world's largest housing boom. In 1953, *Life* magazine sponsored a conference of leaders of the highly competitive building industry. Its purpose was to design a "good-looking, skillfully engineered, $15,000 house." The meeting, coordinated by the National Association of Home Builders, resulted in the creation of the Trade Secrets house. This 1,340 square foot house was designed to be contractor-built all over America, by mass builders applying assembly-line techniques that had been held secret for years. The Trade Secrets house was billed as "a house of today, not a house of tomorrow." It was highly influential in the vernacular Contractor Modern movement.

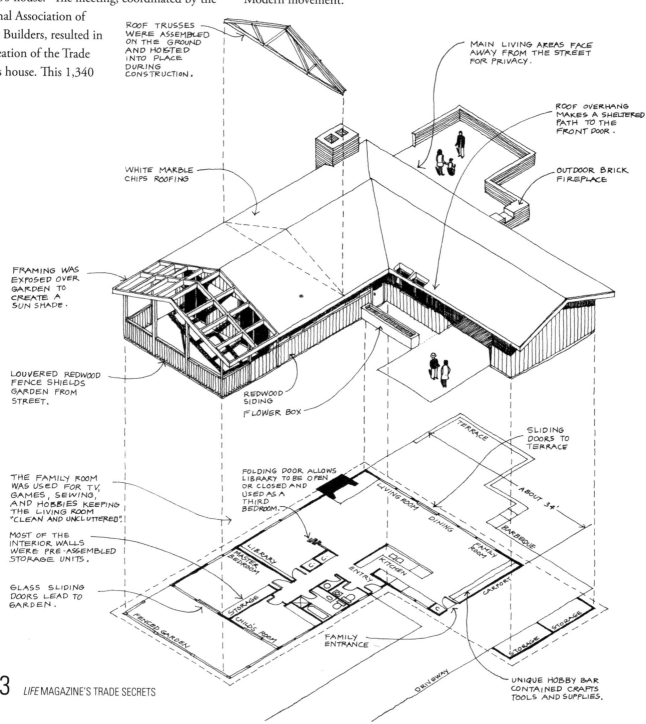

ROOF TRUSSES WERE ASSEMBLED ON THE GROUND AND HOISTED INTO PLACE DURING CONSTRUCTION.

MAIN LIVING AREAS FACE AWAY FROM THE STREET FOR PRIVACY.

ROOF OVERHANG MAKES A SHELTERED PATH TO THE FRONT DOOR.

WHITE MARBLE CHIPS ROOFING

OUTDOOR BRICK FIREPLACE

FRAMING WAS EXPOSED OVER GARDEN TO CREATE A SUN SHADE.

LOUVERED REDWOOD FENCE SHIELDS GARDEN FROM STREET.

REDWOOD SIDING

FLOWER BOX

TERRACE

SLIDING DOORS TO TERRACE

ABOUT 3½'

BARBEQUE

THE FAMILY ROOM WAS USED FOR TV, GAMES, SEWING, AND HOBBIES KEEPING THE LIVING ROOM "CLEAN AND UNCLUTTERED".

FOLDING DOOR ALLOWS LIBRARY TO BE OPEN OR CLOSED AND USED AS A THIRD BEDROOM.

LIVING ROOM

DINING

FAMILY ROOM

MOST OF THE INTERIOR WALLS WERE PRE-ASSEMBLED STORAGE UNITS.

LIBRARY

MASTER BEDROOM

KITCHEN

ENTRY

CARPORT

GLASS SLIDING DOORS LEAD TO GARDEN.

STORAGE

CHILD'S ROOM

FENCED GARDEN

FAMILY ENTRANCE

STORAGE

STORAGE

DRIVEWAY

UNIQUE HOBBY BAR CONTAINED CRAFTS TOOLS AND SUPPLIES.

1953 *LIFE* MAGAZINE'S TRADE SECRETS

Neocolonial

Countrywide
1955

The simplicity and honest beauty of the early colonial styles have influenced American house design for over 300 years. The Neocolonial Style is a continuation of the Colonial Revival Style begun in 1925 as a return to the image of traditional American ideals. The Neocolonial, Contractor Modern, and Split Level are vernacular styles that gain attention through plans published in home magazines, the modern day pattern book. People interested in building a new house simply choose their favorite design from a series of these magazines and find a contractor to build it. Architects are hired by the pattern book (magazine) companies, not by the owners.

Many of the colonial styles were copied in all parts of the country but each geographical section had its own favorite Neocolonial house, usually based on local heritage. In eastern Pennsylvania, for example, the simple colonial stone buildings of the Germans and Scots were emulated with a new box shaped building connected to a garage with the pent roof, an original colonial amenity (p. 70). It is not uncommon, however, for the saltbox, native to New England, to be built in the South or the Greek Revival, used for the southern Colonial mansion, to be built in the North.

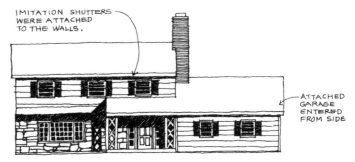

IMITATION SHUTTERS WERE ATTACHED TO THE WALLS.

ATTACHED GARAGE ENTERED FROM SIDE

1950
GERMAN COLONIAL STYLE NEOCOLONIAL HOUSE

A BREEZE WAY WAS OFTEN LOCATED BETWEEN THE HOUSE AND GARAGE.

PENT ROOF

1950
GERMAN COLONIAL STYLE NEOCOLONIAL HOUSE, WALKER RESIDENCE, YARDLEY, PENNSYLVANIA

Neocolonial houses are popular contractor-built homes for suburban one-half acre lot subdivisions all over America. There are hundreds of magazines on the newsstands today extolling the virtues of these nostalgic copies of the past.

SMALL PANED WINDOWS
12" SECOND FLOOR OVERHANG

THE GARAGE WAS ENTERED FROM THE REAR OR SIDE SO THAT IT COULD BE DESIGNED TO LOOK LIKE A KITCHEN WING

1960
GARRISON HOUSE STYLE NEOCOLONIAL HOUSE

1960
MEDIEVAL STYLE NEOCOLONIAL HOUSE

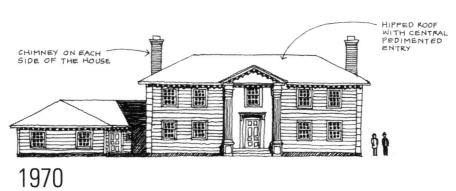

CHIMNEY ON EACH SIDE OF THE HOUSE

HIPPED ROOF WITH CENTRAL PEDIMENTED ENTRY

1970
GEORGIAN STYLE NEOCOLONIAL HOUSE

WROUGHT IRON RAILING

ARCHED OPENINGS
HIPPED ROOF
STUCCO FINISH

1970
SPANISH COLONIAL STYLE NEOCOLONIAL HOUSE

By 1970 the Neocolonial Style house was often a collection of nostalgic features from earlier times. It was common practice for contractors to build homes using ideas cut from a variety of magazines by the owner. Development houses were constructed by the thousands with different "attachments" made to the front of a basic box shape to give a variety of styles. Shown below is an example of how a developer created four different styles from the same building.

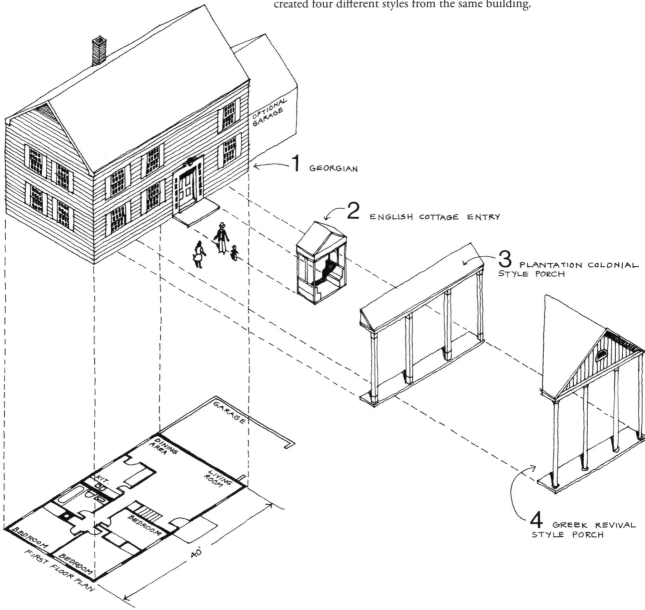

1 GEORGIAN

2 ENGLISH COTTAGE ENTRY

3 PLANTATION COLONIAL STYLE PORCH

4 GREEK REVIVAL STYLE PORCH

OPTIONAL GARAGE

GARAGE

DINING AREA

LIVING ROOM

KIT.

BEDROOM

BEDROOM

BEDROOM

FIRST FLOOR PLAN

40'

1970

FOUR DIFFERENT NEOCOLONIAL STYLES FROM THREE DIFFERENT "ATTACHMENTS"

Developers looking for expedient ways to build have, often unknowingly, eliminated many of the key parts of the original dwelling, often changing the architectural character to such a degree that the new building looks quite different. Shown below, the removal of the entablature (the beam holding up the gable roof) from the front facade of the Greek Revival house changes the aesthetic from solid to fragile. The saltbox without its enormous chimney has lost its "anchor."

These changes and other less common ones are the keys to future development of the vernacular Neocolonial Style. Will contractors continue to design new features based on expediency, or will a new demand for authenticity cause the Neocolonial house to look like its original counterpart again?

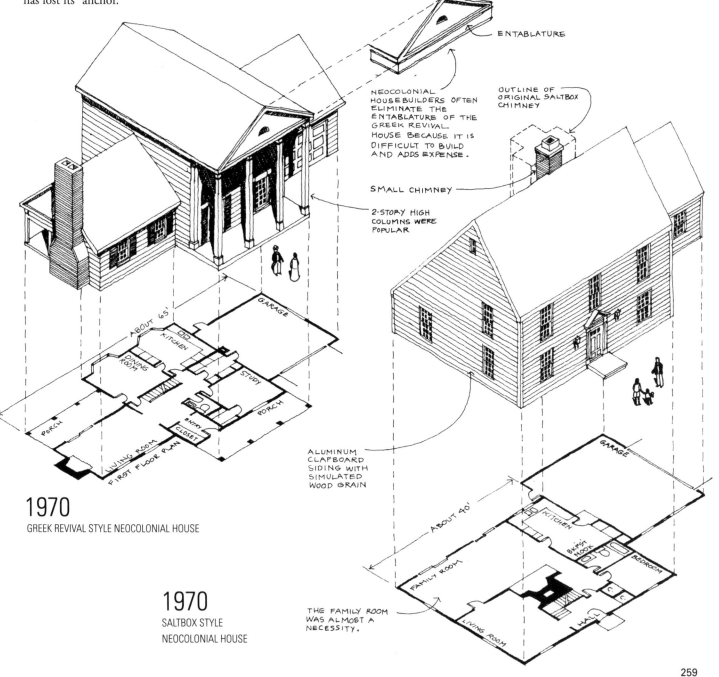

ENTABLATURE

NEOCOLONIAL HOUSEBUILDERS OFTEN ELIMINATE THE ENTABLATURE OF THE GREEK REVIVAL HOUSE BECAUSE IT IS DIFFICULT TO BUILD AND ADDS EXPENSE.

OUTLINE OF ORIGINAL SALTBOX CHIMNEY

SMALL CHIMNEY

2-STORY HIGH COLUMNS WERE POPULAR

ALUMINUM CLAPBOARD SIDING WITH SIMULATED WOOD GRAIN

ABOUT 65'

GARAGE

KITCHEN

DINING ROOM

STUDY

PORCH

PORCH

ENTRY

CLOSET

LIVING ROOM

FIRST FLOOR PLAN

1970
GREEK REVIVAL STYLE NEOCOLONIAL HOUSE

1970
SALTBOX STYLE
NEOCOLONIAL HOUSE

ABOUT 40'

GARAGE

KITCHEN

BKFST NOOK

BEDROOM

FAMILY ROOM

C.

C.

LIVING ROOM

HALL

THE FAMILY ROOM WAS ALMOST A NECESSITY.

PLATFORM FRAME CONSTRUCTION

The platform frame, sometimes called the western frame, is the name given to the method of building over 95 percent of America's houses today. It has been ingeniously developed by contractors and developers interested in fast, economical construction. It is used primarily in building houses in the Contractor Modern, Split Level, and Neocolonial Styles.

Its basic difference from the balloon frame (p. 122), from which it evolved, is that its walls are built at ceiling height to support platforms or floors. The balloon frame's walls are built as a continuous membrane with the floors supported within. Below are seven simplified steps showing how platform frame construction works.

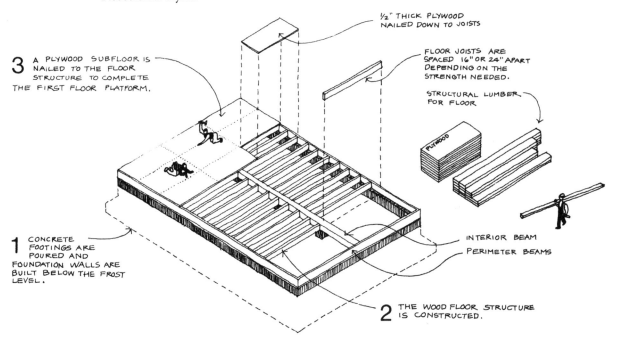

½" THICK PLYWOOD NAILED DOWN TO JOISTS

FLOOR JOISTS ARE SPACED 16" OR 24" APART DEPENDING ON THE STRENGTH NEEDED.

STRUCTURAL LUMBER FOR FLOOR

3 A PLYWOOD SUBFLOOR IS NAILED TO THE FLOOR STRUCTURE TO COMPLETE THE FIRST FLOOR PLATFORM.

1 CONCRETE FOOTINGS ARE POURED AND FOUNDATION WALLS ARE BUILT BELOW THE FROST LEVEL.

INTERIOR BEAM
PERIMETER BEAMS

2 THE WOOD FLOOR STRUCTURE IS CONSTRUCTED.

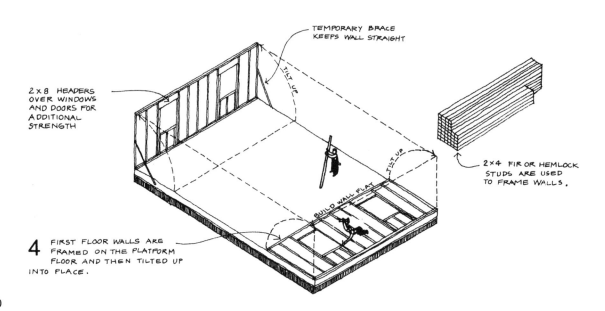

TEMPORARY BRACE KEEPS WALL STRAIGHT

TILT UP

2 X 8 HEADERS OVER WINDOWS AND DOORS FOR ADDITIONAL STRENGTH

2×4 FIR OR HEMLOCK STUDS ARE USED TO FRAME WALLS.

BUILD WALL FLAT

4 FIRST FLOOR WALLS ARE FRAMED ON THE PLATFORM FLOOR AND THEN TILTED UP INTO PLACE.

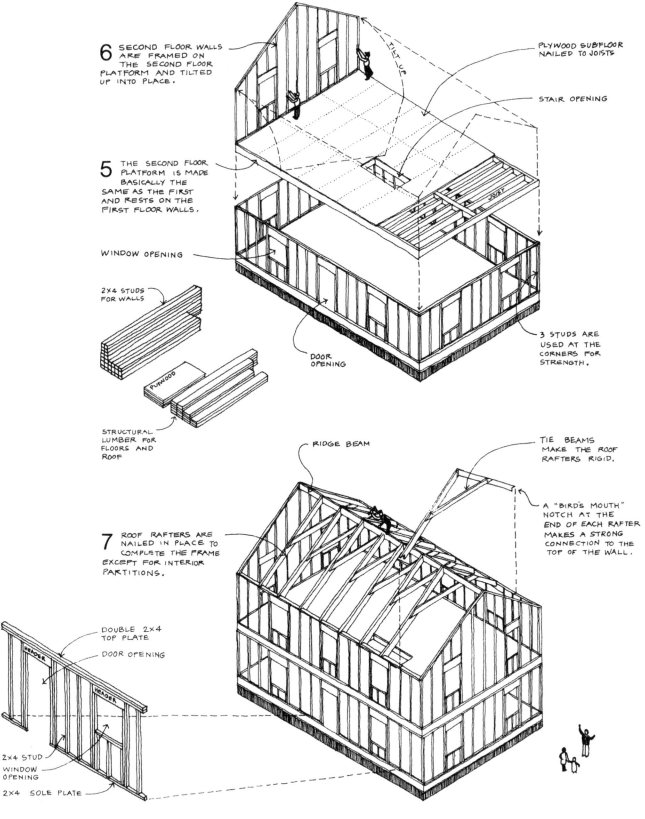

6 SECOND FLOOR WALLS ARE FRAMED ON THE SECOND FLOOR PLATFORM AND TILTED UP INTO PLACE.

PLYWOOD SUBFLOOR NAILED TO JOISTS

STAIR OPENING

TILT UP

5 THE SECOND FLOOR PLATFORM IS MADE BASICALLY THE SAME AS THE FIRST AND RESTS ON THE FIRST FLOOR WALLS.

JOIST

WINDOW OPENING

2×4 STUDS FOR WALLS

PLYWOOD

DOOR OPENING

3 STUDS ARE USED AT THE CORNERS FOR STRENGTH.

STRUCTURAL LUMBER FOR FLOORS AND ROOF

RIDGE BEAM

TIE BEAMS MAKE THE ROOF RAFTERS RIGID.

A "BIRD'S MOUTH" NOTCH AT THE END OF EACH RAFTER MAKES A STRONG CONNECTION TO THE TOP OF THE WALL.

7 ROOF RAFTERS ARE NAILED IN PLACE TO COMPLETE THE FRAME EXCEPT FOR INTERIOR PARTITIONS.

DOUBLE 2×4 TOP PLATE

DOOR OPENING

HEADER

HEADER

2×4 STUD

WINDOW OPENING

2×4 SOLE PLATE

FRAMING FOR DOORS AND WINDOWS

Split Level

Countrywide
1960

The Split Level Style house was a response to the late 1950s and early 1960s culture that necessitated the separation of the formal, informal, and sleeping areas of the house. The formal rooms (living room and dining room) were used primarily for entertaining and quiet times with friends. The informal areas (the kitchen and the family room) were used for recreation, informal dining, and children. The three areas, one noisy, one quiet, and one for sleep, when separated from one another on different levels, created a unique, livable house.

A new American institution, television, was responsible for the development of the family room from the lightly used recreation room of the California Ranch Style (p. 232) to the most important room of the house. It became the hub and usually had direct access to an outdoor terrace and the entry. By placing the entry and stairs in the middle of the building, at the level change, all areas could be reached immediately from the front entrance. This advantage made the split level a favorite among new home buyers in the 1960s.

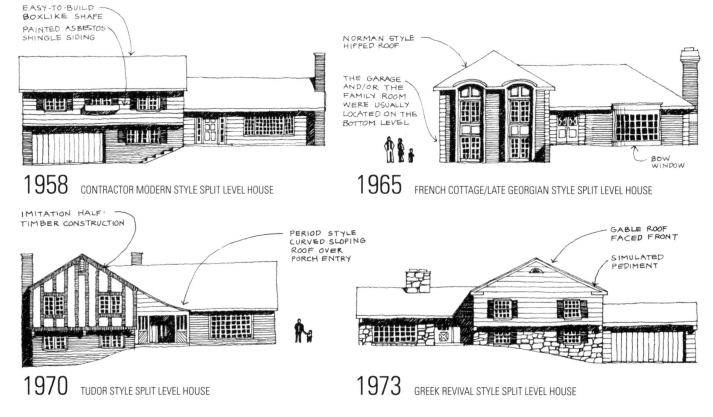

EASY-TO-BUILD BOXLIKE SHAPE
PAINTED ASBESTOS SHINGLE SIDING

1958 CONTRACTOR MODERN STYLE SPLIT LEVEL HOUSE

NORMAN STYLE HIPPED ROOF
THE GARAGE AND/OR THE FAMILY ROOM WERE USUALLY LOCATED ON THE BOTTOM LEVEL
BOW WINDOW

1965 FRENCH COTTAGE/LATE GEORGIAN STYLE SPLIT LEVEL HOUSE

IMITATION HALF-TIMBER CONSTRUCTION
PERIOD STYLE CURVED SLOPING ROOF OVER PORCH ENTRY

1970 TUDOR STYLE SPLIT LEVEL HOUSE

GABLE ROOF FACED FRONT
SIMULATED PEDIMENT

1973 GREEK REVIVAL STYLE SPLIT LEVEL HOUSE

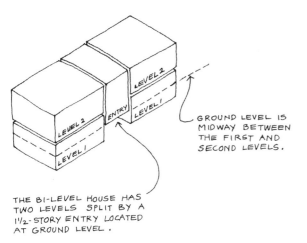

GROUND LEVEL IS MIDWAY BETWEEN THE FIRST AND SECOND LEVELS.

THE BI-LEVEL HOUSE HAS TWO LEVELS SPLIT BY A 1½-STORY ENTRY LOCATED AT GROUND LEVEL.

The split level house, because of its simple boxlike shape, could be manipulated to adapt to almost any style, as shown in the next four illustrations.

In the late 1960s, a new type of multilevel house evolved called the bi-level. It was basically a two-story dwelling with the lower level sunk about four feet below grade. This allows an entry, placed on ground level, to be located one-half a flight of stairs below the main level and one-half a flight above the lower level. Once inside the bi-level, it functions as a simple two-story house. Its advantages are cost (a two-story building for the price of a one-and-one-half one) and a rather elegant one-and-one-half story high entry lobby area. Two examples of the bi-Ievel are illustrated below.

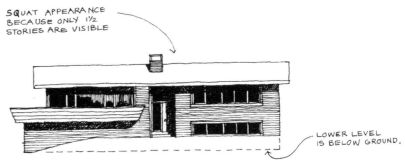

SQUAT APPEARANCE BECAUSE ONLY 1½ STORIES ARE VISIBLE

LOWER LEVEL IS BELOW GROUND.

1975 PRAIRIE STYLE BI-LEVEL HOUSE

HALF HEIGHT WINDOWS PROVIDE NATURAL LIGHT INTO THE LOWER LEVEL.

THE ENTRANCE IS LOCATED BETWEEN THE LOWER AND UPPER LEVELS (HALF A FLIGHT OF STAIRS UP OR DOWN).

1975 PLANTATION COLONIAL STYLE BI-LEVEL HOUSE

The most common split level houses, speculatively built by the millions in American suburban developments, were primarily designed by contractors as they learned, over the years, what sold and what did not. Cost, of course, was a key factor so the roof line and the basic shape were kept simple. As in the Contractor Modern Style (p. 252), a variety of exterior cladding materials and small decorative devices like flower boxes, street lamps, fixed, painted shutters, and fancy doorbells were used to make the house attractive and more saleable. Below and on the opposite page are two of the most popular split levels of the 1960s.

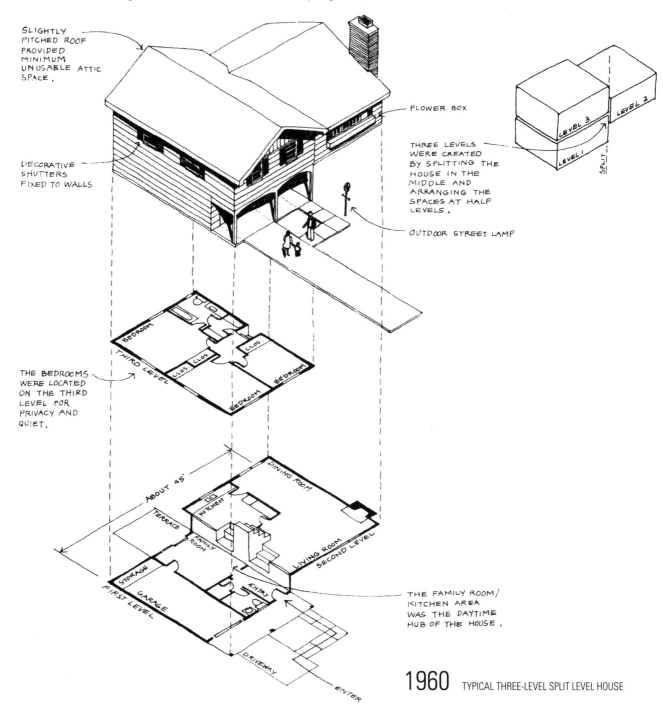

SLIGHTLY PITCHED ROOF PROVIDED MINIMUM UNUSABLE ATTIC SPACE.

DECORATIVE SHUTTERS FIXED TO WALLS

FLOWER BOX

THREE LEVELS WERE CREATED BY SPLITTING THE HOUSE IN THE MIDDLE AND ARRANGING THE SPACES AT HALF LEVELS.

LEVEL 3   LEVEL 2   LEVEL 1   SPLIT

OUTDOOR STREET LAMP

THE BEDROOMS WERE LOCATED ON THE THIRD LEVEL FOR PRIVACY AND QUIET.

BEDROOM   THIRD LEVEL   CLOS   CLOS   CLOS   BEDROOM   BEDROOM

ABOUT 45'

DINING ROOM   KITCHEN   TERRACE   FAMILY ROOM   LIVING ROOM   SECOND LEVEL

STORAGE   FIRST LEVEL   GARAGE   ENTRY

THE FAMILY ROOM/ KITCHEN AREA WAS THE DAYTIME HUB OF THE HOUSE.

DRIVEWAY   ENTER

1960 TYPICAL THREE-LEVEL SPLIT LEVEL HOUSE

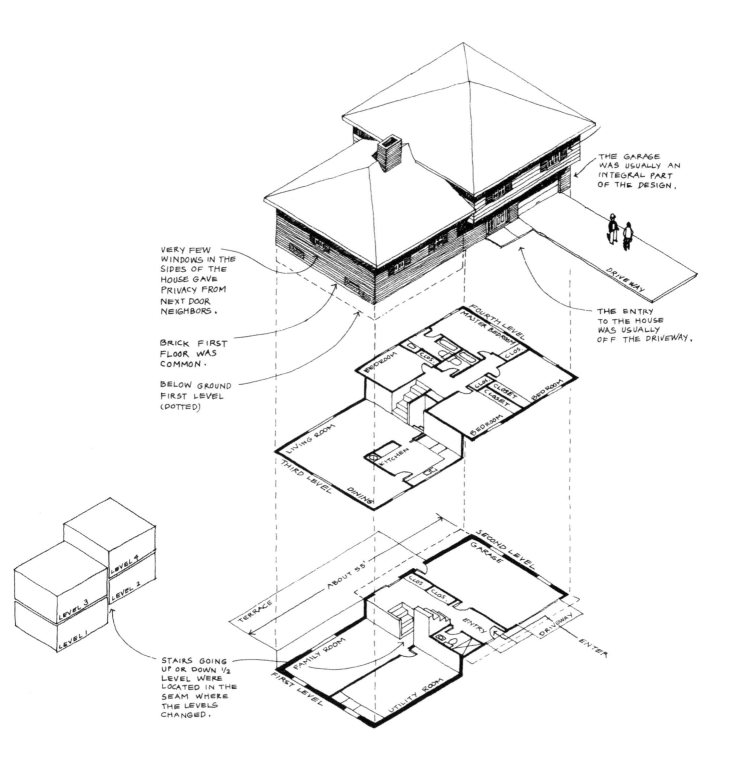

THE GARAGE WAS USUALLY AN INTEGRAL PART OF THE DESIGN.

VERY FEW WINDOWS IN THE SIDES OF THE HOUSE GAVE PRIVACY FROM NEXT DOOR NEIGHBORS.

BRICK FIRST FLOOR WAS COMMON.

BELOW GROUND FIRST LEVEL (DOTTED)

THE ENTRY TO THE HOUSE WAS USUALLY OFF THE DRIVEWAY.

DRIVEWAY

FOURTH LEVEL
MASTER BEDROOM
BEDROOM
CLOS.
CLOS.
CLOS.
CLOSET
CLOSET
BEDROOM
BEDROOM
LIVING ROOM
KITCHEN
THIRD LEVEL
DINING

SECOND LEVEL
GARAGE
ABOUT 55'
CLOS
CLOS
TERRACE
FAMILY ROOM
ENTRY
DRIVEWAY
ENTER
FIRST LEVEL
UTILITY ROOM

LEVEL 4
LEVEL 2
LEVEL 3
LEVEL 1

STAIRS GOING UP OR DOWN ½ LEVEL WERE LOCATED IN THE SEAM WHERE THE LEVELS CHANGED.

1962 TYPICAL FOUR-LEVEL SPLIT LEVEL HOUSE

Converted Train Car

Countrywide 1960

Americans have been converting obsolete train and trolley cars into homes for over one hundred years. They have provided compact, instant, livable space with walls, floor, ceiling, doors, and windows. Trolleys and Pullman and parlor cars require the installation of heat, cooking, and bathroom facilities before the home is complete. The caboose, however, usually contains the necessary plumbing and heating facilities for immediate occupancy.

The adoption of steam-powered trains in place of horse-drawn railcars for urban transportation created the first surplus of obsolete train cars. During the 1880s and 1890s many of these cars were converted into summer homes. Often two or three cars were attached to create multiroomed houses and "carville" villages were not common.

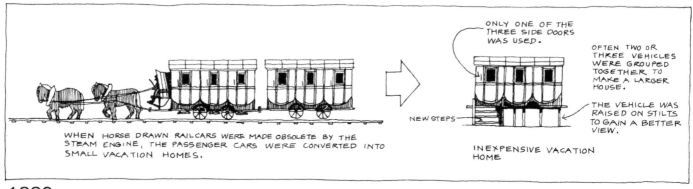

ONLY ONE OF THE THREE SIDE DOORS WAS USED.

OFTEN TWO OR THREE VEHICLES WERE GROUPED TOGETHER TO MAKE A LARGER HOUSE.

NEW STEPS

THE VEHICLE WAS RAISED ON STILTS TO GAIN A BETTER VIEW.

WHEN HORSE DRAWN RAILCARS WERE MADE OBSOLETE BY THE STEAM ENGINE, THE PASSENGER CARS WERE CONVERTED INTO SMALL VACATION HOMES.

INEXPENSIVE VACATION HOME

1880 THE FIRST CONVERTED TRAIN CARS

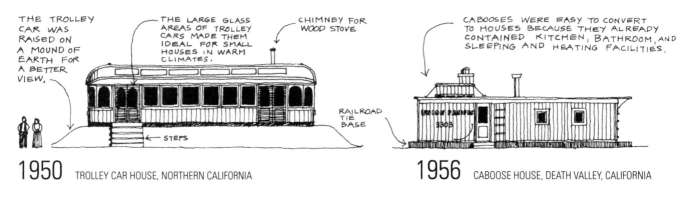

THE TROLLEY CAR WAS RAISED ON A MOUND OF EARTH FOR A BETTER VIEW.

THE LARGE GLASS AREAS OF TROLLEY CARS MADE THEM IDEAL FOR SMALL HOUSES IN WARM CLIMATES.

CHIMNEY FOR WOOD STOVE

STEPS

RAILROAD TIE BASE

CABOOSES WERE EASY TO CONVERT TO HOUSES BECAUSE THEY ALREADY CONTAINED KITCHEN, BATHROOM, AND SLEEPING AND HEATING FACILITIES.

1950 TROLLEY CAR HOUSE, NORTHERN CALIFORNIA

1956 CABOOSE HOUSE, DEATH VALLEY, CALIFORNIA

Over the years as trains grow in size and gain advanced technology, more and more cars become obsolete. Railroad cars are sold to the highest bidders in many locals, usually at scrap iron prices. In many cases converting old cabooses or trolley cars into new homes becomes a historical preservation project. Transportation expenses (usually involving a crane and up to three large trucks) sometimes costs several thousand dollars since most obsolete cars are no longer trackworthy. But to converted train car owners, the privilege of owning a piece of American history is worth the inconvenience.

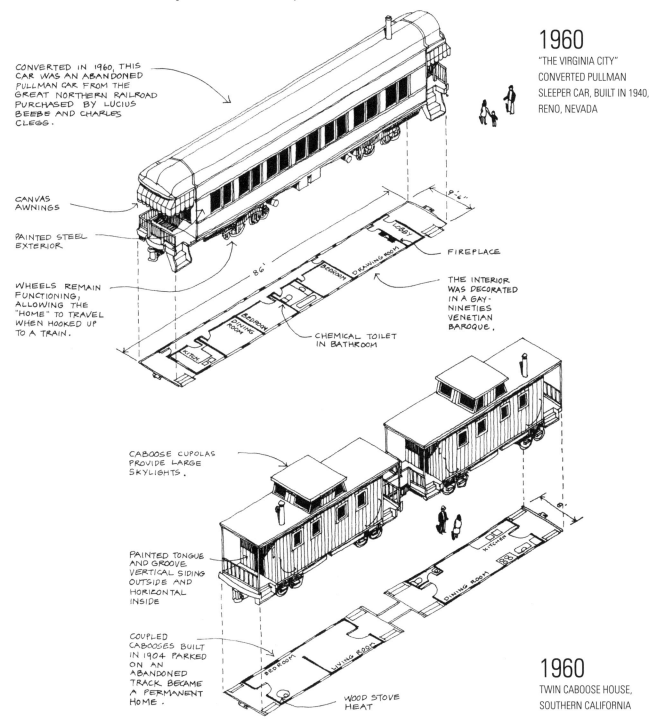

CONVERTED IN 1960, THIS CAR WAS AN ABANDONED PULLMAN CAR FROM THE GREAT NORTHERN RAILROAD PURCHASED BY LUCIUS BEEBE AND CHARLES CLEGG.

CANVAS AWNINGS

PAINTED STEEL EXTERIOR

WHEELS REMAIN FUNCTIONING, ALLOWING THE "HOME" TO TRAVEL WHEN HOOKED UP TO A TRAIN.

1960

"THE VIRGINIA CITY" CONVERTED PULLMAN SLEEPER CAR, BUILT IN 1940, RENO, NEVADA

9'-6"

86'

LOBBY

BEDROOM   DRAWING ROOM

BEDROOM

DINING ROOM

KITCH.

FIREPLACE

THE INTERIOR WAS DECORATED IN A GAY-NINETIES VENETIAN BAROQUE.

CHEMICAL TOILET IN BATHROOM

CABOOSE CUPOLAS PROVIDE LARGE SKYLIGHTS.

PAINTED TONGUE AND GROOVE VERTICAL SIDING OUTSIDE AND HORIZONTAL INSIDE

COUPLED CABOOSES BUILT IN 1904 PARKED ON AN ABANDONED TRACK BECAME A PERMANENT HOME.

KITCHEN

DINING ROOM

LIVING ROOM

BEDROOM

WOOD STOVE HEAT

1960

TWIN CABOOSE HOUSE, SOUTHERN CALIFORNIA

Pole House

Countrywide 1960

In the early 1960s, the Federal Housing Administration produced a booklet entitled *Pole House Construction* as part of its search to lower the cost of housing. The thesis of the booklet was that by "hanging" a house in a framework supported by thick, chemically treated wooden poles it becomes possible to utilize steep hillside lots that are virtually unbuildable by conventional methods because of grade, soil condition, or inaccessability. Since these lots are often undesirable, substantial savings can often be made in their purchase price. The booklet inspired many second home designs including the *Popular Science* "Lockbox" House (shown here) but has never become a significant construction method because of the problems in dealing with the large, heavy poles.

The poles (protected from rot with pressure treated chemicals) must be erected by professionals (the telephone company has pole installation equipment and is usually willing to help) or by a group of people with a rope and pulley system. After they are level and straight (plumb), concrete is poured through the poles by a team of builders. A conventional house is then built within the pole-supported frame.

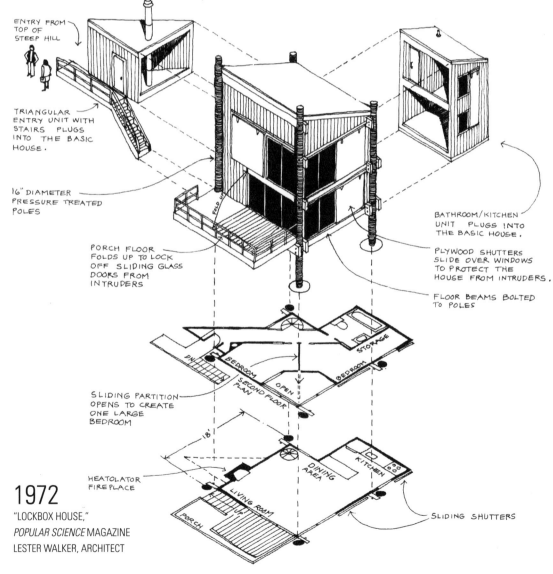

ENTRY FROM TOP OF STEEP HILL

TRIANGULAR ENTRY UNIT WITH STAIRS PLUGS INTO THE BASIC HOUSE.

16" DIAMETER PRESSURE TREATED POLES

PORCH FLOOR FOLDS UP TO LOCK OFF SLIDING GLASS DOORS FROM INTRUDERS

BATHROOM/KITCHEN UNIT PLUGS INTO THE BASIC HOUSE.

PLYWOOD SHUTTERS SLIDE OVER WINDOWS TO PROTECT THE HOUSE FROM INTRUDERS.

FLOOR BEAMS BOLTED TO POLES

FOLD UP

SECOND FLOOR PLAN

BEDROOM

STORAGE

BEDROOM

OPEN

SLIDING PARTITION OPENS TO CREATE ONE LARGE BEDROOM

HEATOLATOR FIREPLACE

18'

DINING AREA

KITCHEN

LIVING ROOM

PORCH

UP

SLIDING SHUTTERS

1972

"LOCKBOX HOUSE,"
POPULAR SCIENCE MAGAZINE
LESTER WALKER, ARCHITECT

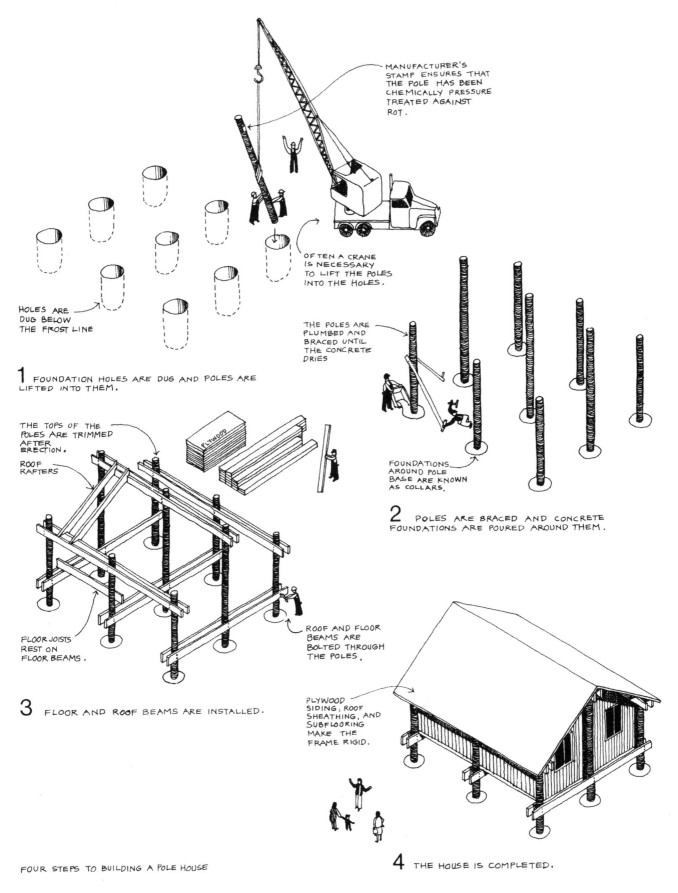

MANUFACTURER'S STAMP ENSURES THAT THE POLE HAS BEEN CHEMICALLY PRESSURE TREATED AGAINST ROT.

OFTEN A CRANE IS NECESSARY TO LIFT THE POLES INTO THE HOLES.

HOLES ARE DUG BELOW THE FROST LINE

1 FOUNDATION HOLES ARE DUG AND POLES ARE LIFTED INTO THEM.

THE POLES ARE PLUMBED AND BRACED UNTIL THE CONCRETE DRIES

FOUNDATIONS AROUND POLE BASE ARE KNOWN AS COLLARS.

2 POLES ARE BRACED AND CONCRETE FOUNDATIONS ARE POURED AROUND THEM.

THE TOPS OF THE POLES ARE TRIMMED AFTER ERECTION.

ROOF RAFTERS

PLYWOOD

FLOOR JOISTS REST ON FLOOR BEAMS.

ROOF AND FLOOR BEAMS ARE BOLTED THROUGH THE POLES.

3 FLOOR AND ROOF BEAMS ARE INSTALLED.

PLYWOOD SIDING, ROOF SHEATHING, AND SUBFLOORING MAKE THE FRAME RIGID.

FOUR STEPS TO BUILDING A POLE HOUSE

4 THE HOUSE IS COMPLETED.

Brutalism

Countrywide 1960

The adjective "brutal" as applied to architecture is not meant to be derogatory but simply descriptive: blocky, strong, massive, and not given to frivolous ornament. The Brutalist Style, developed in the late 1950s in England, uses heavy, unadorned, rough forms almost like the bones of a mammoth skeleton.

The Brutalist Style caught the imagination of American designers after a long era of Miesian steel framed buildings. Concrete was malleable and lent itself to a more sculptural statement. Exposed concrete left in its rough state—or sometimes, as in Paul Rudolph's Yale Art and Architecture Building, artificially roughened (shown below)—is common to most Brutalist buildings. But brick, concrete block, and even rough-cut wood siding can be used if the structure is designed with mass, weight, and solidity in mind. Many Brutalist houses constructed after 1970 were made of wood due to the high cost of concrete or brick, but they always managed to look like concrete buildings covered with a wood veneer.

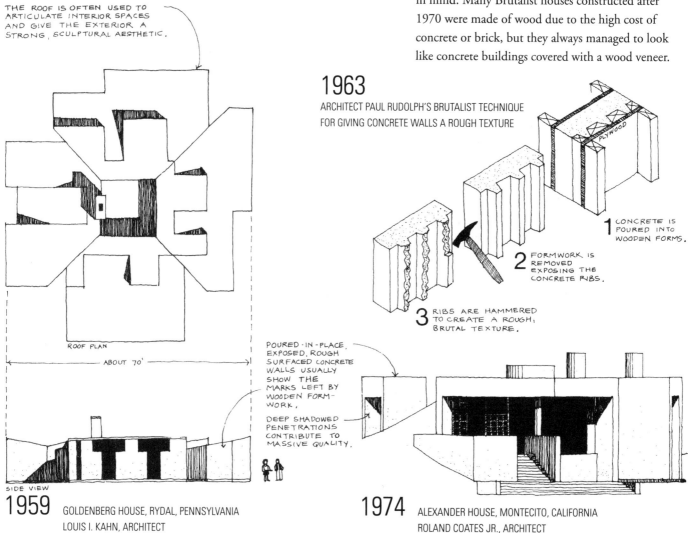

THE ROOF IS OFTEN USED TO ARTICULATE INTERIOR SPACES AND GIVE THE EXTERIOR A STRONG, SCULPTURAL AESTHETIC.

ROOF PLAN

ABOUT 70'

SIDE VIEW

1959   GOLDENBERG HOUSE, RYDAL, PENNSYLVANIA
LOUIS I. KAHN, ARCHITECT

POURED-IN-PLACE, EXPOSED, ROUGH SURFACED CONCRETE WALLS USUALLY SHOW THE MARKS LEFT BY WOODEN FORM-WORK.

DEEP SHADOWED PENETRATIONS CONTRIBUTE TO MASSIVE QUALITY.

1963
ARCHITECT PAUL RUDOLPH'S BRUTALIST TECHNIQUE FOR GIVING CONCRETE WALLS A ROUGH TEXTURE

PLYWOOD

1 CONCRETE IS POURED INTO WOODEN FORMS.

2 FORMWORK IS REMOVED EXPOSING THE CONCRETE RIBS.

3 RIBS ARE HAMMERED TO CREATE A ROUGH, BRUTAL TEXTURE.

1974   ALEXANDER HOUSE, MONTECITO, CALIFORNIA
ROLAND COATES JR., ARCHITECT

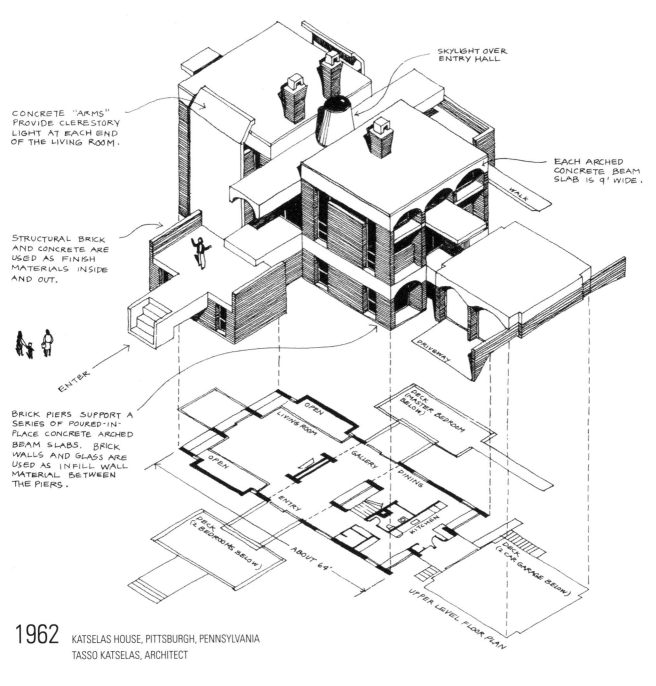

CONCRETE "ARMS" PROVIDE CLERESTORY LIGHT AT EACH END OF THE LIVING ROOM.

SKYLIGHT OVER ENTRY HALL

EACH ARCHED CONCRETE BEAM SLAB IS 9' WIDE.

WALK

STRUCTURAL BRICK AND CONCRETE ARE USED AS FINISH MATERIALS INSIDE AND OUT.

DRIVEWAY

ENTER

BRICK PIERS SUPPORT A SERIES OF POURED-IN-PLACE CONCRETE ARCHED BEAM SLABS. BRICK WALLS AND GLASS ARE USED AS INFILL WALL MATERIAL BETWEEN THE PIERS.

OPEN

LIVING ROOM

OPEN

GALLERY

DINING

ENTRY

DECK (MASTER BEDROOM BELOW)

DECK (2 BEDROOMS BELOW)

ABOUT 64'

KITCHEN

DECK (2 CAR GARAGE BELOW)

UPPER LEVEL FLOOR PLAN

1962 KATSELAS HOUSE, PITTSBURGH, PENNSYLVANIA
TASSO KATSELAS, ARCHITECT

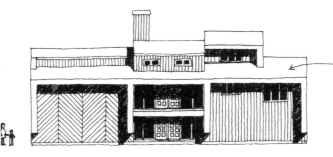

MANY NEW BRUTALIST STYLE HOMES ARE BUILT OF WOOD, FOR ECONOMY, BUT THE FORMS ARE STILL HEAVY AND MASSIVE TO SIMULATE A CONCRETE BUILDING

1975 DESIGN #D 2392, HOME PLANNERS, INC. PATTERN BOOK

Free Form

Countrywide
1965

Since the beginning of the twentieth century when the Spanish architect, Antonio Gaudi, began using concrete in such a creative, free fashion, architects have been intrigued by an architecture that is organic, that grows from a clear description of the function of the building, like a flower. This organic expressionism would qualify free form structures as a kind of Fantasy Style (p. 200) but is separated here because of the newness and distinct nature of its construction (sprayed concrete or plastic fiber glass) and its direct connection to traditional sculpture.

In 1959, architect Frederick Kiesler, a theoretical designer, in a reaction against glass houses, designed a free form house that had a cave-like quality on the inside and an eggshell look on the outside. This house was known as the "Endless House" because of the expected sense of endless space once inside this cornerless dwelling. Kiesler's "Endless House" was erected in the Museum of Modern Art in 1960 and immediately caused a "Why not?" reaction among architectural students and public alike. It could have been the beginning of the end for the overwhelming popularity of the rigidity of the International Style professed in architectural circles.

Free form design is as close to large-scale sculpture as architecture gets. In fact, most free form buildings are owner/architect built, not contractor built, since it is almost impossible for a designer to convey his or her thoughts to a builder with the necessary complexity of architectural drawings. It is also difficult for a designer to imagine a free form space well enough to draw it before it is built.

Free Form Style houses are very rare because they are expensive and difficult to insulate. Sprayed concrete requires highly skilled professionals, and the steel grid necessary to support the concrete until it dries and becomes rigid can be quite expensive. Insulation, when necessary, is usually sprayed urethane foam, an excellent insulation material but a dangerous fire hazard.

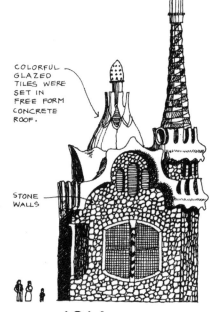

COLORFUL GLAZED TILES WERE SET IN FREE FORM CONCRETE ROOF.

STONE WALLS

1914
GATEHOUSE OF THE PARK GUELL, BARCELONA, SPAIN
ANTONIO GAUDI, ARCHITECT

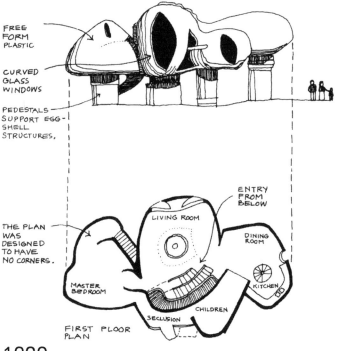

FREE FORM PLASTIC

CURVED GLASS WINDOWS

PEDESTALS SUPPORT EGG-SHELL STRUCTURES.

THE PLAN WAS DESIGNED TO HAVE NO CORNERS.

ENTRY FROM BELOW

LIVING ROOM

DINING ROOM

KITCHEN

MASTER BEDROOM

CHILDREN

SECLUSION

FIRST FLOOR PLAN

1960   "THE ENDLESS HOUSE" BY FREDERICK KIESLER

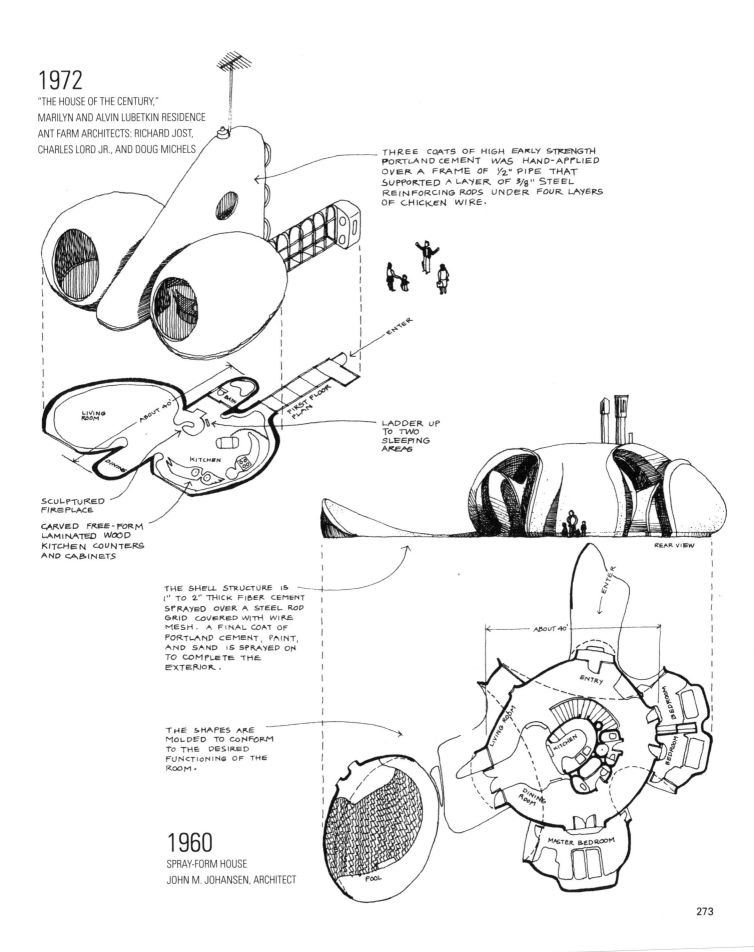

1972

"THE HOUSE OF THE CENTURY,"
MARILYN AND ALVIN LUBETKIN RESIDENCE
ANT FARM ARCHITECTS: RICHARD JOST,
CHARLES LORD JR., AND DOUG MICHELS

THREE COATS OF HIGH EARLY STRENGTH
PORTLAND CEMENT WAS HAND-APPLIED
OVER A FRAME OF ½" PIPE THAT
SUPPORTED A LAYER OF 3/8" STEEL
REINFORCING RODS UNDER FOUR LAYERS
OF CHICKEN WIRE.

ENTER

LIVING
ROOM

ABOUT 40'

BATH

FIRST FLOOR PLAN

DINING

KITCHEN

LADDER UP
TO TWO
SLEEPING
AREAS

SCULPTURED
FIREPLACE

CARVED FREE-FORM
LAMINATED WOOD
KITCHEN COUNTERS
AND CABINETS

REAR VIEW

THE SHELL STRUCTURE IS
1" TO 2" THICK FIBER CEMENT
SPRAYED OVER A STEEL ROD
GRID COVERED WITH WIRE
MESH. A FINAL COAT OF
PORTLAND CEMENT, PAINT,
AND SAND IS SPRAYED ON
TO COMPLETE THE
EXTERIOR.

THE SHAPES ARE
MOLDED TO CONFORM
TO THE DESIRED
FUNCTIONING OF THE
ROOM.

ENTER

ABOUT 40'

ENTRY

BEDROOM

LIVING ROOM

KITCHEN

BEDROOM

DINING
ROOM

MASTER BEDROOM

POOL

1960

SPRAY-FORM HOUSE
JOHN M. JOHANSEN, ARCHITECT

Geodesic Dome

Countrywide
1970

The geodesic dome is a geometrical joining of an array of surface materials in such a way that it creates a part of a sphere that can provide lightweight shelter. The geodesic dome was invented by Dr. Walter Bauersfeld in Jena, Germany, in 1922. R. Buckminster Fuller patented the same type of dome in America in 1954 and built a variety of them for the military and at colleges as test structures. In his worldwide lectures in the 1950s and 1960s, he popularized geodesic domes as a breakthrough in building technology as the most efficient structures yet invented. Fuller envisioned dome components being mass produced on assembly lines and set up a few small factories of his own for this purpose. His factory-made domes never really caught on as he had hoped. Then in the late 1960s, geodesic domes became associated with a new lifestyle, the subculture interested in doing more with less. In 1967 Drop City was founded on the outskirts

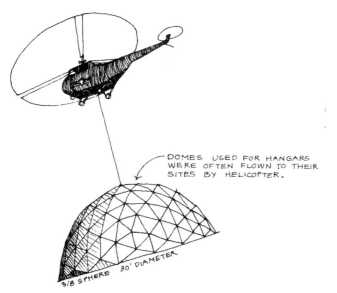

DOMES USED FOR HANGARS WERE OFTEN FLOWN TO THEIR SITES BY HELICOPTER.

3/8 SPHERE 30' DIAMETER

1954
LIGHTWEIGHT DOME MADE FROM
MAGNESIUM AND PLASTIC FOR
THE U.S. MARINE CORPS
DESIGNED BY R. BUCKMINSTER FULLER

THE COMPLETE GROUNDS OF THE HOUSE WERE ENCLOSED ALLOWING A FREE, MULTILEVELED, UNROOFED, GARDENED DWELLING WITHIN THE DOME.

THE DOME WAS RAISED AND LOWERED ON JACKS DEPENDING ON THE WEATHER.

½ SPHERE

1952
"SKYBREAK DWELLING," BY R. B. FULLER AND M.I.T. STUDENTS,
MODEL SHOWN AT MUSEUM OF MODERN ART IN 1952

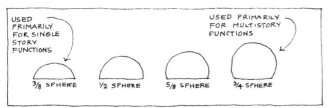

THE FOUR MOST POPULAR DOME SHAPES

USED PRIMARILY FOR SINGLE STORY FUNCTIONS

USED PRIMARILY FOR MULTISTORY FUNCTIONS

3/8 SPHERE 1/2 SPHERE 5/8 SPHERE 3/4 SPHERE

of Trinidad, Colorado, and began building geodesic dome structures largely on the inspiration of a Fuller lecture. In 1968 the mass media found that geodesic domes photograph well and the dome movement was on. Fuller's "sun dome," published in *Popular Science* magazine in 1966 as a thin wooden dome frame covered with a stapled stretched clear vinyl skin, gave amateur dome builders inexpensive plans for making domes of 16½-foot, 25-foot, and 30-foot diameters. By 1970 over 80,000 sets of these plans were sold and used for a variety of dome adaptions. In 1969 *Domebook 1* was published by a group of relatively experienced West Coast dome builders and followed in 1971 by *Domebook 2* with plans, suggestions, and photographs of geodesic domes. With these two handbooks, any do-it-yourselfer could design and construct his or her own dome shelter.

GEODESIC GEOMETRY

The problem facing the original geodesic dome designer was to construct a pattern of manageable surface parts that, when placed together, would make a spherical shape. Below are several regular geometric solids and their patterns. The icosahedron is ideal for dome construction because each of its vertices (points on the icosahedron) would touch a surrounding area.

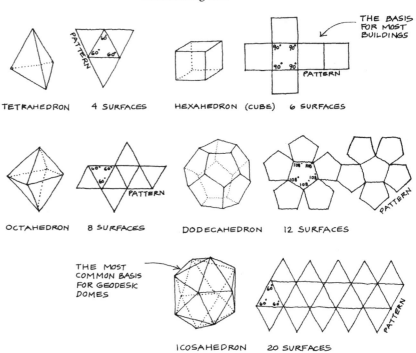

TETRAHEDRON   4 SURFACES

HEXAHEDRON (CUBE)   6 SURFACES

THE BASIS FOR MOST BUILDINGS

OCTAHEDRON   8 SURFACES

DODECAHEDRON   12 SURFACES

THE MOST COMMON BASIS FOR GEODESIC DOMES

ICOSAHEDRON   20 SURFACES

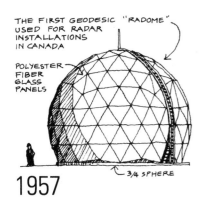

THE FIRST GEODESIC "RADOME" USED FOR RADAR INSTALLATIONS IN CANADA

POLYESTER FIBER GLASS PANELS

3/4 SPHERE

1957
30' DIAMETER "RADOME" BY FULLER'S GEODESIC CO.

FULLER'S "SUN DOME" PLANS WERE MADE AVAILABLE BY POPULAR SCIENCE MAGAZINE IN 1966. IT MADE AN EXCELLENT GREENHOUSE OR SMALL SUMMER SHELTER.

THIN WOOD STRUTS WITH STRETCHED CLEAR PLASTIC SKIN

3/8 SPHERE

1966
25' DIAMETER "SUN DOME"

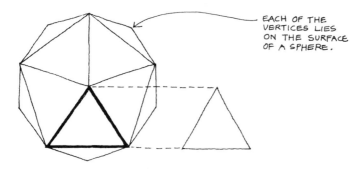

EACH OF THE VERTICES LIES ON THE SURFACE OF A SPHERE.

BASIC ICOSAHEDRON AS SHOWN ABOVE
SINGLE-FREQUENCY DOME (TOP VIEW)

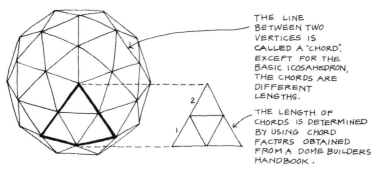

THE LINE BETWEEN TWO VERTICES IS CALLED A "CHORD". EXCEPT FOR THE BASIC ICOSAHEDRON, THE CHORDS ARE DIFFERENT LENGTHS.

THE LENGTH OF CHORDS IS DETERMINED BY USING CHORD FACTORS OBTAINED FROM A DOME BUILDERS HANDBOOK.

TWO-FREQUENCY DOME (TOP VIEW)

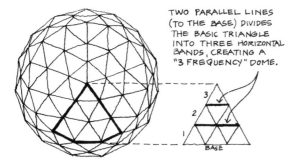

TWO PARALLEL LINES (TO THE BASE) DIVIDES THE BASIC TRIANGLE INTO THREE HORIZONTAL BANDS, CREATING A "3 FREQUENCY" DOME.

THREE-FREQUENCY DOME (TOP VIEW)

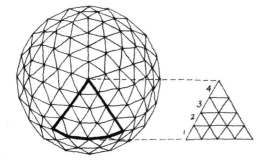

FOUR-FREQUENCY DOME (TOP VIEW)

Each of the twenty surfaces of the icosahedron can be broken down into more triangles to make smaller parts. The more the basic triangle surface is divided, the closer it gets to becoming a sphere, as shown below. Each division of the basic triangle is known as a frequency. The twenty-sided icosahedron is a single frequency dome. When each surface is divided with a horizontal parallel line, a two-frequency dome results, and when the surface is divided with two horizontal parallel lines, a three-frequency dome results. There are several ways to divide the basic icosahedron surface. The one shown here is called the alternate method. It is the most popular because it is easy to conceptualize and to build.

Geodesic domes were extremely popular among do-it-yourself builders in the early 1970s. Dome building kits were, and still are, readily available from a variety of construction companies around the country. These kits save the builder all the tedious and time-consuming cutting and piecing work necessary in constructing an accurate, watertight dome. They are the least difficult of the kit-built houses (p. 240) to erect. The frame erects like a huge toy usually in one or two days by four unskilled workers. Many done owners buy the basic shell and design and construct the interior partitions at their leisure. The dome structures, when complete, usually cost between six and eight dollars per square foot. The difficulty with geodesic dome kit construction is insulating and leakproofing at the seams. The interior is usually sprayed with one-inch of urethane foam by a professional insulator. The leaking problem is solved by occasional caulking by the owner.

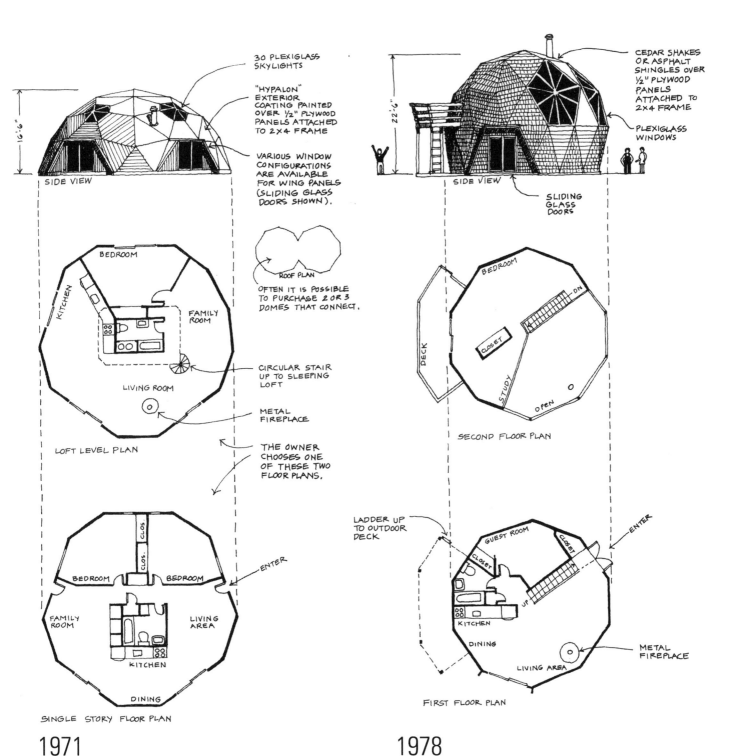

SIDE VIEW

30 PLEXIGLASS SKYLIGHTS

"HYPALON" EXTERIOR COATING PAINTED OVER ½" PLYWOOD PANELS ATTACHED TO 2x4 FRAME

VARIOUS WINDOW CONFIGURATIONS ARE AVAILABLE FOR WING PANELS (SLIDING GLASS DOORS SHOWN).

16'-6"

BEDROOM

KITCHEN

FAMILY ROOM

LIVING ROOM

LOFT LEVEL PLAN

ROOF PLAN

OFTEN IT IS POSSIBLE TO PURCHASE 2 OR 3 DOMES THAT CONNECT.

CIRCULAR STAIR UP TO SLEEPING LOFT

METAL FIREPLACE

THE OWNER CHOOSES ONE OF THESE TWO FLOOR PLANS.

CLOS.

CLOS.

BEDROOM

BEDROOM

FAMILY ROOM

LIVING AREA

ENTER

KITCHEN

DINING

SINGLE STORY FLOOR PLAN

1971

MODEL D-39, 39' DIAMETER, 3/8 SPHERE DOME, GEODESIC STRUCTURES, INC.

SIDE VIEW

CEDAR SHAKES OR ASPHALT SHINGLES OVER ½" PLYWOOD PANELS ATTACHED TO 2x4 FRAME

PLEXIGLASS WINDOWS

22'-6"

SLIDING GLASS DOORS

BEDROOM

DN

DECK

CLOSET

STUDY

OPEN

SECOND FLOOR PLAN

LADDER UP TO OUTDOOR DECK

GUEST ROOM

CLOSET

CLOSET

ENTER

KITCHEN

UP

DINING

LIVING AREA

METAL FIREPLACE

FIRST FLOOR PLAN

1978

30' DIAMETER, ¾ SPHERE DOME, SPACE STRUCTURES INTERNATIONAL CO.

The *Popular Science* Sun Dome in 1966, Domebook 1 in 1969, Domebook 2 in 1971, and two twenty-four foot diameter insulated domes published in *Popular Science* in 1972 gave the energetic do-it-yourself dome builder plenty of information to construct a dome from scratch. The dome's economy, ability to heat and cool, and interesting building technique quickly aligned it with an "alternate" subculture that was seeking less expensive, more sensible shelter. Geodesic domes sprung up in wooded areas all over America, but by 1976 their popularity had waned because of leaking, lack of acoustical privacy, and problems of furniture placement.

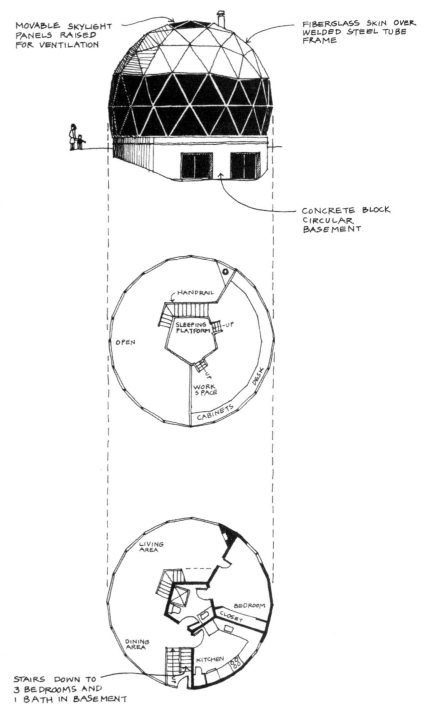

MOVABLE SKYLIGHT PANELS RAISED FOR VENTILATION

FIBERGLASS SKIN OVER WELDED STEEL TUBE FRAME

CONCRETE BLOCK CIRCULAR BASEMENT

HANDRAIL

SLEEPING PLATFORM — UP

OPEN

DESK

WORK SPACE

UP

CABINETS

LIVING AREA

BEDROOM

CLOSET

DINING AREA

KITCHEN

STAIRS DOWN TO 3 BEDROOMS AND 1 BATH IN BASEMENT

1975
JAY AND BEVERLY JAMES HANDMADE 32' DIAMETER 5/8 SPHERE DOME

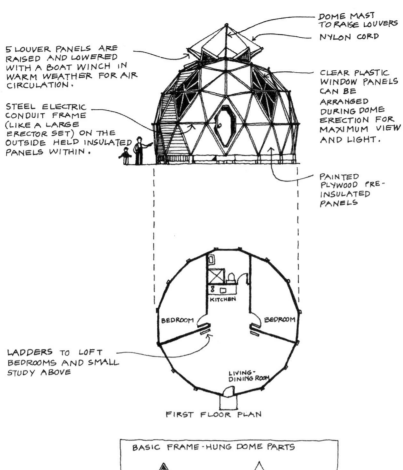

DOME MAST TO RAISE LOUVERS

NYLON CORD

5 LOUVER PANELS ARE RAISED AND LOWERED WITH A BOAT WINCH IN WARM WEATHER FOR AIR CIRCULATION.

CLEAR PLASTIC WINDOW PANELS CAN BE ARRANGED DURING DOME ERECTION FOR MAXIMUM VIEW AND LIGHT.

STEEL ELECTRIC CONDUIT FRAME (LIKE A LARGE ERECTOR SET) ON THE OUTSIDE HELD INSULATED PANELS WITHIN.

PAINTED PLYWOOD PRE-INSULATED PANELS

KITCHEN

BEDROOM

BEDROOM

LADDERS TO LOFT BEDROOMS AND SMALL STUDY ABOVE

LIVING-DINING ROOM

FIRST FLOOR PLAN

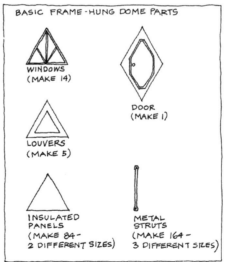

BASIC FRAME-HUNG DOME PARTS

WINDOWS (MAKE 14)

DOOR (MAKE 1)

LOUVERS (MAKE 5)

INSULATED PANELS (MAKE 84 - 2 DIFFERENT SIZES)

METAL STRUTS (MAKE 164 - 3 DIFFERENT SIZES)

THE FRAME HUNG DOME IS MADE FROM A KIT OF INTERCHANGEABLE PARTS, FABRICATED IN A SMALL WORKSHOP.

1972

POPULAR SCIENCE FRAME-HUNG DOME, 24' DIAMETER 5/8 SPHERE DESIGNED BY LESTER WALKER

Modular

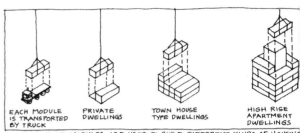

EACH MODULE IS TRANSPORTED BY TRUCK   PRIVATE DWELLINGS   TOWN HOUSE TYPE DWELLINGS   HIGH RISE APARTMENT DWELLINGS

FACTORY MADE MODULES ARE USED TO BUILD DIFFERENT KINDS OF HOUSING

Countrywide 1970

A module is a box-shaped element that when attached to other similar elements makes a complete dwelling unit. Each module is made in a factory using assembly line techniques, much like the mobile home, but is trucked to a building site where it is placed on a permanent foundation.

The advantages of this type of construction are cost (less expensive than traditional construction methods but more expensive than mobile homes), and speed of erection (very little on-site labor). The disadvantages include the design limitations of the twelve-foot-wide box (twelve feet is the maximum width allowed by law on America's highways), and lack of building code conformity (some parts of the nation require a building supervisor to inspect during all phases of construction).

After Moshe Safdie's "Habitat" at the 1967 Montreal World's Fair (an arrangement of factory-made modules stacked to create a large apartment complex) modular construction has become well-known. The system has been used for various types of housing projects, large and small. Its popularity in the private home market has been dramatically increasing, especially with the standard two-module home (below), since its beginnings in the mid-1960s.

HELICOPTERS ARE OFTEN USED TO TRANSPORT VACATION MODULES TO WILDERNESS SITES.

1968
THE "NUTSHELL" HOUSE, ACORN CO. SOLD THROUGH SELECTED DEPARTMENT STORES

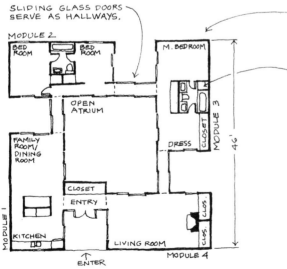

SLIDING GLASS DOORS SERVE AS HALLWAYS.

MODULE 2

BED ROOM   BED ROOM

M. BEDROOM

OPEN ATRIUM

MODULE 3

DRESS

CLOSET

FAMILY ROOM/ DINING ROOM

CLOSET

ENTRY

46'

MODULE 1

KITCHEN

LIVING ROOM

CLOS

MODULE 4

↑ ENTER

1964
"CENTURY 21 HOUSE," DESIGNED BY R. M. ENGLEBRECHT FOR U.S. PLYWOOD CORP. AND THE SEATTLE WORLD'S FAIR COMMISSION

FOUR 12'X24'X9' HIGH FACTORY FINISHED MODULES ARE ARRANGED AROUND AN ATRIUM PATIO.

EACH MODULE IS TRANSFORMED INTO BEDROOMS, KITCHEN, AND OTHER ROOMS BY ADDING PREFABRICATED SECONDARY COMPONENTS, SUCH AS A BATHROOM PACKAGE, A STORAGE WALL, OR A KITCHEN UNIT.

A 3-BEDROOM HOUSE IS MADE FROM TWO 12'X44' MODULES. (THE 2 BEDROOM HOUSE IS MADE FROM TWO 12'X36' MODULES.)

FRONT

44'

DINING   KITCHEN

BEDROOM

CLOS. CL.

UTIL.

CL.

CL CLOS

MODULE 2

LIVING ROOM

CL. CL.

BEDROOM

BEDROOM

MODULE 1

FLOOR PLAN

1970
STANDARD TWO-MODULE MODULAR HOME

About 85 percent to 95 percent of work on a modular home is completed in a factory. On-site work includes providing a foundation, utility lines, rough plumbing and electrical work, attaching the modules to the foundation, some minor finishing work, plumbing and electrical hookups, entrance steps and decks, and landscaping. Modular home building companies claim that once the modules arrive on the site, it is only a matter of two days before occupancy is possible. Below is the sequence of this two-day period.

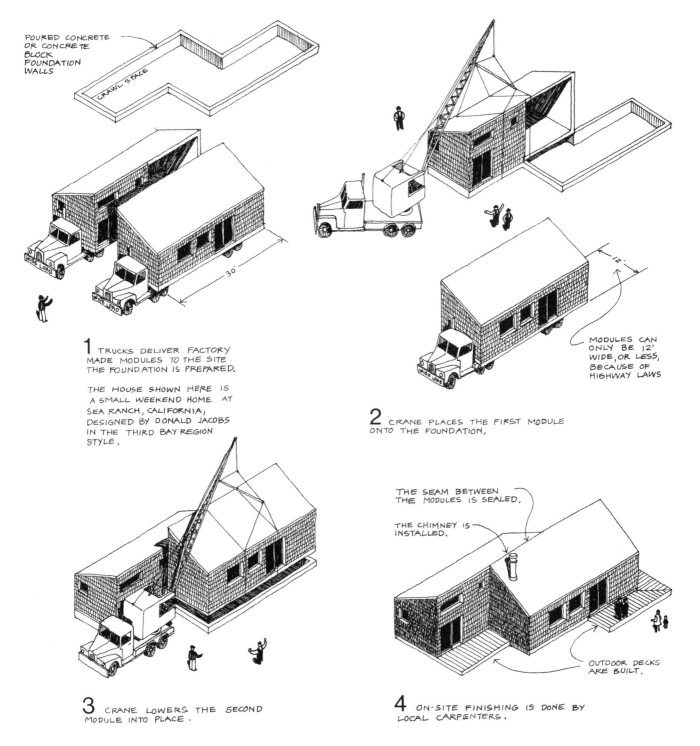

POURED CONCRETE OR CONCRETE BLOCK FOUNDATION WALLS

CRAWL SPACE

30'

1 TRUCKS DELIVER FACTORY MADE MODULES TO THE SITE. THE FOUNDATION IS PREPARED.

THE HOUSE SHOWN HERE IS A SMALL WEEKEND HOME AT SEA RANCH, CALIFORNIA, DESIGNED BY DONALD JACOBS IN THE THIRD BAY REGION STYLE.

12'

MODULES CAN ONLY BE 12' WIDE, OR LESS, BECAUSE OF HIGHWAY LAWS

2 CRANE PLACES THE FIRST MODULE ONTO THE FOUNDATION.

3 CRANE LOWERS THE SECOND MODULE INTO PLACE.

THE SEAM BETWEEN THE MODULES IS SEALED.

THE CHIMNEY IS INSTALLED.

OUTDOOR DECKS ARE BUILT.

4 ON-SITE FINISHING IS DONE BY LOCAL CARPENTERS.

Silo and Yurt

Countrywide 1970

With the rising cost of housebuilding in the early 1970s, many young people turned to unique, inexpensive, do-it-yourself construction methods. Two such methods, the silo and the yurt, are grouped together here because they are both built like a barrel—vertical wooden slats held in a cylinder shape by steel hoops. Both structures have a long history.

The silo has been a popular grain storage unit for the American farmer for over 200 years. It was also used for water storage tanks on large urban buildings in the early 1900s. It makes a unique, round, roofed house shell that is very inexpensive, easy to erect, but hard to insulate (often two silos are used with a six-inch diameter difference to provide insulation space), difficult to light (wide windows destroy the silo's strength), and the round walls make it hard to furnish.

The yurt is the traditional portable home of the shepherds of Inner Asia, the equivalent of the American tipi. It is ingeniously constructed with light poles for a roof, a sapling lattice for walls and a thick felt exterior skin. The weight of the roof forces

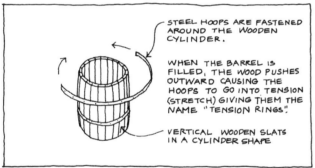

STEEL HOOPS ARE FASTENED AROUND THE WOODEN CYLINDER.

WHEN THE BARREL IS FILLED, THE WOOD PUSHES OUTWARD CAUSING THE HOOPS TO GO INTO TENSION (STRETCH) GIVING THEM THE NAME "TENSION RINGS".

VERTICAL WOODEN SLATS IN A CYLINDER SHAPE

THE STRUCTURAL PRINCIPLE OF THE BARREL IS THE SAME AS THE SILO AND THE YURT.

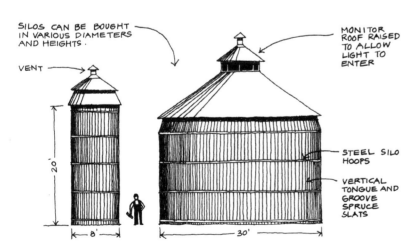

SILOS CAN BE BOUGHT IN VARIOUS DIAMETERS AND HEIGHTS.

VENT

MONITOR ROOF RAISED TO ALLOW LIGHT TO ENTER

STEEL SILO HOOPS

VERTICAL TONGUE AND GROOVE SPRUCE SLATS

20'

8'

30'

TWO SILOS BY UNADILLA LAMINATED PRODUCTS, UNADILLA, NEW YORK

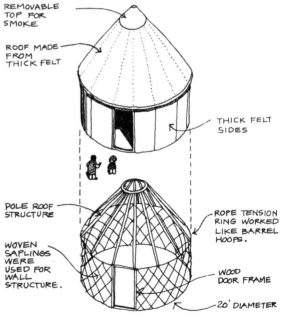

REMOVABLE TOP FOR SMOKE

ROOF MADE FROM THICK FELT

THICK FELT SIDES

POLE ROOF STRUCTURE

WOVEN SAPLINGS WERE USED FOR WALL STRUCTURE.

ROPE TENSION RING WORKED LIKE BARREL HOOPS.

WOOD DOOR FRAME

20' DIAMETER

1700 TRADITIONAL ASIAN NOMADIC YURT

the walls outward, creating a need for a "tension ring" or strap that will hold the circular wall rigid like the hoop of a barrel. This is done with a simple rope made from yak, camel, or sheep hair, stretched around the wall top perimeter. The yurt, still a familiar Asian housing form, never really gained much popularity in America. While it is unique, easy to build, and quite beautiful inside, it also is hard to insulate and to furnish.

Below are examples of a modern silo house and an American adaption of the traditional yurt. The silo house is interesting because its designers, Mr. and Mrs. Louis Audette, chose to retain the simplicity of the silo and add dormer and stairway appendages. Their silo cost $2,300 delivered in 1969. The modern yurt retains the same principle as the Asian yurt except for portability.

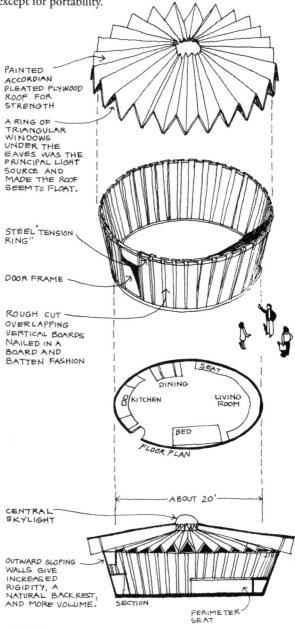

ASPHALT SHINGLES

THREE DORMERS WERE ADDED TO THE BASIC SILO ROOF TO GAIN LIGHT AND SPACE IN THE THIRD FLOOR.

LARGE, WIDE WINDOWS WEAKEN THE STRUCTURE SO NARROW ONES (THE WIDTH OF A SINGLE VERTICAL BOARD) ARE USED.

STEEL SILO HOOPS WERE TIGHTENED AFTER ONE YEAR.

AN 18' DIAMETER GRAIN SILO WAS USED FOR THE SECOND FLOOR.

LIVING ROOM · UP DN · MASTER BEDROOM · SECOND FLOOR

THE STAIR ENCLOSURE WAS MADE FROM A ONE HALF 24' DIAMETER SILO.

A 16' DIAMETER GRAIN SILO WAS USED FOR THE FIRST FLOOR.

CLOSET · KITCHEN · UP · DINING · FIRST FLOOR · ENTER

PAINTED ACCORDIAN PLEATED PLYWOOD ROOF FOR STRENGTH

A RING OF TRIANGULAR WINDOWS UNDER THE EAVES WAS THE PRINCIPAL LIGHT SOURCE AND MADE THE ROOF SEEM TO FLOAT.

STEEL "TENSION RING"

DOOR FRAME

ROUGH CUT OVERLAPPING VERTICAL BOARDS NAILED IN A BOARD AND BATTEN FASHION

SEAT · DINING · KITCHEN · LIVING ROOM · BED · FLOOR PLAN

ABOUT 20'

CENTRAL SKYLIGHT

OUTWARD SLOPING WALLS GIVE INCREASED RIGIDITY, A NATURAL BACKREST, AND MORE VOLUME.

SECTION · PERIMETER SEAT

1970

AUDETTE HOUSE, MARBORO, VERMONT, SILOS PURCHASED FROM THE UNADILLA LAMINATED PRODUCTS CO., UNADILLA, NEW YORK

1973

A MODERN YURT, PUBLISHED IN *SHELTER*, 1973

Floating House

West Coast, Florida, and the Gulf Coast
1970

The earliest residential floating houses were built on the West Coast in the 1880s by mill workers, gold rushers, and other new settlers. By the early 1900s more affluent families had begun to see the recreational possibilities of floating dwellings and had built a large number of floating weekend cottages. By 1920 there were an estimated 2,500 floating houses in Seattle. During the Great Depression, floating houses boomed because they were the least expensive form of housing with the advantage of fishing for food. In the 1950s and 1960s many ordinances were passed, primarily concerning sewerage, taxes, and zoning, causing a large drop in their number, but by the 1970s there was a resurgence in construction by people who enjoy the lifestyle around the water. Permanent floating house colonies can be found in many parts of America, but they are most popular in California and Florida because of the climate.

There are two basic types of floating houses. The first requires a substantial hull and is always anchored or permanently fixed close to shore, adjacent to a dock. This dwelling is a house built on the water instead of the ground and is aptly called a floating house. The second type is a floating home designed for recreational travel, usually factory-built, popularly called a houseboat. There are about two million recreational boats in America that are of the size and shape that permit living aboard. These houseboats are constructed like the early mobile homes but they travel on water and are primarily used as a second home for recreational purposes. Their key advantage over the floating house is that of mobility.

A few examples of the houseboat are shown below and on the opposite page.

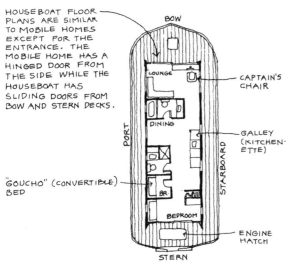

HOUSEBOAT FLOOR PLANS ARE SIMILAR TO MOBILE HOMES EXCEPT FOR THE ENTRANCE. THE MOBILE HOME HAS A HINGED DOOR FROM THE SIDE WHILE THE HOUSEBOAT HAS SLIDING DOORS FROM BOW AND STERN DECKS.

BOW

LOUNGE

CAPTAIN'S CHAIR

DINING

PORT

STARBOARD

GALLEY (KITCHEN-ETTE)

"GOUCHO" (CONVERTIBLE) BED

BR.

BEDROOM

ENGINE HATCH

STERN

PLANS TO BUILD HOUSEBOATS LIKE THIS ARE AVAILABLE TO THE AMATEUR BUILDER FROM MANY HOUSEBOAT COMPANIES

GALLEY (KITCHENETTE)

25'

CABIN

HELM

INBOARD OR OUTBOARD MOTORS

SETTEE FORMS UPPER AND LOWER BERTH BEDS

1970 TYPICAL HOUSEBOAT FLOOR PLAN

1972 25' DELTA QUEEN, GLEN L-MARINE DESIGNS, CALIFORNIA

1970 TYPICAL LUXURIOUS FACTORY MADE HOUSEBOAT

PAINTED ALUMINUM SIDING

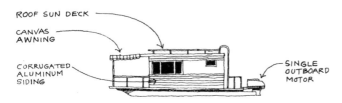

ROOF SUN DECK

CANVAS AWNING

CORRUGATED ALUMINUM SIDING

SINGLE OUTBOARD MOTOR

1972 TYPICAL SMALL FACTORY-MADE HOUSEBOAT

VARIOUS TYPES OF BOATS ARE OFTEN RECYCLED FROM THEIR ORIGINAL USE TO INTERESTING FLOATING DWELLINGS.

1973 CONVERTED TUGBOAT HOUSEBOAT, BAYOU SORRELL, LOUISIANA

In the mid-1970s the trailerable houseboat became a popular recreation vehicle. It was used as a conventional camper-trailer on land and a houseboat on water giving, in effect, two recreational vehicles for the price of one. An example is shown below.

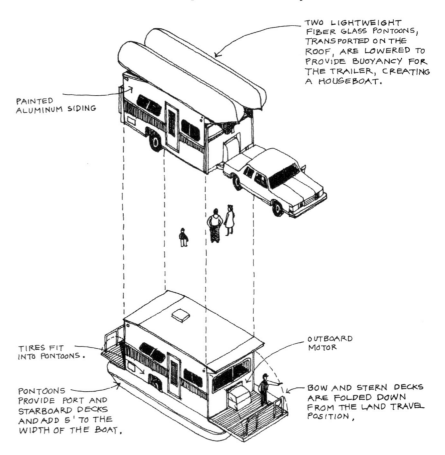

TWO LIGHTWEIGHT FIBER GLASS PONTOONS, TRANSPORTED ON THE ROOF, ARE LOWERED TO PROVIDE BUOYANCY FOR THE TRAILER, CREATING A HOUSEBOAT.

PAINTED ALUMINUM SIDING

TIRES FIT INTO PONTOONS.

PONTOONS PROVIDE PORT AND STARBOARD DECKS AND ADD 5' TO THE WIDTH OF THE BOAT.

OUTBOARD MOTOR

BOW AND STERN DECKS ARE FOLDED DOWN FROM THE LAND TRAVEL POSITION.

1972 25' LAND TRAILER/HOUSEBOAT, TRAIL OR FLOAT CORP., GRESHAM, OREGON

During the Great Depression, poor fishermen living in the tidal mud flats of the Skagit River Estuary in the state of Washington built floating small houses called floatshacks, built on large logs that gave the house buoyancy during the two or three hours per day that the tide was in. These simple gable roof shingled cottages were abandoned after the Depression but have lately been "discovered" and renovated by local artists.

Some of the most innovative floating houses in the country were built in the late 1960s and 1970s in the small water-oriented community of Waldo Point in Sausalito, California. Floating houses were made from unused World War II hardware, lifeboats, cars, old bargebottoms, and scrapwood by hippies and other disaffected young people with little money or building talent and lots of imagination. This community continues to be a creative center for floating home building, among other things, but is sporadically threatened by developers and politicians.

A DRIFTWOOD FENCE WAS USED TO KEEP POSSESSIONS FROM FLOATING AWAY.

LOGS GAVE BUOYANCY AT HIGH TIDE

1935 FLOATSHACK, SKAGIT RIVER, WASHINGTON

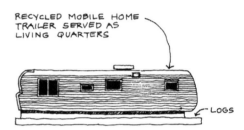

RECYCLED MOBILE HOME TRAILER SERVED AS LIVING QUARTERS

LOGS

1970 CONVERTED MOBILE HOME, WALDO POINT, SAUSALITO, CALIFORNIA

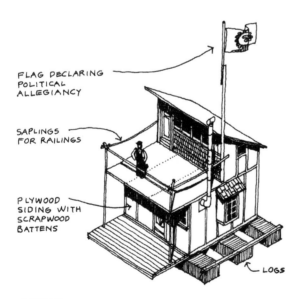

FLAG DECLARING POLITICAL ALLEGIANCY

SAPLINGS FOR RAILINGS

PLYWOOD SIDING WITH SCRAPWOOD BATTENS

LOGS

1978 HANDCRAFTED FLOATING HOUSE, WALDO POINT, SAUSALITO, CALIFORNIA

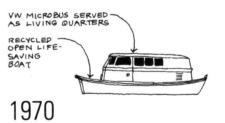

VW MICROBUS SERVED AS LIVING QUARTERS

RECYCLED OPEN LIFE-SAVING BOAT

1970 CONVERTED VAN, WALSO POINT, SAUSALITO, CALIFORNIA

With ocean-front property selling at staggering prices, increasing numbers of home owners are building their dream houses in a variety of styles on bargelike hulls that offer the advantages of the water without the initial property cost. These dwellings usually are required to hook up to sewerage, water, and electric systems at their mooring site and, in effect, taxes are paid through the moorage fees. But to the floating home owner, this cost is offset by the water, the sun, the views, and the ability to relocate the dwelling.

SKYLIGHTS, BAY WINDOWS, AND OTHER HANDMADE DETAILS

ROUGHCUT NATURAL CEDAR SHINGLE SIDING

1975
CALIFORNIA BAY REGION STYLE FLOATING HOUSE, SKAGIT RIVER, WASHINGTON

ROUGHCUT NATURAL CEDAR SHINGLE SIDING

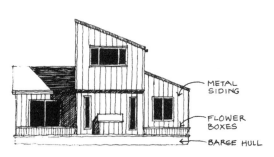

METAL SIDING

FLOWER BOXES

BARGE HULL

1972
SPLIT LEVEL STYLE FLOATING HOUSE, INDIAN CREEK, FLORIDA

MANY WEST COAST FLOATING HOUSES WERE INFLUENCED BY THE RUSTIC BAY REGION STYLE.

ABOUT 20'

BEDROOM

STUDY

STORAGE

DN

SECOND FLOOR

DINING

LIVING ROOM

KITCHEN

ENTRY

STAIR.

UP

DOCK

FIRST FLOOR

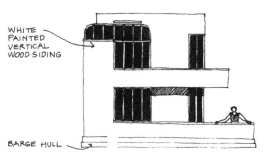

WHITE PAINTED VERTICAL WOOD SIDING

BARGE HULL

1977
INTERNATIONAL STYLE FLOATING HOUSE, SEATTLE, WASHINGTON

1978
MANSARD ROOFED FLOATING HOUSE, SEATTLE, WASHINGTON

New Shingle

Countrywide 1970

The New Shingle Style evolved very quickly in the mid-1960s greatly inspired by the work of Charles Moore and Robert Venturi. These two architects were particularly influential because of their ability to distort the form of a building, to carve away its excess, until it became a tight, economical shape that fit the owners' requirements and the constraints of the site. Their architecture was rooted in the vernacular, especially that of colonial America as was the original Shingle Style architects of the 1890s. Thus the name, New Shingle Style.

Moore's and Venturi's work was widely published as a new direction, opposed to the rigid glass box and white stuccoed cubist forms of the International Style. Both Moore and Venturi were educators and prolific writers. They gave young architects of the 1960s new ways of seeing and designing buildings, of, as Louis I. Kahn professed, "allowing the building to be what it wants to be." Later, Charles Moore's list of "ways to assemble rooms" in his book *Dimensions*, co-authored by Gerald Allen, became familiar design technique to students and practitioners alike.

New Shingle Syle architects worked with two basic forms: the gabled and the shed roof structure and most New Shingle Style houses comprise one or more of them. Unpretentious materials like the wood shingle, the clapboard, small-paned windows, and metal chimneys and vernacular forms like the dormer and the bay window were revived. Unlike the original Shingle Style, small budgets kept the size of New Shingle Style houses down. But the ideology of the two styles was quite similar.

Here is an example of an early house by Robert Venturi. The obvious delight which he takes in distorting what began as a rigid building was an exciting breakthrough in the 1960s, comparable to the Early Gothic Revival Style's breaking away from the constraining forms of the Greek Revival in 1840.

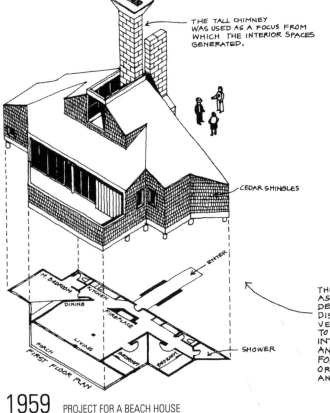

THE TALL CHIMNEY WAS USED AS A FOCUS FROM WHICH THE INTERIOR SPACES GENERATED.

CEDAR SHINGLES

M. BEDROOM · KITCHEN · DINING · FIREPLACE · LIVING · PORCH · FIRST FLOOR PLAN · BEDROOM · BEDROOM · ENTER · SHOWER

THE HOUSE BEGAN AS A SYMETRICAL DESIGN AND WAS DISTORTED BY VENTURI TO ADAPT TO VARYING INTERIOR DEMANDS AND EXTERIOR FORCES OF ORIENTATION AND VIEW.

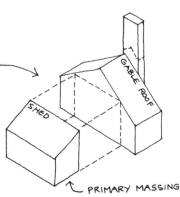

GABLE ROOF

SHED

PRIMARY MASSING

1959 PROJECT FOR A BEACH HOUSE
ROBERT VENTURI, ARCHITECT

While the American Victorian house of the mid-nineteenth century was an explosion of forms (when space was needed, the designer allowed the plan to push out in the necessary direction), the New Shingle Style often was an implosion of forms (when space was needed, the designer added or "clipped on" space from the outside). Most of the houses in this chapter are examples of this idea, but the house by Hugh Hardy shown below is the most obvious. Here, the character of the building is obtained by a "collision" of three simple gable roofed forms. After the collision, the forms were allowed to distort until all programmatic requirements were met.

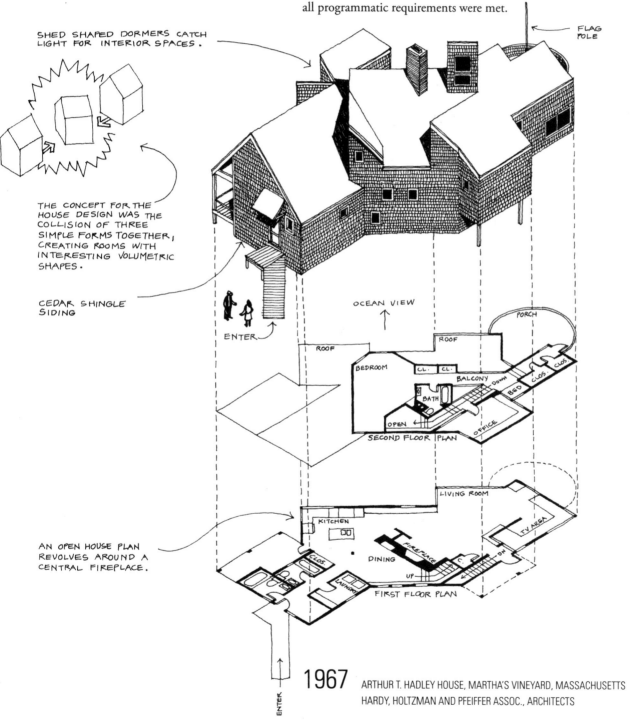

SHED SHAPED DORMERS CATCH LIGHT FOR INTERIOR SPACES.

THE CONCEPT FOR THE HOUSE DESIGN WAS THE COLLISION OF THREE SIMPLE FORMS TOGETHER, CREATING ROOMS WITH INTERESTING VOLUMETRIC SHAPES.

CEDAR SHINGLE SIDING

ENTER

FLAG POLE

OCEAN VIEW

PORCH

ROOF

ROOF

BEDROOM

CL. CL.

BALCONY

BATH

CLOS. CLOS.

BED

DOWN

OPEN

OFFICE

SECOND FLOOR PLAN

LIVING ROOM

KITCHEN

TV AREA

AN OPEN HOUSE PLAN REVOLVES AROUND A CENTRAL FIREPLACE.

CLOS.

FIREPLACE

DINING

UP

LAUNDRY

FIRST FLOOR PLAN

ENTER

1967   ARTHUR T. HADLEY HOUSE, MARTHA'S VINEYARD, MASSACHUSETTS
HARDY, HOLTZMAN AND PFEIFFER ASSOC., ARCHITECTS

One of the most common techniques for creating a New Shingle Style house is to combine several shed structures, a method used by many California Bay Area architects in the early 1960s. One of the most influential, certainly the most widely published, was an award-winning beach cottage that Hobart Betts built for himself in 1965. In *Progressive Architecture*'s 1965 design awards issue, the house was discussed: "The simplest, clearest, and most controlled use of an idiom that now seems to be everywhere....These houses are like Pop Art. That's why they're replacing the box...."

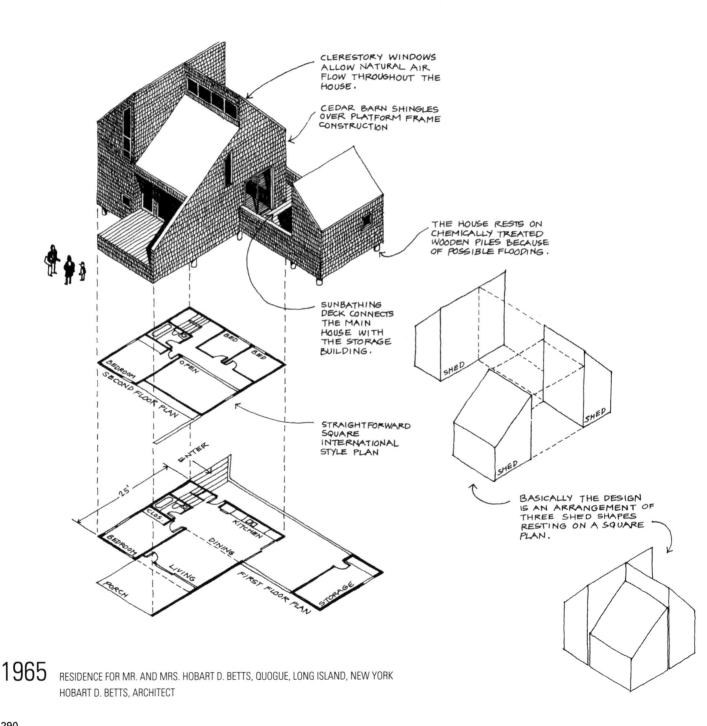

CLERESTORY WINDOWS ALLOW NATURAL AIR FLOW THROUGHOUT THE HOUSE.

CEDAR BARN SHINGLES OVER PLATFORM FRAME CONSTRUCTION

THE HOUSE RESTS ON CHEMICALLY TREATED WOODEN PILES BECAUSE OF POSSIBLE FLOODING.

SUNBATHING DECK CONNECTS THE MAIN HOUSE WITH THE STORAGE BUILDING.

STRAIGHTFORWARD SQUARE INTERNATIONAL STYLE PLAN

BASICALLY THE DESIGN IS AN ARRANGEMENT OF THREE SHED SHAPES RESTING ON A SQUARE PLAN.

BEDROOM
SECOND FLOOR PLAN
BED
BED
OPEN

ENTER
25'
BEDROOM
CLOS.
KITCHEN
DINING
LIVING
PORCH
FIRST FLOOR PLAN
STORAGE

SHED
SHED
SHED

1965
RESIDENCE FOR MR. AND MRS. HOBART D. BETTS, QUOGUE, LONG ISLAND, NEW YORK
HOBART D. BETTS, ARCHITECT

In 1964 two Yale architecture graduates, David Sellers and William Reineke moved to Prickly Mountain, Vermont, near Sugarbush, and began building, with their own hands, a series of steep-slanted roofed houses (to shed the snow) that were to become the forerunners of the popular modern ski house. Their use of materials borrowed from Vermont farm building vernacular and the simplicity and geometric strength of their forms are reason enough to classify them as New Shingle Style.

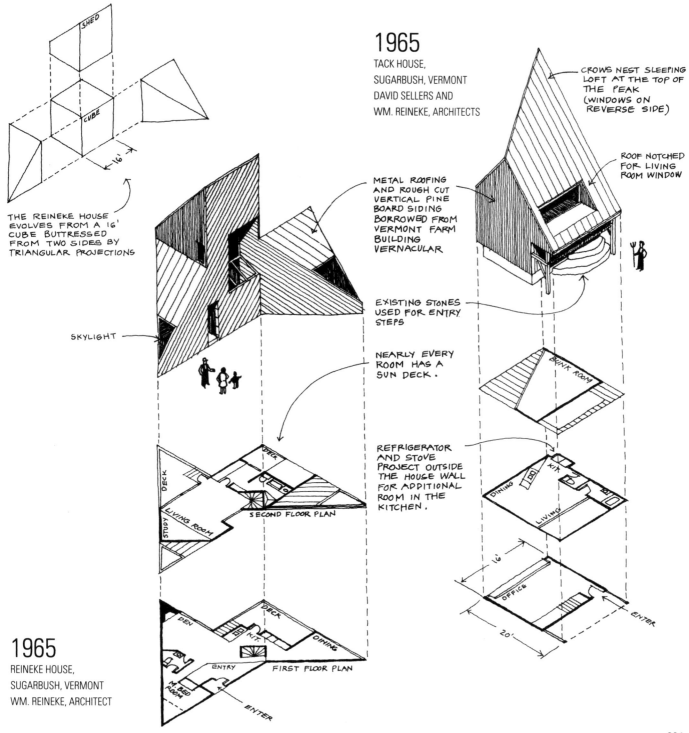

THE REINEKE HOUSE EVOLVES FROM A 16' CUBE BUTTRESSED FROM TWO SIDES BY TRIANGULAR PROJECTIONS

SKYLIGHT

SECOND FLOOR PLAN

DECK
LIVING ROOM
STUDY

1965
REINEKE HOUSE,
SUGARBUSH, VERMONT
WM. REINEKE, ARCHITECT

DEN
DECK
KIT.
DINING
ENTRY
FIRST FLOOR PLAN
M. BED ROOM
ENTER

1965
TACK HOUSE,
SUGARBUSH, VERMONT
DAVID SELLERS AND
WM. REINEKE, ARCHITECTS

METAL ROOFING AND ROUGH CUT VERTICAL PINE BOARD SIDING BORROWED FROM VERMONT FARM BUILDING VERNACULAR

CROWS NEST SLEEPING LOFT AT THE TOP OF THE PEAK (WINDOWS ON REVERSE SIDE)

ROOF NOTCHED FOR LIVING ROOM WINDOW

EXISTING STONES USED FOR ENTRY STEPS

NEARLY EVERY ROOM HAS A SUN DECK.

REFRIGERATOR AND STOVE PROJECT OUTSIDE THE HOUSE WALL FOR ADDITIONAL ROOM IN THE KITCHEN.

BUNK ROOM

DINING
KIT.
LIVING

OFFICE
ENTER

Robert Venturi, one of America's most influential modern architects, is well-known for the use of conventional, vernacular images in his work. As Andy Warhol showed us with his Campbell soup can that common everyday objects can be interesting and worthy of our attention as art, Venturi made us see beauty and architectural validity in popular vernacular architecture like the roadside fast food restaurant, the Las Vegas nightclub, the beach bungalow, and billboards.

The Trubek and Wislocki houses shown below are examples of Venturi's use of the New England fisherman's cottage vernacular. The houses are very simple gable roof structures but the plans are

1972
TRUBEK AND WISLOCKI HOUSES,
NANTUCKET, MASSACHUSETTS
ROBERT VENTURI, ARCHITECT

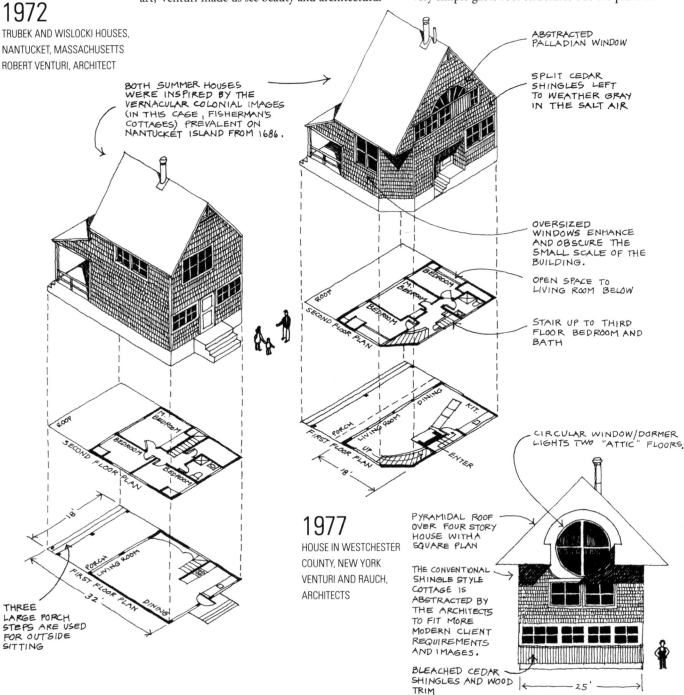

BOTH SUMMER HOUSES WERE INSPIRED BY THE VERNACULAR COLONIAL IMAGES (IN THIS CASE, FISHERMAN'S COTTAGES) PREVALENT ON NANTUCKET ISLAND FROM 1686.

ABSTRACTED PALLADIAN WINDOW

SPLIT CEDAR SHINGLES LEFT TO WEATHER GRAY IN THE SALT AIR

OVERSIZED WINDOWS ENHANCE AND OBSCURE THE SMALL SCALE OF THE BUILDING.

OPEN SPACE TO LIVING ROOM BELOW

STAIR UP TO THIRD FLOOR BEDROOM AND BATH

THREE LARGE PORCH STEPS ARE USED FOR OUTSIDE SITTING

1977
HOUSE IN WESTCHESTER COUNTY, NEW YORK
VENTURI AND RAUCH, ARCHITECTS

CIRCULAR WINDOW/DORMER LIGHTS TWO "ATTIC" FLOORS.

PYRAMIDAL ROOF OVER FOUR STORY HOUSE WITH A SQUARE PLAN

THE CONVENTIONAL SHINGLE STYLE COTTAGE IS ABSTRACTED BY THE ARCHITECTS TO FIT MORE MODERN CLIENT REQUIREMENTS AND IMAGES.

BLEACHED CEDAR SHINGLES AND WOOD TRIM

complex like those of the nineteenth-century Shingle Style, necessitated somewhat by the rigidness of the exterior form. The Westchester house is his abstraction of a small Shingle Style house.

Some of the more interesting New Shingle Style homes are arrangements of separate structures as illustrated in the house designed by Edward L. Barnes, shown below. Each of the four elements: a laundry/studio tower; a one-bedroom house with living, dining and kitchen; a two-story guest house; and a high ceilinged library/study, is shaped in simple gable or shed roof vernacular forms finished in cedar shingles. The buildings are artfully placed in relation to each other, just as the dock buildings of nearby Deer Island, Maine, fishing villages might have developed. This house is an excellent example of the modest, human scale that most New Shingle Style architects strive for.

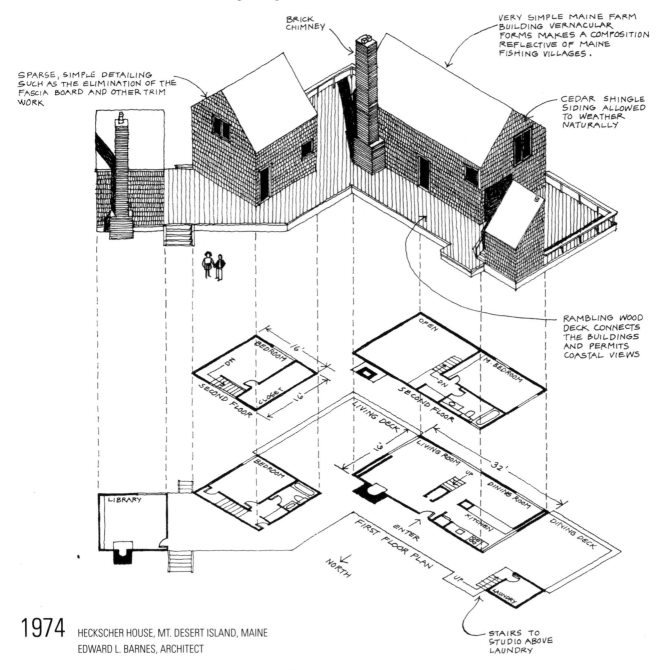

BRICK CHIMNEY

VERY SIMPLE MAINE FARM BUILDING VERNACULAR FORMS MAKES A COMPOSITION REFLECTIVE OF MAINE FISHING VILLAGES.

SPARSE, SIMPLE DETAILING SUCH AS THE ELIMINATION OF THE FASCIA BOARD AND OTHER TRIM WORK

CEDAR SHINGLE SIDING ALLOWED TO WEATHER NATURALLY

RAMBLING WOOD DECK CONNECTS THE BUILDINGS AND PERMITS COASTAL VIEWS

BEDROOM 16'
DN
CLOSET 16'
SECOND FLOOR

OPEN
M. BEDROOM
DN
SECOND FLOOR

LIVING DECK
LIVING ROOM
UP
DINING ROOM
32'
DINING DECK

BEDROOM
LIBRARY
ENTER
FIRST FLOOR PLAN
KITCHEN
NORTH
UP
LAUNDRY

STAIRS TO STUDIO ABOVE LAUNDRY

1974 HECKSCHER HOUSE, MT. DESERT ISLAND, MAINE
EDWARD L. BARNES, ARCHITECT

The two houses shown below are examples of further development of the New Shingle Style. Both architects related the various facades of their buildings to different aspects of the site—seeing the building not as a consistent volume but as a space with four sides, each having its own separate job. The tiny (640 square feet) Walker house has an English cottage-like facade facing the entry and a stark, primarily glass facade facing a spectacular natural view. The Riley house has the same kind of "cute" entry facade, more Neocolonial in style, and an energy-conscious, primarily glass (greenhouse), south-facing facade. Both architects used vernacular forms and obviously appreciate the original Shingle Style and its roots.

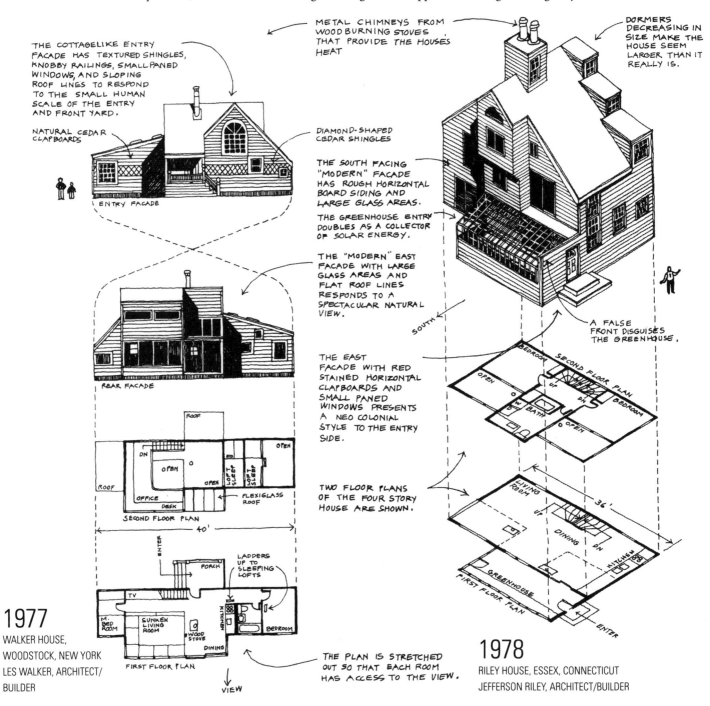

THE COTTAGELIKE ENTRY FACADE HAS TEXTURED SHINGLES, KNOBBY RAILINGS, SMALL PANED WINDOWS, AND SLOPING ROOF LINES TO RESPOND TO THE SMALL HUMAN SCALE OF THE ENTRY AND FRONT YARD.

NATURAL CEDAR CLAPBOARDS

ENTRY FACADE

METAL CHIMNEYS FROM WOOD BURNING STOVES THAT PROVIDE THE HOUSES HEAT

DORMERS DECREASING IN SIZE MAKE THE HOUSE SEEM LARGER THAN IT REALLY IS.

DIAMOND-SHAPED CEDAR SHINGLES

THE SOUTH FACING "MODERN" FACADE HAS ROUGH HORIZONTAL BOARD SIDING AND LARGE GLASS AREAS.

THE GREENHOUSE ENTRY DOUBLES AS A COLLECTOR OF SOLAR ENERGY.

THE "MODERN" EAST FACADE WITH LARGE GLASS AREAS AND FLAT ROOF LINES RESPONDS TO A SPECTACULAR NATURAL VIEW.

REAR FACADE

SOUTH

A FALSE FRONT DISGUISES THE GREENHOUSE.

THE EAST FACADE WITH RED STAINED HORIZONTAL CLAPBOARDS AND SMALL PANED WINDOWS PRESENTS A NEO COLONIAL STYLE TO THE ENTRY SIDE.

SECOND FLOOR PLAN

BEDROOM · OPEN · BATH · DN · UP · OPEN · BEDROOM

ROOF · DN · OPEN · OPEN · LOFT SLEEP · LOFT SLEEP · OPEN · ROOF · OFFICE · DESK · PLEXIGLASS ROOF

SECOND FLOOR PLAN

40'

TWO FLOOR PLANS OF THE FOUR STORY HOUSE ARE SHOWN.

LIVING ROOM · UP · DINING · DN · KITCHEN · 36'

ENTER · PORCH · LADDERS UP TO SLEEPING LOFTS · TV · M. BED ROOM · SUNKEN LIVING ROOM · WOOD STOVE · KITCHEN · DINING · BEDROOM

GREENHOUSE · FIRST FLOOR PLAN · ENTER

FIRST FLOOR PLAN

1977
WALKER HOUSE, WOODSTOCK, NEW YORK
LES WALKER, ARCHITECT/BUILDER

THE PLAN IS STRETCHED OUT SO THAT EACH ROOM HAS ACCESS TO THE VIEW.

VIEW

1978
RILEY HOUSE, ESSEX, CONNECTICUT
JEFFERSON RILEY, ARCHITECT/BUILDER

The work of Charles Moore and the California Bay Region architects was a primary influence in the development of the New Shingle Style. It represented a real break with the International Style in favor of more human, local, vernacular designs.

The Saz house, shown below, clearly illustrates how Moore begins with a relatively simple form and distorts it and/or adds to it to create spaces that not only fit site and client requirements but have such great human character.

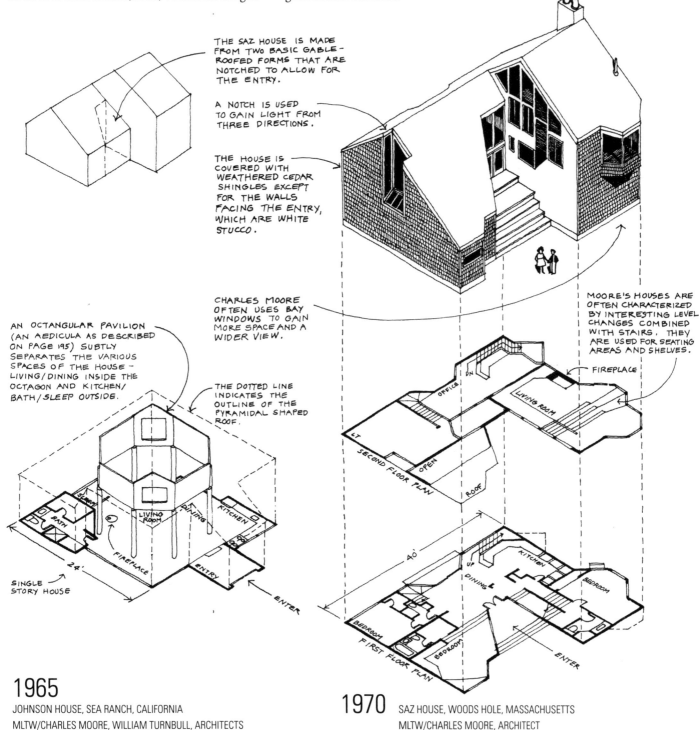

THE SAZ HOUSE IS MADE FROM TWO BASIC GABLE-ROOFED FORMS THAT ARE NOTCHED TO ALLOW FOR THE ENTRY.

A NOTCH IS USED TO GAIN LIGHT FROM THREE DIRECTIONS.

THE HOUSE IS COVERED WITH WEATHERED CEDAR SHINGLES EXCEPT FOR THE WALLS FACING THE ENTRY, WHICH ARE WHITE STUCCO.

CHARLES MOORE OFTEN USES BAY WINDOWS TO GAIN MORE SPACE AND A WIDER VIEW.

MOORE'S HOUSES ARE OFTEN CHARACTERIZED BY INTERESTING LEVEL CHANGES COMBINED WITH STAIRS. THEY ARE USED FOR SEATING AREAS AND SHELVES.

AN OCTANGULAR PAVILION (AN AEDICULA AS DESCRIBED ON PAGE 195) SUBTLY SEPARATES THE VARIOUS SPACES OF THE HOUSE – LIVING/DINING INSIDE THE OCTAGON AND KITCHEN/BATH/SLEEP OUTSIDE.

THE DOTTED LINE INDICATES THE OUTLINE OF THE PYRAMIDAL SHAPED ROOF.

FIREPLACE

OFFICE
DN
LT
SECOND FLOOR PLAN
OPEN
ROOF
LIVING ROOM

SINGLE STORY HOUSE

BATH
LIVING ROOM
DINING
KITCHEN
FIREPLACE
ENTRY
ENTER
24'

40'
UP
DINING
KITCHEN
BEDROOM
BEDROOM
BEDROOM
FIRST FLOOR PLAN
ENTER

1965
JOHNSON HOUSE, SEA RANCH, CALIFORNIA
MLTW/CHARLES MOORE, WILLIAM TURNBULL, ARCHITECTS

1970
SAZ HOUSE, WOODS HOLE, MASSACHUSETTS
MLTW/CHARLES MOORE, ARCHITECT

International Revival

Countrywide 1970

Inspired by the pioneering work of the early Internationalists, especially Le Corbusier, a few architects continued working with this style since its inception in America in the 1930s (p. 214) and saw it experience a revival in the late 1970s. It has been called Cubism because of the blockiness of its forms, Minimalism or Exclusivism because it seeks to eliminate or exclude all ornamentation or extraneous shapes, Neo Corbusian because it is based on the work of the master, Le Corbusier, Late International Style because it often seems like the end of a continuation of the original style, and Cardboard Corbu because of the similarity between house and white cardboard model.

The 1970s revival of the International Style is exemplified in the work of a loose collective of architects known as The New York Five. In their 1972 book, *Five Architects*, they—Peter Eisenman, Michael Graves, Charles Gwathmey, John Hejduk, and Richard Meier—published essays, drawings, and photographs of completed private dwellings, most of them stark white and steeped in the vocabulary of Le Corbusier. *Time* magazine in 1978 called them "the cutting edge of their profession." Their work has had great influence among architects across the country.

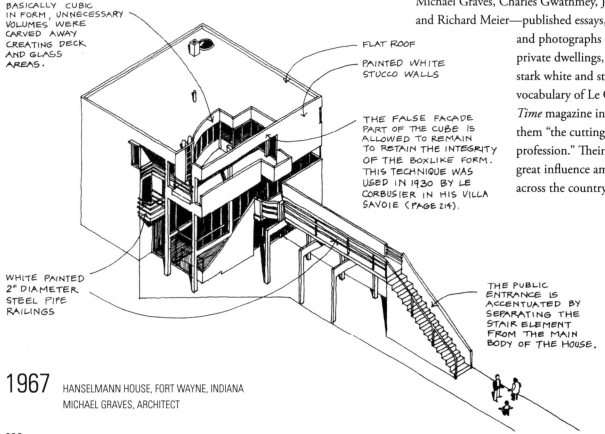

BASICALLY CUBIC IN FORM, UNNECESSARY VOLUMES WERE CARVED AWAY CREATING DECK AND GLASS AREAS.

FLAT ROOF

PAINTED WHITE STUCCO WALLS

THE FALSE FACADE PART OF THE CUBE IS ALLOWED TO REMAIN TO RETAIN THE INTEGRITY OF THE BOXLIKE FORM. THIS TECHNIQUE WAS USED IN 1930 BY LE CORBUSIER IN HIS VILLA SAVOIE (PAGE 214).

WHITE PAINTED 2" DIAMETER STEEL PIPE RAILINGS

THE PUBLIC ENTRANCE IS ACCENTUATED BY SEPARATING THE STAIR ELEMENT FROM THE MAIN BODY OF THE HOUSE.

1967 HANSELMANN HOUSE, FORT WAYNE, INDIANA
MICHAEL GRAVES, ARCHITECT

International Revival Style houses have been criticized as elitist and as being beautiful to view in the "high art" sense but cold and inhuman to live in. Jacquelin Robertson has suggested that they are like "machines in a garden," looking "more like equipment than houses," that they are precious objects, things, and not part of a larger context.

Influences of the Shingle Style have distinguished the work of Charles Gwathmey from the basic International Style, but his use of simple, pure geometric forms, the flat roof, the smooth surface, and the simplicity of his plans, are strong reasons for listing him here. His design for his artist father's house is shown here.

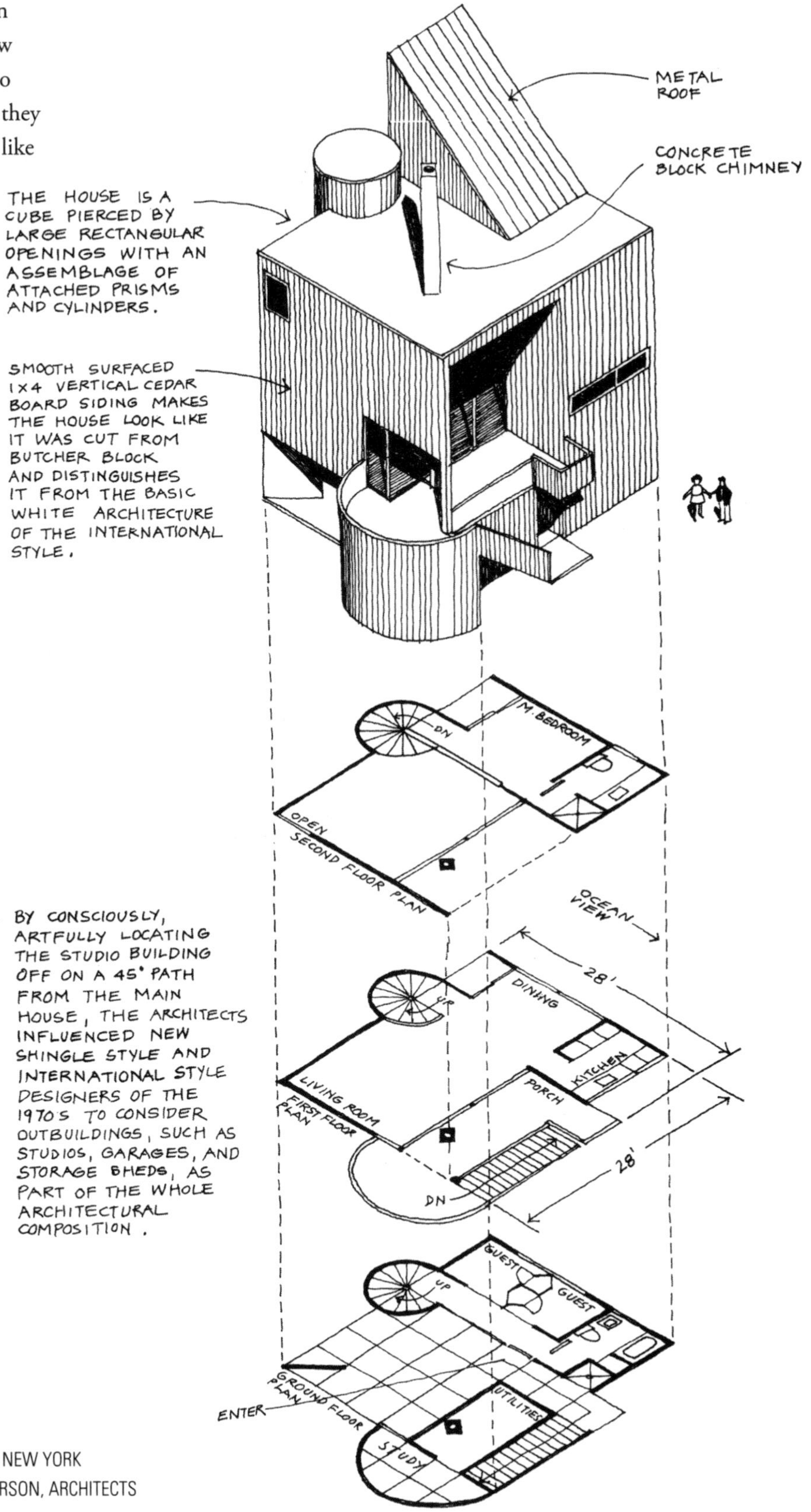

THE HOUSE IS A CUBE PIERCED BY LARGE RECTANGULAR OPENINGS WITH AN ASSEMBLAGE OF ATTACHED PRISMS AND CYLINDERS.

METAL ROOF

CONCRETE BLOCK CHIMNEY

SMOOTH SURFACED 1×4 VERTICAL CEDAR BOARD SIDING MAKES THE HOUSE LOOK LIKE IT WAS CUT FROM BUTCHER BLOCK AND DISTINGUISHES IT FROM THE BASIC WHITE ARCHITECTURE OF THE INTERNATIONAL STYLE.

STUDIO BUILDING (ROOF)

PATH

BY CONSCIOUSLY, ARTFULLY LOCATING THE STUDIO BUILDING OFF ON A 45° PATH FROM THE MAIN HOUSE, THE ARCHITECTS INFLUENCED NEW SHINGLE STYLE AND INTERNATIONAL STYLE DESIGNERS OF THE 1970s TO CONSIDER OUTBUILDINGS, SUCH AS STUDIOS, GARAGES, AND STORAGE SHEDS, AS PART OF THE WHOLE ARCHITECTURAL COMPOSITION.

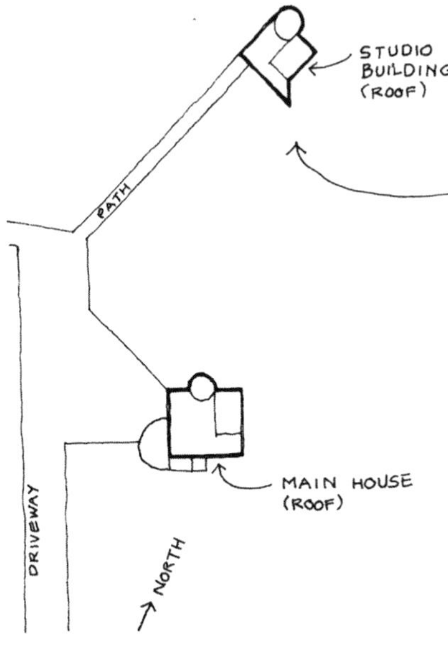

DRIVEWAY

NORTH

MAIN HOUSE (ROOF)

GWATHMEY HOUSE SITE PLAN

M. BEDROOM
DN
OPEN SECOND FLOOR PLAN

OCEAN VIEW

DINING
UP
LIVING ROOM
FIRST FLOOR PLAN
PORCH
KITCHEN
28'
28'
DN

GUEST
UP
GUEST
ENTER
GROUND FLOOR PLAN
UTILITIES
STUDY

1967 ROBERT GWATHMEY HOUSE, AMAGANSETT, NEW YORK
CHARLES GWATHMEY AND RICHARD HENDERSON, ARCHITECTS

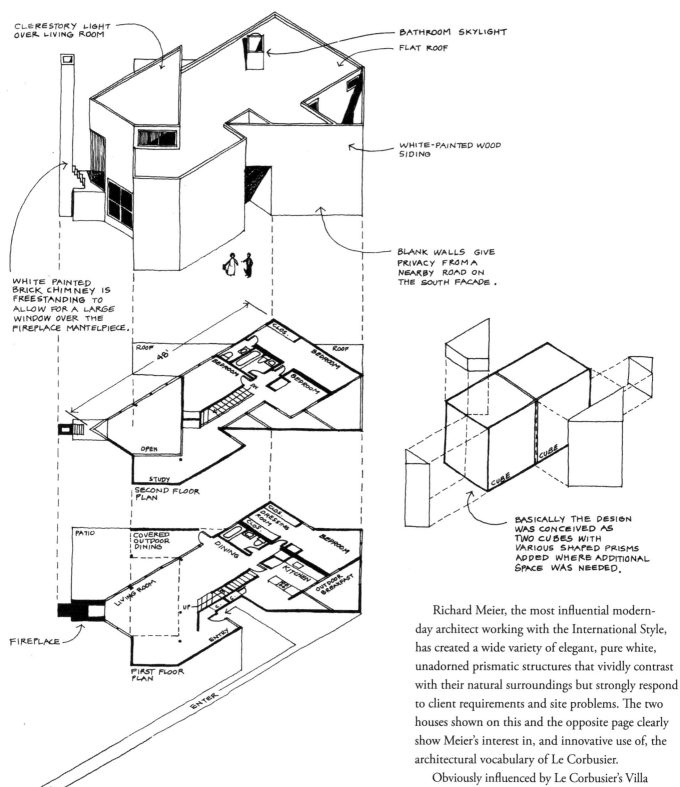

CLERESTORY LIGHT OVER LIVING ROOM

BATHROOM SKYLIGHT

FLAT ROOF

WHITE-PAINTED WOOD SIDING

BLANK WALLS GIVE PRIVACY FROM A NEARBY ROAD ON THE SOUTH FACADE.

WHITE PAINTED BRICK CHIMNEY IS FREESTANDING TO ALLOW FOR A LARGE WINDOW OVER THE FIREPLACE MANTELPIECE.

ROOF

48'

BEDROOM

BEDROOM

ROOF

BEDROOM

DN

OPEN

STUDY

SECOND FLOOR PLAN

PATIO

COVERED OUTDOOR DINING

CLOS.

DRESSING ROOM

CLOS.

BEDROOM

DINING

KITCHEN

LIVING ROOM

UP

CLOS.

OUTDOOR BREAKFAST

FIREPLACE

ENTRY

FIRST FLOOR PLAN

ENTER

PATH

CUBE

CUBE

BASICALLY THE DESIGN WAS CONCEIVED AS TWO CUBES WITH VARIOUS SHAPED PRISMS ADDED WHERE ADDITIONAL SPACE WAS NEEDED.

1964 HOFFMAN HOUSE, EAST HAMPTON, NEW YORK
RICHARD MEIER, ARCHITECT

Richard Meier, the most influential modern-day architect working with the International Style, has created a wide variety of elegant, pure white, unadorned prismatic structures that vividly contrast with their natural surroundings but strongly respond to client requirements and site problems. The two houses shown on this and the opposite page clearly show Meier's interest in, and innovative use of, the architectural vocabulary of Le Corbusier.

Obviously influenced by Le Corbusier's Villa Savoie (p. 214) and quite similar in construction method, the Saltzman residence (often called Villa Saltaman), shown opposite, is an excellent example of the architecture that present-day International Style designers have evolved. Meier, however, does not stress the logic of the steel frame as did Le Corbusier and the exterior facade has been made much smoother and whiter than earlier International Style buildings.

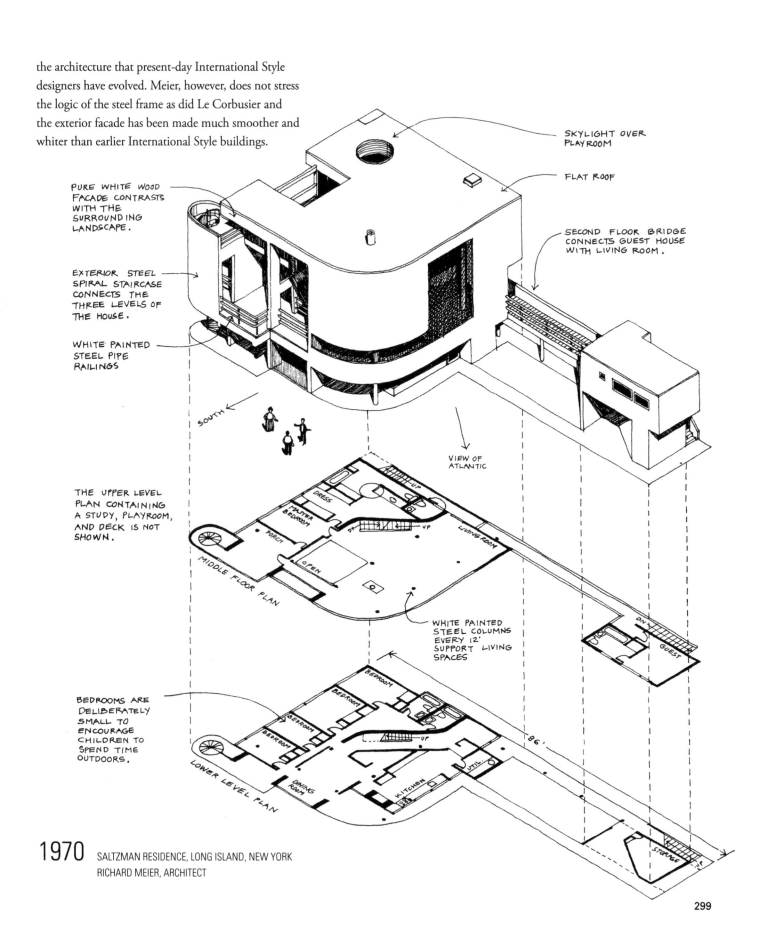

SKYLIGHT OVER PLAYROOM

FLAT ROOF

PURE WHITE WOOD FACADE CONTRASTS WITH THE SURROUNDING LANDSCAPE.

SECOND FLOOR BRIDGE CONNECTS GUEST HOUSE WITH LIVING ROOM.

EXTERIOR STEEL SPIRAL STAIRCASE CONNECTS THE THREE LEVELS OF THE HOUSE.

WHITE PAINTED STEEL PIPE RAILINGS

SOUTH

VIEW OF ATLANTIC

THE UPPER LEVEL PLAN CONTAINING A STUDY, PLAYROOM, AND DECK IS NOT SHOWN.

MIDDLE FLOOR PLAN

MASTER BEDROOM

DRESS

PORCH

OPEN

UP

UP

LIVING ROOM

GUEST

WHITE PAINTED STEEL COLUMNS EVERY 12' SUPPORT LIVING SPACES

BEDROOMS ARE DELIBERATELY SMALL TO ENCOURAGE CHILDREN TO SPEND TIME OUTDOORS.

BEDROOM

BEDROOM

BEDROOM

UP

86'

LOWER LEVEL PLAN

DINING ROOM

KITCHEN

UTIL.

STORAGE

UP

1970 SALTZMAN RESIDENCE, LONG ISLAND, NEW YORK
RICHARD MEIER, ARCHITECT

Inflatable

Countrywide
1975

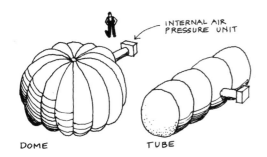

DOME   INTERNAL AIR PRESSURE UNIT   TUBE

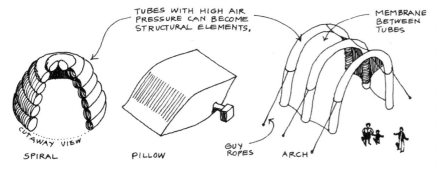

TUBES WITH HIGH AIR PRESSURE CAN BECOME STRUCTURAL ELEMENTS.

MEMBRANE BETWEEN TUBES

SPIRAL   CUTAWAY VIEW   PILLOW   GUY ROPES   ARCH

Inflatables are defined as air-supported structures that have a space-enclosing membrane anchored to the ground and kept in tension (filled with air) by internal air pressure so that it can support applied loads (wind, rain, and sometimes snow). Because of their short lifespan and their inability to be insulated, they have rarely been used for homes in America; rather, their primary use has been to enclose swimming pools and tennis courts. However, their unique qualities may lead to future developments in their use in the private house.

In the early 1970s inflatables had a brief period of popularity with the people seeking alternate forms to the existing culture. The inflatable provided a very inexpensive, exciting, easy-to-build shelter—more for less. Work by the Chrysalis Corporation, a group of English designers working in Los Angeles with air-supported structures, made quite an impact on young architects.

Ant Farm, a group of architects working in Texas, published *Inflatocookbook*, a how-to guide for inflatable builders in 1970 and soon, a wide variety of experimental structures were popping up all around the country. The inflatable's value for quick , exciting, inexpensive shelter was instantly discovered. By cutting patterns and attaching the pieces together, an infinite amount of volumetric shapes were possible (see left).

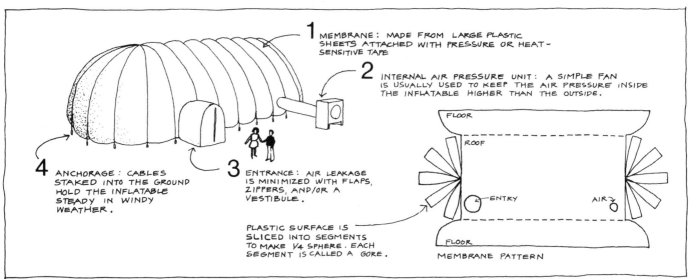

1 MEMBRANE: MADE FROM LARGE PLASTIC SHEETS ATTACHED WITH PRESSURE OR HEAT-SENSITIVE TAPE

2 INTERNAL AIR PRESSURE UNIT: A SIMPLE FAN IS USUALLY USED TO KEEP THE AIR PRESSURE INSIDE THE INFLATABLE HIGHER THAN THE OUTSIDE.

3 ENTRANCE: AIR LEAKAGE IS MINIMIZED WITH FLAPS, ZIPPERS, AND/OR A VESTIBULE.

4 ANCHORAGE: CABLES STAKED INTO THE GROUND HOLD THE INFLATABLE STEADY IN WINDY WEATHER.

PLASTIC SURFACE IS SLICED INTO SEGMENTS TO MAKE 1/4 SPHERE. EACH SEGMENT IS CALLED A GORE.

FLOOR   ROOF   ENTRY   AIR   FLOOR   MEMBRANE PATTERN

THE FOUR BASIC COMPONENTS OF AN INFLATABLE STRUCTURE

The life expectancy of most factory-made inflatables is about five years, but this varies greatly with weather and air conditions. Areas with great temperature changes, air pollution, and snow reduce the time to about three years. In most cases, the inflatable can be resprayed with a protecting synthetic coating and have its life-span increased to as much as ten years. This relatively short life expectancy, the requirement of a constant power supply, and the inability to be insulated are the three primary reasons inflatable structures are rarely used for homes. These disadvantages more than offset the advantages of low cost, unobstructed clear span, speed and ease of erection, portability, and low maintenance, for the housebuilder.

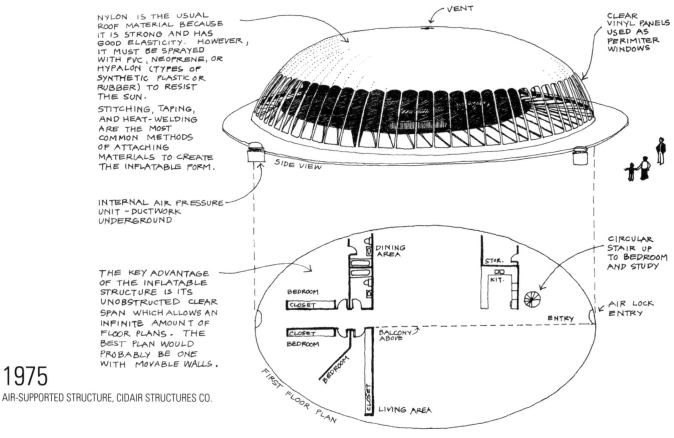

NYLON IS THE USUAL ROOF MATERIAL BECAUSE IT IS STRONG AND HAS GOOD ELASTICITY. HOWEVER, IT MUST BE SPRAYED WITH PVC, NEOPRENE, OR HYPALON (TYPES OF SYNTHETIC PLASTIC OR RUBBER) TO RESIST THE SUN.

STITCHING, TAPING, AND HEAT-WELDING ARE THE MOST COMMON METHODS OF ATTACHING MATERIALS TO CREATE THE INFLATABLE FORM.

INTERNAL AIR PRESSURE UNIT - DUCTWORK UNDERGROUND

VENT

CLEAR VINYL PANELS USED AS PERIMITER WINDOWS

SIDE VIEW

THE KEY ADVANTAGE OF THE INFLATABLE STRUCTURE IS ITS UNOBSTRUCTED CLEAR SPAN WHICH ALLOWS AN INFINITE AMOUNT OF FLOOR PLANS. THE BEST PLAN WOULD PROBABLY BE ONE WITH MOVABLE WALLS.

DINING AREA

BEDROOM
CLOSET

CLOSET
BEDROOM

BEDROOM
CLOSET

BALCONY ABOVE

LIVING AREA

FIRST FLOOR PLAN

STOR.
KIT.

ENTRY

CIRCULAR STAIR UP TO BEDROOM AND STUDY

AIR LOCK ENTRY

1975

AIR-SUPPORTED STRUCTURE, CIDAIR STRUCTURES CO.

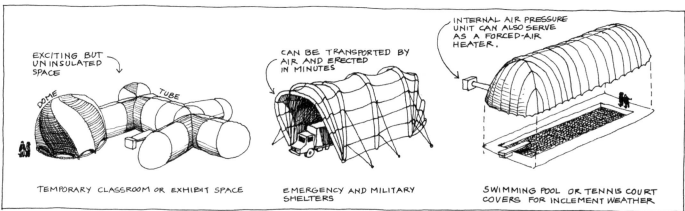

EXCITING BUT UNINSULATED SPACE

DOME

TUBE

TEMPORARY CLASSROOM OR EXHIBIT SPACE

CAN BE TRANSPORTED BY AIR AND ERECTED IN MINUTES

EMERGENCY AND MILITARY SHELTERS

INTERNAL AIR PRESSURE UNIT CAN ALSO SERVE AS A FORCED-AIR HEATER.

SWIMMING POOL OR TENNIS COURT COVERS FOR INCLEMENT WEATHER

SOME POPULAR USES FOR INFLATABLES

Passive Solar

Countrywide 1975

A passive solar house is designed to obtain part or all of its heating from the sun, using conventional building parts to collect, store, and distribute heat without energy-using pumps or fans. Sunlight enters the building through south-facing glass or plastic and is absorbed by dense material such as brick, block, concrete, stone, adobe, or water. Living spaces are arranged so that they are in direct thermal contact with this storage mass allowing them to be heated without the expense of special plumbing or forced hot air distribution systems. Such buildings require careful site planning. As shown below, such natural elements as wind direction, deciduous trees, ponds, contours, and evergreen trees are all keys to the proper functioning of an energy conscious house. The choice of the passive solar heating system (six are shown below) is made after an analysis of the site, with an emphasis on temperature. Colder temperatures necessitate larger, more elaborate heating systems.

The challenge facing the house designer interested in utilizing passive solar energy is to provide an energy-absorbing system on the south wall of the building without eliminating natural light and view. The house shown opposite is an

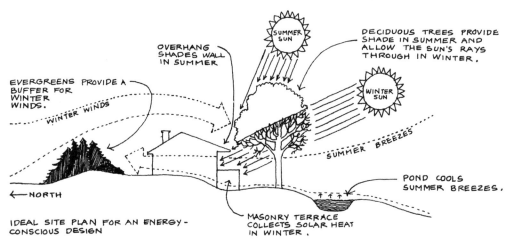

OVERHANG SHADES WALL IN SUMMER

DECIDUOUS TREES PROVIDE SHADE IN SUMMER AND ALLOW THE SUN'S RAYS THROUGH IN WINTER.

EVERGREENS PROVIDE A BUFFER FOR WINTER WINDS.

WINTER WINDS

SUMMER SUN

WINTER SUN

SUMMER BREEZES

POND COOLS SUMMER BREEZES.

← NORTH

IDEAL SITE PLAN FOR AN ENERGY-CONSCIOUS DESIGN

MASONRY TERRACE COLLECTS SOLAR HEAT IN WINTER.

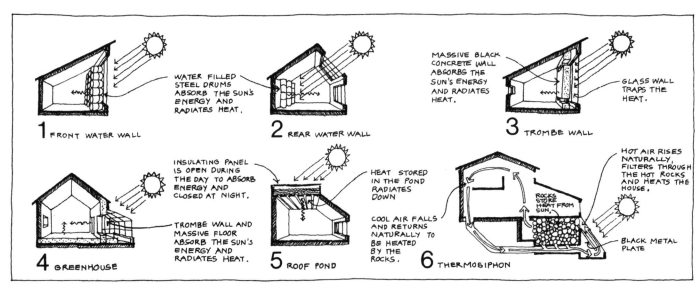

WATER FILLED STEEL DRUMS ABSORB THE SUN'S ENERGY AND RADIATES HEAT.

1 FRONT WATER WALL

2 REAR WATER WALL

MASSIVE BLACK CONCRETE WALL ABSORBS THE SUN'S ENERGY AND RADIATES HEAT.

GLASS WALL TRAPS THE HEAT.

3 TROMBE WALL

INSULATING PANEL IS OPEN DURING THE DAY TO ABSORB ENERGY AND CLOSED AT NIGHT.

TROMBE WALL AND MASSIVE FLOOR ABSORB THE SUN'S ENERGY AND RADIATES HEAT.

4 GREENHOUSE

HEAT STORED IN THE POND RADIATES DOWN

COOL AIR FALLS AND RETURNS NATURALLY TO BE HEATED BY THE ROCKS.

5 ROOF POND

HOT AIR RISES NATURALLY, FILTERS THROUGH THE HOT ROCKS AND HEATS THE HOUSE.

ROCKS STORE HEAT FROM SUN.

BLACK METAL PLATE

6 THERMOSIPHON

SIX WAYS TO HEAT A HOUSE PASSIVELY WITH SOLAR ENERGY

admirable example of how one architect achieved both goals. He punched holes in his fifteen-inch-thick concrete wall and double-glazed them for windows and created additional space, light, and heat with an attached greenhouse on the south wall. His back up fuel costs throughout the 1976–1977 winter were only $75.00.

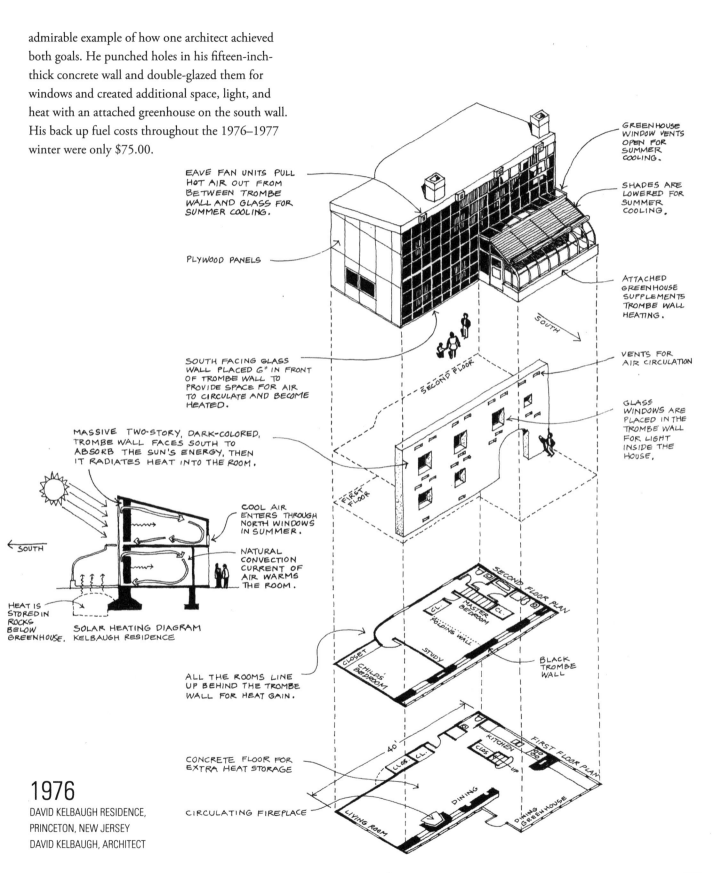

GREENHOUSE WINDOW VENTS OPEN FOR SUMMER COOLING.

SHADES ARE LOWERED FOR SUMMER COOLING.

EAVE FAN UNITS PULL HOT AIR OUT FROM BETWEEN TROMBE WALL AND GLASS FOR SUMMER COOLING.

PLYWOOD PANELS

ATTACHED GREENHOUSE SUPPLEMENTS TROMBE WALL HEATING.

SOUTH

SOUTH FACING GLASS WALL PLACED 6" IN FRONT OF TROMBE WALL TO PROVIDE SPACE FOR AIR TO CIRCULATE AND BECOME HEATED.

VENTS FOR AIR CIRCULATION

GLASS WINDOWS ARE PLACED IN THE TROMBE WALL FOR LIGHT INSIDE THE HOUSE.

SECOND FLOOR

FIRST FLOOR

MASSIVE TWO-STORY, DARK-COLORED, TROMBE WALL FACES SOUTH TO ABSORB THE SUN'S ENERGY, THEN IT RADIATES HEAT INTO THE ROOM.

SOUTH

COOL AIR ENTERS THROUGH NORTH WINDOWS IN SUMMER.

NATURAL CONVECTION CURRENT OF AIR WARMS THE ROOM.

HEAT IS STORED IN ROCKS BELOW GREENHOUSE.

SOLAR HEATING DIAGRAM KELBAUGH RESIDENCE

SECOND FLOOR PLAN

CL.

MASTER BEDROOM

CL.

CLOSET

CHILDS BEDROOM

FOLDING WALL

STUDY

BLACK TROMBE WALL

ALL THE ROOMS LINE UP BEHIND THE TROMBE WALL FOR HEAT GAIN.

FIRST FLOOR PLAN

KITCHEN

CLOS

UP

40'

CLOS CL.

CONCRETE FLOOR FOR EXTRA HEAT STORAGE

CIRCULATING FIREPLACE

DINING

LIVING ROOM

DINING GREENHOUSE

1976

DAVID KELBAUGH RESIDENCE,
PRINCETON, NEW JERSEY
DAVID KELBAUGH, ARCHITECT

Active Solar

Countrywide
1975

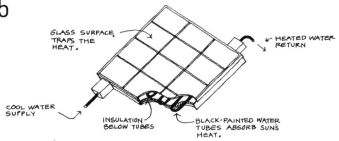

GLASS SURFACE TRAPS THE HEAT.

HEATED WATER RETURN

COOL WATER SUPPLY

INSULATION BELOW TUBES

BLACK-PAINTED WATER TUBES ABSORB SUNS HEAT.

1 FLAT PLATE (WATER) COLLECTOR

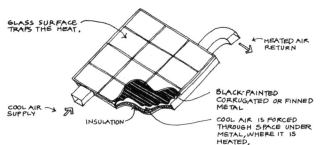

GLASS SURFACE TRAPS THE HEAT.

HEATED AIR RETURN

COOL AIR SUPPLY

INSULATION

BLACK-PAINTED CORRUGATED OR FINNED METAL

COOL AIR IS FORCED THROUGH SPACE UNDER METAL, WHERE IT IS HEATED.

2 FLAT PLATE (AIR) COLLECTOR

The rising cost of fuel and the environmental problems associated with most conventional heating systems have played important roles in causing solar energy to capture the imagination of the American housebuilder. By 1975 many new houses were incorporating solar energy into home design as a prime heating source. An active solar heating system is like a furnace with the sun as the heat source. Like a furnace, and unlike a passive solar heating system, it consists of moving mechanical components such as thermostats, fans, pumps, and valves, powered by electricity, to collect and distribute heat.

The two basic kinds of active systems (shown left) are distinguished by the different heat-transfer fluids they use: air or water with antifreeze. Both fluids are heated when forced through collector panels facing the sun. These panels are called flat plate collectors because of their flat metal energy-absorbing plate components. They are usually arranged in rows on the roof of the house, tilted to

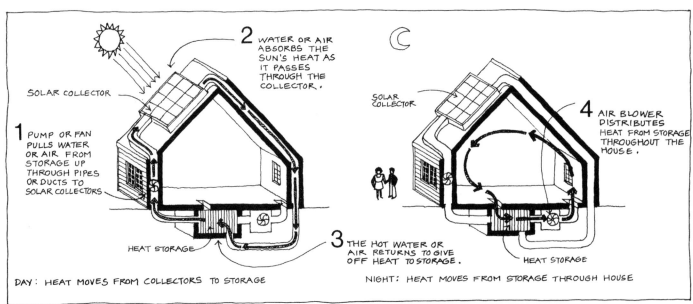

2 WATER OR AIR ABSORBS THE SUN'S HEAT AS IT PASSES THROUGH THE COLLECTOR.

SOLAR COLLECTOR

1 PUMP OR FAN PULLS WATER OR AIR FROM STORAGE UP THROUGH PIPES OR DUCTS TO SOLAR COLLECTORS

HEAT STORAGE

DAY: HEAT MOVES FROM COLLECTORS TO STORAGE

3 THE HOT WATER OR AIR RETURNS TO GIVE OFF HEAT TO STORAGE.

SOLAR COLLECTOR

4 AIR BLOWER DISTRIBUTES HEAT FROM STORAGE THROUGHOUT THE HOUSE.

HEAT STORAGE

NIGHT: HEAT MOVES FROM STORAGE THROUGH HOUSE

FOUR STEPS TO HEATING AN ACTIVE SOLAR HOUSE

be perpendicular to the low winter sun. There are many variations on these systems.

Basically, as shown opposite, during a sunny day, the heat-transfer fluid flows from collector to a water tank or rock bin storage unit. Here it heats the water or rocks and is pumped back to the collector to be heated again. During cloudy days or at night, the stored heat is then distributed throughout the house.

The problem of utilizing the south-facing wall to provide an energy-absorbing system without totally eliminating natural light and view is as difficult for a designer using an active solar system as a passive one. The design shown below, for a cool-temperature climate, ingeniously combines collectors, greenhouse living space, windows, doors, and a second floor sun porch on the south-facing wall. All other walls are heavily insulated and have a minimum of windows.

The shape of a solar house is dictated by the amount of collectors necessary to heat the house comfortably. A few alternatives

(shown below) from a study by Donald Watson in his book *The Solar House* illustrates the many possibilities for placement of collectors in various climates. In all examples, the first floor facing south is free of collectors to be used for windows, doors, patios, and greenhouse living space.

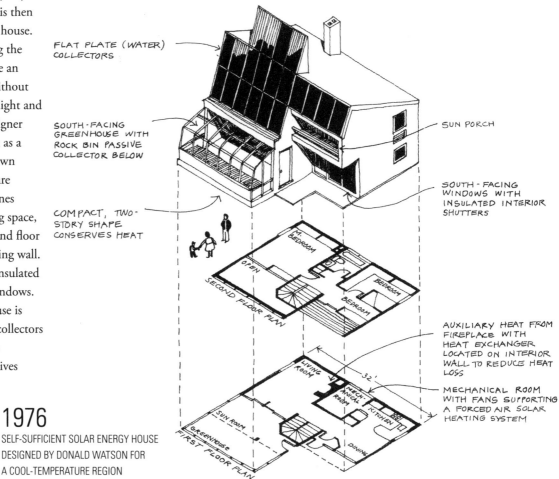

FLAT PLATE (WATER) COLLECTORS

SOUTH-FACING GREENHOUSE WITH ROCK BIN PASSIVE COLLECTOR BELOW

COMPACT, TWO-STORY SHAPE CONSERVES HEAT

SUN PORCH

SOUTH-FACING WINDOWS WITH INSULATED INTERIOR SHUTTERS

AUXILIARY HEAT FROM FIREPLACE WITH HEAT EXCHANGER LOCATED ON INTERIOR WALL TO REDUCE HEAT LOSS

MECHANICAL ROOM WITH FANS SUPPORTING A FORCED AIR SOLAR HEATING SYSTEM

1976

SELF-SUFFICIENT SOLAR ENERGY HOUSE DESIGNED BY DONALD WATSON FOR A COOL-TEMPERATURE REGION

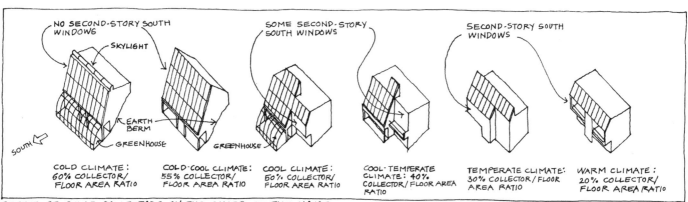

COLD CLIMATE: 60% COLLECTOR/ FLOOR AREA RATIO

COLD-COOL CLIMATE: 55% COLLECTOR/ FLOOR AREA RATIO

COOL CLIMATE: 50% COLLECTOR/ FLOOR AREA RATIO

COOL-TEMPERATE CLIMATE: 40% COLLECTOR/FLOOR AREA RATIO

TEMPERATE CLIMATE: 30% COLLECTOR/ FLOOR AREA RATIO

WARM CLIMATE: 20% COLLECTOR/ FLOOR AREA RATIO

EFFECT OF SOLAR COLLECTORS ON THE SHAPE OF THE HOUSE

Earth Sheltered

Countrywide 1975

The earth sheltered house is another form of passive solar energy design. The goal of the earth sheltered house is to keep or improve on the comfort of conventional houses while pulling the earth as a blanket around as much of the house as possible. The earth then acts as a barrier to wind chill and direct heat loss. Since the temperature of the earth below the frost line stays around 55° F, earth sheltered houses are warm in the winter and cool in the summer.

There are three basic kinds of earth sheltered houses: The first type is completely underground with earth covered rooms usually facing an open-to-the-sky atrium. This type is the most efficient in gaining or losing heat from or to the earth but it is also the most claustrophobic with no view and little natural light. The second type is called bermed, after the term describing the mounds of earth pushed around the sides of the house. Berming is a common practice for energy conscious house designs. The third type is the house that is built into a hillside. This is the most desirable because it can absorb heating and cooling energy from the earth and still

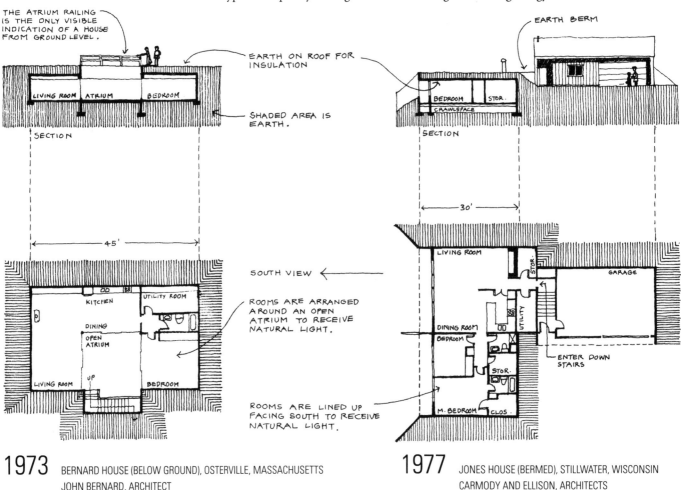

1973 BERNARD HOUSE (BELOW GROUND), OSTERVILLE, MASSACHUSETTS
JOHN BERNARD, ARCHITECT

1977 JONES HOUSE (BERMED), STILLWATER, WISCONSIN
CARMODY AND ELLISON, ARCHITECTS

306

have at least one wall (ideally facing south to gain maximum energy from the sun) with a view.

Opposite are examples of the first two types of the earth sheltered house and on this page is an example of the third type.

Many earth sheltered homes incorporate an earth covered (usually eighteen-inch-thick) roof into their design as shown in the hillside house below. This is an expensive method of insulating because of the structure and waterproofing necessary to hold the heavy, wet earth. But the aesthetics and/or the psychological sensation of having grass growing on the roof can be quite special.

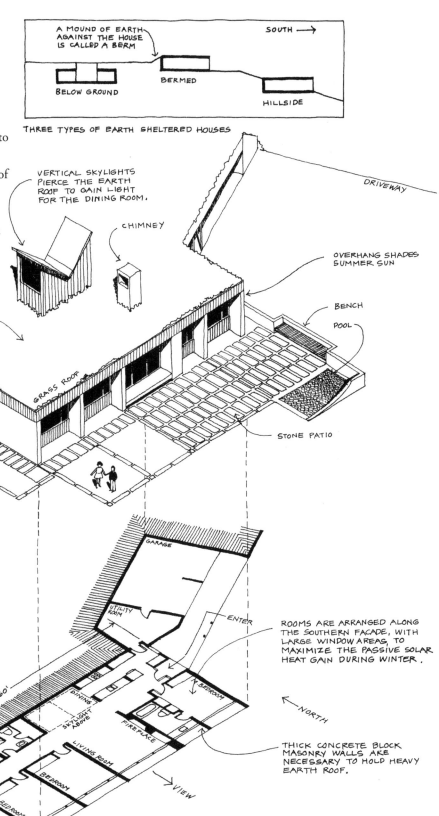

A MOUND OF EARTH AGAINST THE HOUSE IS CALLED A BERM

SOUTH →

BELOW GROUND

BERMED

HILLSIDE

THREE TYPES OF EARTH SHELTERED HOUSES

VERTICAL SKYLIGHTS PIERCE THE EARTH ROOF TO GAIN LIGHT FOR THE DINING ROOM.

CHIMNEY

DRIVEWAY

OVERHANG SHADES SUMMER SUN

BENCH

POOL

THE HOUSE IS BUILT INTO A MOUNTAINSIDE FACING SOUTH.

12-15"- THICK PLANTED EARTH ROOF FOR EXTRA INSULATION

POURED CONCRETE RETAINING WALL HOLDS BACK HILLSIDE.

GRASS ROOF

STONE PATIO

GARAGE

UTILITY ROOM

ENTER

ROOMS ARE ARRANGED ALONG THE SOUTHERN FACADE, WITH LARGE WINDOW AREAS, TO MAXIMIZE THE PASSIVE SOLAR HEAT GAIN DURING WINTER.

NORTH

SHADED AREAS INDICATE EARTH

60'

DINING

SKYLIGHT ABOVE

BEDROOM

FIREPLACE

LIVING ROOM

BEDROOM

THICK CONCRETE BLOCK MASONRY WALLS ARE NECESSARY TO HOLD HEAVY EARTH ROOF.

ENTER

BEDROOM

VIEW

1972
WINSTON HOUSE (HILLSIDE), LYME, NEW HAMPSHIRE
DON METZ, ARCHITECT

Post Modern

Countrywide 1978

By the late 1960s, the "modern" International Style had become, to many, the ultimate corporate style. The glass box, a radical idea in the 1940s was viewed as conservative, establishment architecture. Robert Venturi wrote in his *Complexity and Contradiction in Architecture*, "I like the elements which are hybrid rather than 'pure,' compromising rather than 'clean,' distorted rather than 'straightforward.'" Mies Van der Rohe's famous International Style axiom, "Less is more" became "Less is a bore" to the antimodern or Post Modern architects.

Post Modernists indirectly imitate many historical styles (an important one is the Shingle Style discussed on page 288 in the New Shingle Style chapter), use ornament, and often mix various styles and periods from different cultures. Charles Moore has written, "I hope future historians will note the late twentieth-century architectural wisdom of absorbing and enjoying the influences available to us."

Post Modern architects have sought inspiration from sources as diverse as the "Pop" vernacular American highway strip to Italian hill towns. They use images from their own travels and studies and often include the client's ideas of his or her

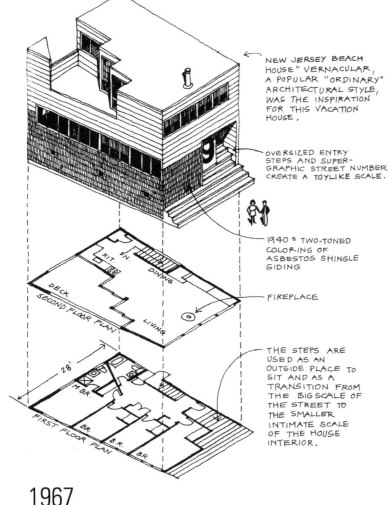

NEW JERSEY BEACH HOUSE" VERNACULAR, A POPULAR "ORDINARY" ARCHITECTURAL STYLE, WAS THE INSPIRATION FOR THIS VACATION HOUSE.

OVERSIZED ENTRY STEPS AND SUPER-GRAPHIC STREET NUMBER CREATE A TOYLIKE SCALE.

1940ˢ TWO-TONED COLORING OF ASBESTOS SHINGLE SIDING

FIREPLACE

THE STEPS ARE USED AS AN OUTSIDE PLACE TO SIT AND AS A TRANSITION FROM THE BIG SCALE OF THE STREET TO THE SMALLER INTIMATE SCALE OF THE HOUSE INTERIOR.

SECOND FLOOR PLAN
KIT. B.N. DINING
DECK
LIVING

FIRST FLOOR PLAN
28'
M. BR.
BR.
BR.

1967
LIEB HOUSE, LOVELADIES, NEW JERSEY
VENTURI AND RAUCH, ARCHITECTS

"DESIGN JOKES" SHOWING IRREVERANCE TO "MINIMAL" ARCHITECTURE, THE USE OF DECORATIVE ELEMENTS, AND HUMOR IN BUILDINGS, BEGAN THE BREAKDOWN OF THE INTERNATIONAL STYLE.

10'

THE SCREEN WALL JOGS UPAND DOWN TO ACCOMMODATE COLUMNS OF UNEQUAL HEIGHT. AN INTERNATIONAL STYLE ARCHITECT WOULD HAVE TWO SLENDER STEEL COLUMNS OF EQUAL HEIGHT SUPPORTING A SIMPLE RECTANGULAR WALL.

1967
SCREEN WALL, MLTW OFFICES, NEW HAVEN, CONNECTICUT
CHARLES MOORE, ARCHITECT

dream house. The Lang House, shown below, is a composition of elements from the Mediterranean Villa Style, the Italian Baroque, the English manor house, with many of the structural qualities of the International Style—ideas brought to the project by the client and the architect.

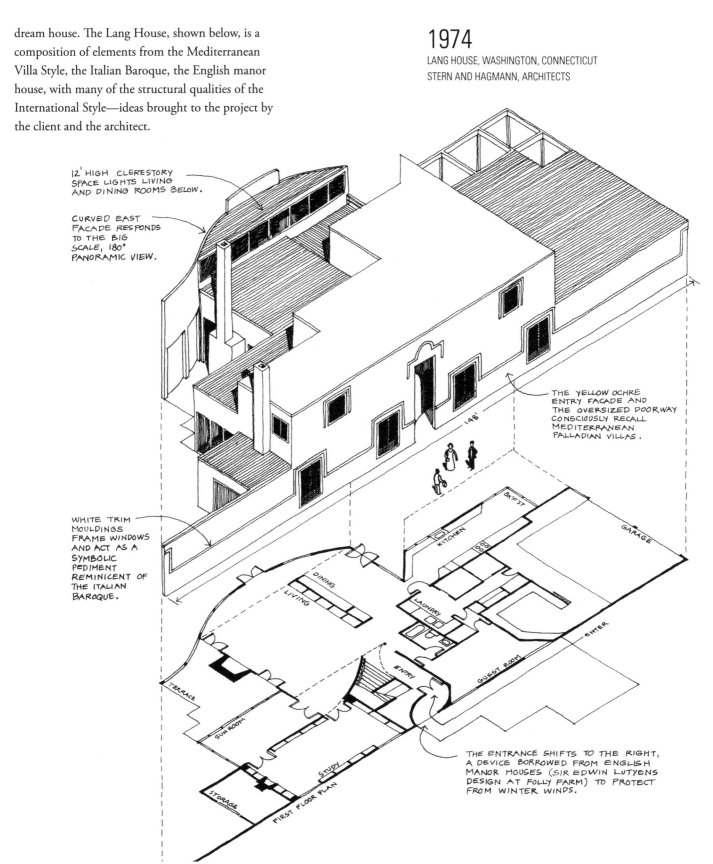

12' HIGH CLERESTORY SPACE LIGHTS LIVING AND DINING ROOMS BELOW.

CURVED EAST FACADE RESPONDS TO THE BIG SCALE, 180° PANORAMIC VIEW.

THE YELLOW OCHRE ENTRY FACADE AND THE OVERSIZED DOORWAY CONSCIOUSLY RECALL MEDITERRANEAN PALLADIAN VILLAS.

WHITE TRIM MOULDINGS FRAME WINDOWS AND ACT AS A SYMBOLIC PEDIMENT REMINICENT OF THE ITALIAN BAROQUE.

THE ENTRANCE SHIFTS TO THE RIGHT, A DEVICE BORROWED FROM ENGLISH MANOR HOUSES (SIR EDWIN LUTYENS DESIGN AT FOLLY FARM) TO PROTECT FROM WINTER WINDS.

DINING

LIVING

BK'FST

KITCHEN

GARAGE

LAUNDRY

ENTER

GUEST ROOM

ENTRY

TERRACE

SUN ROOM

STUDY

STORAGE

FIRST FLOOR PLAN

148'

Words and phrases like "romanticism," "tongue-in-cheek allusions," "a return to ornament," "neoeclecticism," "humorous architecture," and "mixing architectural metaphors" are all used to describe Post Modern buildings. The house shown below is an example of all of these. A classical, thick-corniced, rustic Bay Region styled building with a large overhead gas station door dominating the key elevation.

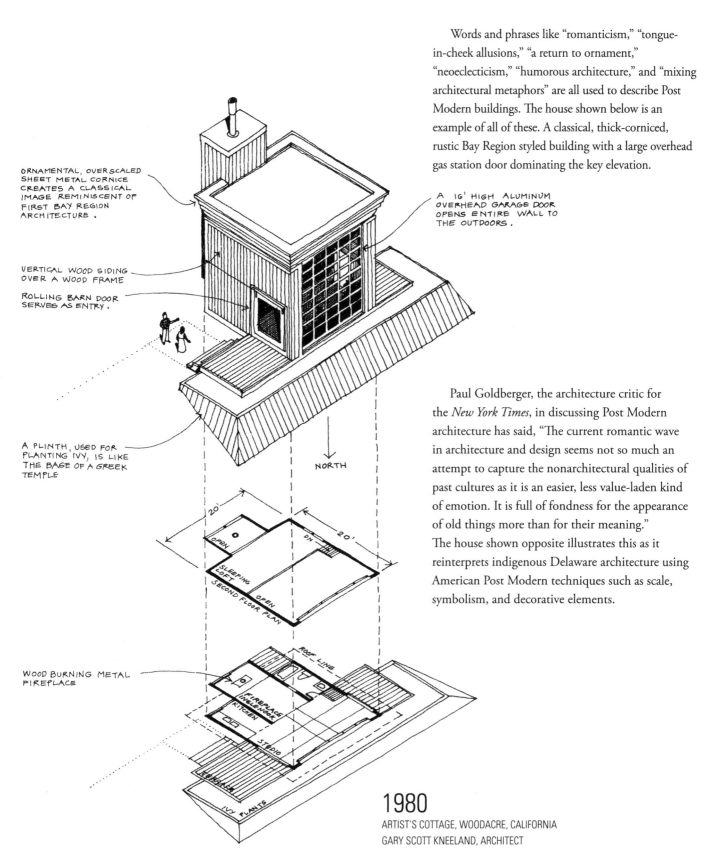

ORNAMENTAL, OVERSCALED SHEET METAL CORNICE CREATES A CLASSICAL IMAGE REMINISCENT OF FIRST BAY REGION ARCHITECTURE .

A 16' HIGH ALUMINUM OVERHEAD GARAGE DOOR OPENS ENTIRE WALL TO THE OUTDOORS .

VERTICAL WOOD SIDING OVER A WOOD FRAME

ROLLING BARN DOOR SERVES AS ENTRY .

A PLINTH, USED FOR PLANTING IVY, IS LIKE THE BASE OF A GREEK TEMPLE

NORTH

WOOD BURNING METAL FIREPLACE

20'

20'

OPEN

ON

SLEEPING LOFT OPEN

SECOND FLOOR PLAN

ROOF LINE

FIREPLACE INGLENOOK

KITCHEN

STUDIO

LIBRARY

IVY PLANTS

Paul Goldberger, the architecture critic for the *New York Times*, in discussing Post Modern architecture has said, "The current romantic wave in architecture and design seems not so much an attempt to capture the nonarchitectural qualities of past cultures as it is an easier, less value-laden kind of emotion. It is full of fondness for the appearance of old things more than for their meaning." The house shown opposite illustrates this as it reinterprets indigenous Delaware architecture using American Post Modern techniques such as scale, symbolism, and decorative elements.

1980
ARTIST'S COTTAGE, WOODACRE, CALIFORNIA
GARY SCOTT KNEELAND, ARCHITECT

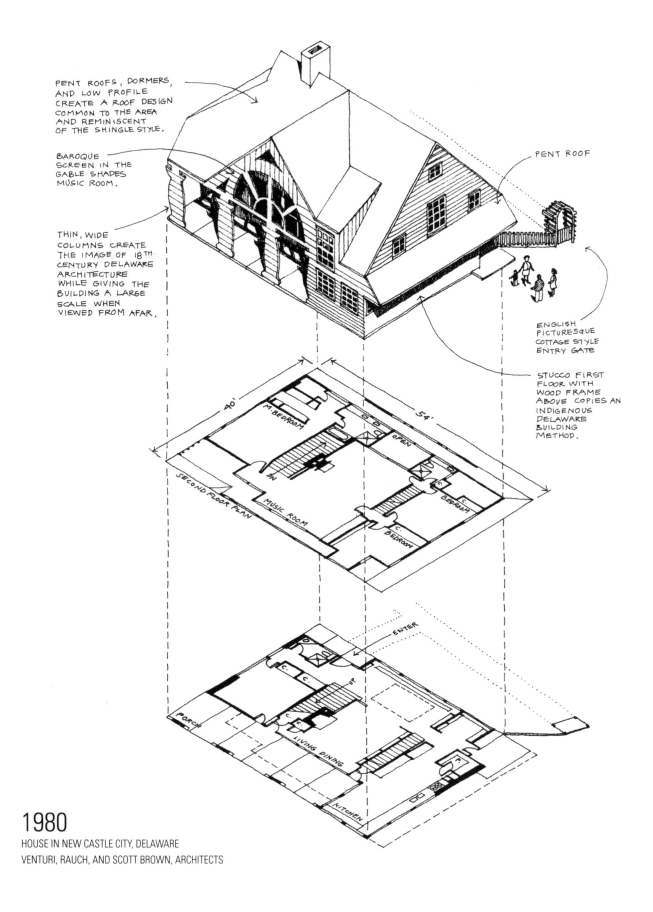

PENT ROOFS, DORMERS, AND LOW PROFILE CREATE A ROOF DESIGN COMMON TO THE AREA AND REMINISCENT OF THE SHINGLE STYLE.

BAROQUE SCREEN IN THE GABLE SHADES MUSIC ROOM.

THIN, WIDE COLUMNS CREATE THE IMAGE OF 18TH CENTURY DELAWARE ARCHITECTURE WHILE GIVING THE BUILDING A LARGE SCALE WHEN VIEWED FROM AFAR.

PENT ROOF

ENGLISH PICTURESQUE COTTAGE STYLE ENTRY GATE

STUCCO FIRST FLOOR WITH WOOD FRAME ABOVE COPIES AN INDIGENOUS DELAWARE BUILDING METHOD.

40'

54'

SECOND FLOOR PLAN

M. BEDROOM

OPEN

IN

MUSIC ROOM

BEDROOM

C.

BEDROOM

C.

ENTER

C.   C.

C.

PORCH

LIVING DINING

KITCHEN

1980
HOUSE IN NEW CASTLE CITY, DELAWARE
VENTURI, RAUCH, AND SCOTT BROWN, ARCHITECTS

Deconstruction

Countrywide 1988

The term "deconstruction" began as a twentieth-century philosophical method of analysis primarily used for text, and was later used as the title of the 1988 Museum of Modern Art (MOMA) exhibit produced by Philip Johnson and Mark Wigley.

The philosophy of deconstructive method was first developed by Jacques Derrida, an Algerian Jew who moved to Paris as a young man to study and teach philosophy at the prestigious Ecole Normale Superieure. Deconstruction, as a philosophical method, means to pick something apart in order to ascertain its failings. It challenges the idea of belief, that the world is simple and can be known with certainty, and reveals the limits of human thought. Referring to the 1988 MOMA exhibit, Mark Wigley stated, "It is the ability to disturb our thinking about form that makes these projects deconstructive…they emerge from within the architectural tradition and happen to exhibit some deconstructive qualities."

As an architectural term, or "style," deconstruction means something different, relating more to the work of the Russian Constructivists than the philosophy of Derrida. Around the turn of the century, during the birth of the European modern movement, the Russian avant garde introduced a radical new set of formal strategies. Questioning the traditional role of the object and the relationship of its parts, the constructivists began by composing simple forms to produce geometry of instability and disorder. Their works were exemplified by artists such as Malevich, El Lissitzky, Tatlin, and Kandinsky. Although influential in European modernism, the work of the constructivists was seen by the Communist regime as rebellious, and was suppressed. It wasn't until the 1988 MOMA show that this distinct school of thought resurfaced in the formal strategies of the architects involved.

Similar to the way Derrida analyzes text to reveal its conflicts and contradictions, a deconstructivist architecture attempts to exaggerate the conflict inherently possible in geometric composition; that is, to elicit and exemplify what architects have traditionally subverted. Although meaning is inevitable in the method, this "meaning" is willingly lost to the multitude of possible interpretations believed by the deconstructivists to be inherent in all forms. The fragmentation undermines any single interpretation and emphasizes the possibility of many. Anthony Vidler, an architectural historian, has summed up the movement's tenets quite eloquently:

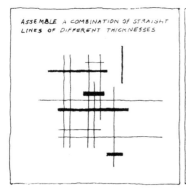

ASSEMBLE A COMBINATION OF STRAIGHT LINES OF DIFFERENT THICKNESSES

COMPILE MANY STRAIGHT LINES WITH A DYNAMIC SLOPE

ASSEMBLE A DYNAMIC ORNAMENT WITH CURVED LINES

MAKE A RECTILINEAR CONFIGURATION WITH POLYGONAL PLANES

SELECTED PROJECTS TAKEN FROM THE TEACHING PROGRAM OF THE RUSSIAN CONSTRUCTIVIST ARCHITECT IAKOV CHERNIKOV IN 1925

"Deconstruction gains all its force by challenging the very values of harmony, unity and stability and proposing instead a different view of structure: the view that flaws are intrinsic to the structure."

The single most influential house designed in what many scholars would call the Deconstruction Style is a small pink asbestos shingled California bungalow that architect Frank Gehry has transformed into a new, larger, "more important" home for himself. A new shell of rough, raw hard-edge materials, like chain link fence panels, wire glass, and untreated plywood, wraps the original house on three sides intentionally creating the image of an unfinished building. As Gehry explains it, "The very finished building has security, and it's predictable. I wanted to try something different. I like playing at the edge of disaster."

ORIGINAL PINK DUTCH REVIVAL HOUSE

CHAIN LINK FENCE

INTERSECTING POLYGONAL CHAIN LINK SCREEN PANELS

INTERSECTING CONCRETE RECTILINEAR PLANES CREATE ENTRY STEPS

LOW CONCRETE BLOCK WALL

PICKET FENCE

WINDOW OPENING CUT IN WALL PROVIDES VIEW TO BACK YARD

CORRUGATED METAL WALL

POLYGONAL GLASS VOLUME CREATES A SKYLIGHT THAT "READS AS A CUBE FALLING OUT OF A BOX.

A NEW SHELL WRAPS THE ORIGINAL DUTCH REVIVAL HOUSE ON THREE SIDES

HOUSE

SHELL

BEDROOM

CLOS

MASTER BEDROOM

OUTDOOR DECK

OUTDOOR DECK

LOGGIA OPENING TO BACK YARD

BEDROOM

BEDROOM

ENTRY

LIVING AREA

KITCHEN

BKFST AREA

DINING AREA

1979
GEHRY HOUSE,
SANTA MONICA, CALIFORNIA,
FRANK GEHRY, ARCHITECT

MAKE AN ELEMENT IN SPACE WITH A BENT SINGLE PLANE

MAKE AN ELEMENT IN SPACE WITH INTERSECTING RECTILINEAR PLANES

MAKE A COMPOSITION WITH LINEAR ELEMENTS AND A CIRCLE

MAKE A VOLUMETRIC COMPOSITION WITH CIRCULAR AND RECTANGULAR FORMS

313

Another house that gives an international appearance of being unfinished is "Home Sweet Home," situated on a small 35' x 60' lot in San Diego, California, shown here. Rooms are formed with planes, views are framed with a wide variety of window devices, passage between spaces is accomplished with flat, bridge-like panels, and a roof is retractable. The building effectively dissolves preconceived notions of what is interior and what is exterior, what is finished and what is unfinished. It, like the Gehry house, attempts to discover the "in-between" of these and other opposing ideas.

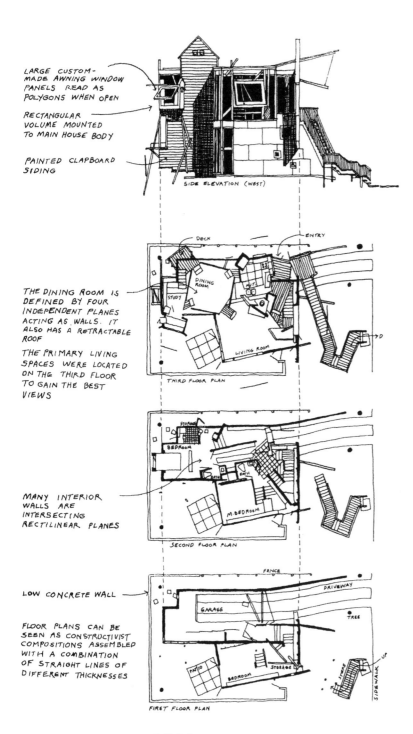

LARGE CUSTOM-MADE AWNING WINDOW PANELS READ AS POLYGONS WHEN OPEN

RECTANGULAR VOLUME MOUNTED TO MAIN HOUSE BODY

PAINTED CLAPBOARD SIDING

SIDE ELEVATION (WEST)

DECK

ENTRY

DINING ROOM

STUDY

LIVING ROOM

D

THE DINING ROOM IS DEFINED BY FOUR INDEPENDENT PLANES ACTING AS WALLS. IT ALSO HAS A RETRACTABLE ROOF

THE PRIMARY LIVING SPACES WERE LOCATED ON THE THIRD FLOOR TO GAIN THE BEST VIEWS

THIRD FLOOR PLAN

STORAGE

BEDROOM

BATH

BATH

M.BEDROOM

MANY INTERIOR WALLS ARE INTERSECTING RECTILINEAR PLANES

SECOND FLOOR PLAN

FENCE

DRIVEWAY

GARAGE

TREE

LOW CONCRETE WALL

FLOOR PLANS CAN BE SEEN AS CONSTRUCTIVIST COMPOSITIONS ASSEMBLED WITH A COMBINATION OF STRAIGHT LINES OF DIFFERENT THICKNESSES

PATIO

BEDROOM

STORAGE

STEPS

SIDEWALK

UP

FIRST FLOOR PLAN

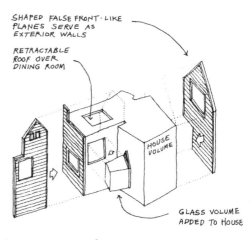

SHAPED FALSE FRONT-LIKE PLANES SERVE AS EXTERIOR WALLS

RETRACTABLE ROOF OVER DINING ROOM

HOUSE VOLUME

GLASS VOLUME ADDED TO HOUSE

"HOME SWEET HOME" MASSING DIAGRAM

1989
"HOME SWEET HOME," SAN DIEGO, CALIFORNIA
RICHARD DALRYMPLE, ARCHITECT, PACIFIC ASSOCIATES PLANNERS ARCHITECTS

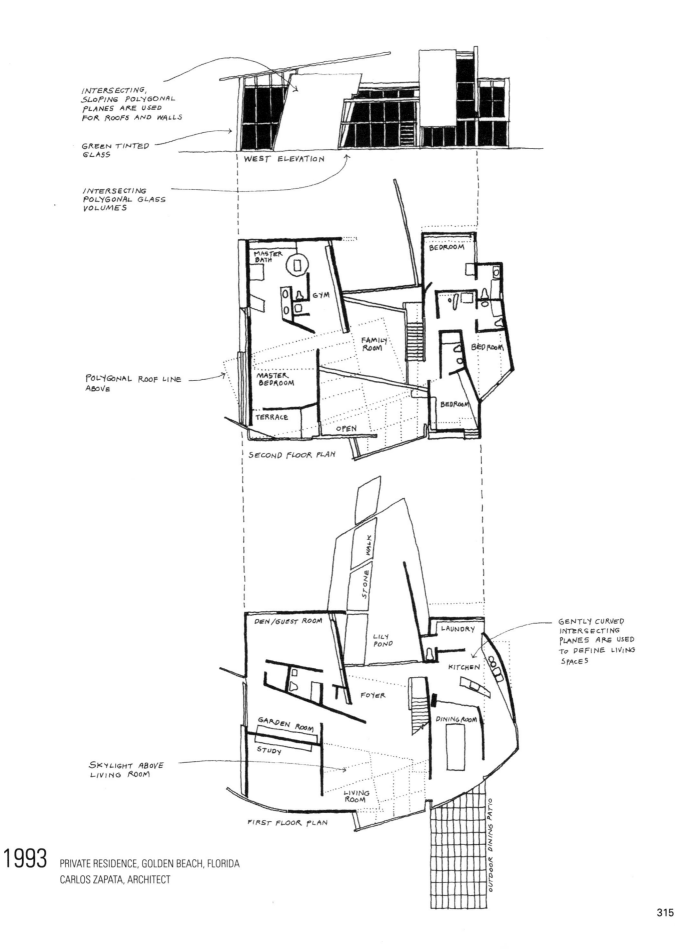

INTERSECTING, SLOPING POLYGONAL PLANES ARE USED FOR ROOFS AND WALLS

GREEN TINTED GLASS

WEST ELEVATION

INTERSECTING POLYGONAL GLASS VOLUMES

MASTER BATH

GYM

BEDROOM

FAMILY ROOM

BEDROOM

POLYGONAL ROOF LINE ABOVE

MASTER BEDROOM

BEDROOM

TERRACE

OPEN

BEDROOM

SECOND FLOOR PLAN

STONE WALK

DEN/GUEST ROOM

LILY POND

LAUNDRY

GENTLY CURVED INTERSECTING PLANES ARE USED TO DEFINE LIVING SPACES

KITCHEN

FOYER

DINING ROOM

GARDEN ROOM

STUDY

SKYLIGHT ABOVE LIVING ROOM

LIVING ROOM

OUTDOOR DINING PATIO

FIRST FLOOR PLAN

1993 PRIVATE RESIDENCE, GOLDEN BEACH, FLORIDA
CARLOS ZAPATA, ARCHITECT

Neomodern

California 1990

The Neomodern Style began as a kind of "architecture as art" movement with beach bungalows, studios, and small restaurants and shops in the West Side of Los Angeles. It is recognized worldwide as a more abstract, sculptural, heroic kind of modern architecture. Its roots are in the International Style, which rejects history (page 214), the Post Modern Style, which embraces history (page 208), and most recently in the Deconstructivist Movement (page 312). As one of the most published California architects, Mark Mack, has said, "For me, Modernism doesn't mean a negation of the past, it just means to live in our time, which always includes previous times and is a continuum."

The Neomodern Style celebrates fragmented, juxtaposed, angular forms, clad with a wide variety of usually raw materials, textures, and bright colors—much different from the finished white buildings of the earlier Modern movement (International Style). Glass prisms, slanted walls, odd shaped trapezoidal windows, and unusually fine detailing and craftsmanship are hallmarks. The style's most influential practitioners are Frank Gehry, Frank Israel,

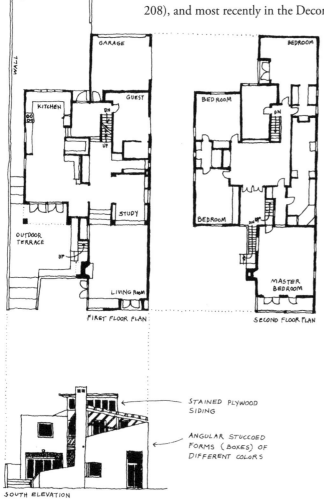

STAINED PLYWOOD SIDING

ANGULAR STUCCOED FORMS (BOXES) OF DIFFERENT COLORS

SOUTH ELEVATION

1990
SUMMERS RESIDENCE, SANTA MONICA, CALIFORNIA, MARK MACK, ARCHITECT

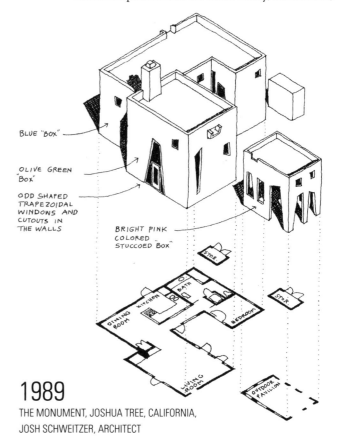

BLUE "BOX"

OLIVE GREEN "BOX"

ODD SHAPED TRAPEZOIDAL WINDOWS AND CUTOUTS IN THE WALLS

BRIGHT PINK COLORED STUCCOED BOX

1989
THE MONUMENT, JOSHUA TREE, CALIFORNIA, JOSH SCHWEITZER, ARCHITECT

and Eric Owen Moss of Los Angeles, architects who reject the conventional and sentimental ideas of house design. Their houses challenge the owners with a sense of disorder and uncertainty combined with the unusual and the unexpected.

Neomodernists like Frank Gehry are much more expressive and resilient with their planning and their forms than the earlier Modernists. As illustrated here, the architecture of the Schnabel Residence is a village of rooms, each with its own vastly different interior and exterior character.

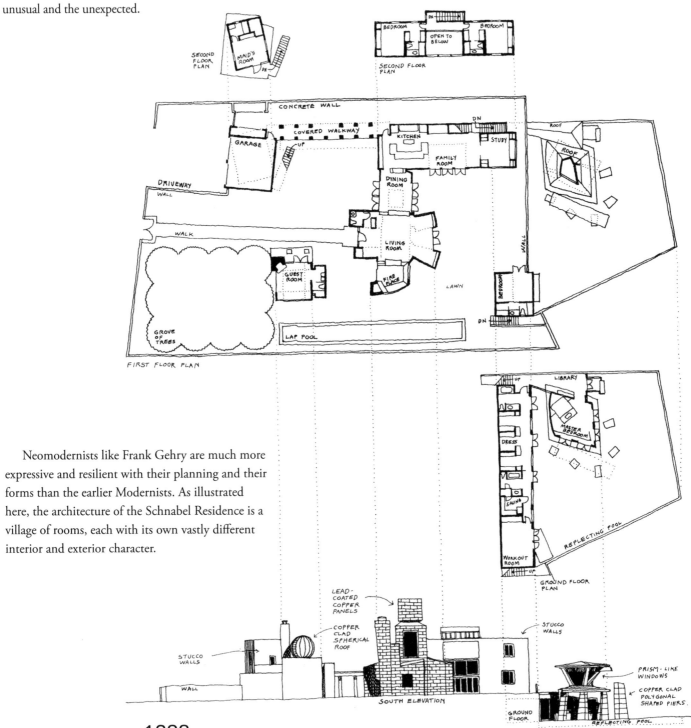

1988 SCHNABEL RESIDENCE, LOS ANGELES, CALIFORNIA, FRANK GEHRY, ARCHITECT

The two small Neomodern houses shown below illustrate a more traditional Modernist approach to the design of the house, but they both utilize vernacular industrial construction methods and materials, and they both are uniquely sculpted for the particular constraints of their sites.

The Studio House, built on a small urban lot with buildings on each side a few feet away, has mostly blank side walls and entries at each end. The corrugated metal used for the curved roof, a steel stair and handrail, a hanging industrial heater, the corner skylights, and the bright colored doors and windows are particular to the new Modernists' work.

The McDonald Residence is specially designed to take advantage of a seashore view while at the same time giving privacy and protection from Pacific northwest winds. The seemingly temporary framing of the carport, the irregular plan shape, the odd shaped windows, and the particle board floors are common traits of the Neomodern Style.

The Drager Residence, designed by Frank Israel and shown on the opposite page, is one of the most widely published and controversial houses in recent times. As Paul Goldberger of *The New York Times* has written. "It is not a spaceship or an explosion or a piece of sculpture. It is more like an essay on the continuing evolution of Modernism, a structure that gracefully melds the sensibility of early Modernism with that of today."

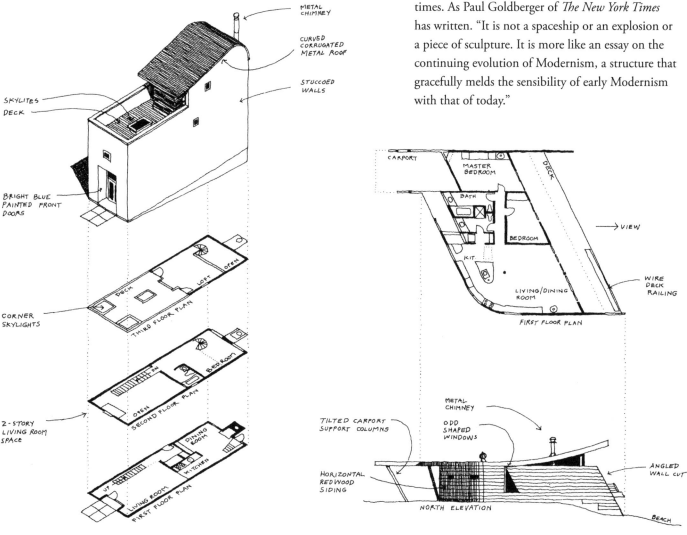

1990
STUDIO PROTOTYPE HOUSE, TORONTO, CANADA
STEVEN FONG, ARCHITECT

1989
McDONALD RESIDENCE, STINSON BEACH, CALIFORNIA
STANLEY SAITOWITZ, ARCHITECT

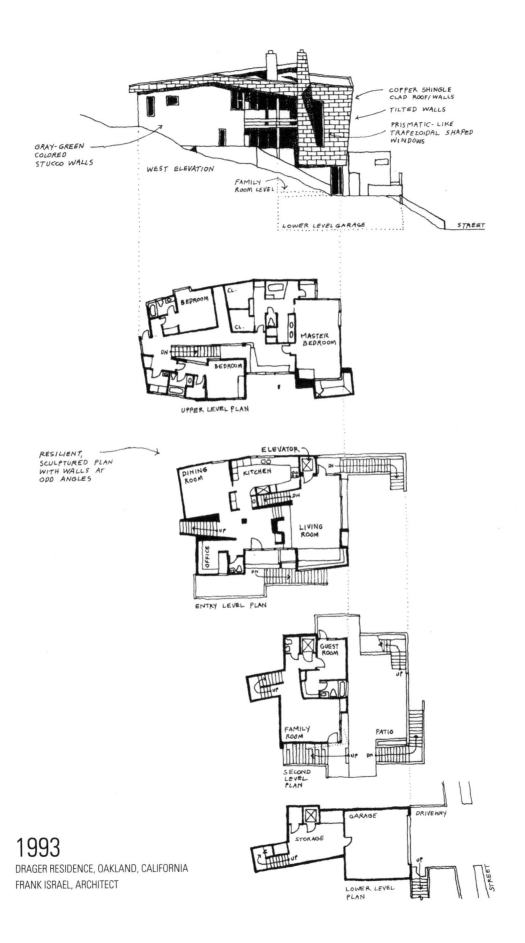

COPPER SHINGLE
CLAD ROOF/WALLS

TILTED WALLS

PRISMATIC-LIKE
TRAPEZOIDAL SHAPED
WINDOWS

GRAY-GREEN
COLORED
STUCCO WALLS

WEST ELEVATION

FAMILY
ROOM LEVEL

LOWER LEVEL GARAGE

STREET

BEDROOM

CL.

CL.

MASTER
BEDROOM

DN

BEDROOM

UPPER LEVEL PLAN

RESILIENT,
SCULPTURED PLAN
WITH WALLS AT
ODD ANGLES

ELEVATOR

DINING
ROOM

KITCHEN

DN

DN

OFFICE

UP

LIVING
ROOM

DN

ENTRY LEVEL PLAN

GUEST
ROOM

UP

UP

FAMILY
ROOM

PATIO

UP   DN

SECOND
LEVEL
PLAN

GARAGE

DRIVEWAY

STORAGE

UP

UP

LOWER LEVEL
PLAN

STREET

1993
DRAGER RESIDENCE, OAKLAND, CALIFORNIA
FRANK ISRAEL, ARCHITECT

Everyday and the Ordinary

Countrywide
1992

METAL FLUE

CORRUGATED ASPHALT ROOF

VERNACULAR COTTAGE DETAILING

BARN SILO SHAPE

CEDAR SHINGLE SIDING

WEST ELEVATION

ROOF

BEDROOM

DN

STUDY DN

O OPEN

ROOF

SECOND FLOOR PLAN

DECK

PORCH

BEDROOM

DINING ROOM

KITCHEN

ENTRY UP

DECK

UP

LIVING ROOM

FIRST FLOOR PLAN

1989
MR. AND MRS. EDWARD BENNETT, JR. RESIDENCE,
WASHINGTON ISLAND, WISCONSIN
FREDERICK PHILLIPS AND ASSOCIATES, ARCHITECTS

The Everyday and the Ordinary Style is an architecture that seeks to combine a range of familiar local vernacular—and, to some, often unheroic and unexciting-building types. Like the Post Modern Style (page 308) it is a reaction against the abstract formalism that dominates modern architecture.

VERMONT VERNAGULAR FARMHOUSE SHAPES

METAL FLUE

PAINTED CLAPBOARD SIDING

OPEN PORCH

SOUTH ELEVATION

CL. CL.

ROOF

DN

ROOF

BEDROOM

OPEN

ROOF

SECOND FLOOR PLAN

PORCH

ENTRY

DD

KITCHEN

DINING ROOM

BEDROOM

UP

LIVING ROOM

DECK

DN

PORCH

FIRST FLOOR PLAN

1991
DENNISON/PEEK HOUSE, MONKTON, VERMONT
TURNER BROOKS, ARCHITECT

320

Everyday and the Ordinary houses are designed by architects who appreciate the more common buildings they see, like Turner Brooks in Vermont or Fernau and Hartman in California, who are influenced by local farm outbuildings, or Steven Harris's references to Florida's motels, lifeguard towers, and boardwalk arcades.

The style is exciting not only because it reflects historical precedents but because a collection of ordinary building types, often with their qualities exaggerated, brightly colored, and detailed with ordinary materials, can be quite extraordinary.

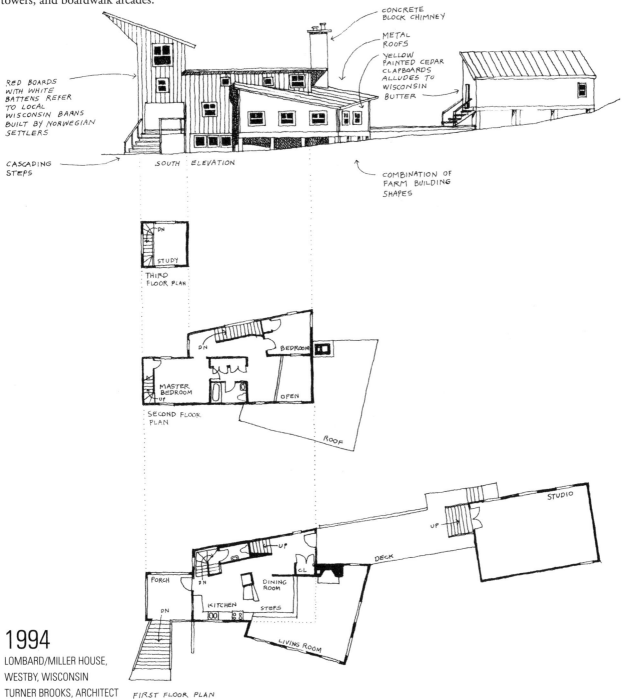

CONCRETE BLOCK CHIMNEY

METAL ROOFS

YELLOW PAINTED CEDAR CLAPBOARDS ALLUDES TO WISCONSIN BUTTER

RED BOARDS WITH WHITE BATTENS REFER TO LOCAL WISCONSIN BARNS BUILT BY NORWEGIAN SETTLERS

CASCADING STEPS

SOUTH ELEVATION

COMBINATION OF FARM BUILDING SHAPES

DN
STUDY
THIRD FLOOR PLAN

DN
BEDROOM
MASTER BEDROOM
UP
OPEN
SECOND FLOOR PLAN
ROOF

STUDIO
UP
DECK
PORCH
DN
UP
CL
DINING ROOM
KITCHEN
STEPS
DN
LIVING ROOM

1994
LOMBARD/MILLER HOUSE, WESTBY, WISCONSIN
TURNER BROOKS, ARCHITECT

FIRST FLOOR PLAN

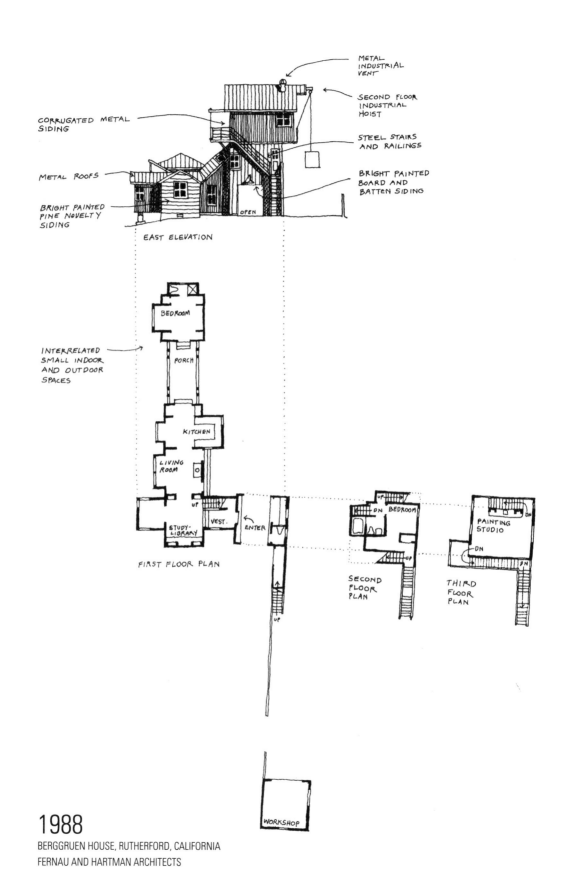

METAL
INDUSTRIAL
VENT

SECOND FLOOR
INDUSTRIAL
HOIST

CORRUGATED METAL
SIDING

STEEL STAIRS
AND RAILINGS

METAL ROOFS

BRIGHT PAINTED
BOARD AND
BATTEN SIDING

BRIGHT PAINTED
PINE NOVELTY
SIDING

OPEN

EAST ELEVATION

INTERRELATED
SMALL INDOOR
AND OUTDOOR
SPACES

BEDROOM

PORCH

KITCHEN

LIVING
ROOM

UP

STUDY-
LIBRARY

VEST.

ENTER

UP

FIRST FLOOR PLAN

UP

UP

DN

BEDROOM

PAINTING
STUDIO

DN

DN

SECOND
FLOOR
PLAN

UP

THIRD
FLOOR
PLAN

DN

WORKSHOP

1988

BERGGRUEN HOUSE, RUTHERFORD, CALIFORNIA
FERNAU AND HARTMAN ARCHITECTS

The Berggruen House, shown on the opposite page, and the Slesin/Steinberg House, shown below, are excellent examples of how architects, working in different parts of the country, can use their own local vernacular precedents to evoke a collection of small buildings in one large house. Both homes exhibit an innovative combination of simple, familiar shapes, inspired by modest local building types, strong colors, industrial materials, and exquisite interior detailing done in simple utilitarian fashion.

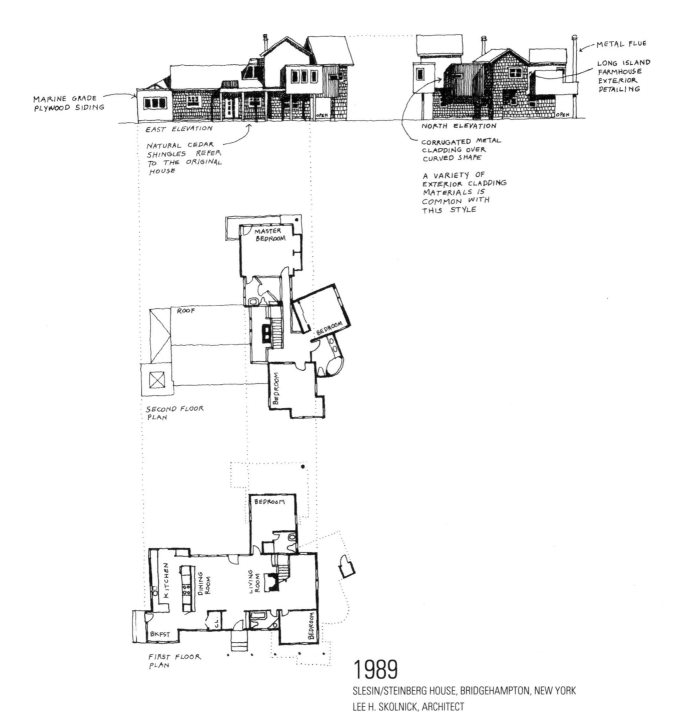

MARINE GRADE PLYWOOD SIDING

EAST ELEVATION

NATURAL CEDAR SHINGLES REFER TO THE ORIGINAL HOUSE

NORTH ELEVATION

METAL FLUE

LONG ISLAND FARMHOUSE EXTERIOR DETAILING

CORRUGATED METAL CLADDING OVER CURVED SHAPE

A VARIETY OF EXTERIOR CLADDING MATERIALS IS COMMON WITH THIS STYLE

MASTER BEDROOM

ROOF

BEDROOM

BEDROOM

SECOND FLOOR PLAN

BEDROOM

KITCHEN

DINING ROOM

LIVING ROOM

BEDROOM

BKFST

CL.

FIRST FLOOR PLAN

1989

SLESIN/STEINBERG HOUSE, BRIDGEHAMPTON, NEW YORK
LEE H. SKOLNICK, ARCHITECT

Steven Harris, a Florida native, has designed two wonderful houses, shown below and on the opposite page, that make a most fitting end point to this book. Done in the Everyday and the Ordinary Style, these buildings are eclectic collections of North Florida vernacular structures that exhibit a love for all architecture. They clearly illustrate how a combination of ordinary, everyday buildings like motels, watchtowers, garages, bungalows, pool sheds, and brightly-colored lifeguard stands can be configured into extraordinary homes.

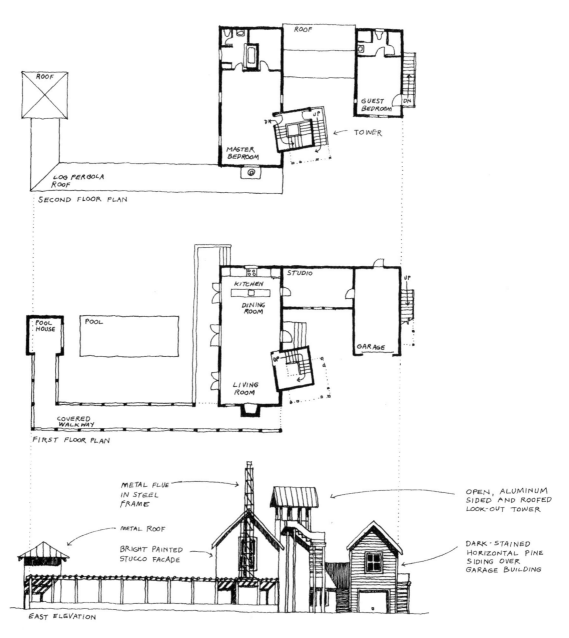

1987 KAUFMANN HOUSE, ATLANTIC BEACH, FLORIDA
STEVEN HARRIS, ARCHITECT

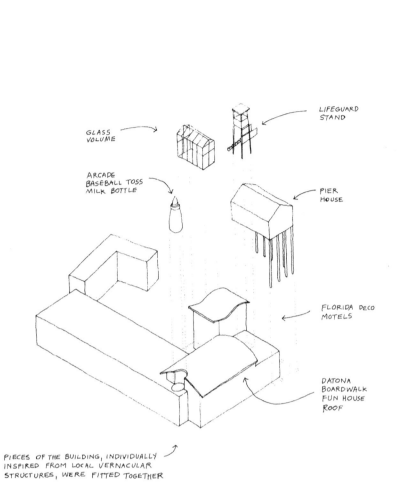

GLASS VOLUME

LIFEGUARD STAND

ARCADE BASEBALL TOSS MILK BOTTLE

PIER HOUSE

FLORIDA DECO MOTELS

DATONA BOARDWALK FUN HOUSE ROOF

PIECES OF THE BUILDING, INDIVIDUALLY INSPIRED FROM LOCAL VERNACULAR STRUCTURES, WERE FITTED TOGETHER

ROOF

GLASS ROOF

CLOSET

MASTER BEDROOM

OPEN

ROOF

PORCH

SECOND FLOOR PLAN

GARAGE

POOL HOUSE

POOL

BEDROOM

BEDROOM

ENTRY

KITCHEN

LIVING ROOM

DINING ROOM

FIRST FLOOR PLAN

RED PAINTED STEEL LOOK-OUT TOWER

THIRD FLOOR METAL CLAD GUEST ROOM

PINK STUCCO CHIMNEY

METAL ROOF

YELLOW STUCCO WALL

ACQUA STUCCO WALL

EAST ELEVATION

1991 ROOT GUEST HOUSE, ORMOND BEACH, FLORIDA
STEVEN HARRIS, ARCHITECT

Space

A 1975 report entitled *Space Settlements* by the National Aeronautics and Space Administration and the American Society for Engineering Education has made it possible to construct a convincing picture of how humans might permanently sustain life in space on a large scale.

The settlement described in the report is a space colony where 10,000 people work, raise families, and live out normal human lives. The wheel-like structure in which they live orbits the earth in the same orbit as the moon, at a point in space called L5, and is made from a 427-foot diameter tube bent into a wheel; it is more than one mile in diameter. People live inside the ring-shaped tube, which is connected by large access routes (spokes) to a central hub where incoming spacecraft dock. These spokes provide entry and exit to the living and agriculture areas in the tubular region. The entire habitat rotates at one revolution per minute to simulate the earth's gravity and is heated and lit with natural sunshine.

Materials for the colony would, of course, come from earth (except for some raw materials found on the moon) and would be transported by space shuttle vehicles to L5 where it would take about thirty years to build a complete colony. The houses

2000
A SIMPLIFIED VIEW OF HOW HOUSES MIGHT BE BUILT IN SPACE

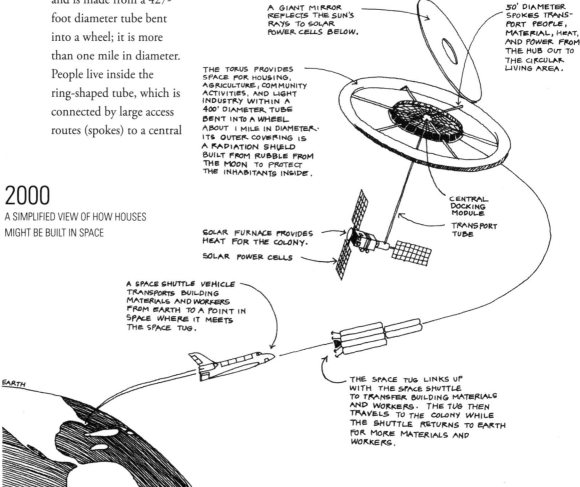

A GIANT MIRROR REFLECTS THE SUN'S RAYS TO SOLAR POWER CELLS BELOW.

50' DIAMETER SPOKES TRANSPORT PEOPLE, MATERIAL, HEAT, AND POWER FROM THE HUB OUT TO THE CIRCULAR LIVING AREA.

THE TORUS PROVIDES SPACE FOR HOUSING, AGRICULTURE, COMMUNITY ACTIVITIES, AND LIGHT INDUSTRY WITHIN A 400' DIAMETER TUBE BENT INTO A WHEEL ABOUT 1 MILE IN DIAMETER. ITS OUTER COVERING IS A RADIATION SHIELD BUILT FROM RUBBLE FROM THE MOON TO PROTECT THE INHABITANTS INSIDE.

CENTRAL DOCKING MODULE

TRANSPORT TUBE

SOLAR FURNACE PROVIDES HEAT FOR THE COLONY.

SOLAR POWER CELLS

A SPACE SHUTTLE VEHICLE TRANSPORTS BUILDING MATERIALS AND WORKERS FROM EARTH TO A POINT IN SPACE WHERE IT MEETS THE SPACE TUG.

EARTH

THE SPACE TUG LINKS UP WITH THE SPACE SHUTTLE TO TRANSFER BUILDING MATERIALS AND WORKERS. THE TUG THEN TRAVELS TO THE COLONY WHILE THE SHUTTLE RETURNS TO EARTH FOR MORE MATERIALS AND WORKERS.

shown here would be made with large prefabricated lightweight (primarily aluminum) materials very similar to those shown on page 240 developed by the American prefabricated housing industry. It is presumed that industry would assume the responsibility for prebuilding the house parts on earth for shipment to the colony.

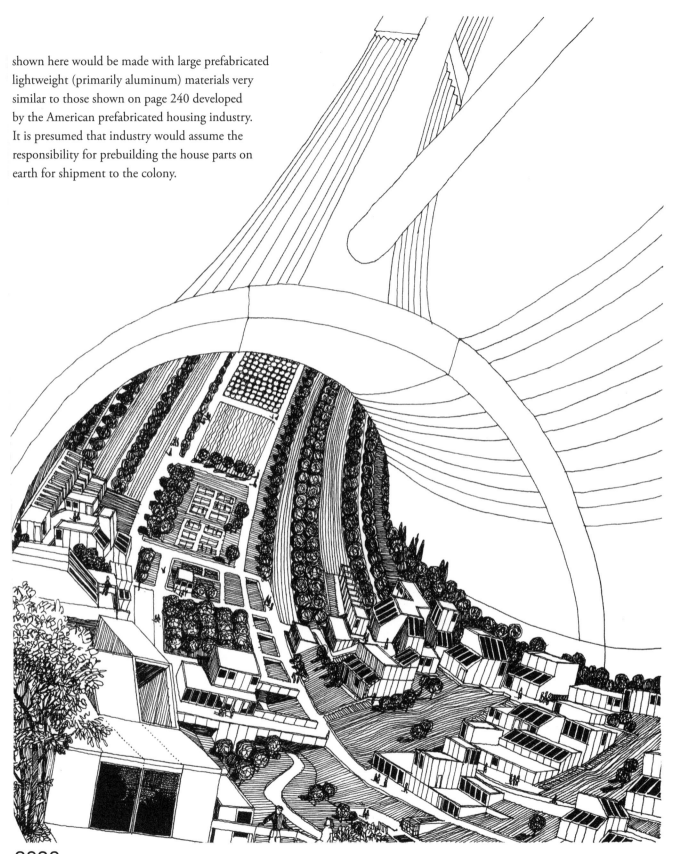

2030 A CONCEPTUAL VIEW OF THE INSIDE OF THE SETTLEMENT, NATIONAL SPACE AND AERONAUTICS ADMINISTRATION

GLOSSARY

ADOBE Clay bricks dried in the sun used as a building material for walls in warm dry climates.

AGGREGATE A material, usually sand or gravel, that is mixed with water and cement to make concrete.

APPLIQUE Ornament, usually carved wood, fastened to a surface of a building.

ARCADE A passageway with a roof supported by arched columns.

ARCH A curved structure made of wedge-shaped stones or bricks, spanning an opening and capable of bearing the weight of the material above it.

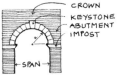

ROUNDED ARCH

TUDOR ARCH

POINTED (GOTHIC) ARCH

OGEE ARCH

ASBESTOS SHINGLES Thin, synthetic, fireproof, waterproof, factory-made material used as exterior siding on buildings.

ASHLAR Hewn, square edged, even-faced stone laid in horizontal courses with vertical joints when constructing walls.

ATRIUM A hall or court located in the heart or central portion of a building.

BALLOON FRAME A method of timber-frame construction popular in America during the nineteenth and early part of the twentieth centuries. See page 122.

BALUSTRADE A handrail supported by short posts or pillars (balusters).

BARGEBOARD Projecting boards placed against the slope of the roof gable of a building; often decorated.

BAROQUE The architectural style of the seventeenth and eighteenth centuries characterized by exuberant decoration, curvaceous forms, and spatially complex compositions.

BAR JOISTS Horizontal structural members, laid parallel to each other to support a floor or roof; made from thin welded steel rods (bars).

BATTEN A strip of wood attached (usually nailed) over the adjoining edge of parallel vertical boards on the surface of a wall or door.

BATTERED A wall that is slanted gradually backward from its base.

BATTLEMENT A notched wall at the top of a medieval styled building originally for the purpose of fortification.

BAUHAUS An art school founded in 1919 in Weimar, Germany, by Walter Gropius. Artists, craftsmen, and architects worked together striving for direct functional forms for the building of the future.

BOARD AND BATTEN A method of siding a building with parallel vertical boards whose seams are weatherproofed with a thin vertical strip of wood (batten). See page 125.

BRACKET A small flat piece of wood or stone projecting from a wall as a support for a shelf, balcony, or roof. See page 128.

BREEZEWAY A roofed passage open at the sides between separate buildings, such as a house and a garage.

BROKEN PEDIMENT

A pediment in which one or both cornices are not continuous.

TOP CORNICE
PEDIMENT
BOTTOM CORNI

BROKEN PEDIMENT
(TOP CORNICE BROKEN)
OFTEN USED OVER DOORWAYS

CANTILEVER

A projecting beam that is supported at one end only. It usually supports a structure, like a balcony, where supports cannot be placed or are not desired.

BROKEN PEDIMENT
(BOTTOM CORNICE BROKEN)
OFTEN USED ON THE GABLE EN
OF GREEK REVIVAL HOUSES

CAPITAL The top part of a column, usually decorated, and larger than the shaft of the column. See page 106.

CLADDING The process of overlaying a finish material over an unfinished wall or roof surface.

CLAPBOARD (pronounced "kla'berd") A thin board that when laid horizontally and overlapped, creates a weathertight outer wall surface on a wooden building.

CLASSICAL Having to do with the style of the ancient Greek or Roman periods.

COLONNADE A series of columns set the same distance apart usually supporting a roof.

distance apart usually supporting a roof.

COLUMN   A slender, upright post consisting of a nearly cylindrical shaft, with a base and capital used as a support or ornament in building.

COPING   The top layer of a brick or stone wall usually built with a slight slope to shed water.

CORNICE   An ornamental molding that projects along the top of a wall, pillar, or side of a building, often a decorative development of the eave of a roof.

CRENELATION   A pattern of square indentations, often called battlements.

CRESTING   An ornamental finish, usually of wood or metal, at the top of a building, such as the ridge of a roof or the top of a wall.

CUPOLA   A small tower on a roof of a building with louvered and/or windowed sides to let air and/or light into the building.

DENTILS   Small projecting blocks or "teeth" used in rows in classical cornices as ornament. See page 000.

GABLED DORMER WHOLLY IN ROOF SPACE

2 GABLED DORMER WINDOW ABOVE EAVES

3 GABLED DORMER WINDOW BELOW EAVES

4 SHED DORMER

5 HIPPED DORMER

6 PEDIMENTED DORMER

7 EYEBROW DORMER

8 JACOBEAN STYLE DORMER

DORMER   An upright window that projects from a sloping roof.

EARTH BERM   An artificially created mound of soil or earth.

EAVES   The lower edge of a roof that projects beyond the wall underneath.

ELEVATION   Any of the sides of a building. The east elevation of a building faces east. The south elevation faces south, and so forth.

ENTABLATURE   The part of a building resting on the top of columns. The classical entablature consists of an architrave, frieze, and cornice. See page 106.

FACADE   The front, or chief elevation, of a building.

FACTORY SASH   A steel window frame used to hold panes in place commonly used in factories.

FANLIGHT   A fan-shaped transom or window over a door.

FASCIA BOARD   A plain horizontal band of trimwork along the eaves of a roof.

FINIAL   An ornament at the crest of a roof, or top of a tower or canopy.

FLASHING   Pieces of sheet metal, such as copper or aluminum, used around windows and chimneys or roof joints to make them waterproof.

FlUE   An enclosed passage for conveying smoke, hot air, or other exhaust outside a building. A chimney often has several flues.

FRAME   The support, usually made of parts joined together, over which other materials are attached to create a building.

FROND   The divided leaf of a fern, palm, or cycad.

FROST LINE   The maximum depth to which winter frost penetrates the ground in a given locality.

GABLE   The triangular portion of the end wall of a building under a ridge roof.

GALERIE   A long, narrow, platform or open passage projecting from a wall of a building.

GALVANIZED SHEET METAL   A steel roofing material covered with a thin coating of zinc, which resists rust.

GEODESIC   Having to do with a system of mathematics used to study curves, such as the curvature of the earth or dome structures.

GINGERBREAD   Ornate wood decoration used in Victorian style buildings.

GIRT   A horizontal supporting beam.

GLAZED BRICK   Brick that has been coated with a glossy coating on one surface to alter the other.

HALF-TIMBER   A type of construction in which spaces formed by a timber frame are filled in with stone, bricks, or wattle and daub, the frame left exposed.

HEADER   A beam forming part of a framework around an opening of a floor, roof, window, or door. See page 260.

ICOSAHSDRON   A solid having twenty faces of an equilateral triangular shape. See page 275.

INDIGENOUS   Originating in the region or country where found; native.

JAMB   The upright piece forming the side of a doorway or window frame.

JOIST   Intermediate parallel beams that support a floor or ceiling.

LAMINATED WOOD BEAM   A thick beam made by gluing together layer on layer of thin wood planks.

LATH   One of the thin, narrow wood strips placed over the frame of a wall, ceiling, or roof to support plaster.

LEAN-TO   A supplementary structure added to a building usually covered by a roof with a single slope.

LIGHTWEIGHT CONCRETE   Concrete that uses lightweight aggregates, generally produced by artificial means, to create a material having many of the properties of concrete but is appreciably lighter in weight.

LINTEL   A horizontal beam of stone above a door or window to support the structure above it.

LOGGIA   A gallery or arcade open to the air on at least one side.

MASONRY   Construction using stone or brick with mortar.

MODULE   A prefabricated, standardized, interchangeable piece or part of a dwelling unit. See page 280.

MULLION   A vertical bar between the panes of a window.

NICHE   A recess or hollow in a wall, usually for a statue or vase.

ORDER   Anyone of several styles of columns and architecture having differences in proportion and decoration.

OUTSHOT   A projection of, or an addition to, a building.

OVERHEAD DOOR   A term used to describe a garage door that stores horizontally along the ceiling when in the open position.

PALISADE   A fence of stakes set firmly into the ground to enclose or defend.

PARAPET   A low wall placed to protect any spot where there is a sudden drop, for example, at the edge of a balcony or house top.

PEDIMENT   A low triangular part, framed by horizontal and sloping cornices, usually found at the two gable ends of a Greek temple between the frieze and the roof. See page 106.

PENDANT   An ornament hanging down from an arch, ceiling, or roof.

PENT ROOF   A narrow roof sloping in one direction only.

PIAZZA   A large porch along one or more sides of a house.

PIER   A vertical support of masonry.

PILASTER   A flat vertical support usually used as decoration.

PINNACLE   An ornamental slender turret or spire at the top of a pyramidal or conical shaped roof.

PITCH   The angle or steepness of a roof.

PIT SAWN   Wood that has been cut into boards with a large, two-man saw, one of the men working in a pit. See page 41.

PLATFORM FRAME CONSTRUCTION   A system of framing a building where the floor joists of each story rest on the walls of the story below. See page 260.

PLINTH   The lower, square part of the base of a column.

POLYCHROMY   The art of decorating in several colors.

POLYGONAL   Having more than three angles and three sides.

PORTICO   An entrance porch, usually with columns and a roof.

POST AND BEAM CONSTRUCTION   A system of framing where heavy timber posts and beams are used. See page 234.

PURLIN   Horizontal roof beams used to support roof rafters between the roof ridge and the eave.

QUOIN   A rectangle of stone, wood, or brick used in vertical series to decorate corners of buildings.

RAFTER   One of a series of parallel sloping roof members designed to support the roof. The rafters of a flat roof are often called joists.

RETAINING WALL   Any wall subjected to lateral pressure such as a bank of earth.

RIDGE POLE   The horizontal timber along the top of a roof.

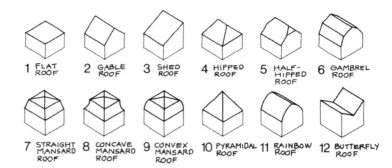

1 FLAT ROOF 2 GABLE ROOF 3 SHED ROOF 4 HIPPED ROOF 5 HALF-HIPPED ROOF 6 GAMBREL ROOF 7 STRAIGHT MANSARD ROOF 8 CONCAVE MANSARD ROOF 9 CONVEX MANSARD ROOF 10 PYRAMIDAL ROOF 11 RAINBOW ROOF 12 BUTTERFLY ROOF

RIGID INSULATION   Stiff, one-inch to three-inch thick panels, when attached to a wall, roof, or floor of a building serve to insulate.

ROOF   The top covering of a building.

ROOF DECKING   The covering material that is attached to the roof rafters to receive the finish, weatherproof roofing material.

ROOF RIDGE   The horizontal line at the junction of the top edges of two roof surfaces.

SASH   The framework that holds the glass in a window.

SEGMENTED ARCH   An arch having the profile of a circular arc substantially less than a full semicircle.

SHEATHING   The first covering of boards or plywood on a house, nailed to the roof and walls of the frame.

SHELL STRUCTURE   A thin, self-supporting membrane structure on the eggshell principle, usually constructed with lightweight concrete.

SHINGLE   A thin piece of wood or other material, used to cover the roof and walls of a house. Shingles are laid in overlapping rows with the thicker ends showing. See page 161.

SILL PLATE   The lowest member of the frame of a structure, resting on the foundation and supporting the uprights of the frame.

SILO   A cylindrical, airtight tower of wood or metal in which green fodder for livestock is preserved and stored.

SOD   A piece or layer of ground covered with grass and its roots.

STEPPED GABLE   The gable end of a building that is constructed with a series of steps along the roof slope but independent of it. See page 56.

STOOP   A porch or platform at the entrance of a house.

STUCCO   Plaster finish for exterior walls.

STUD   One of a series of vertical wood or metal structural members in wall frames.

STYROFOAM   A polystyrene (plastic) foam that is used as lightweight rigid insulation.

TAR PAPER   Heavy paper covered or impregnated with tar, used especially for waterproofing and windproofing buildings.

TENSION RING   A circular device that controls the pull or strain of a circular roof structure.

THATCH   Straw, rushes, palm leaves, or the like woven into a roof covering.

THERMAL   Of or having to do with heat; determined, measured, or operated by heat.

THERMOSTAT   An automatic device for regulating temperature.

THERMOSIPHON   A siphon attachment by which the circulation in a system of hot-water pipes is increased or induced.

TIE BEAM   A horizontal timber beam so situated that it ties the principal rafters of a roof together and prevents them from thrusting out of line.

TOP PLATE   A horizontal member placed on the top of a framed wall to carry the roof rafters of the frame.

TOTEM POLE   A pole carved and painted with representations of totems, erected by the Indians of the Northwestern American coast.

TRACERY   A pattern of intersecting bars or a plate with leaflike decoration in the upper part of a Gothic window.

TRANSOM   A series of panes or lights above a door.

TRELLIS   A frame of light strips of wood or metal crossing one another with open spaces in between with the purpose of supporting growing vines.

TROMBE WALL   A massive masonry wall, usually painted black, used to absorb and store the sun's heat in energy conscious houses.

TRUSS   A structural unit consisting of members usually arranged to form triangles to provide rigid support over wide spans with a minimum amount of material.

TURRET   A small tower often on the corner of a building and projecting above it.

VERANDA   A large porch along one or more sides of

a house.

VERNACULAR Native or peculiar to a certain country or locality.

VERTICES The points opposite to and furthest from the base of a triangle, pyramid, or other figure having a base.

VESTIBULE A passage, hall, or chamber immediately between the outer door and the inside of a building.

VIGA A beam that supports the roof in Indian and Spanish type dwellings.

WATTLE AND DAUB A building material that is a mixture of mud, stones, and sticks.

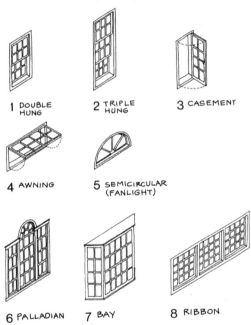

1 DOUBLE HUNG   2 TRIPLE HUNG   3 CASEMENT

4 AWNING   5 SEMICIRCULAR (FANLIGHT)

6 PALLADIAN   7 BAY   8 RIBBON

WINDOW An opening in a wall or roof to let in light or air usually enclosed by a frame that holds a movable sash or sashes fitted with panes of glass.

WROUGHT IRON A tough, durable form of iron with little carbon in it, that is malleable and soft enough to be forged and welded easily.

BIBLIOGRAPHY

American Builder, *Most Popular Homes in America*, Vol. 2 (Chicago: American Builder Publications, 1927)

American Institute of Architects, *A Guide to New Orleans Architecture* (Washington, D.C.: American Institute of Architects, 1959)

Architectural Record, Mid-May issues 1950 through 1996 (New York: Architectural Record)

Bailey, Rosalie F., *Pre-Revolutionary Dutch Houses and Families in Northern New Jersey and Southern New York* (New York: Dover Publications, 1968)

Blake, Peter, *Marcel Breuer* (New York: Dodd, Mead, and Co., 1949)

Blaser, Werner, *Mies van der Rohe* (New York: Praeger, 1965)

Blumenson, John J.G., *Identifying American Architecture* (Nashville, Tennessee: American Association for State and Local History, 1977)

Brooks, H. Allen, *The Prairie School* (Toronto: University of Toronto Press, 1972)

Brooks, H. Allen, *Prairie School Architecture* (Toronto: University of Toronto Press, 1975)

Cherner, Norman, *Fabricating Houses from Component Parts* (New York: Reinhold, 1957)

Collins, George R., *Antonio Gaudi* (New York: George Braziller, 1960)

Conrads, Ulrick, *The Architecture of Fantasy* (New York: Praeger, 1962)

Davidson, Marshall B., *Notable American Houses* (New York: American Heritage, 1971)

Foley, Mary Mix, *The American House* (New York: Harper and Row, 1980)

Forman, Henry Chandlee, *Tidewater Maryland Architecture and Gardens* (New York: Architectural Book Publishing Co., 1956)

Forman, Henry Chandlee, *The Architecture of the Old South* (New York: Russell and Russell, 1948)

Fracchia, Charles, *Converted into Houses* (New York: Viking, 1976)

Frary, I.T., *Thomas Jefferson: Architect and Builder* (Richmond, Virginia: Garrett and Massey, 1931)

Fuller, R. Buckminster, and Robert Marks, *The Dymaxion World of Buckminster Fuller* (Garden City, New York: Anchor Books, 1973)

Gabor, Mark, *House Boats* (New York: Ballantine Books, 1979)

Gebhard, David, *Schindler* (New York: Viking, 1971)

Gebhard, David, and Harriette Von Breton, *Architecture in California* (Santa Barbara: University of California Regents, 1968)

Greif, Martin, *Depression Modern* (New York: Universe Books, 1975)

Grow, Lawrence, *Old House Plans* (New York: Universe Books, 1978)

Guiness, Desmond, and Julius Trousdale Sadler, Jr., *Mr. Jefferson, Architect* (New York: Viking, 1973)

Hammett, Ralph W., *Architecture in the United States* (New York: John Wiley, 1976)

Harrison, Henry S., *Houses* (Chicago: National Institute of Real Estate Brokers, 1973)

Henderson, Andrew, *The Family House in England* (London, England: Phoenix House, 1964)

Herzog, Thomas, *Pneumatic Structures* (New York: Oxford University Press, 1976)

Historic Savannah Foundation, Inc., *Historic Savannah* (Savannah, Georgia: Historic Savannah Foundation, Inc., 1968)

Hitchcock, Henry Russell, Jr., *Built in USA: Post-War Architecture* (New York: Museum of Modern Art, 1968)

Holling, Holling C., *The Book of Indians* (New York: Platt and Munk, 1966)

Ison, Walter, and Leonora Ison, *English Architecture through the Ages* (New York: Coward-McCann, 1966)

Jencks, Charles, *Post Modern Architecture* (New York: Rizzoli,1977)

Junior League of Kingston, N.Y., Inc., *Early Architecture in Ulster County* (Kingston, New York: Junior League of Kingston, N.Y., Inc., 1974)

Karp, Ben, *Wood Motifs in American Domestic Architecture* (Cranbury, New Jersey: A.S. Barnes, 1966)

Kauffman, Henry J., *The American Farmhouse* (New York: Hawthorn Books, 1975)

Kelly, Burnham, *The Prefabrication of Houses* (New York: John Wiley, 1951)

Kelley, J. Frederick, *The Early Domestic Architecture of Connecticut* (New York: Dover, 1963)

Kimball, Fiske, *Domestic Architecture of the American Colonies and Early Republic* (New York: Dover, 1927)

Kinney, Jean, *47 Creative Homes* (Scranton, Pennsylvania: Funk and Wagnalls, 1974)

Kirker, Harold, *California's Architectural Frontier* (San Marino, California: The Hintington Library, 1960)

LaFarge, Oliver, *The American Indian (*New York: Golden Press, 1962)

Lancaster, Clay, *The Architecture of Historic Nantucket* (New York: McGraw-Hill, 1972)

Lancaster, Clay, *Architectural Follies in America* (Rutland, Vermont: Charles Tuttle, 1960)

Lancaster, Clay, *Ante Bellum Houses of the Bluegrass* (Lexington: University of Kentucky Press, 1961)

Laubin, Gladys, and Reginald Laubin, *The Indian Tipi* (Norman, Oklahoma: University of Oklahoma Press, 1957)

Lidz, Jane, *Rolling Homes* (New York: A and W Visual Library, 1979)

Loth, Calder, and Julius Trousdale Sadler, Jr., *The Only Proper Style* (New York: New York Graphic Society, 1975)

Los Angeles County Museum of Art, *Architecture in Southern California* (Los Angeles: Los Angeles County Museum of Art, 1968)

Maass, John, *The Gingerbread Age* (New York: Reinhart, 1957)

Maass, John, *The Victorian Home in America* (New York: Hawthorn Books, 1972)

Makinson, Randell L., *Greene and Greene* (Santa Barbara, California: Peregine Smith, 1977)

Malo, John W., *The Complete Guide to Houseboating* (New York: MacMillan, 1974)

McArdle, Alma deC., and Deirdre Bartlett, *Carpenter Gothic* (New York: Whitney Library of Design, 1978)

McCall, Wayne, Herb Andree, and Noel Young, *Santa Barbara Architecture* (Santa Barbara, California: Capra Press, 1975)

McCoy, Esther, *Richard Nuetra* (New York: George Braziller, 1960)

McCoy, Esther, *Craig Ellwood* (New York: Walker and Co., 1968)

McCoy, Esther, *Five California Architects* (New York: Reinhold, 1960)

McCoy, Esther, *Modern California Architects* (New York: Reinhold, 1958)

McDole, Brad, and Chris Jerome, *Kit Houses by Mail* (New York: Grosset and Dunlap, 1979)

Merrill, Anthony F., *The Rammed Earth House* (New York: Harper and Row, 1947)

Moore, Charles, Gerald Allen, and Donlyn Lyndon, *The Place of Houses* (New York: Holt, Rinehart, Winston, 1974)

Moore, Charles, and Gerald Allen, *Dimensions* (New York: Architectural Record Books, 1976)

Morrison, Hugh, *Early American Architecture* (New York: Oxford University Press, 1952)

Mother Earth News, *The, Monthly Publication* (Hendersonville, North Carolina: Mother Earth News)

Museum of Modern Art, *Five Architects* (New York: Wittenborn, 1972)

Museum of Modern Art, *Modern Architecture International Exhibition* (New York: Arno Press, 1969)

National Aeronautics and Space Administration, *Space Settlements* (Washington, D.C.: National Aeronautics and Space Administration, 1976)

Nebraska State Historical Society. *The Sod House*, Educational Leaflet No.3 (Lincoln, Nebraska: Nebraska State Historical Society, 1967)

New York Times, Special Magazine Section (New York: New York Times, March 12, 1995)

Nulsen, Robert H., *Mobile Home Manual*, Volume One (Beverly Hills, California: Trail-R-Club of America, 1967)

Old House Journal, The, Monthly Publication (Brooklyn, New York: Old House Journal)

Pacific Domes, *Domebook One* (Los Gatos, California: Pacific Domes, 1970)

Pacific Domes, *Domebook Two* (Los Gatos, California: Pacific Domes, 1972)

Papadakis, Andreas, Catherine Cook, and Andrew Benjamin, *Deconstruction* (New York: Rizzoli, 1989)

Pawley, Martin, *Garbage Housing* (New York: 1975)

Pevsner, Nikolaus, John Fleming, and Hugh Honour, *A Dictionary of Architecture* (Woodstock, New York: Overlook Press, 1976)

Pickering, Ernest, *The Homes of America* (New York: Reinhart, 1954)

Pillsbury, Richard, *A Field Guide to the Folk Architecture of the North East United States* (Hanover, New Hampshire: Geography Publications, Dartmouth University, 1970)

Poblet, Josep M., *Gaudi* (Barcelona: Bruguera, 1973)

POINT, *Co Evolution Quarterly* (Sausalito, California: POINT)

Poppeliers, John, and S. Allen Chambers, *What Style Is It?* (Washington, D.C.: The Preservation Press of the National Trust for Historic Preservation, 1977)

Price, Cedric, *Air Structures* (London, England.: Directorate General of Research and Development, Department of the Environment, 1971)

Rabb, Bernard, and Judith Rabb, *Good Shelter* (New York: Quadrangle, 1975)

Randall, Anne, and Robert Foley, *Newport* (Newport, Rhode Island: Catboat Press, 1970)

Reiff, Daniel D., *Architecture in Fredonia* (Fredonia, New York: Rockefeller Arts Center Gallery, State University of New York, 1972)

Reynolds, Helen Wilkinson, *Dutch Houses in the Hudson Valley before 1776* (New York: Dover Publications, 1965)

Richman, Irwin, *Pennsylvania Architecture* (University Park, Pennsylvania: Pennsylvania Historical Association, 1969)

Robinson, E.F., and T.P. Robinson, *Houses in America* (New York: Viking, 1966)

Sandbank, Harold, and Alfred Bruce, *A History of Prefabrication* (New York: Arno Press, 1972)

Sanford, Trent Elwood, *The Architecture of the Southwest* (New York: Norton, Inc., 1950)

Saylor, Henry, *Bungalows* (Philadelphia, Pennsylvania: John C. Winston, 1911)

Schmidt, Carl F., *The Octagon Fad* (Scottsville, New York: Carl F. Schmidt, 1958)

Scully, Vincent, *The Shingle Style* (New Haven, Connecticut: Yale University Press, 1971)

Scully, Vincent, *The Shingle Style Today* (New York: George Braziller, 1974)

Scully, Vincent, *Modern Architecture* (New York: George Braziller, 1961)

Shelter Publications, *Shelter One* (Bolinas, California: Shelter Publications, 1973)

Shelter Publications, *Shelter Two* (Bolinas California: Shelter Publications, 1978)

Shurtleff, Harold R., *The Log Cabin Myth* (Cambridge, Massachusetts: Harvard University Press, 1939)

Smith, C. Ray, *Supermannerism* (New York: Dutton, 1977)

Stedman, Wilfred, and Myrtle Stedman, *Adobe Architecture* (Santa Fe, New Mexico: Sunstone Press, 1973)

Stoehr, C. Eric, *Bonanza Victorian* (Albuquerque: University of New Mexico Press, 1975)

Strand, Janann, *A Greene and Greene Guide* (Pasadena, California: Castle Press, 1974)

Sunset Magazine, *Western Ranch Houses* (San Francisco, California: Lane Publishing Company, 1946)

Twombly, Robert C., *Frank Lloyd Wright* (New York: John Wiley, 1968)

University of Minnesota Underground Space Center, *Earth Sheltered Housing Design* (Minneapolis, Minnesota: University of Minnesota Underground Space Center, 1978)

United States Department of Housing and Urban Development, *The First Passive Solar Home Awards* (Washington, D.C.: United States Department of Housing and Urban Development, 1979)

United States Department of Housing and Urban Development, Office of Policy Development and Research, *Solar Dwelling Design Concepts* (Washington, D.C.: United States Department of Housing and Urban Development, 1976)

United States Department of Housing and Urban Development, *Handbook for Building Homes of Earth* (Washington, D.C.: United States Department of Housing and Urban Development, 1979)

United States Federal Housing Administration, *FHA Pole House Construction* (Washington, D.C.: United States Department of Housing and Urban Development, 1969)

Wagner, Walter, *Great Houses* (New York: McGraw·Hill, 1976)

Wagner, Willis H. *Modern Carpentry* (South Holland, Illinois: Goodheart Wilcox Co., 1969)

Wampler, Jan, *All Their Own* (New York: John Wiley, 1977)

Watson, Donald, *Designing and Building a Solar House* (Charlotte, Vermont: Garden Way Publishing Co., 1977)

Welsch, Roger, *The Nebraska Soddy* Nebraska History, Volume 48, Number 4 (Lincoln, Nebraska: Nebraska Historical Society, 1967)

Whiffen, Marcus, *American Architecture Since 1780* (Boston, Massachusetts: M.I.T. Press, 1969)

Woodall, Ronald, and T.H. Watkins, *Taken by the Wind* (New York: New York Graphic Society, 1977)

Wrenn, Tony, and Elizabeth D. Mulloy, *America's Forgotten Architecture* (New York: Pantheon, 1976)

Wright, Frank Lloyd, *The Robie House* (Palos Park, Illinois: Prairie School Press, 1968)

Yale University Architectural Journal, *Perspecta 7, 10, 11, and 12* (New Haven, Connecticut: Yale University Architectural Journal, 1961·1968)

INDEX TO ARCHITECTS

Aalto, Alvar, 215
Allen, Gerald, 63,192, 288
Ant Farm, 273, 300
Architects Collaborative, The, 215

Barnes, Edward L., 293
Barry, Charles, 142
Beman, Solon Spencer, 169
Bernard, John, 306
Betts, Hobart D., 290
Breuer, Marcel, 215–216, 250
Brittelle, W. Miles, 197
Brooks, Turner, 320, 321
Brown, A. Page, 172
Brown, Denise Scott, 200, 311
Bulfinch, Charles, 102

Campbell and Wong, 224, 225
Carmody and Ellison, 306
Catalano, Eduardo, 250
Chrysalis, 300
Clayton, Nicholas J, 169
Coates, Roland Jr., 270
Coxhead, Ernest, 190,192

Da Cortona, Domenico, 168
Dabney, William H. Jr, 160
Dalrymple, Richard, 314
Davis, Alexander Jackson, 114, 120, 121, 125–126, 132
Davis, Pierpont, 210
Dietrich, E.G.W, 164
Dorn, R.H, 146
Downing, Andrew Jackson, 120, 123–126, 132, 133, 134, 144
Drummond, Walter, 194
Drummond, William, 195

Eames, Charles, 248, 249
Eastlake, Charles L., 154
Eisenman, Peter, 296
Ellwood, Craig, 238, 247
Elmslie, George C, 194–195
Emerson, Ralph, 165
Englebrecht, R. M., 280
Esherick, Homsey, and Dodge, 192
Esherick, Joseph, 192, 193

Fernau and Hartman, 321, 322
Fong, Stephen, 318
Fowler, Orson Squire, 138
Franzen, Ulrich, 250, 251
Fuller, R. Buckminster, 240, 242, 274–275
Furness, Frank, 149

Gaudi, Antonio, 272
Gehry, Frank, 313–314, 316–317
Gill, Irving, 173, 215
Goff, Bruce, 203, 206, 207
Goodhue, Bertram, 177, 208
Graves, Michael, 296
Greene and Greene, 178, 179
Griffin, Walter Burley, 194
Gropius, Walter, 183, 214, 216, 236, 328
Gwathmey, Charles, 296–297

Hardy, Holtzman & Pfieffer, 289
Hardy, Hugh, 289
Harris, Steven, 324, 325
Hays, Jay Acker, 189
Hejduk, John, 296
Henderson, Richard, 297
Hibben, Tom, 222, 223
Hill, Albert H, 191
Hill, James, 231
Homsey, George, 192
Hunt, Richard Morris, 143–144, 145, 168–169, 176

Israel, Frank, 316, 318, 319
Izenour, Steven, 200

Jay, William, 104–105
Jefferson, Thomas, 17, 98–100, 102
Johansen, John M., 273
Johnson, Philip, 236–237, 312
Jones, Inigo, 44, 94
Jost, Richard, 273

Kahn, Louis I., 270, 288
Katselas, Tasso, 271
Kautzky, Theodore, 213
Keck, George, 243
Kelbaugh, David, 303
Kiesler, Frederick, 272
Kneeland, Gary Scott, 310
Kocher and Frey, 247
Kraetsch and Kraetsch, 219

Lafferty, James V., 201
Lamb and Wheeler, 151
Latrobe, Benjamin, 102, 106
Le Corbusier, 182, 210, 214–215, 236, 296, 298–299
Little, Arthur, 161, 163
Lowell, Guy, 187

Mack, Mark, 316
Maher, George, 194
Mansart, Francois, 146

May, Cliff, 191, 233
Maybeck, Bernard, 176, 178, 190, 192
McFarland, C. T, 171
McGoodwin, Robert R., 211
McIntire, Samuel, 96, 97
McKim, Mead, and White, 158, 159, 165, 170, 171
Meier, Richard, 296, 298–299
Mendelsohn and Chermayeff, 216
Metz, Don, 307
Michels, Doug, 273
Mies van der Rohe, Ludwig, 182–183, 214–215, 236–237, 247
Montgomery and Mullary, 196
Moore, Charles, 192, 288, 295, 308
Moore, Lester S., 172
Moore, Lyndon, Turnbull, and Whitaker, 192
Morin, Roi L., 212
Morris, William, 178
Moss, Eric Owen, 317
Mould and McNichol, 156

Nash, John, 124
Neff, Wallace, 209
Neutra, Richard, 183, 215
Newsom, Samuel and Joseph, 155
Notman, John, 132, 142
Noyes, Eliot, 216, 217

Palladio, Andrea, 94
Peabody and Sterns, 162
Phillips, Frederick, 320
Polk, Willis, 190
Pollman, Richard, 220, 221
Price, Bruce, 164, 165
Pugin, Augustus, W. N., 120
Purcell, William, 194, 195

Reineke, William, 291
Richardson, H. H., 156–157, 160, 165, 176
Riddell, John, 137
Riggs, Lutah M., 209
Riley, Jefferson, 294
Robertson, Jacquelin, 297
Rudolph, Paul, 216, 251
Ruskin, John, 120, 148
Russell, Archimedes, 148

Safdie, Moshe, 280
Saitowitz, Stanley, 318
Schindler, Rudolph, 215
Schulitz, Helmut, 249

Schweinfurth, A. C., 196
Schweitzer, Josh, 316
Sellers, David, 291
Shaw, Richard Norman, 150, 160, 174
Shoppell, R. W, 153
Skolnick, Lee H., 323
Sloan, Samuel, 139
Soane, John, 104
Soldwedel and Tatto, 175
Spencer, Robert, 194
Steele, William, 194
Stern and Hagmann, 309
Stewardson, John, 176
Stickley, Gustave, 178
Stone, Edward D., 218
Storey, Ellsworth, 220
Striebinger, F.W., 177
Sullivan, Louis, 176, 194, 220

Town, Isthiel, 126
Trost, Henry, 173

Vaux, Calvert, 124
Venturi, Robert, 200, 288, 292, 308, 311
Venturi and Rauch, 292, 308
Vidler, Anthony, 312
Voysey, C. F. A., 178

Walker, Lester, 268, 279, 294
Watson, Donald, 305
Wheeler, Gervase, 144
Wigley, Mark, 312
Wilson, F. W, 187
Woodward, George E., 126
Wright, Frank Lloyd, 163, 178, 180–183, 194–195, 220
Wurster, Bernardi, and Emmons, 191
Wurster, William, 191–192

Young, Ammi B., 142, 143

Zapata, Carlos, 315